SRA
Open Court Reading

Book 6

Perseverance

•

Uncovering the Past

•

Taking a Stand

•

Beyond the Notes

•

Ecology

•

A Question of Value

SRA Open Court Reading

Book 6

Program Authors

Carl Bereiter

Marilyn Jager Adams

Michael Pressley

Marsha Roit

Robbie Case

Anne McKeough

Jan Hirshberg

Marlene Scardamalia

Ann Brown

Joe Campione

Iva Carruthers

Gerald H. Treadway, Jr.

A Division of The McGraw-Hill Companies

Columbus, Ohio

Acknowledgments

Jose Aruego: THE DAY THEY PARACHUTED CATS OUT ON BORNEO: A DRAMA OF ECOLOGY by Charlotte Pomerantz, illustrations by Jose Aruego. Illustrations copyright © 1971 by Jose Aruego. Reprinted with permission of Jose Aruego.

Atheneum Books for Young Readers, an imprint of Simon & Schuster Children's Publishing Division: **THE GOLD COIN by Alma Flor Ada, illustrated by Neil Waldman.** *Text copyright © 1991, by Alma Flor Ada. Illustrations copyright © 1991, by Neil Waldman.* Reprinted with permission of Atheneum Books for Young Readers, Simon & Schuster Children's Publishing Division. All rights reserved. **"The Grimke Sisters" from GREAT LIVES: HUMAN RIGHTS by William Jay Jacobs.** *Copyright © 1990 William Jay Jacobs.* Reprinted with the permission of Atheneum Books for Young Readers, an imprint of Simon & Schuster Children's Publishing Division.

David Berreby: "The Man Who Wrote Messiah" by David Berreby, from April 1992 issue of *Reader's Digest.* Copyright © 1992 by David Berreby. Reprinted with permission of David Berreby.

Broadside Press: "Martin Luther King, Jr." by Gwendolyn Brooks from BLACK OUT LOUD: AN ANTHOLOGY OF MODERN POEMS BY BLACK AMERICANS, edited by Arnold Adoff. Copyright © 1970 by Arnold Adoff, copyright © 1970 The Macmillan Co. Reprinted with permission of Broadside Press.

Carolrhoda Books, Inc.: "Lady Merida" from STORIES FROM THE BLUE ROAD by Emily Crofford. Text copyright © 1982 by Emily Crofford. Reprinted with permission of Carolrhoda Books, Inc., Minneapolis, MN. All rights reserved. SAVING THE PEREGRINE FALCON by Caroline Arnold, photographs by Richard R. Hewett. Text copyright © 1985 by Caroline Arnold. Photographs copyright © 1985 by Richard R. Hewett. Reprinted with permission of Carolrhoda Books, Inc., Minneapolis, MN. All rights reserved.

Children's Press, Inc.: MIDORI: BRILLIANT VIOLINIST by Charnan Simon. Copyright © 1993 by Children's Press, Inc. Reprinted with permission of Children's Press, Inc.

Chronicle Books: ALEJANDRO'S GIFT by Richard Albert, illustrations by Sylvia Long. Text copyright © 1994 by Richard E. Albert. Illustrations copyright © 1994 by Sylvia Long. Reprinted with permission of Chronicle Books.

Dial Books for Young Readers, a division of Penguin Putnam Inc.: "The Pretty Pennies Picket," from PHILIP HALL LIKES ME, I RECKON MAYBE by Bette Greene. Copyright © 1974 by Bette Greene. Used by permission of Dial Books for Young Readers, a division of Penguin Putnam Inc.

Doubleday, a division of Bantam Doubleday Dell Publishing Group, Inc: "Money Matters" from TOUGH TIFFANY by Belinda Hurmence. Copyright © 1980 by Belinda Hurmence. Used by permission of Doubleday, a division of Bantam Doubleday Dell Publishing Group, Inc. "What is Music" from MUSIC IS MY MISTRESS by Duke Ellington. Copyright © 1973 by Duke Ellington, Inc. Used by permission of Doubleday, a division of Bantam Doubleday Dell Publishing Group, Inc.

Funsten and Franzen: An excerpt entitled "Ray and Mr. Pit" from BROTHER RAY: RAY CHARLES' OWN STORY by Ray Charles and David Ritz. Copyright © 1978 by Ray Charles and David Ritz. Reprinted with permission of Funsten and Franzen.

Roy A. Gallant: "The Island of the Bulls" from LOST CITIES by Roy A. Gallant. Copyright © 1985 by Roy A. Gallant. Reprinted with permission of Roy A. Gallant.

Harcourt Brace & Company: "The No-Guitar Blues" from BASEBALL IN APRIL AND OTHER STORIES, copyright © 1990 by Gary Soto, reprinted by permission of Harcourt Brace & Company.

HarperCollins Publishers: "AMAROQ, THE WOLF" from JULIE OF THE WOLVES by JEAN CRAIGHEAD GEORGE. TEXT COPYRIGHT © 1972 BY JEAN CRAIGHEAD GEORGE. Used by permission of HarperCollins Publishers. From HIS MAJESTY, QUEEN HATSHEPSUT by DOROTHY SHARP CARTER. TEXT COPYRIGHT © 1987 BY DOROTHY SHARP CARTER. Used by permission of HarperCollins Publishers. "THE PASSENGER PIGEON" from I AM PHOENIX by PAUL FLEISCHMAN. TEXT COPYRIGHT © 1985 BY PAUL FLEISCHMAN. Used by permission of HarperCollins Publishers. "THE SHOESHINE STAND" from SHOESHINE GIRL by CLYDE ROBERT BULLA. COPYRIGHT © 1975 BY CLYDE ROBERT BULLA. Used by permission of HarperCollins

Publishers. THE SILK ROUTE: 7000 MILES OF HISTORY by JOHN MAJOR, illustrations by STEPHEN FIESER. TEXT COPYRIGHT © 1995 BY JOHN S. MAJOR. ILLUSTRATIONS COPYRIGHT © 1995 BY STEPHEN FIESER. Used by permission of HarperCollins Publishers.

Holiday House, Inc.: "Back to the Drawing Board" by Russell Freedman. Copyright © 1991 by Russell Freedman. All rights reserved. Reprinted from THE WRIGHT BROTHERS: HOW THEY INVENTED THE AIRPLANE by permission of Holiday House, Inc. Text copyright © 1992 by David A. Adler. Illustrations copyright © 1992 by Robert Casilla. All rights reserved. Reprinted from A PICTURE BOOK OF JESSE OWENS by permission of Holiday House, Inc.

Henry Holt and Company, Inc.: From ON TOP OF THE WORLD: THE CONQUEST OF MT. EVEREST by MARY ANN FRASER, © 1991 by MARY ANN FRASER, text and illustrations. Reprinted by permission of Henry Holt and Company, Inc.

Houghton Mifflin Co.: "The Great Musician" from GREEK MYTHS. Copyright © 1949, renewed 1977 by Olivia E. Coolidge. Reprinted by permission of Houghton Mifflin Co. All rights reserved.

International Creative Management: THE NIGHTINGALE by Hans Christian Andersen, translated by Eva Le Gallienne. Translation copyright © 1965 by Eva Le Gallienne. Reprinted with permission of International Creative Management.

Alfred A. Knopf, Inc: "Mother to Son" from COLLECTED POEMS by Langston Hughes. Copyright

SRA/McGraw-Hill

*A Division of The **McGraw·Hill** Companies*

Send all inquiries to:
SRA/McGraw-Hill
8787 Orion Place
Columbus, Ohio 43240

Printed in the United States of America.

ISBN 0-02-830958-8

6 7 8 9 VHP 04 03 02

Program Authors

Carl Bereiter, Ph.D.
University of Toronto

Marilyn Jager Adams, Ph.D.
BBN Technologies

Michael Pressley, Ph.D.
University of Notre Dame

Marsha Roit, Ph.D.
National Reading Consultant

Robbie Case, Ph.D.
University of Toronto

Anne McKeough, Ph.D.
University of Toronto

Jan Hirshberg, Ed.D.
Reading Consultant

Marlene Scardamalia, Ph.D.
University of Toronto

Ann Brown, Ph.D.
University of California at Berkeley

Joe Campione, Ph.D.
University of California at Berkeley

Iva Carruthers, Ph.D.
Northeastern Illinois University

Gerald H. Treadway, Jr., Ed.D.
San Diego State University

Table *of* Contents

Table *of* Contents

Table *of* Contents

11

Table *of* Contents

Table *of* Contents

Table *of* Contents

Perseverance

Have you ever tried to learn something really, really hard for you? How long did it take? Did you keep trying until you got it? How important is perseverance? What can the ability to keep trying do for our lives?

19

The Fire Builder

from ***Hatchet***
by Gary Paulsen
illustrated by Renee Reichert

Three days ago, Brian Robeson, age thirteen, boarded a Cessna 406 airplane to visit his father who lives in the Canadian wilderness. During the flight, the pilot suffered a heart attack and died. Despite Brian's desperate attempts to make radio contact and to land the plane safely, the plane crashed into a lake in the northern Canadian woods. Brian, the only passenger, survived.

Now that he has survived the crash, he must survive the Canadian wilderness. In the past three days, he has been attacked by hordes of vicious mosquitos and flies, has been racked with hunger, and has seen a bear. The only tool he has is the hatchet his mother gave him before he boarded the airplane in New York. So far he has found a rock shelter and has managed to satisfy some of his hunger with berries.

It is the third night of Brian's ordeal and he is sleeping in his shelter.

At first he thought it was a growl. In the still darkness of the shelter in the middle of the night his eyes came open and he was awake and he thought there was a growl. But it was the wind, a medium wind in the pines had made some sound that brought him up, brought him awake. He sat up and was hit with the smell.

It terrified him. The smell was one of rot, some musty rot that made him think only of graves with cobwebs and dust and old death. His nostrils widened and he opened his eyes wider but he could see nothing. It was too dark, too hard dark with clouds covering even the small light from the stars, and he could not see. But the smell was alive, alive and full and in the shelter. He thought of the bear, thought of Bigfoot and every monster he had ever seen in every fright movie he had ever watched, and his heart hammered in his throat.

Then he heard the slithering. A brushing sound, a slithering brushing sound near his feet——and he kicked out as hard as he could, kicked out and threw the hatchet at the sound, a noise coming from his throat. But the hatchet missed, sailed into the wall where it hit the rocks with a shower of sparks, and his leg was instantly torn with pain, as if a hundred needles had been driven into it. "Unnnngh!"

Now he screamed, with the pain and fear, and skittered on his backside up into the corner of the shelter, breathing through his mouth, straining to see, to hear.

The slithering moved again, he thought toward him at first, and terror took him, stopping his breath. He felt he could see a low dark form, a bulk in the darkness, a shadow that lived, but now it moved away, slithering and scraping it moved away and he saw or thought he saw it go out of the door opening.

He lay on his side for a moment, then pulled a rasping breath in and held it, listening for the attacker to return. When it was apparent that the shadow wasn't coming back he felt the calf of his leg, where the pain was centered and spreading to fill the whole leg.

His fingers gingerly touched a group of needles that had been driven through his pants and into the fleshy part of his calf. They were stiff and very sharp on the ends that stuck out, and he knew then what the attacker had been. A porcupine had stumbled into his shelter and when he had kicked it the thing had slapped him with its tail of quills.

He touched each quill carefully. The pain made it seem as if dozens of them had been slammed into his leg, but there were only eight, pinning the cloth against his skin. He leaned back against the wall for a minute. He couldn't leave them in, they had to come out, but just touching them made the pain more intense.

So fast, he thought. So fast things change. When he'd gone to sleep he had satisfaction and in just a moment it was all different. He grasped one of the quills, held his breath, and jerked. It sent pain signals to his brain in tight waves, but he grabbed another, pulled it, then another quill. When he had pulled four of them he stopped for a moment. The pain had gone from being a pointed injury pain to spreading in a hot smear up his leg and it made him catch his breath.

Some of the quills were driven in deeper than others and they tore when they came out. He breathed deeply twice, let half of the breath out, and went back to work. Jerk, pause, jerk——and three more times before he lay back in the darkness, done. The pain filled his leg now, and with it came new waves of self-pity. Sitting alone in the dark, his leg aching, some mosquitos finding him again, he started crying. It was all too much, just too much, and he couldn't take it. Not the way it was.

I can't take it this way, alone with no fire and in the dark, and next time it might be something worse, maybe a bear, and it wouldn't be just quills in the leg, it would be worse. I can't do this, he thought, again and again. I can't. Brian pulled himself up until he was sitting upright back in the corner of the cave. He put his head down on his arms across his knees, with stiffness taking his left leg, and cried until he was cried out.

He did not know how long it took, but later he looked back on this time of crying in the corner of the dark cave and thought of it as when he learned the most important rule of survival, which was that feeling sorry for yourself didn't work. It wasn't just that it was wrong to do, or that it was considered incorrect. It was more than that——it didn't work. When he sat alone in the darkness and cried and was done, was all done with it, nothing had changed. His leg still hurt, it was still dark, he was still alone and the self-pity had accomplished nothing.

At last he slept again, but already his patterns were changing and the sleep was light, a resting doze more than a deep sleep, with small sounds awakening him twice in the rest of the night. In the last doze period before daylight, before he awakened finally with the morning light and the clouds of new mosquitos, he dreamed, of his father at first and then of his friend Terry.

In the initial segment of the dream his father was standing at the side of a living room looking at him and it was clear from his expression that he was trying to tell Brian something. His lips moved but there was no sound, not a whisper. He waved his hands at Brian, made gestures in front of his face as if he were scratching something, and he worked to make a word with his mouth but at first Brian could not see it. Then the lips made an *mmmmm* shape but no sound came. *Mmmmm——maaaa.* Brian could not hear it, could not understand it and he wanted to so badly; it was so important to understand his father, to know what he was saying. He was trying to help, trying so hard, and when Brian couldn't understand he looked cross, the way he did when Brian asked questions more than once, and he faded. Brian's father faded into a fog place Brian could not see and the dream was almost over, or seemed to be, when Terry came.

He was not gesturing to Brian but was sitting in the park at a bench looking at a barbecue pit and for a time nothing happened. Then he got up and poured some charcoal from a bag into the cooker, then some starter fluid, and he took a flick type of lighter and lit the fluid. When it was burning and the charcoal was at last getting hot he turned, noticing Brian for the first time in the dream. He turned and smiled and pointed to the fire as if to say, see, a fire.

But it meant nothing to Brian, except that he wished he had a fire. He saw a grocery sack on the table next to Terry. Brian thought it must contain hot dogs and chips and mustard and he could think only of the food. But Terry shook his head and pointed again to the fire, and twice more he pointed to the fire, made Brian see the flames, and Brian felt his frustration and anger rise and he thought all right, all right, I see the fire but so what? I don't have a fire. I know about fire; I know I need a fire.

I know that.

His eyes opened and there was light in the cave, a gray dim light of morning. He wiped his mouth and tried to move his leg, which had stiffened like wood. There was thirst, and hunger, and he ate some raspberries from the jacket. They had spoiled a bit, seemed softer and mushier, but still had a rich sweetness. He crushed the berries against the roof of his mouth with his tongue and drank the sweet juice as it ran down his throat. A flash of metal caught his eye and he saw his hatchet in the sand where he had thrown it at the porcupine in the dark.

He scootched up, wincing a bit when he bent his stiff leg, and crawled to where the hatchet lay. He picked it up and examined it and saw a chip in the top of the head.

The nick wasn't large, but the hatchet was important to him, was his only tool, and he should not have thrown it. He should keep it in his hand, and make a tool of some kind to help push an animal away. Make a staff, he thought, or a lance, and save the hatchet. Something came then, a thought as he held the hatchet, something about the dream and his father and Terry, but he couldn't pin it down.

"Ahhh . . ." He scrambled out and stood in the morning sun and stretched his back muscles and his sore leg. The hatchet was still in his hand, and as he stretched and raised it over his head it caught the first

rays of the morning sun. The first faint light hit the silver of the hatchet and it flashed a brilliant gold in the light. Like fire. That is it, he thought. What they were trying to tell me.

Fire. The hatchet was the key to it all. When he threw the hatchet at the porcupine in the cave and missed and hit the stone wall it had showered sparks, a golden shower of sparks in the dark, as golden with fire as the sun was now.

The hatchet was the answer. That's what his father and Terry had been trying to tell him. Somehow he could get fire from the hatchet. The sparks would make fire.

Brian went back into the shelter and studied the wall. It was some form of chalky granite, or a sandstone, but imbedded in it were large pieces of a darker stone, a harder and darker stone. It only took him a moment to find where the hatchet had struck. The steel had nicked into the edge of one of the darker stone pieces. Brian turned the head backward so he would strike with the flat rear of the hatchet and hit the black rock gently. Too gently, and nothing happened. He struck harder, a glancing blow, and two or three weak sparks skipped off the rock and died immediately.

He swung harder, held the hatchet so it would hit a longer, sliding blow, and the black rock exploded in fire. Sparks flew so heavily that several of them skittered and jumped on the sand beneath the rock and he smiled and struck again and again.

There could be fire here, he thought. I will have a fire here, he thought, and struck again——I will have fire from the hatchet.

Brian found it was a long way from sparks to fire.

Clearly there had to be something for the sparks to ignite, some kind of tinder or kindling——but what? He brought some dried grass in, tapped sparks into it and watched them die. He tried small twigs, breaking them into little pieces, but that was worse than the grass. Then he tried a combination of the two, grass and twigs.

Nothing. He had no trouble getting sparks, but the tiny bits of hot stone or metal——he couldn't tell which they were——just sputtered and died.

He settled back on his haunches in exasperation, looking at the pitiful clump of grass and twigs.

He needed something finer, something soft and fine and fluffy to catch the bits of fire.

Shredded paper would be nice, but he had no paper.

"So close," he said aloud, "so close . . ."

He put the hatchet back in his belt and went out of the shelter, limping on his sore leg. There had to be something, had to be. Man had made fire. There had been fire for thousands, millions of years. There had to be a way. He dug in his pockets and found a twenty-dollar bill in his wallet. Paper. Worthless paper out here. But if he could get a fire going . . .

He ripped the twenty into tiny pieces, made a pile of pieces, and hit sparks into them. Nothing happened. They just wouldn't take the sparks. But there had to be a way——some way to do it.

Not twenty feet to his right, leaning out over the water were birches and he stood looking at them for a full half-minute before they registered on his mind. They were a beautiful white with bark like clean, slightly speckled paper.

Paper.

He moved to the trees. Where the bark was peeling from the trunks it lifted in tiny tendrils, almost fluffs. Brian plucked some of them loose, rolled them in his fingers. They seemed flammable, dry and nearly powdery. He pulled and twisted bits off the trees, packing them in one hand while he picked them with the other, picking and gathering until he had a wad close to the size of a baseball.

Then he went back into the shelter and arranged the ball of birchbark peelings at the base of the black rock. As an afterthought he threw in the remains of the twenty-dollar bill. He struck and a stream of sparks fell into the bark and quickly died. But this time one spark fell on one small hair of dry bark——almost a thread of bark——and seemed to glow a bit brighter before it died.

The material had to be finer. There had to be a soft and incredibly fine nest for the sparks.

I must make a home for the sparks, he thought. A perfect home or they won't stay, they won't make fire.

He started ripping the bark, using his fingernails at first, and when that didn't work he used the sharp edge of the hatchet, cutting the bark in thin slivers, hairs so fine they were almost not there. It was painstaking work, slow work, and he stayed with it for over two hours. Twice he stopped for a handful of berries and once to go to the lake for a drink. Then back to work, the sun on his back, until at last he had a ball of fluff as big as a grapefruit——dry birchbark fluff.

He positioned his spark nest——as he thought of it——at the base of the rock, used his thumb to make a small depression in the middle, and slammed the back of the hatchet down across the black rock. A cloud of sparks rained down, most of them missing the nest, but some, perhaps thirty or so, hit in the depression and of those six or seven found fuel and grew, smoldered and caused the bark to take on the red glow.

Then they went out.

Close——he was close. He repositioned the nest, made a new and smaller dent with his thumb, and struck again.

More sparks, a slight glow, then nothing.

It's me, he thought. I'm doing something wrong. I do not know this——a cave dweller would have had a fire by now, a Cro-Magnon man would have a fire by now——but I don't know this. I don't know how to make a fire.

Maybe not enough sparks. He settled the nest in place once more and hit the rock with a series of blows, as fast as he could. The sparks poured like a golden waterfall. At first they seemed to take, there were several, many sparks that found life and took briefly, but they all died.

Starved.

He leaned back. They are like me. They are starving. It wasn't quantity, there were plenty of sparks, but they needed more.

I would kill, he thought suddenly, for a book of matches. Just one book. Just one match. I would kill.

What makes fire? He thought back to school. To all those science classes. Had he ever learned what made a fire? Did a teacher ever stand up there and say, "This is what makes a fire . . ."

He shook his head, tried to focus his thoughts. What did it take? You have to have fuel, he thought——and he had that. The bark was fuel. Oxygen——there had to be air.

He needed to add air. He had to fan on it, blow on it.

He made the nest ready again, held the hatchet backward, tensed, and struck four quick blows. Sparks came down and he leaned forward as fast as he could and blew.

Too hard. There was a bright, almost intense glow, then it was gone. He had blown it out.

Another set of strikes, more sparks. He leaned and blew, but gently this time, holding back and aiming the stream of air from his mouth to hit the brightest spot. Five or six sparks had fallen in a tight mass of bark hair and Brian centered his efforts there.

The sparks grew with his gentle breath. The red glow moved from the sparks themselves into the bark, moved and grew and became worms, glowing red worms that crawled up the bark hairs and caught other threads of bark and grew until there was a pocket of red as big as a quarter, a glowing red coal of heat.

And when he ran out of breath and paused to inhale, the red ball suddenly burst into flame.

"Fire!" He yelled. "I've got fire! I've got it, I've got it, I've got it . . ."

But the flames were thick and oily and burning fast, consuming the ball of bark as fast as if it were gasoline. He had to feed the flames, keep them going. Working as fast as he could he carefully placed the dried grass and wood pieces he had tried at first on top of the bark and was gratified to see them take.

But they would go fast. He needed more, and more. He could not let the flames go out.

He ran from the shelter to the pines and started breaking off the low, dead small limbs. These he threw in the shelter, went back for more, threw those in, and squatted to break and feed the hungry flames. When the small wood was going well he went out and found larger wood and did not relax until that was going. Then he leaned back against the wood brace of his door opening and smiled.

I have a friend, he thought——I have a friend now. A hungry friend, but a good one. I have a friend named fire.

"Hello, fire . . ."

The curve of the rock back made an almost perfect drawing flue that carried the smoke up through the cracks of the roof but held the heat. If he kept the fire small it would be perfect and would keep anything like the porcupine from coming through the door again.

A friend and a guard, he thought.

So much from a little spark. A friend and a guard from a tiny spark.

The Fire Builder

Meet the Author

Gary Paulsen was an "Army brat," so his family moved around a lot. Nature became an escape for Paulsen. He is very proud to have finished the Iditarod, a 1,200-mile dog-sled race in Alaska, twice. Says Paulsen, "The overriding concern among kids is honesty." He thinks that to protect kids from the truth is unfair to them. For this reason, his stories are often about tough reality and tough children.

Meet the Illustrator

Renee Reichert received her degree in art from the University of Massachusetts at Amherst. Her work has been displayed at the Society of Illustrators 41st Annual Exhibition, and the Vincent Louis Galleries in Greenwich Village. It has also been included in numerous other exhibitions on Long Island. Ms. Reichert says she is "inspired by both the beautiful and the absurd." She shares her home on Long Island with her husband, two children, and their pets.

Theme Connections

Think About It

Visualize the environment Brian was in. Imagine how he felt. What would you have done if you were in his place?

Record Ideas

Record in your Writing Journal specific ideas of how you could use your imagination in discovering resources to help you to survive a plane crash in the wilderness.

Make a New Ending

In the story, we are led to believe that Brian probably survived because he had been able to build a fire. Make up another ending that would leave us with a different impression, and explain how a different ending changes the story.

Amaroq, the Wolf

from *Julie of the Wolves*
by Jean Craighead George
illustrated by Anthony Carnabuci

Miyax pushed back the hood of her sealskin parka and looked at the Arctic sun. It was a yellow disc in a lime-green sky, the colors of six o'clock in the evening and the time when the wolves awoke. Quietly she put down her cooking pot and crept to the top of a dome-shaped frost heave, one of the many earth buckles that rise and fall in the crackling cold of the Arctic winter. Lying on her stomach, she looked across a vast lawn of grass and moss and focused her attention on the wolves she had come upon two sleeps ago. They were wagging their tails as they awoke and saw each other.

Her hands trembled and her heartbeat quickened, for she was frightened, not so much of the wolves, who were shy and many harpoon-shots away, but because of her desperate predicament. Miyax was lost. She had been lost without food for many sleeps on the North Slope of Alaska. The barren slope stretches for three hundred miles from the Brooks Range to the Arctic Ocean, and for more than eight hundred miles from the Chukchi to the Beaufort Sea. No roads cross it; ponds and lakes freckle its immensity. Winds scream across it, and the view in every direction is exactly the same. Somewhere in this cosmos was Miyax; and the very life in her body, its spark and warmth, depended upon these wolves for survival. And she was not so sure they would help.

Miyax stared hard at the regal black wolf, hoping to catch his eye. She must somehow tell him that she was starving and ask him for food. This could be done she knew, for her father, an Eskimo hunter, had done so. One year he had camped near a wolf den while on a hunt. When a month had passed and her father had seen no game, he told the leader of the wolves that he was hungry and needed food. The next night the wolf called him from far away and her father went to him and found a freshly killed caribou. Unfortunately, Miyax's father never explained to her how he had told the wolf of his needs. And not long afterward he paddled his kayak into the Bering Sea to hunt for seal, and he never returned.

She had been watching the wolves for two days, trying to discern which of their sounds and movements expressed goodwill and friendship. Most animals had such signals. The little Arctic ground squirrels flicked their tails sideways to notify others of their kind that they were friendly. By imitating this signal with her forefinger, Miyax had lured many a squirrel to

her hand. If she could discover such a gesture for the wolves she would be able to make friends with them and share their food, like a bird or a fox.

Propped on her elbows with her chin in her fists, she stared at the black wolf, trying to catch his eye. She had chosen him because he was much larger than the others, and because he walked like her father, Kapugen, with his head high and his chest out. The black wolf also possessed wisdom, she had observed. The pack looked to him when the wind carried strange scents or the birds cried nervously. If he was alarmed, they were alarmed. If he was calm, they were calm.

Long minutes passed, and the black wolf did not look at her. He had ignored her since she first came upon them, two sleeps ago. True, she moved slowly and quietly, so as not to alarm him; yet she did wish he would see the kindness in her eyes. Many animals could tell the difference between hostile hunters and friendly people by merely looking at them. But the big black wolf would not even glance her way.

A bird stretched in the grass. The wolf looked at it. A flower twisted in the wind. He glanced at that. Then the breeze rippled the wolverine ruff on Miyax's parka and it glistened in the light. He did not look at that. She waited. Patience with the ways of nature had been instilled in her by her father. And so she knew better than to move or shout. Yet she must get food or die. Her hands shook slightly and she swallowed hard to keep calm.

Miyax was a classic Eskimo beauty, small of bone and delicately wired with strong muscles. Her face was pearl-round and her nose was flat. Her black eyes, which slanted gracefully, were moist and sparkling. Like the beautifully formed polar bears and foxes of the north, she was slightly short-limbed. The frigid environment of the Arctic has sculptured life into compact shapes. Unlike the long-limbed, long-bodied animals of the south that are cooled by dispensing heat on extended surfaces, all live things in the Arctic tend toward compactness, to conserve heat.

The length of her limbs and the beauty of her face were of no use to Miyax as she lay on the lichen-speckled frost heave in the midst of the bleak tundra. Her stomach ached and the royal black wolf was carefully ignoring her.

"*Amaroq, ilaya,* wolf, my friend," she finally called. "Look at me. Look at me."

She spoke half in Eskimo and half in English, as if the instincts of her father and the science of the *gussaks,* the white-faced, might evoke some magical combination that would help her get her message through to the wolf.

Amaroq glanced at his paw and slowly turned his head her way without lifting his eyes. He licked his shoulder. A few matted hairs sprang apart and twinkled individually. Then his eyes sped to each of the three adult wolves that made up his pack and finally to the five pups who were sleeping in a fuzzy mass near the den entrance. The great wolf's eyes softened at the sight of the little wolves, then quickly hardened into brittle yellow jewels as he scanned the flat tundra.

Not a tree grew anywhere to break the monotony of the gold-green plain, for the soils of the tundra are permanently frozen. Only moss, grass, lichens, and a few hardy flowers take root in the thin upper layer that thaws briefly in summer. Nor do many

species of animals live in this rigorous land, but those creatures that do dwell here exist in bountiful numbers. Amaroq watched a large cloud of Lapland longspurs wheel up into the sky, then alight in the grasses. Swarms of crane flies, one of the few insects that can survive the cold, darkened the tips of the mosses. Birds wheeled, turned, and called. Thousands sprang up from the ground like leaves in a wind.

The wolf's ears cupped forward and tuned in on some distant message from the tundra. Miyax tensed and listened, too. Did he hear some brewing storm, some approaching enemy? Apparently not. His ears relaxed and he rolled to his side. She sighed, glanced at the vaulting sky, and was painfully aware of her predicament.

Here she was, watching wolves——she, Miyax, daughter of Kapugen, adopted child of Martha, citizen of the United States, pupil at the Bureau of Indian Affairs School in Barrow, Alaska, and thirteen-year-old wife of the boy Daniel. She shivered at the thought of Daniel, for it was he who had driven her to this fate. She had run away from him exactly seven sleeps ago, and because of this she had one more title by gussak standards—— the child divorcée.

The wolf rolled to his belly.

"Amaroq," she whispered. "I am lost and the sun will not set for a month. There is no North Star to guide me."

Amaroq did not stir.

"And there are no berry bushes here to bend under the polar wind and point to the south. Nor are there any birds I can follow." She looked up. "Here the birds are buntings and longspurs. They do not fly to the sea twice a day like the puffins and sandpipers that my father followed."

The wolf groomed his chest with his tongue.

"I never dreamed I could get lost, Amaroq," she went on, talking out loud to ease her fear. "At home on Nunivak Island where I was born, the plants and birds pointed the way for wanderers. I thought they did so everywhere . . . and so, great black Amaroq, I'm without a compass."

It had been a frightening moment when two days ago she realized that the tundra was an ocean of grass on which she was circling around and around. Now as that fear overcame her again she closed her eyes. When she opened them her heart skipped excitedly. Amaroq was looking at her!

"*Ee-lie,*" she called and scrambled to her feet. The wolf arched his neck and narrowed his eyes. He pressed his ears forward. She waved. He drew back his lips and showed his teeth. Frightened by what seemed a snarl, she lay down again. When she was flat on her stomach, Amaroq flattened his ears and wagged his tail once. Then he tossed his head and looked away.

Discouraged, she wriggled backward down the frost heave and arrived at her camp feet first. The heave was between herself and the wolf pack and so she relaxed, stood up, and took stock of her home. It was a simple affair, for she had not been able to carry much when she ran away; she took just those things she would need for the journey——a backpack, food for a week or so, needles to mend clothes, matches, her sleeping skin, and ground cloth to go under it, two knives, and a pot.

She had intended to walk to Point Hope. There she would meet the *North Star,* the ship that brings supplies from the States to the towns on the Arctic Ocean in August when the ice pack breaks up. The ship could always use dishwashers or laundresses, she had heard, and so she would work her way to San Francisco where Amy, her pen pal, lived. At the end of every letter Amy always wrote: "When are you coming to San Francisco?" Seven days ago she had been on her way——on her way to the glittering, white, postcard city that sat on a hill among trees, those enormous plants she had never seen. She had been on her way to see the television and carpeting in Amy's school, the glass buildings, traffic lights, and stores full of fruits; on her way to the harbor that never froze and the Golden Gate Bridge. But primarily she was on her way to be rid of Daniel, her terrifying husband.

She kicked the sod at the thought of her marriage; then shaking her head to forget, she surveyed her camp. It was nice. Upon discovering the wolves, she had settled down to live near them in the hope of sharing their food, until the sun set and the stars came out to guide her. She had built a house of sod, like the summer homes of the old Eskimos. Each brick had been cut with her *ulo,* the half-moon shaped woman's knife, so versatile it can trim a baby's hair, slice a tough bear, or chip an iceberg.

Her house was not well built for she had never made one before, but it was cozy inside. She had windproofed it by sealing the sod bricks with mud from the pond at her door, and she had made it beautiful by spreading her caribou ground cloth on the floor. On this she had placed her sleeping skin, a moosehide bag lined with soft white rabbit skins. Next to her bed she had built a low table of sod on which to put her clothes when she slept. To decorate the house she had made three flowers of bird feathers and stuck them in the top of the table. Then she had built a fireplace outdoors and placed her pot beside it. The pot was empty, for she had not found even a lemming to eat.

Last winter, when she had walked to school in Barrow, these mice-like rodents were so numerous they ran out from under her feet wherever she stepped. There were thousands and thousands of them until December, when they suddenly vanished. Her teacher said that the lemmings had a chemical similar to antifreeze in their blood, that kept them active all winter when other little mammals were hibernating. "They eat grass and multiply all winter," Mrs. Franklin had said in her singsong voice. "When there are too many, they grow nervous at the sight of each other. Somehow this shoots too much antifreeze into their bloodstreams and it begins to poison them. They become restless, then crazy. They run in a frenzy until they die."

Of this phenomenon Miyax's father had simply said, "The hour of the lemming is over for four years."

Unfortunately for Miyax, the hour of the animals that prey on the lemmings was also over. The white fox, the snowy owl, the weasel, the jaeger, and the siskin had virtually disappeared. They had no food to eat and bore few or no young. Those that lived preyed on each other. With the passing of the lemmings, however, the grasses had grown high again and the hour of the caribou was upon the land. Healthy fat caribou cows gave birth to many calves. The caribou population increased, and this in turn increased the number of wolves who prey on the caribou. The abundance of the big deer of the north did Miyax no good, for she had not brought a gun on her trip. It had never occurred to her that she would not reach Point Hope before her food ran out.

A dull pain seized her stomach. She pulled blades of grass from their sheaths and ate the sweet ends. They were not very satisfying, so she picked a handful of caribou moss, a lichen. If the deer could survive in winter on this food, why not she? She munched, decided the plant might taste better if cooked, and went to the pond for water.

As she dipped her pot in, she thought about Amaroq. Why had he bared his teeth at her? Because she was young and he knew she couldn't hurt him? No, she said to herself, it was because he was speaking to her! He had told her to lie down. She had even understood and obeyed him. He had talked to her not with his voice, but with his ears, eyes, and lips; and he had even commended her with a wag of his tail.

She dropped her pot, scrambled up the frost heave and stretched out on her stomach.

"Amaroq," she called softly, "I understand what you said. Can you understand me? I'm hungry——very, very hungry. Please bring me some meat."

The great wolf did not look her way and she began to doubt her reasoning. After all, flattened ears and a tail-wag were scarcely a conversation. She dropped her forehead against the lichens and rethought what had gone between them.

"Then why did I lie down?" she asked, lifting her head and looking at Amaroq. "Why did I?" she called to the yawning wolves. Not one turned her way.

Amaroq got to his feet, and as he slowly arose he seemed to fill the sky and blot out the sun. He was enormous. He could swallow her without even chewing.

"But he won't," she reminded herself. "Wolves do not eat people. That's gussak talk. Kapugen said wolves are gentle brothers."

The black puppy was looking at her and wagging his tail. Hopefully, Miyax held out a pleading hand to him. His tail wagged harder. The mother rushed to him and stood above him sternly. When he licked her cheek apologetically, she pulled back her lips from her fine white teeth. They flashed as she smiled and forgave her cub.

"But don't let it happen again," said Miyax sarcastically, mimicking her own elders. The mother walked toward Amaroq.

"I should call you Martha after my stepmother," Miyax whispered. "But you're much too beautiful. I shall call you Silver instead."

Silver moved in a halo of light, for the sun sparkled on the guard hairs that grew out over the dense underfur and she seemed to glow.

The reprimanded pup snapped at a crane fly and shook himself. Bits of lichen and grass spun off his fur. He reeled unsteadily, took a wider stance, and looked down at his sleeping sister. With a yap he jumped on her and rolled her to her feet. She whined. He barked and picked up a bone. When he was sure she was watching, he ran down the slope with it. The sister tagged after him. He stopped and she grabbed the bone, too. She pulled; he pulled; then he pulled and she yanked.

Miyax could not help laughing. The puppies played with bones like Eskimo children played with leather ropes.

"I understand *that*," she said to the pups. "That's tug-o-war. Now how do you say, 'I'm hungry'?"

Amaroq was pacing restlessly along the crest of the frost heave as if something were about to happen. His eyes shot to Silver, then to the gray wolf Miyax had named Nails. These glances seemed to be a summons, for Silver and Nails glided to him, spanked the ground with their forepaws, and bit him gently under the chin. He wagged his tail furiously and took Silver's slender nose in his mouth. She crouched before him, licked his cheek, and lovingly bit his lower jaw. Amaroq's tail flashed high as her mouthing charged him with vitality. He nosed her affectionately. Unlike the fox who met his mate only in the breeding season, Amaroq lived with his mate all year.

Next, Nails took Amaroq's jaw in his mouth and the leader bit the top of his nose. A third adult, a small male, came slinking up. He got down on his belly before Amaroq, rolled trembling to his back, and wriggled.

"Hello, Jello," Miyax whispered, for he reminded her of the quivering gussak dessert her mother-in-law made.

She had seen the wolves mouth Amaroq's chin twice before and so she concluded that it was a ceremony, a sort of "Hail to the Chief." He must indeed be their leader for he was clearly the wealthy wolf; that is, wealthy as she had known the meaning of the word on Nunivak Island. There the old Eskimo hunters she

had known in her childhood thought the riches of life were intelligence, fearlessness, and love. A man with these gifts was rich and was a great spirit who was admired in the same way that the gussaks admired a man with money and goods.

The three adults paid tribute to Amaroq until he was almost smothered with love; then he bayed a wild note that sounded like the wind on the frozen sea. With that the others sat around him, the puppies scattered between them. Jello hunched forward and Silver shot a fierce glance at him. Intimidated, Jello pulled his ears together and back. He drew himself down until he looked smaller than ever.

Amaroq wailed again, stretching his neck until his head was high above the others. They gazed at him affectionately and it was plain to see that he was their great spirit, a royal leader who held his group together with love and wisdom.

Any fear Miyax had of the wolves was dispelled by their affection for each other. They were friendly animals and so devoted to Amaroq that she needed only to be accepted by him to be accepted by all. She even knew how to achieve this— bite him under the chin. But how was she going to do that?

She studied the pups hoping they had a simpler way of expressing their love for him. The black puppy approached the leader, sat, then lay down and wagged his tail vigorously.

He gazed up at Amaroq in pure adoration, and the royal eyes softened.

Well, that's what I'm doing! Miyax thought. She called to Amaroq. "I'm lying down gazing at you, too, but you don't look at *me* that way!"

When all the puppies were wagging his praises, Amaroq yipped, hit a high note, and crooned. As his voice rose and fell, the other adults sang out and the puppies yipped and bounced.

The song ended abruptly. Amaroq arose and trotted swiftly down the slope. Nails followed, and behind him ran Silver, then Jello. But Jello did not run far. Silver turned and looked him straight in the eye. She pressed her ears forward aggressively and lifted her tail. With that, Jello went back to the puppies and the three sped away like dark birds.

Miyax hunched forward on her elbows, the better to see and learn. She now knew how to be a good puppy, pay tribute to the leader, and even to be a leader by biting others on the top of the nose. She also knew how to tell Jello to baby-sit. If only she had big ears and a tail, she could lecture and talk to them all.

Flapping her hands on her head for ears, she flattened her fingers to make friends, pulled them together and back to express fear, and shot them forward to display her aggression and dominance. Then she folded her arms and studied the puppies again.

The black one greeted Jello by tackling his feet. Another jumped on his tail, and before he could discipline either, all five were upon him. He rolled and tumbled with them for almost an hour; then he ran down the slope, turned, and stopped. The pursuing pups plowed into him, tumbled, fell, and lay still. During a minute of surprised recovery there was no action. Then the black pup flashed his tail like a semaphore signal and they all jumped on Jello again.

Miyax rolled over and laughed aloud. "That's funny. They're really like kids."

When she looked back, Jello's tongue was hanging from his mouth and his sides were heaving. Four of the puppies had collapsed at his feet and were asleep. Jello flopped down, too, but the black pup still looked around. He was not the least bit tired. Miyax watched him, for there was something special about him.

He ran to the top of the den and barked. The smallest pup, whom Miyax called Sister, lifted her head, saw her favorite brother in action and, struggling to her feet, followed him devotedly. While they romped, Jello took the opportunity to rest behind a clump of sedge, a moisture-loving plant of the tundra. But hardly was he settled before a pup tracked him to his hideout and pounced on him. Jello narrowed his eyes, pressed his ears forward, and showed his teeth.

"I know what you're saying," she called to him. "You're saying, 'lie down.'" The puppy lay down, and Miyax got on all fours and looked for the nearest pup to speak to. It was Sister.

"Ummmm," she whined, and when Sister turned around she narrowed her eyes and showed her white teeth. Obediently, Sister lay down.

"I'm talking wolf! I'm talking wolf!" Miyax clapped, and tossing her head like a pup, crawled in a happy circle. As she was coming back she saw all five puppies sitting in a row watching her, their heads cocked in curiosity. Boldly the black pup came toward her, his fat backside swinging as he trotted to the bottom of her frost heave, and barked.

"You are *very* fearless and *very* smart," she said. "Now I know why you are special. You are wealthy and the leader of the puppies. There is no doubt what you'll grow up to be. So I shall name you after my father Kapugen, and I shall call you Kapu for short."

Kapu wrinkled his brow and turned an ear to tune in more acutely on her voice.

"You don't understand, do you?"

Hardly had she spoken than his tail went up, his mouth opened slightly, and he fairly grinned.

"Ee-lie!" she gasped. "You do understand. And that scares me." She perched on her heels. Jello whined an undulating note and Kapu turned back to the den.

Miyax imitated the call to come home. Kapu looked back over his shoulder in surprise. She giggled. He wagged his tail and jumped on Jello.

She clapped her hands and settled down to watch this language of jumps and tumbles, elated that she was at last breaking the wolf code. After a long time she decided they were not talking but roughhousing, and so she started home. Later she changed her mind. Roughhousing was very important to wolves. It occupied almost the entire night for the pups.

"Ee-lie, okay," she said. "I'll learn to roughhouse. Maybe then you'll accept me and feed me." She pranced, jumped, and whimpered; she growled, snarled, and rolled. But nobody came to roughhouse.

Sliding back to her camp, she heard the grass swish and looked up to see Amaroq and his hunters sweep around her frost heave and stop about five feet away. She could smell the sweet scent of their fur.

The hairs on her neck rose and her eyes widened. Amaroq's ears went forward aggressively and she remembered that wide eyes meant fear to him. It was not good to show him she was afraid. Animals attacked the fearful. She tried to narrow them, but remembered that was not right either. Narrowed eyes were mean. In desperation she recalled that Kapu had moved forward when challenged. She pranced right up to Amaroq. Her heart beat furiously as she grunt-whined the sound of the puppy begging adoringly for attention. Then she got down on her belly and gazed at him with fondness.

The great wolf backed up and avoided her eyes. She had said something wrong! Perhaps even offended him. Some slight gesture that meant nothing to her had apparently meant something to the wolf. His ears shot forward angrily and it seemed all was lost. She wanted to get up and run, but she gathered her courage and pranced closer to him. Swiftly she patted him under the chin.

The signal went off. It sped through his body and triggered emotions of love. Amaroq's ears flattened and his tail wagged in friendship. He could not react in any other way to the chin pat, for the roots of this signal lay deep in wolf history. It was inherited from generations and generations of leaders before him. As his eyes softened, the sweet odor of ambrosia arose from the gland on the top of his tail and she was drenched lightly in wolf scent. Miyax was one of the pack.

Amaroq, the Wolf

Meet the Author

Jean Craighead George's family owned a beautiful Pennsylvania farm where George and her twin brothers spent their summers swimming and fishing in its ponds. She and her brothers used to go into the woods with their father, who was a forester. He taught them how to catch catfish and find plants and roots that were good to eat. Many of her books are about kids who use their knowledge of nature and wildlife to survive on their own in the wilds.

Meet the Illustrator

Anthony Carnabuci was always encouraged by his family to create. They used to visit the museum every Sunday when he was young. His mother painted, and he remembers a still life she had done that looked incredibly real. He says, "I thought that I could reach out and touch the objects in the painting." Carnabuci graduated from the Rhode Island School of Design with a degree in art, and his work has been recognized by the Society of Illustrators and *Parents* magazine. He believes that "art is really communication" and he hopes his work is able to accomplish this.

Theme Connections

Think About It

- What were the events that led to Miyax's becoming lost on the Arctic tundra?
- What happened in her past that helped her survive her ordeal?

Record Ideas

In your Writing Journal, write a goal you want to achieve. What knowledge or experience will help you stick to your goal and achieve it?

Tell a Story

Work with a partner to plan the next and final chapter of Miyax's story. Join with another pair of students and share your stories. Discuss how they are similar and different and why.

On Top of the World

The Conquest of Mount Everest
by Mary Ann Fraser

It was May 28th, 1953. With feelings of loneliness and excitement, Edmund Hillary and Tenzing Norgay watched the last of their companions head down the mountain. It had taken eight months, an army of men, and three tons of supplies to get them to where they now stood, 1,100 feet from the summit. In the morning they hoped to be the first ever to climb the highest mountain in the world——Mount Everest.

As their companions faded from view, Hillary and Tenzing began preparations for the night. Already they had climbed many miles from Katmandu, the expedition's starting point. But over the next twenty-four hours would come their greatest obstacles.

Straddling the border between Tibet and Nepal, Everest rises 29,028 feet out of the world's youngest——and highest——mountain range, the Himalayas. Near the top of the world, the air has only one third the oxygen found at sea level. Breathing the thin air, climbers can suffer physically and mentally. But the weight of oxygen tanks and frames also makes climbing more difficult.

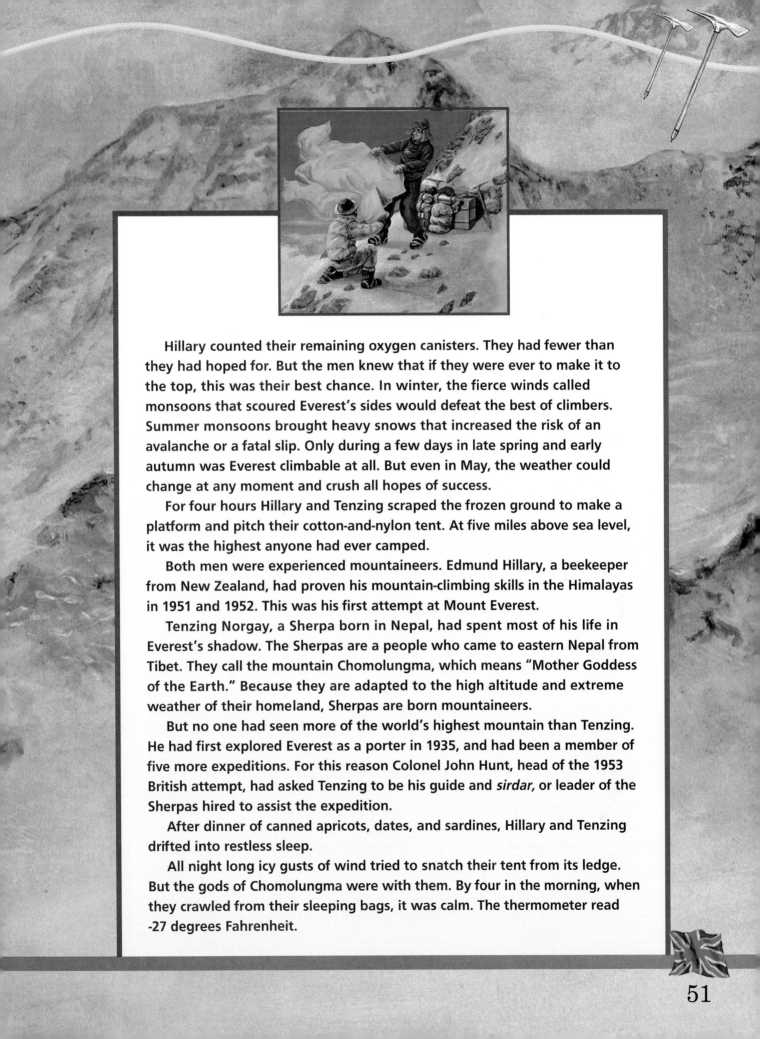

Hillary counted their remaining oxygen canisters. They had fewer than they had hoped for. But the men knew that if they were ever to make it to the top, this was their best chance. In winter, the fierce winds called monsoons that scoured Everest's sides would defeat the best of climbers. Summer monsoons brought heavy snows that increased the risk of an avalanche or a fatal slip. Only during a few days in late spring and early autumn was Everest climbable at all. But even in May, the weather could change at any moment and crush all hopes of success.

For four hours Hillary and Tenzing scraped the frozen ground to make a platform and pitch their cotton-and-nylon tent. At five miles above sea level, it was the highest anyone had ever camped.

Both men were experienced mountaineers. Edmund Hillary, a beekeeper from New Zealand, had proven his mountain-climbing skills in the Himalayas in 1951 and 1952. This was his first attempt at Mount Everest.

Tenzing Norgay, a Sherpa born in Nepal, had spent most of his life in Everest's shadow. The Sherpas are a people who came to eastern Nepal from Tibet. They call the mountain Chomolungma, which means "Mother Goddess of the Earth." Because they are adapted to the high altitude and extreme weather of their homeland, Sherpas are born mountaineers.

But no one had seen more of the world's highest mountain than Tenzing. He had first explored Everest as a porter in 1935, and had been a member of five more expeditions. For this reason Colonel John Hunt, head of the 1953 British attempt, had asked Tenzing to be his guide and *sirdar,* or leader of the Sherpas hired to assist the expedition.

After dinner of canned apricots, dates, and sardines, Hillary and Tenzing drifted into restless sleep.

All night long icy gusts of wind tried to snatch their tent from its ledge. But the gods of Chomolungma were with them. By four in the morning, when they crawled from their sleeping bags, it was calm. The thermometer read -27 degrees Fahrenheit.

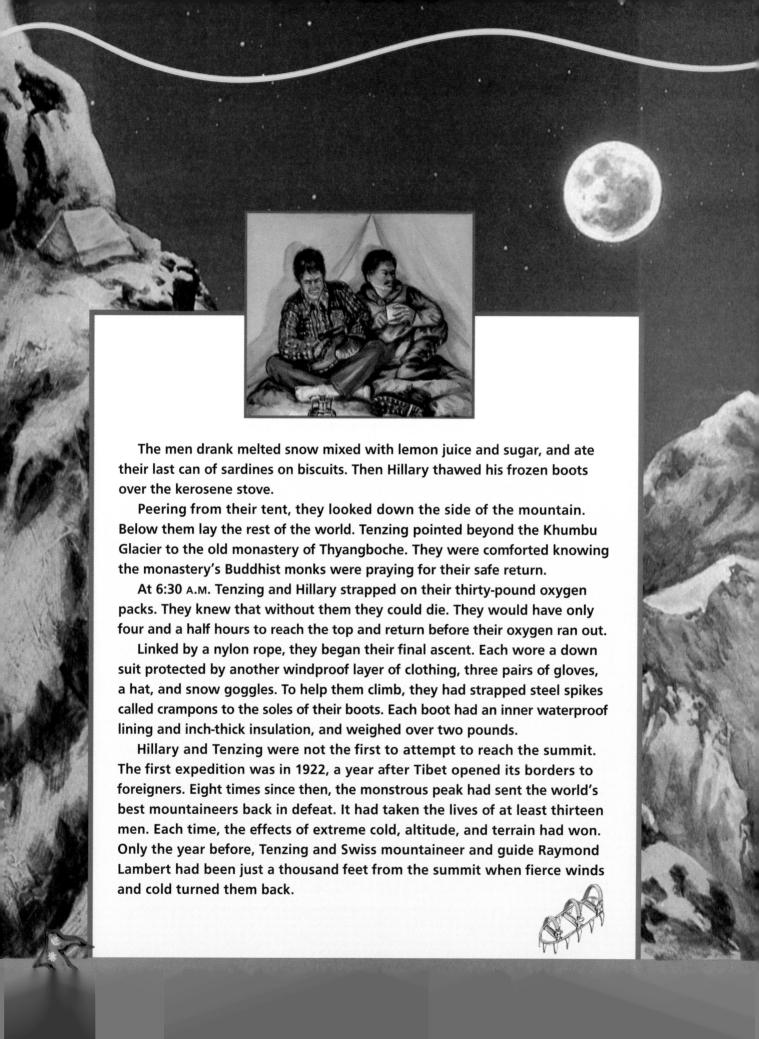

The men drank melted snow mixed with lemon juice and sugar, and ate their last can of sardines on biscuits. Then Hillary thawed his frozen boots over the kerosene stove.

Peering from their tent, they looked down the side of the mountain. Below them lay the rest of the world. Tenzing pointed beyond the Khumbu Glacier to the old monastery of Thyangboche. They were comforted knowing the monastery's Buddhist monks were praying for their safe return.

At 6:30 A.M. Tenzing and Hillary strapped on their thirty-pound oxygen packs. They knew that without them they could die. They would have only four and a half hours to reach the top and return before their oxygen ran out.

Linked by a nylon rope, they began their final ascent. Each wore a down suit protected by another windproof layer of clothing, three pairs of gloves, a hat, and snow goggles. To help them climb, they had strapped steel spikes called crampons to the soles of their boots. Each boot had an inner waterproof lining and inch-thick insulation, and weighed over two pounds.

Hillary and Tenzing were not the first to attempt to reach the summit. The first expedition was in 1922, a year after Tibet opened its borders to foreigners. Eight times since then, the monstrous peak had sent the world's best mountaineers back in defeat. It had taken the lives of at least thirteen men. Each time, the effects of extreme cold, altitude, and terrain had won. Only the year before, Tenzing and Swiss mountaineer and guide Raymond Lambert had been just a thousand feet from the summit when fierce winds and cold turned them back.

But on the clear, frosty morning of May 29th, Tenzing and Hillary had the strongest start yet. From the start of the 1953 expedition, all fifty-three members had worked to advance supplies from camp to camp up the mountain. They knew that the higher the final camp was, the more likely the men would reach the summit before their oxygen ran out.

Colonel John Hunt had decided to send Tom Bourdillon, an excellent rock climber, and Charles Evans, an experienced mountaineer, to try for the summit first. On May 23, this First Team left for Camp VIII, at the South Col. In the meantime, the remaining men moved supplies farther up the mountain. If the First Team failed, Tenzing and Hillary would try for the top from an even higher location.

Three days later Bourdillon and Evans stumbled back to the South Col, where the others were waiting. They had run out of oxygen, energy, and time three hundred feet from the top of Everest.

The next day the Second Team was moved into position, at Camp IX. It was now up to them alone to climb the last 1,100 feet.

Steadily they kicked steps in the snow, breathing from the oxygen canisters secured to their backs. The strain of each movement prevented them from speaking, yet they worked together as a team.

About four hundred feet from the South Peak's face, the men came to an abrupt stop. Which way should they go? Bourdillon and Evans had taken the ridge, but its loose snow made it dangerous. Hillary and Tenzing decided to take the face route. Cautiously they chipped steps straight up the mountainside, knowing that if they zigzagged, the undercut snow could avalanche.

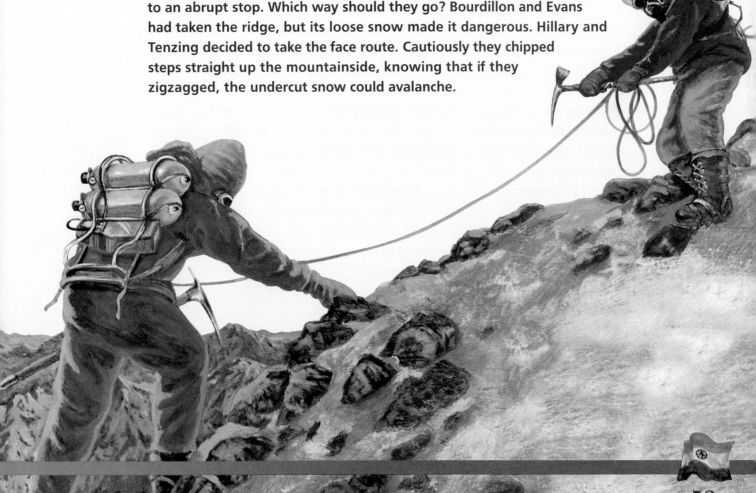

They were halfway up Everest's treacherous Southeast Ridge when suddenly the powdery snow broke away. Hillary slid several feet before he could stop his fall with his ice ax.

"I don't like this," he gasped. "Shall we go on?"

Tenzing replied, "Just as you wish."

They knew the risks were great, but the goal was worth it. This was not a competition to see who could reach the top of the world first. It was more like a relay race, with each expedition, each man, passing on new gains in experience and knowledge to the next. Now it was Tenzing and Hillary's turn to carry on the work of all who had tried before.

Carefully they pushed on.

Finally, at 9 A.M., they reached the 28,700-foot South Peak. No one had ever gone higher.

After a brief rest to check their oxygen supply and study the ridge ahead, they continued their dangerous climb. To their relief the snow was firm.

Their axes rang out in unison as they chopped steps up the razor-like ridge. They had to be more careful than ever now. To their right, great overhanging cornices of snow stuck out like twisted fingers above a 10,000-foot drop. To their left were plunging cliffs of windswept rock.

They could see the tents of Camp IV more than a mile below. Like a giant bird Hillary flapped his arms, but he knew he was too far away for the men at the camp to see him.

As they continued on, step by icy step, Tenzing began fumbling with his oxygen equipment. Hillary stopped, and discovered that ice had completely blocked the tube through which Tenzing was exhaling. Quickly Hillary cleared it so his partner could get fresh oxygen again. He then checked his own equipment and cleaned out the ice from the exhaust tubes.

But with one danger averted, they found themselves staring at an even greater barrier: A giant rock, forty feet high, blocked the ridge. There seemed to be no way over it and no way around it. Had Everest won again?

Then they noticed a small crack that rose like a chimney between the rock and cornice of ice. Hillary wedged himself into the chimney. Pushing with each part of his body and kicking with his boots, he slowly wriggled his way upward. At any moment the cornice could split away. His only safety lay in the rope Tenzing had wrapped around his ax and driven into the snow.

At last Hillary dragged himself over the top of the rock and onto a wide ledge. Then, securing his end of the rope, he motioned for Tenzing to follow.

Hillary heaved with all his might until Tenzing, too, collapsed at the top of the chimney.

At the height of almost twenty Empire State Buildings, any movement was very tiring. It took several minutes for them to catch their breaths.

Ahead, the ridge rolled in a series of seemingly never-ending humps. As the men climbed over one, another always loomed ahead. Their boots felt like lead, and their packs grew heavier with each step. Time was quickly passing, and there was still no sign of the summit. With each bite of the ax, shards of ice and rock were hurled into the air.

It was now 11:30 A.M. Their oxygen supply was dwindling, and in a few minutes they would have to turn back defeated.

Once more Hillary looked ahead, and suddenly realized the ridge didn't rise up, but fell sharply away. With a glimmer of hope the two climbers whacked more steps in the firm snow.

Beyond them lay a dome of ice. It stood like an island surrounded by an ocean of snow-capped peaks. The summit. But was it safe? Could it break away?

Probing with their axes, they cautiously staggered the last few yards. At last they stood on the highest point on earth, 29,028 feet above the sea. From the top of the world, they could see four countries: Tibet to the north, Sikkim to the east, India to the south, and Nepal to the south and west.

The moment was too great for words. Tenzing threw his arms around Hillary and thumped him on the back.

Then Tenzing unwound from his ax a string of flags: one for the United Nations, one for Britain, one for Nepal, and one for India. Hillary turned off his oxygen and removed his mask. Then he pulled out the camera he had kept warm beneath his shirt and took some pictures. These would be proof that they had made it. They were on top of the world!

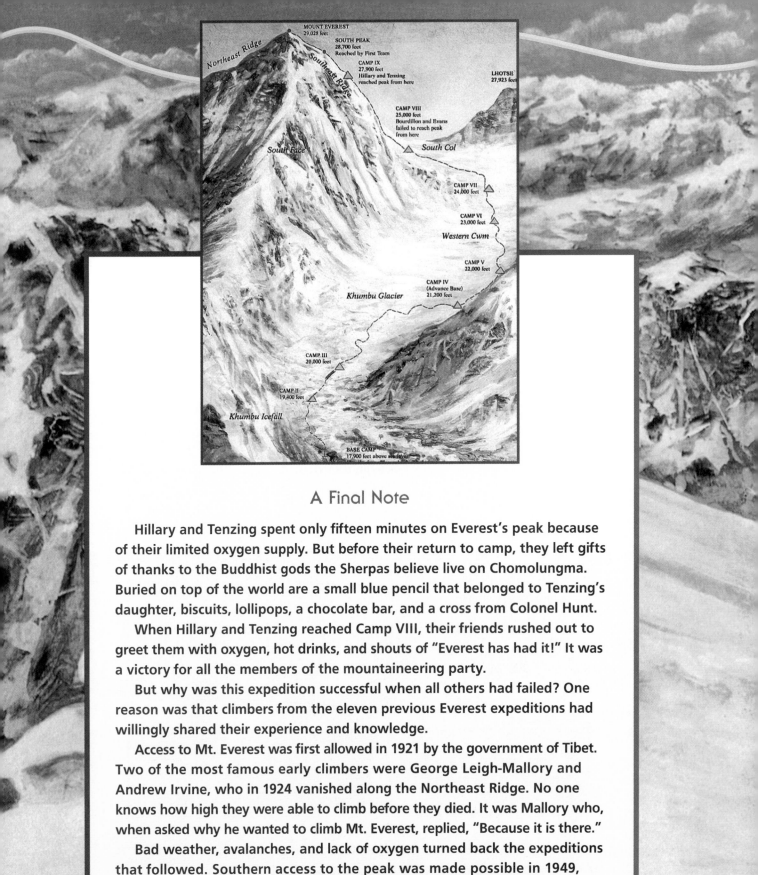

A Final Note

Hillary and Tenzing spent only fifteen minutes on Everest's peak because of their limited oxygen supply. But before their return to camp, they left gifts of thanks to the Buddhist gods the Sherpas believe live on Chomolungma. Buried on top of the world are a small blue pencil that belonged to Tenzing's daughter, biscuits, lollipops, a chocolate bar, and a cross from Colonel Hunt.

When Hillary and Tenzing reached Camp VIII, their friends rushed out to greet them with oxygen, hot drinks, and shouts of "Everest has had it!" It was a victory for all the members of the mountaineering party.

But why was this expedition successful when all others had failed? One reason was that climbers from the eleven previous Everest expeditions had willingly shared their experience and knowledge.

Access to Mt. Everest was first allowed in 1921 by the government of Tibet. Two of the most famous early climbers were George Leigh-Mallory and Andrew Irvine, who in 1924 vanished along the Northeast Ridge. No one knows how high they were able to climb before they died. It was Mallory who, when asked why he wanted to climb Mt. Everest, replied, "Because it is there."

Bad weather, avalanches, and lack of oxygen turned back the expeditions that followed. Southern access to the peak was made possible in 1949, when Nepal opened its borders to foreigners. The most helpful of the later expeditions was made by the Swiss. It was on their climb in 1952 that Tenzing and Raymond Lambert came within a thousand feet of the summit.

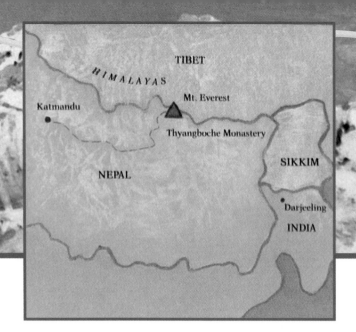

Another reason for Hillary and Tenzing's success was the superior planning by Colonel Hunt, the expedition's leader. When selecting climbers, he looked for men between the ages of twenty-five and forty with experience scaling the Himalayas and the ability to work selflessly with others. Fourteen men were chosen, including Michael Ward, who was to be the doctor. It was his responsibility to help prevent the illnesses that had plagued earlier expeditions. In addition, thirty-eight Sherpas were hired to carry supplies up the mountain.

Colonel Hunt had the men make practice climbs in Wales, the Alps, and the Himalayas. These treks enabled them to come together as a team and test new equipment and rations.

Superior supplies also gave the 1953 expedition an advantage over earlier teams. Improvements included tents made of a new cotton-nylon weave, two new styles of boots designed to prevent frostbite, and sleeping bags with both an inner and outer layer of down.

The use of more efficient and reliable oxygen sets, both closed circuit and open circuit, was the greatest improvement of all. Hillary and Tenzing used the open circuit, which mixed oxygen with the outside air. The closed circuit, used by Evans and Bourdillon, fed pure oxygen through a bag. The new systems allowed the climbers to conserve energy and climb faster, with less risk of depleting their oxygen supply.

Many countries have since sent people to Mt. Everest's summit, using further technological advancements. In 1963, Americans made the first traverse of the mountain, and six men reached the summit. Twenty-five years later, the Japanese made the first television broadcast from the top. In 1989, the first two women, both Americans, reached the peak. And in 1990, Sir Edmund Hillary's son, Peter, followed in his father's footsteps to stand on the world's highest point.

The conquest of Mt. Everest was the ultimate mountaineering test for Hillary and Tenzing. But it was also the fulfillment of a dream for those who had tried before, and an inspiration for all mountain adventurers to follow.

On Top of the World

Meet the Author and Illustrator

Mary Ann Fraser is both a writer and an illustrator. She wrote *On Top of the World: The Conquest of Mount Everest* because of the "amazement [she] felt for people's ability to reach new goals."

Theme Connections

Think About It

- How did teamwork and perseverance contribute to Edmund Hillary's success?

- Does teamwork help us persevere to reach our goals in everyday situations as well? When and how?

Record Ideas

 Record in your Writing Journal what you learned from your readings and classmates about the role of teamwork in perseverance.

Write a Letter

Write a thank-you letter to someone who has helped you persevere. Tell the person how he or she helped you and why it was important to you.

Saint George and the Dragon

from *The Faerie Queene* by Edmund Spenser
retold by Margaret Hodges
illustrated by Trina Schart Hyman

In the days when monsters and giants and fairy folk lived in England, a noble knight was riding across a plain. He wore heavy armor and carried an ancient silver shield marked with a red cross. It was dented with the blows of many battles fought long ago by other brave knights.

The Red Cross Knight had never yet faced a foe, and did not even know his name or where he had been born. But now he was bound on a great adventure, sent by the Queen of the Fairies to try his young strength against a deadly enemy, a dragon grim and horrible.

Beside him, on a little white donkey, rode a princess leading a white lamb, and behind her came a dwarf carrying a small bundle of food. The lady's lovely face was veiled and her shoulders were covered with a black cloak, as if she had a hidden sorrow in her heart. Her name was Una.

The dreadful dragon was the cause of her sorrow. He was laying waste to her land so that many frightened people had left their homes and run away. Others had shut themselves inside the walls of a castle with Una's father and mother, the king and queen of the country. But Una had set out alone from the safety of the castle walls to look for a champion who would face the terrible dragon. She had traveled a long, long way before she found the Red Cross Knight.

Like a sailor long at sea, under stormy winds and fierce sun, who begins to whistle merrily when he sees land, so Una was thankful.

Now the travelers rode together, through wild woods and wilderness, perils and dangers, toward Una's kingdom. The path they had to follow was straight and narrow, but not easy to see. Sometimes the Red Cross Knight rode too far ahead of Una and lost his way. Then she had to find him and guide him back to the path. So they journeyed on. With Una by his side, fair and faithful, no monster or giant could stand before the knight's bright sword.

After many days the path became thorny and led up a steep hillside, where a good old hermit lived in a little house by himself. While Una rested, the Red Cross Knight climbed with the hermit to the top of the hill and looked out across the valley. There against the evening sky they saw a mountaintop that touched the highest heavens. It was crowned with a glorious palace, sparkling like stars and circled with walls and towers of pearls and precious stones. Joyful angels were coming and going between heaven and the High City.

Then the Red Cross Knight saw that a little path led up the distant mountain to that city, and he said, "I thought that the fairest palace in the world was the crystal tower in the city of the Fairy Queen. Now I see a palace far more lovely. Una and I should go there at once."

But the old hermit said, "The Fairy Queen has sent you to do brave deeds in this world. That High City that you see is in another world. Before you climb the path to it and hang your shield on its wall, go down into the valley and fight the dragon that you were sent to fight.

"It is time for me to tell you that you were not born of fairy folk, but of English earth. The fairies stole you away as a baby while you slept in your cradle. They hid you in a farmer's field, where a plowman found you. He called you George, which means 'Plow the Earth' and 'Fight the Good Fight.' For you were born to be England's friend and patron saint, Saint George of Merry England."

Then George, the Red Cross Knight, returned to Una, and when morning came, they went together down into the valley. They rode through farmlands, where men and women working in their fields looked up and cheered because a champion had come to fight the dragon, and children clapped their hands to see the brave knight and the lovely lady ride by.

"Now we have come to my own country," said Una. "Be on your guard. See, there is the city and the great brass tower that my parents built strong enough to stand against the brassy-scaled dragon. There are my father and mother looking out from the walls, and the watchman stands at the top, waiting to call out the good news if help is coming."

Then they heard a hideous roaring that filled the air with terror and seemed to shake the ground. The dreadful dragon lay stretched on the sunny side of a great hill, like a great hill himself, and when he saw the knight's armor glistening in the sunlight, he came eagerly to do battle. The knight bade his lady stand apart, out of danger, to watch the fight, while the beast drew near, half flying, half running. His great size made a wide shadow under his huge body as a mountain casts a shadow on a valley. He reared high, monstrous, horrible, and vast, armed all over with scales of brass fitted so closely that no sword or spear could pierce them. They clashed with every movement. The dragon's wings stretched out like two sails when the wind fills them. The clouds fled before him. His huge, long tail, speckled red and black, wound in a hundred folds over his scaly back and swept the land behind him for almost half a mile. In his tail's end, two sharp stings were fixed. But sharper still were his cruel claws. Whatever he touched or drew within those claws was in deadly danger. His head was more hideous than tongue can tell, for his deep jaws gaped wide, showing three rows of iron teeth ready to devour his prey. A cloud of smothering smoke and burning sulfur poured from his throat, filling the air with its stench. His blazing eyes, flaming with rage, glared out from deep in his head. So he came toward the knight, raising his speckled breast, clashing his scales, as he leaped to greet his newest victim.

The knight on horseback fiercely rode at the dragon with all his might and couched his spear, but as they passed, the pointed steel glanced off the dragon's hard hide. The wrathful beast, surprised at the strength of the blow, turned quickly, and, passing the knight again, brushed him with his long tail so that horse and man fell to the ground.

Once more the Red Cross Knight mounted and attacked the dragon. Once more in vain. Yet the beast had never before felt such a mighty stroke from the hand of any man, and he was furious for revenge. With his waving wings spread wide, he lifted himself high from the ground, then, stooping low, snatched up both horse and man to carry them away. High above the plain he bore them as far as a bow can shoot an arrow, but even then the knight still struggled until the monster was forced to lower his paws so that both horse

and rider fought free. With the strength of three men, again the knight struck. The spear glanced off the scaly neck, but it pierced the dragon's left wing, spread broad above him, and the beast roared like a raging sea in a winter storm. Furious, he snatched the spear in his claws and broke it off, throwing forth flames of fire from his nostrils. Then he hurled his hideous tail about and wrapped it around the legs of the horse, until, striving to loose the knot, the horse threw its rider to the ground.

Quickly, the knight rose. He drew his sharp sword and struck the dragon's head so fiercely that it seemed nothing could withstand the blow. The dragon's crest was too hard to take a cut, but he wanted no more such blows. He tried to fly away and could not because of his wounded wing.

Loudly he bellowed——the like was never heard before——and from his body, like a wide devouring oven, sent a flame of fire that scorched the knight's face and heated his armor red-hot. Faint, weary, sore, burning with heat and wounds, the knight fell to the ground, ready to die, and the dragon clapped his iron wings in victory, while the lady, watching from afar, fell to her knees. She thought that her champion had lost the battle.

But it happened that where the knight fell, an ancient spring of silvery water bubbled from the ground. In that cool water the knight lay resting until the sun rose. Then he, too, rose to do battle again. And when the dragon saw him, he could hardly believe his eyes. Could this be the same knight, he wondered, or another who had come to take his place?

The knight brandished his bright blade, and it seemed sharper than ever, his hands even stronger. He smote the crested head with a blow so mighty that the dragon reared up like a hundred raging lions. His long, stinging tail threw down high trees and tore rocks to pieces. Lashing forward, it pierced the knight's shield and its point stuck fast in his shoulder. He tried to free himself from that barbed sting, but when he saw that his struggles were in vain, he raised his fighting sword and struck a blow that cut off the end of the dragon's tail.

Heart cannot think what outrage and what cries, with black smoke and flashing fire, the beast threw forth, turning the whole world to darkness. Gathering himself up, wild for revenge, he fiercely fell upon the sunbright shield and gripped it fast with his paws. Three times the knight tried and failed to pull the shield free. Then, laying about him with his trusty sword, he struck so many blows that fire flew from the dragon's coat like sparks from an anvil, and the beast raised one paw to defend himself. Striking with might and main, the knight severed the other paw, which still clung to the shield.

Now from the furnace inside himself, the dragon threw huge flames that covered all the heavens with smoke and brimstone so that the knight was forced to retreat to save his body from the scorching fire. Again, weary and wounded with his long fight, he fell. When gentle Una saw him lying motionless, she trembled with fear and prayed for his safety.

But he had fallen beneath a fair apple tree, its spreading branches covered with red fruit, and from that tree dropped a healing dew that the deadly dragon did not dare to come near. Once more the daylight faded and night spread over the earth. Under the apple tree the knight slept.

Then dawn chased away the dark, a lark mounted up to heaven, and up rose the brave knight with all his hurts and wounds healed, ready to fight again. When the dragon saw him, he began to be afraid. Still he rushed upon the knight, mouth gaping wide to swallow him whole. And the knight's bright weapon, taking advantage of that open

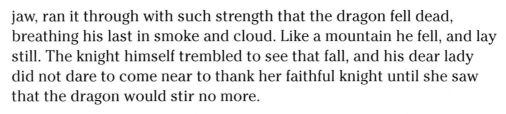

jaw, ran it through with such strength that the dragon fell dead, breathing his last in smoke and cloud. Like a mountain he fell, and lay still. The knight himself trembled to see that fall, and his dear lady did not dare to come near to thank her faithful knight until she saw that the dragon would stir no more.

Now our ship comes into port. Furl the sails and drop anchor. Safe from storm, Una is at her journey's end.

The watchman on the castle wall called out to the king and queen that the dragon was dead, and when the old king saw that it was true, he ordered the castle's great brass gates to be opened so that the tidings of peace and joy might spread through all the land. Trumpets sounded the news that the great beast had fallen. Then the king and queen came out of the city with all their nobles to meet the Red Cross Knight. Tall young men led the way, carrying laurel branches to lay at the hero's feet. Pretty girls wore wreaths of flowers and made music on tambourines. The children came dancing, laughing and singing, with a crown of flowers for Una. They gazed in wonder at the victorious knight.

But when the people saw where the dead dragon lay, they dared not come near to touch him. Some ran away, some pretended not to be afraid. One said the dragon might still be alive; one said he saw fire in the eyes. Another said the eyes were moving. When a foolish child ran forward to touch the dragon's claws, his mother scolded him. "How can I tell?" she said. "Those claws might scratch my son, or tear his tender hand." At last someone of the bolder men began to measure the dragon to prove how many acres his body covered.

The old king embraced and kissed his daughter. He gave gifts of gold and ivory and a thousand thanks to the dragonslayer. But the knight told the king never to forget the poor people, and gave the rich gifts to them. Then back to the palace all the people went, still singing, to feast and to hear the story of the knight's adventures with Una.

When the tale ended the king said, "Never did living man sail through such a sea of deadly dangers. Since you are now safely come to shore, stay here and live happily ever after. You have earned your rest."

But the brave knight answered, "No, my lord, I have sworn to give knight's service to the Fairy Queen for six years. Until then, I cannot rest."

The king said, "I have promised that the dragonslayer should have Una for his wife, and be king after me. If you love each other, my daughter is yours now. My kingdom shall be yours when you have done your service for the Fairy Queen and returned to us."

Then he called Una, who came no longer wearing her black cloak and her veil, but dressed in a lily-white gown that shimmered like silver. Never had the knight seen her so beautiful. Whenever he looked at the brightness of her sunshiny face, his heart melted with pleasure.

So Una and the Red Cross Knight were married and lived together joyfully. But the knight did not forget his promise to serve the Fairy Queen, and when she called him into service, off he rode on brave adventures until at last he earned his name, Saint George of Merry England.

That is how it is when jolly sailors come into a quiet harbor. They unload their cargo, mend ship, and take on fresh supplies. Then away they sail on another long voyage, while we are left on shore, waving good-bye and wishing them Godspeed.

Saint George and the Dragon

Meet the Author

Margaret Hodges' father asked her older cousin, Margaret Carlisle, to move in with the family after his wife died. It was Cousin Margaret and Hodges' father who helped lead Hodges down the path to writing by giving her many books to read. While at public school Number 60 in Indianapolis, Indiana, she wrote a poem. It was published in the children's magazine, *St. Nicholas*. Hodges even had her own television show for ten years as the storyteller on "Tell Me a Story." It aired locally in Pittsburgh, Pennsylvania.

Meet the Illustrator

Trina Shart Hyman worked many years before she became a famous children's illustrator. She started drawing when she was young and went on to art schools in her hometown of Philadelphia, Pennsylvania. While living in Sweden, Hyman got her first job illustrating *Pippi Longstocking*. It took her only two weeks. She later returned to the United States and had many rejections before getting work as an illustrator. She won a Caldecott Award, one of the most important awards for children's books, for *Saint George and the Dragon*. Hyman is known for using people from her life, including her neighbors, friends, their children, and her own children, in her illustrations.

Theme Connections

Think About It

- What does this selection teach us about being persistent?

- Is perseverance different from bravery? Why or why not?

- What in the knight's backgound prepared him for his challenge?

Record Ideas

 Work with a partner and imagine you are reporters about to interview St. George about his battle with the dragon. What questions will you ask him?

Role-Play an Interview

Join another pair of students and interview each other. Working with your original partner, decide who will be the reporter and who will be the knight. If you are the reporter, interview the other knight. If you are the knight, let the other reporter interview you.

FINE Art

Brittany Children. c.1892. **Enella Benedict.** Oil on canvas. $31\frac{5}{8} \times 24\frac{1}{8}$ in. The National Museum of Women in the Arts, Washington, DC. Gift of Elizabeth Sita.

On the Dogger Bank. William Clarkson Stanfield. Oil on canvas. Victoria and Albert Museum. Photo: By courtesy of The Board of Trustees of the Victoria and Albert Museum, London/ET Archive, London/Superstock.

Four Jockeys Riding Hard. c.1815. **Théodore Géricault.** Museé Bonnat, Bayonne, France. Photo: Giraudon/Art Resource, NY.

A Picture Book of Jesse Owens

David A. Adler

illustrated by Robert Casilla

Jesse Owens was born on September 12, 1913, on a small farm in Oakville, Alabama. His given name was James Cleveland. His nickname was J.C.

J.C.'s grandparents had been slaves. His parents, Henry and Mary Emma Owens, were sharecroppers. They farmed on another man's land and shared with him their small crop of corn and cotton.

J.C.'s parents lived with their many children in a house that J.C. later described as "wooden planks thrown together." The roof leaked. In winter, cold wind blew through the walls. In summer, the house was so hot, J.C. felt he could hardly breathe.

J.C. was skinny and often sick with what his family called a "devil's cold." It was probably pneumonia. There was no money for doctors or medicine, so to cure J.C.'s illness, his mother wrapped him in cloth and put him by the fireplace.

A large lump once appeared on J.C.'s leg. His mother cut it out with a hot kitchen knife. J.C. said later that's when he learned "the meaning of pain."

When J.C. was about nine his family moved to what his mother said would be "a better life." They moved north to Cleveland, Ohio.

On J.C.'s first day of school in Cleveland, his teacher asked him his name. "J.C. Owens," he said. She thought he said "Jesse" and wrote that in her book. From then on he was known as Jesse Owens.

In Cleveland Jesse's father and older brothers worked in a steel mill. His mother worked washing clothes and cleaning

houses. Jesse worked, too——sweeping floors, shining shoes, watering plants, and delivering groceries. Even with the whole family working, the Owenses were still very poor.

In 1927 Jesse entered Fairmount Junior High School. There he met Charles Riley, a gym teacher and coach of the track team. Riley saw Jesse run in gym class and asked him to train for the track team. Because Jesse worked afternoons, he met the coach every morning before school. Jesse felt very close to Coach Riley and called him "Pop."

Coach Riley taught Jesse to run as if the ground were on fire. He said Jesse should train not just for the next race, but to be the best runner he could be. He told Jesse to always train for the future——"for four years from next Friday."

With a lot of work and with what Jesse later called his "lucky legs," he ran so fast and with such grace that he was called a "floating wonder." One newspaper reporter wrote that when Jesse Owens ran, it seemed like he was about to "soar into the air."

In 1928 Jesse Owens set the junior high school record for the long jump and the high jump. In 1933 he set high school records for the long jump and for the 220-yard dash.

He went to Ohio State University and was on the track team there, too. On May 25, 1935, at the Big Ten Championship meet, Jesse had what has been called the greatest day in track-and-field history. He set three world records and tied a fourth, all within forty-five minutes.

Several weeks later, on July 5, 1935, Jesse Owens married Minnie Ruth Solomon, a young woman he had met at Fairmount Junior High School. He said later, "I fell in love with her the first time we talked, and a little more every time after that." She was quiet, smart, a loving and supportive wife for Jesse, and a good mother to their three daughters, Gloria, Marlene, and Beverly.

In 1936 the Olympic games were held in Berlin, Germany. Adolf Hitler, the German Nazi leader at the time, said native Germans were part of a "master race"; that blacks and especially Jews were inferior. Jesse Owens and other athletes proved he was wrong. Jesse Owens won four gold medals and was the hero of the 1936 Olympics.

He tied the Olympic record of 10.3 seconds for the 100-meter race, set a new world record of 20.7 seconds for 200 meters around a curve, and was part of the team to set a record for the 400-meter relays.

With a long jump of 26 feet, 5 5/16 inches (8.06 meters), Jesse Owens set a new Olympic record, too.

He "seemed to be jumping clear out of Germany," wrote one reporter.

Lutz Long, the popular German jumper who came in second, ran over to shake Jesse's hand. The picture of the two athletes——a black American and a white German in the midst of all the hate and prejudice around them——is one of the lasting images of the 1936 Olympics.

There was a parade in Cleveland to welcome Jesse Owens home, and in New York City, he rode at the head of a ticker-tape parade of the entire Olympic team. But there was prejudice, too, and Jesse said later that when he returned to the United States, "I couldn't ride in the front of the bus . . . I couldn't live where I wanted."

In the years following Jesse's great victories at the 1936 Olympics, he worked as a playground director, made speeches, appeared on radio programs, and led a band of black musicians. He started the Jesse Owens Dry Cleaning

Company in 1938, but it went out of business a year later. He continued to run, too, in exhibition races against baseball players, cars, motorcycles, dogs, and horses. Years later he wrote that sometimes those races made him feel more like a spectacle than an athlete, but he also wrote, "At least it was an honest living. I had to eat."

Jesse Owens gave hundreds of speeches on the value of family, religion, and hard work. He was warm and friendly, and audiences loved to listen to him.

Jesse Owens also wrote his autobiography and two books on issues facing the black community. In the first one, *Blackthink: My Life as Black Man and White Man,* he wrote, "If the Negro doesn't succeed in today's America, it is because he has chosen to fail." Two years later, in *I Have Changed,* he seemed more aware of the prejudice blacks faced every day and showed more understanding for those who fought for equality.

For many years, Jesse Owens was called the "World's Fastest Human," and he won many awards. In 1950 he was named the all-time greatest track-and-field athlete by the Associated Press. In 1976 President Gerald R. Ford gave him the Presidential Medal of Freedom. In 1979 President Jimmy Carter gave him the Living Legends Award.

Jesse Owens died of lung cancer on March 31, 1980, in Tucson, Arizona. People all over the world were saddened as they remembered his great victories and his warm smile. The races Jesse Owens ran were over in seconds, but the story of his rise from a poor sharecropper's son to a world hero has inspired young people to dream and to work hard to make their dreams come true.

A Picture Book of Jesse Owens

Meet the Author

David Adler was born into a family with five brothers and sisters. They all had their own hobbies. One brother liked to make rock candy. Another brother made dirt clean. As a group, the Adler children liked to collect things, including baseball cards, bottle caps, and autographs. Being raised in this kind of family helped mold Adler into a very successful writer of stories for children.

Meet the Illustrator

Robert Casilla was born in Jersey City, New Jersey. He began illustrating after graduating from the School of Visual Arts. He said, "I find great rewards and satisfaction in illustrating for children." He enjoys working with watercolors for his illustrations. Many of his illustrations are for biographies. When he illustrates a biography, he tries to learn a lot about the person. Knowing the person very well helps him when he works on the art.

Theme Connections

Think About It

- How do the illustrations contribute to this biography?

Record Ideas

 What have you learned about perseverance from this selection? Write your thoughts in your Writing Journal.

Bring in a Photograph

Work with a classmate to find a photograph or a picture of someone you believe has persevered to achieve his or her goals and dreams. Join a small group of your classmates and tell them who the person is, what he or she has accomplished, and how he or she has persevered.

Mother to Son

Langston Hughes
illustrated by Anna Rich

Well, son, I'll tell you:
Life for me ain't been no crystal stair.
It's had tacks in it,
And splinters,
And boards torn up,
And places with no carpet on the floor——
Bare.
But all the time
I'se been a-climbin' on,
And reachin' landin's,
And turnin' corners,
And sometimes goin' in the dark
Where there ain't been no light.
So boy, don't you turn back.
Don't you set down on the steps
'Cause you finds it's kinder hard.
Don't you fall now——
For I'se still goin', honey,
I'se still climbin',
And life for me ain't been no crystal stair.

Back to the Drawing Board

from *The Wright Brothers: How They Invented the Airplane*
by Russell Freedman
with original photographs by Wilbur and Orville Wright

The year was 1899. In the workroom of their bicycle shop in Dayton, Ohio, two brothers designed and built their first experimental aircraft——a biplane glider flown as a kite. With its successful flight, Wilbur and Orville Wright's next step was to build a man-carrying glider. The performance of this glider, which they tested at Kitty Hawk, North Carolina, in the fall of 1900, left the brothers hopeful. They returned to Kitty Hawk in July 1901, to test a bigger, newly designed glider, but experienced one problem after another. By the end of August, Wilbur and Orville, puzzled and discouraged, went back to Dayton. Wilbur later wrote, "We doubted that we would ever resume our experiments. When we looked at the time and money which we had expended, and considered the progress made and the distance yet to go, we considered our experiments a failure. At this time I made the prediction that man would sometime fly, but that it would not be in our lifetime."

Flying a glider as a kite.

The experiments that Wilbur and Orville had carried out with their latest glider in 1901 were far from encouraging. Reflecting on their problems, Wilbur observed: "We saw that the calculations upon which all flying machines had been based were unreliable, and that all were simply groping in the dark. Having set out with absolute faith in the existing scientific data, we were driven to doubt one thing after another, till finally, after two years of experiment, we cast it all aside, and decided to rely entirely on our own investigations."

In the gaslit workroom behind their bicycle shop, Wilbur and Orville began to compile their own data. They wanted to test different types of wing surfaces and obtain accurate air-pressure tables. To do this, they built a wind tunnel ——a wooden box 6 feet long with a glass viewing window on top and a fan at one end. It wasn't the world's first wind tunnel, but it would be the first to yield valuable results for the construction of a practical airplane.

The materials needed to make model wings, or airfoils, and the tools to shape them were right at hand. Using tin shears, hammers, files, and a soldering iron, the brothers fashioned as many as two hundred miniature wings out of tin, galvanized iron, steel, solder, and wax. They made wings that were thick or thin, curved or flat, wings with rounded tips and pointed tips, slender wings and stubby wings. They attached these experimental airfoils to balances made of bicycle spokes and

A replica of the Wrights' pioneering wind tunnel.

old hacksaw blades. Then they tested the wings in their wind tunnel to see how they behaved in a moving airstream.

For several weeks they were absorbed in painstaking and systematic lab work——testing, measuring, and calculating as they tried to unlock the secrets of an aircraft wing. The work was tedious. It was repetitious. Yet they would look back on that winter as a time of great excitement, when each new day promised discoveries waiting to be made. "Wilbur and I could hardly wait for morning to come," Orville declared, "to get at something that interested us. *That's* happiness."

The Wrights knew that they were exploring uncharted territory with their wind-tunnel tests. Each new bit of data jotted down in their notebooks added to their understanding of how an airfoil works. Gradually they replaced the calculations of others with facts and figures of their own. Their doubts vanished, and their faith in themselves grew. When their lab tests were finally completed, they felt confident that they could calculate in advance the performance of an aircraft's wings with far greater accuracy than had ever before been possible.

Armed with this new knowledge, they designed their biggest glider yet. Its wings, longer and narrower than before, measured 32 feet from tip to tip and 5 feet from front to rear. For the first time, the new glider had a tail——two 6-foot-high vertical fins, designed to help stabilize the machine during turns. The hip cradle developed the year before to control wing warping was retained. The craft weighed just under 120 pounds.

With growing anticipation, Wilbur and Orville prepared for their 1902 trip to the Outer Banks of North Carolina. "They really ought to get away for a while," their sister Katharine wrote to her father. "Will is thin and nervous and so is Orv. They will be all right when they get down in the sand where the salt breezes blow. . . . They think that life at Kitty Hawk cures all ills, you know.

"The flying machine is in process of making now. Will spins the sewing machine around by the hour while Orv squats around marking the places to sew [the cotton wing covering]. There is no place in the house to live but I'll be lonesome enough by this time next week and wish I could have some of their racket around."

The brothers reached the Outer Banks at the end of August with their trunks, baggage, and crates carrying the glider parts. At Kill Devil Hills, their launching site, they found that their wooden shed from the year before had been battered by winter storms. They set to work making repairs and remodeling the building, so they could use it instead of a tent as their new living quarters.

"We fitted up our living arrangements much more comfortably than last year," Wilbur reported. "Our kitchen is immensely improved, and then we have made beds on the second floor and now sleep aloft. It is an improvement over cots. We also have a bicycle which runs much better over the sand than we hoped, so

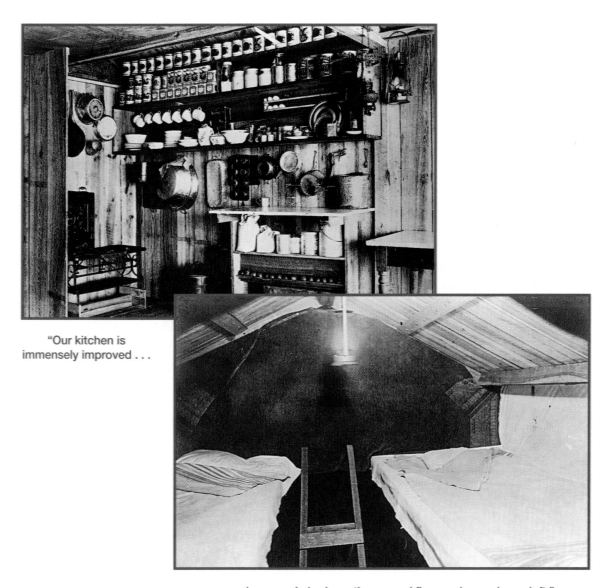

"Our kitchen is immensely improved . . .

. . . we have made beds on the second floor and now sleep aloft."

that it takes only about an hour to make the round trip to Kitty Hawk instead of three hours as before. There are other improvements . . . so we are having a splendid time."

By the middle of September they had assembled their new glider and were ready to try it out. This year they took turns in the pilot's position, giving Orville a chance to fly for the first time. To begin with, they were very cautious. They would launch the machine from the slope on Big Hill and glide only a short distance as they practiced working the controls. Steering to the right or left was accomplished by warping the wings, with the glider always turning toward the lower wing. Up-and-down movements were controlled by the forward elevator.

In a few days they made dozens of short but successful test glides. At this point, things looked more promising than ever. The only mishap occurred one afternoon when Orville was at the controls. That evening he recorded the incident in his diary:

"I was sailing along smoothly without any trouble . . . when I

Wilbur and Dan Tate launch the 1902 glider with Orville at the controls.

96

noticed that one wing was getting a little too high and that the machine was slowly sliding off in the opposite direction. . . . The next thing I knew was that the wing was very high in the air, a great deal higher than before, and I thought I must have worked the twisting apparatus the wrong way. Thinking of nothing else . . . I threw the wingtips to their greatest angle. By this time I found suddenly that I was making a descent backwards toward the low wing, from a height of 25 or 30 feet. . . . The result was a heap of flying machine, cloth and sticks in a heap, with me in the center without a bruise or scratch. The experiments thereupon suddenly came to a close till repairs can be made. In spite of this sad catastrophe we are tonight in a hilarious mood as a result of the encouraging performance of the machine."

A few days' labor made the glider as good as new. It wasn't seriously damaged again during hundreds of test glides, and it repeatedly withstood rough landings at full speed. Wilbur and Orville became more and more confident. "Our new machine is a very great improvement over anything we had built before and over anything anyone has built," Wilbur told his father. "Everything is so much more satisfactory that we now believe that the flying problem is really nearing its solution."

And yet the solution was not yet quite at hand. As they continued their test flights, a baffling new problem arose. On most flights, the glider performed almost perfectly. But every so often——in about one flight out of fifty——it would spin out of control as the pilot tried to level off after a turn.

"We were at a loss to know what the cause might be," wrote Wilbur. "The new machine . . . had a vertical tail while the earlier ones were tailless; and the wing tips were on a line with the center while the old machines had the tips drawn down like a gull's wings. The trouble might be due to either of these differences."

First they altered the wingtips and went back to Big Hill for more test flights. Again, the glider spun out of control during a turn. Then they focused their attention to the machine's 6-foot-high double-vaned tail, which was fixed rigidly in place. They had installed this tail to help stabilize the glider during turns, but now, it seemed, something was wrong.

Lying in bed one sleepless night, Orville figured out what the problem was. The fixed tail worked perfectly well most of the time. During some turns, however——when the airspeed was low and the pilot failed to level off soon enough——pressure was built up on the tail, throwing the glider off balance and into a spin. That's just what happened to Orville the day of his accident. The cure was to make the tail movable——like a ship's rudder or a bird's tail.

The next morning at breakfast, Orville told Wilbur about his idea. After thinking it over for a few minutes, Wilbur agreed. Then he offered an idea of his own. Why not connect the new movable tail to the wing-warping wires? This would allow the pilot to twist the wings and turn the tail at the same time, simply by shifting his hips. With the wings and tail coordinated, the glider would always make a smooth banked turn.

They removed the original tail and installed a movable single-vaned tail 5 feet high. From then on, there were no more problems. The movable tail rudder finally gave the Wright brothers complete control of their glider. "With this improvement our serious troubles ended," wrote Wilbur, "and thereafter we devoted ourselves to the work of gaining skill by continued practice."

As the brothers worked on their glider, their camp was filling up with visitors again. Their older brother Lorin arrived at the end of September to see what Wilbur and Orville were up to. Then Octave Chanute, a civil engineer who had also conducted gliding experiments, showed up, along with two other gliding enthusiasts. Now six bunks were jammed into the narrow sleeping quarters up in the rafters. At night, the sounds of Wilbur's harmonica, Orville's mandolin, and a chorus of male voices drifted across the lonely dunes.

With their movable tail rudder, the Wrights felt confident that their glider could master the winds. They practiced flying at every opportunity, staying on at their camp until late in October, long after all their visitors had left. "Glides were made whenever weather conditions were favorable," Wilbur recalled. "Many days were lost on account of rain. Still more were lost on account of light winds. Whenever the breeze fell below six miles an hour, very hard running was required to get the machine started, and the task of carrying it back up the hill was real labor . . . but when the wind rose to 20 miles an hour, gliding was a real sport, for starting was easy and the labor of carrying the machine back uphill was performed by the wind."

One day they had a wind of about 30 miles an hour and were able to glide in it without any trouble. "That was the highest wind a gliding machine was ever in, so that we now hold all the records!" Orville wrote home. "The largest machine ever handled . . . the longest distance glide (American), the longest time in the air, the smallest angle of descent, and the highest wind!!! Well, I'll leave the rest of the 'blow' till we get home."

That season the Wrights had designed, built, and flown the world's first fully controllable aircraft. The three-dimensional system of aircraft control worked out by the brothers is the basic system used even today in all winged vehicles that depend on the atmosphere for support.

Except for an engine, their 1902 glider flew just as a Boeing 747 airliner or a jet fighter flies. A modern plane "warps" its wings in order to turn or level off by moving the ailerons on the

Lorin Wright took this photo of his brothers and their visitors at Kill Devil Hills in October 1902. From left: Octave Chanute, Orville, Wilbur, Augustus M. Herring, George A. Spratt, Dan Tate.

rear edges of the wings. It makes smooth banking turns with the aid of a movable vertical rudder. And it noses up or down by means of an elevator (usually located at the rear of the plane).

Wilbur and Orville made hundreds of perfectly controlled glides in 1902. They proved that their laboratory tests were accurate. The next step was to build a powered airplane. "Before leaving camp," Orville wrote, "we were already at work on the general design of a new machine which we proposed to propel with a motor."

The Wright brothers could not just take a motor and put it into one of their gliders. First they needed a motor that was light yet powerful. Then they had to design propellers that would produce enough thrust to drive a flying machine through the air. Finally they had to build an aircraft body sturdy enough to carry the weight and withstand the vibrations of the motor and propellers.

Wilbur wrote to several manufacturers of gasoline engines, asking if they could supply an engine that would produce at least 8 horsepower, yet weigh less than 200 pounds. No company was willing to take on the assignment. Wilbur and Orville decided to build the motor themselves with the help of Charlie Taylor, a mechanic they had hired to help out in the bicycle shop.

"We didn't make any drawings," Taylor later recalled. "One of us would sketch out the part we were talking about on a piece of scratch paper and I'd spike the sketch over my bench." In just six weeks, they had the motor on the block testing its power. A marvel of lightness and efficiency, it weighed 179 pounds and generated more than 12 horsepower.

The propellers were much more difficult, since no reliable data on aerial propellers existed. "What at first seemed a simple problem became more complex the longer we studied it," wrote Orville. "With the machine moving forward, the air flying backward, the propellers turning sideways, and nothing standing still, it seemed impossible to find a starting point from which to trace the various simultaneous reactions. . . . Our minds became so obsessed with it that we could do little other work."

During several months of study, experiments, and discussion, Wilbur and Orville filled no less than five notebooks with formulas, diagrams, tables of data, and computations. They were the first to understand that an aerial propeller works like a rotary wing. The same physical laws that produce upward lift when a curved wing slices through the air will also produce forward thrust when a curved propeller blade rotates. Once they had grasped this idea, the Wrights were able to design propeller blades with the right diameter, pitch, and area for their needs.

"Isn't it astonishing that all these secrets have been preserved for so many years just so that we could discover them!!!" Orville told a friend. "Well, our propellers are so different from any that have been used before that they will have to either be a good deal better, or a good deal worse."

They decided to use two propellers turning in opposite directions, so that any twisting effect on the aircraft would be neutralized. The propellers were connected to the motor through a sprocket-and-chain transmission, like the kind used

"They decided to use two propellers turning in opposite directions . . ."

to drive a bicycle. The motor rested on the lower wing, to the right of the pilot, so it would not fall on him in case of a headlong crash. To balance the motor's extra weight, the right wing was 4 inches longer than the left.

In the Wright brothers' gliders, the wing-warping wires had twisted the entire wing up or down. In their new powered machine, the front edge of each wing was fixed rigidly in place. Only the rear outer edges of the wingtips could now be flexed, much like the movements of ailerons on a modern aircraft. The controls were similar to those in the 1902 glider——a padded hip cradle to operate the wing warping and the tail rudder, and a wooden hand lever to control the forward elevator. With a wingspan of just over 40 feet, the new machine was their biggest yet. They called it their first "Flyer."

There wasn't enough space in the bicycle shop workroom to assemble the entire machine. The center section alone was so big that it blocked the passage leading to the front of the shop.

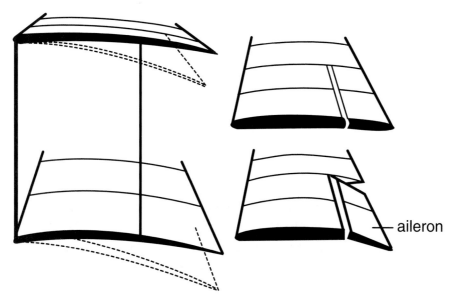

Wing warping in the 1903 Wright Flyer served the same function as ailerons on a modern aircraft.

When a customer walked in, one of the brothers had to go out a side door and walk around to the front to wait on the customer. They didn't see their Flyer in one piece until the parts were shipped to the Outer Banks and assembled there.

Wilbur and Orville returned to their camp at Kill Devil Hills on September 25, 1903, and again found a storm-ravaged camp building. They made repairs and put up a second building to use as a workshop for assembling and housing their Flyer. On days with good winds, they took out their old 1902 glider for practice flights. On calm or rainy days, they worked on the new machine indoors.

Their progress was slowed by frustrating problems with the propeller shafts and the transmission sprocket wheels, which kept coming loose as the motor was being tested. Meanwhile, winter arrived early. Rain, snow, and freezing winds buffeted their camp. The water in their washbasin was frozen solid in the morning. They converted an old carbide can into a woodburning stove and piled on the blankets when they went to bed.

"We have no trouble keeping warm at nights," Wilbur wrote home. "In addition to the classifications of last year, to wit, 1, 2, 3 and 4 blanket nights, we now have 5 blanket nights, & 5 blankets & 2 quilts. Next come 5 blankets, 2 quilts & fire; then 5, 2, fire, & hot-water jug. This is as far as we have got so far. Next come the addition of sleeping without undressing, then shoes & hats, and finally overcoats. We intend to be comfortable while we are here."

The propeller shafts gave them so much trouble that Orville had to go all the way back to Dayton to have new ones made. He was returning to North Carolina on the train when he read a newspaper story about Samuel Pierpont Langley's second and last attempt to launch a man-carrying airplane on December 8, 1903. Once again, the *Great Aerodrome* and its pilot had crashed into the Potomac——and so had the $73,000 Langley had spent on it. So far, the Wrights had spent less than $1,000 on their still untested Flyer.

Orville reached Kill Devil Hills with the new propeller shafts on December 11. The brothers were anxious to test their Flyer before the weather got any worse. To launch the machine, they had built a movable starting track——a 60-foot-long wooden rail made of four 15-foot sections. The top of the rail was covered with a thin metal strip. For takeoff, the Flyer would be placed over this track with its landing skids resting on a small two-wheeled dolly, or "truck" as the Wrights called it, which ran freely along the rail. When the propellers started to turn, the Flyer would ride down the monorail on its truck, heading into the wind until it gained enough airspeed to lift off and fly. The Wrights called this starting track their "Grand Junction Railroad."

They were ready for their first trial on Monday, December 14, but the wind that day wasn't strong enough to permit a launching from level ground. Instead of waiting any longer, they decided to try a downhill launching from the side of Big Kill Devil Hill.

They hoisted a red signal flag to the top of a pole, alerting the lifesaving station a mile away. Before long, five men, two small boys, and a dog came trudging up the beach. The lifesavers had agreed to act as witnesses and help move more than 700 pounds of flying machine over the sand.

Everyone pitched in. Balancing the Flyer by hand, they rolled it along the starting rail, moving each 15-foot section of track from the rear to the front as they went along. When they reached the bottom of Big Hill, the entire 60-foot track was laid

The flyer sits atop its movable 60-foot starting track.

on the hillside. Then the Flyer was pulled up the rail and placed in position. "With the slope of the track, the thrust of the propellers, and the machine starting directly into the wind, we did not anticipate any trouble in getting up flying speed on the 60-foot monorail track," Orville recalled.

They started the motor. The propellers turned over, paddling loudly. The transmission chains clattered. The motor popped and coughed, and the whole machine seemed to shudder and shake. The two small boys took one look, backed away, and went racing across the sand dunes with the dog at their heels.

Wilbur and Orville tossed a coin to decide who should try first. Wilbur won. He lay down on the lower wing, sliding his hips into the padded wing-warping cradle. Orville took a position at one of the wings to help balance the machine as it roared down the starting track. Then Wilbur loosened the restraining rope that held the Flyer in place. The machine shot down the track with such speed that Orville was left behind, gasping for breath.

After a 35- to 40-foot run, the Flyer lifted up from the rail. Once in the air, Wilbur tried to point the machine up at too steep an angle. It climbed a few feet, stalled, settled backward, and smashed into the sand on its left wing. Orville's stopwatch showed that the Flyer had flown for just $3\frac{1}{2}$ seconds.

Wilbur wasn't hurt, but it took two days to repair the damage to the Flyer. They were ready to try again on Thursday, December 17, 1903.

They woke up that morning to freezing temperatures and a blustery 27-mile-an-hour wind. Puddles of rainwater in the sand hollows around their camp were crusted with ice. They spent the early part of the morning indoors, hoping the wind would die down a little. At 10 o'clock, with the wind as brisk as ever, they decided to attempt a flight. "The conditions were very unfavorable," wrote Wilbur. "Nevertheless, as we had set our minds on being home by Christmas, we determined to go ahead."

They hoisted the signal flag to summon the lifesavers. Then, in the biting wind, they laid down all four sections of the starting track on a level stretch of sand just below their camp. They had to go inside frequently to warm their hands by the carbide-can stove.

By the time the starting track was in place, five witnesses had shown up——four men from the lifesaving station and a teenage boy from the nearby village of Nags Head. They helped haul the Flyer over to the launching site.

Now it was Orville's turn at the controls. First he set up his big box camera, focused on a point near the end of the track, and inserted a glass-plate negative. Then he placed the rubber bulb that tripped the shutter in the big hand of John Daniels, one of the lifesaving men, and asked him to squeeze the bulb just as the Flyer took off.

The brothers shook hands. "We couldn't help but notice how they held onto each other's hand," one of the lifesavers recalled, "sort of like two folks parting who weren't sure they'd ever see one another again."

Orville took the pilot's position, his hips in the wing-warping cradle, the toes of his shoes hooked over a small supporting rack behind him. Like his brother, he was wearing a dark suit, a stiff collar, a necktie, and a cap. Wilbur turned to the lifesaving men and told them "not to look so sad, but to . . . laugh and holler and clap . . . and try to cheer Orville up when he started."

"After running the motor a few minutes to heat it up," Orville recalled, "I released the wire that held the machine to the track, and the machine started forward into the wind. Wilbur ran at the side of the machine, holding the wing to balance it on the track. Unlike the start on the 14th, made in a calm, the machine, facing a 27-mile-per-hour wind, started very slowly. Wilbur was able to stay with it till it lifted from the track after a forty-foot run. [John] snapped the camera for us, taking a picture just as the machine had reached the end of the track and had risen to a height of about two feet."

Wilbur had just let go of the wing when John Daniels tripped the shutter. The lifesavers broke into a ragged cheer. The Flyer was flying!

Orville couldn't hear them. He hung on to the control lever and stared straight ahead as the icy wind whistled past his ears and the motor clattered beside him. Buffeted by gusts, the Flyer lurched forward like a drunken bird. "The course of the flight up and down was exceedingly erratic," wrote Orville, "partly due to the irregularity of the air, and partly to lack of experience in handling this machine. . . . As a result the machine would rise suddenly to about ten feet, and then as suddenly dart for the ground. A sudden dart when a little over a hundred feet from the end of the track, or a little over 120 feet from the point at which it rose into the air, ended the flight. . . .

"This flight lasted only 12 seconds, but it was nevertheless the first in the history of the world in which a machine carrying a man had raised itself by its own power into the air in full flight, had sailed forward without reduction of speed, and had finally landed at a point as high as that from which it had started."

It had happened so quickly. A boy could have thrown a ball as far as the Flyer had flown. But the Wright brothers were elated. They had launched a flying machine that could actually fly.

The Wright brothers' first flight.

Back to the Drawing Board

Meet the Author

Russell Freedman grew up in San Francisco, California. His parents were good friends with several authors. Many of these authors came over to discuss the news of the day with the Freedmans. Hearing these discussions helped Freedman learn to develop his own ideas, a skill he would use well as an author. He took the idea for his first book from an article in *The New York Times* about teenagers who had already done amazing things in their lives. He called it *Teenagers Who Made History*.

Theme Connections

Think About It

- How might the world be different if the Wright Brothers hadn't persevered and achieved their goal?

Record Ideas

Make a list of four or five quotations that focus on perseverance you like best in your Writing Journal. Write about how they might influence your life in the future.

Make a Display

Select your favorite quotation from all you have heard. Join with a group of your classmates and decide how to display your quotations in a poster.

Crazy Boys

by Beverly McLoughland

Watching buzzards,
Flying kites,
Lazy, crazy boys
The Wrights. They

Tried to fly
Just like a bird
Foolish dreamers
Strange. Absurd. We

Scoffed and scorned
Their dreams of flight
But we were wrong
And they were Wright.

Bibliography

The Circuit: Stories from the Life of a Migrant Child

by Francisco Jiménez. Panchito is a Mexican-American migrant worker who shares his family's stories of everyday life and everyday struggles.

Ella Enchanted

by Gail Carson Levine. Ella is cursed with the "gift" of obedience: no matter who orders her to do something, she has to do it. But Ella's not giving up until she finds a way to break the curse and live happily ever after.

Littlejim's Dream

by Gloria Houston. Littlejim's father has no interest in his son's dream of attending college until problems in the family are solved by Littlejim's brilliance.

The Moon and I

by Betsy Byars. While describing her humorous encounters with a black snake that prowls around her writing cottage, Byars explains the process by which she writes a book.

Out of the Dust

by Karen Hesse. Life in the dust bowl of Oklahoma is as dry and gritty as the dust that covers everything. Can Billie Jo overcome the unrelenting misery of the country's Depression and find hope?

Sing for Your Father, Su Phan

by Stella Pevsner and Fay Tang. The Vietnamese War was not history to Su Phan; it was reality. This is her story.

Whitewash

by Ntozake Shange. A young black girl is spray-painted white by a vicious gang. How does she find the courage to leave her room and return to the world?

Wilma Unlimited: How Wilma Rudolph Became the World's Fastest Woman

by Kathleen Krull. Wilma Rudolph was partially paralyzed by polio, but she refused to give up until she realized her dreams and became an Olympic gold medallist.

Uncovering the Past

Have you ever wondered how we know anything about people who lived so long ago that there were no books or other written records? What can we learn from old bones and broken pots? Quite a bit, if you know how. It's a kind of detective work called archaeology. In this unit you can learn both how archaeologists work and what they have figured out about some of the fascinating civilizations that existed before there was written history.

Digging Up the Past

from ***Digging Up the Past:***
The Story of an Archaeological Adventure
by Carollyn James
illustrated by Ed Tadiello

Walking up the hill to his friend Joe's, Damien Shea was thinking about Rocky Mountain sheep and what he was going to do for the last three days of spring break.

With one foot on the sidewalk and the other in the road, Damien pretended he was a Rocky Mountain sheep climbing up a rock slide. One false move, one loose rock, and he would tumble off the mountain. He kept his eyes on his feet.

"Ah, ha!" he said. Next to his left shoe, poking out of the leaves at the curb, was a quarter. Before putting it in his pocket along with the two large bolts, the pen, and the screwdriver he'd found since breakfast, Damien looked at the coin closely. It was dated 1973. This quarter is older than I am, he said to himself, thinking it was better to spend it before it got any older.

Before seeing Joe, Damien bought gum at the 7-Eleven. He and Joe would need something to chew on while they explored the woods behind Joe's house.

Joe was lucky to have the town's park for a backyard. The park was all wooded, with a crayfish stream sandwiched between two hills. It was the kind of place two ten-year-olds like Damien and Joe could spend whole days exploring nature on their own. And they often did.

This particular day, Damien and Joe made another secret path to the fort they had made out of scrap pieces of wood a week ago. While they worked, they were on the lookout for anything curious. By sunset, their pockets were full of the day's finds.

Before dinner, Damien showed his mother his discoveries.

"The screwdriver's a little bent," Damien said, "but it'll still work."

"I like this rock," Mrs. Shea said. "Do you think those green veins might be gold?"

"Get real, Mom. It's just copper," he said.

Mrs. Shea held a small piece of blue glass up to the light. "Where did you find this?" she asked. The top was round and fluted, with a bubble of clear glass in the middle. As the light passed through it, the fluted points shone like an exploding star. "This is cobalt blue glass. It might be a hundred years old."

Damien told her he found it in the woods behind Joe's house.

"I think you found yourself an old perfume bottle stopper." She held the glass to her nose. "You can almost smell the perfume."

Damien told her that he found lots of old things in the woods. Last week he found a brown bottle with a medicine label.

"You know what," Mrs. Shea said, "you may have found an *archaeological site.*"

Damien's mother was an archaeologist. Archaeology is the science of studying the life and culture of people of the past. Part of Damien's mother's work as an archaeologist was finding buried places where people had lived and worked hundreds, sometimes thousands, of years ago. She found many of these places, or sites, by carefully looking for archaeological clues lying on the ground's surface. The clues might be things people made long ago——things called artifacts——like a broken piece of a bowl or a nail or an arrowhead. Another clue might be an interesting way rocks are arranged, as if around a campfire. Like Damien, she had to be a keen observer.

"Wow, Mom!" Damien yelled. "You mean like I might have found an old Indian village or Egyptian tomb?"

"No. I mean like an old junkyard," said Damien's mother. "Often junk can tell archaeologists more than treasure can. A long time ago," his mother continued, "our town may have been a farm. It's hard to tell that now, with all the houses and streets and the interstate highway. But maybe what you found is evidence of what it used to be."

Damien slapped his thigh and thought, Well, I'll be doggoned. He wanted to find more clues about his town's past life.

"If we go into the woods as scientists," she told him, "we'll find a whole lot more than just neat stuff, Damien. We'll find out about the people who left all that neat stuff there. And maybe even why they left it there."

But his mother said she wouldn't help unless he promised that he was going to behave like an archaeologist. She explained that there are rules and methods archaeologists follow.

"Without rules," she said, "you destroy the meaning of everything you find and the things you'll find will have no meaning."

Damien nodded and promised he'd behave like a scientist.

"The first step in archaeology is to ask the right questions," his mother said. "All science is a way of looking for answers, Damien. What question do you think we should ask first?"

"Uh . . . why did the farmer dump his garbage in the woods?"

"We're too far ahead of ourselves. We still don't know for sure if there was a farm here. Right now we're simply asking, Did people live or work around here before this was a town? If we can find out that they did, our knowledge of archaeology will help us to ask more questions. Where did they come from? What was their life like? Why did they leave? We'll start looking for answers later. Right now, let's set the table."

After dinner, Damien and his mother went to the library. The town kept its special records at the library in acid-free folders and boxes that preserved the paper from rotting. The town's old photographs, original land deeds, subdivision and tax records, and maps were its history. These documents were like pictures in a family album. They were proof of how the town had grown and changed, and changed some more before it became the place where Damien lived today.

At the librarian's desk, Damien asked if he could see the town's historical documents. He told the librarian he was looking for an archaeological site in the woods, but first he needed to know if anyone used to live there.

The librarian left and came back with a box of old documents. Damien and his mother began to search through them. After a while, Damien found an old picture of Joe's house. It looked different. Instead of a garage, there was a barn, and the big oak in Joe's front yard was much smaller in the photograph.

"In 1867," the librarian told Damien, "a farmer named Matthew Abbott built that house on fifty-five acres of land. It was his grandson who sold the farm to the people who built our town."

In the photograph, the woods looked bigger.

"Damien," Mrs. Shea looked at the photograph, "I think this answers our first archaeological question. Now we're ready to ask another question."

"Right, Mom. What's for dessert?"

The next morning, Damien was over at Joe's before sunrise.

"Wake up!" Damien yelled up at Joe's bedroom window. "You're living in Matthew Abbott's house!"

Joe's father came to the window. "Damien," he said, "do you know what time it is?"

"Sure. Five, six o'clock," Damien said. "Did you know your house is more than a hundred years old?"

"Damien, go home. Now."

When Damien got home, he made his breakfast and read comic books until seven. Then he woke up his mother, who also asked him if he knew what time it was.

At nine o'clock, Damien called the mayor's office. The woods officially belonged to the town, and Damien had to get permission to work there. When the mayor said, "My dear little boy," Damien knew the mayor wasn't taking him seriously. The mayor said that he couldn't possibly give him permission because then every little boy in town would want to dig up the parks. Damien said that he didn't want to dig up the park. He wanted to excavate it!

"This is not a game, sir. Archaeology is a science!" Damien nearly shouted into the telephone.

Then Damien's mother got on the telephone. She told the mayor that as an archaeologist she would make sure that proper archaeological methods were followed in excavating the site if the town gave them permission. She apologized for her son calling him but said she would write him later that day to request permission.

"Today we want to go and surface collect, to make sure that a site exists. If you give us temporary permission," she told the mayor, "we'd like to start mapping it out. And, if there's time, we could start a test pit."

She promised that when they were finished digging and studying their findings, they would give whatever they found to the town. She also promised that they would fill in any holes they created. And she invited the mayor to come and watch.

The mayor said he might like to visit the site and that, yes, they had his permission, temporarily.

By this time Joe had come over to Damien's house, and Damien was talking real fast. Did Joe know there used to be a barn behind his house? That his house used to be a farm? Did he want to see a picture of it? Did he want to be an archaeologist?

Joe said, sure, he wouldn't mind being an archaeologist. But first he'd like to be a pitcher for the Orioles.

"Forget baseball, Joe," Damien said. "Starting today you're going to be an archaeologist."

With Mrs. Shea's help, the boys began collecting the tools they would need for their field kits to map out the site. Into their backpacks they put pencils, markers, graph paper, balls of string, measuring tape, a compass, and a bunch of wooden stakes. "Aahhhgg, ze Count Dracula dies," Damien said, holding one of the stakes to his chest and pretending to faint on the couch.

"All those stakes are going to be useful," his mother said. "You'll need them for marking off the areas you'll be digging in." She added Band-Aids to their kits, and then gave each boy a mason's trowel. "Don't lose these. These trowels are your most important tools," she said.

They went into the garage for a couple of square shovels and the screen they would use to sift the dirt. The loose dirt would be put on top of a window screen table that they would shake back and forth, Damien's mother explained. "If there's something in the dirt we miss seeing when we dig, we'll shake it out with this."

After putting the trowels in their field kits, Joe and Damien carried them along with the screen down to the site. Damien's mother brought the shovels and the buckets.

"Before we begin," she asked, "what question do we try to answer now? What exactly are we looking for in the woods?"

"That's easy. Did Farmer Abbott dump his trash in the woods?" Damien said.

"Well, what you're really asking is, is there any evidence left of the Abbott family in the woods? Probably it will be their trash," she said.

They went across the street, down the block, and through Joe's backyard into the woods. Damien's mother asked where they had found the old medicine bottle and they showed her the spot near a small mound.

"And over there," Damien said, pointing to the right, about ten feet away, "is where I found the perfume stopper."

His mother pointed to a row of daffodils behind them. "How did daffodils get out here?" she asked. "And why do you think they're growing in a long, straight line like that?"

"Because someone planted them that way?" Damien said.

"That's possible," she said. "People often plant daffodils along fence lines. Perhaps the Abbotts did, too." Looking at the mound, and then looking up at Joe's house, Damien realized this looked like a good place to have a backyard fence . . . and a very good place to put a junk pile.

Walking in a line behind the flowers, Joe found a rotted wooden post sticking out of the ground. In the opposite direction, Damien found another. Walking back toward Joe, Damien stumbled over the stub of another post. It was an old fence line, all right.

"When we get back home," Mrs. Shea said, "I have to contact the state historical society, to let them know about this place. But for now, boys, let's start mapping."

"I don't see why we have to draw a map when we already know where the site is," Damien said.

"Because archaeology is about *where* you find things as much as it is about *what* you find," Mrs. Shea answered. "Without a map, nothing will have a place. And archaeologists map what they find vertically as well as horizontally. We're going to be working up and down as well as across. Trust me, we're going to need a record for that. But, like any map, we first need a name for this place."

They decided to call the site Matthew Abbott's Dump One, in case there might be more than one trash pile in the woods. Or "M.A.D. 1" for short.

That settled, they had to figure out where to begin their map. Damien's mother explained, "We can't just draw a map, willy nilly, because then the map could be of any place. We need what's called a datum point for this site. A datum point is something peculiar to this site, and permanent. It will be the map's reference point, the place that we measure everything else on the map from. That way, after we're finished digging, anyone who wants to know where our site was can use maps and our datum point to find it. Let's see . . . is there something around here we can use as a datum point?"

"The daffodils?" Damien asked. Mrs. Shea said that while the daffodils were very noticeable now, archaeologists needed something more permanent. Not only couldn't they find the daffodils in winter, but someone might pull them up.

"How about a tree?" Joe asked.

There was a big oak tree about 15 feet from the center of the mound. They decided to make the tree their datum point.

"Don't you think we should dress up our datum point?" Damien asked. "Like tie a red scarf around it or something?"

"How about tying my sister to it?" Joe laughed and Damien pretended he was Joe's sister begging to be untied.

Damien's mother had drawn a black dot in the middle of a piece of graph paper and marked it Large Oak Tree. "What we really need for our datum point are directions."

Damien took out the compass and stood under the tree. Walking around the tree, he pointed out north, south, east, and west. On the map, his mother drew four straight lines from the datum point. The map was now divided into four squares.

Avoiding the tree's roots, Damien pounded four stakes into the ground in a 10-foot square from the tree. On each stake he tied a long piece of string and gave the other end to Joe. Joe walked straight out from each stake. At the end of the string, he pounded another stake in the ground and tied the string to it. Now, north, south, east, and west were lined out from their datum point.

Working together, they began crisscrossing their string lines with more strings and stakes. First working along the north and south lines, they marked off every 5 feet with a stake. Then going along their east and west lines, they again staked out every five feet. Once the string was tied to their stakes, they had created eighteen squares, five feet by five feet.

"How come five feet, Mom?"

"The squares could have been any size, but I think five by five squares will give you enough room to sit down and work comfortably," she answered.

The squares went beyond where Damien had already found artifacts. But most of them were on and around the mound.

"These squares indicate where we will be digging," Mrs. Shea said. "If we need more squares, we can always make more."

On the map, Mrs. Shea marked off the squares just as they were laid on the ground. She made a note that each square was five by five feet, and then, inside of each mapped square, she wrote two letters and two numbers——using N, S, E, W and 1, 2, 3, 4.

The first letter in each square was an N or S. This meant the square was either north or south of the tree. The other letter was an E or W, for east or west of the tree. The numbers told how close the square was to the tree, with the lowest numbers closest to it.

125

Each square had its own name, like a town on a map. Damien was standing in a square right on top of the mound. It was in the first row of squares south of the datum point and in the second row of squares west of the datum point. "What's this square called?" he asked. On his mother's map, this was square S1 W2. The square next to this one and right next to the tree was S1 W1. The square on the other side of Damien was called S1 W3.

"Archaeologists name each square for where it is from their datum point," Damien's mother explained. "Otherwise, it would take too long to figure out what square they were talking about. Okay, boys. Let's get ready to dig."

"**W**e need a test pit," said Mrs. Shea. "Let's dig it here." It was a square northeast of the tree, called N4 E3. The closest mapped square was N3 E2. "We can't expect to find any artifacts in this square, though."

"Then why dig it up?" Damien thought that was dumb. Who'd want to dig up a square with nothing in it?

"Because N4 E3 is going to teach us how to dig. And——more important——N4 E3 will help us compare the layers, or strata, of soil in the other squares to this one."

"I don't get it."

"Well, it's like comparing two dishes of ice cream. Let's say you have one dish with a scoop of vanilla and a little bit of chocolate sauce on top. And in another dish, you also have one scoop of vanilla and a little bit of chocolate, except that someone has mushed and mixed the sauce in with the ice cream. You only know what the mixed ice cream used to look like by looking at the first dish. . . . "

"You're making me hungry, Mom."

"The Abbots probably didn't dump their trash here, and probably didn't dig up any of the dirt here, either. So we'll learn what the natural ground looks like. This dirt is undisturbed, and it will let us know how much digging the Abbotts did. If they dug a hole to put their trash in, and then if they dug up more dirt to cover their trash, we'll know that because we'll compare it to how the layers of dirt look in this test pit."

The ground was covered with leaves. There were bits and pieces of old wet leaves stuck together under the dry leaves. Using her fingers, Damien's mother picked through the leaves and rubbed them. She found nothing. She piled them outside of the square. The boys did the same.

About an inch under the leaves, they hit dirt. They measured the depth of leaf covering. Damien's mother recorded it in their field notes. She wrote, "M.A.D. 1, N4 E3, leaf cover 0.0 ft–0.1 ft B.S." Then she wrote the date and her initials and showed it to Joe and Damien.

"Archaeologists always put their initials and date on everything they record," she told them. "That's so anyone who looks at their records will know who to talk to if they have any questions."

She told them that B.S. meant below the surface. "But why didn't you just write the leaves covered the square for about an inch?" Damien asked.

"As scientists," his mother said, "we're using scientific measurements and language. We change inches into decimals. And leaf cover 0.0 ft–0.1 ft B.S. is the way archaeologists write down that the leaves did cover the square for about an inch. Now that we've drawn a map of the top of the site, from here on we'll be mapping the *depth* of the site. The very top of the site is 0.0 ft. From there, we measure down."

Once all the leaves were cleared from the square, Damien's mother showed the boys how to dig with a trowel. The flat side of the trowel was used to scrape the ground, a quarter of an inch at a time. "Never use the point to pry anything up," she said. "I can't stress that enough. If there is something in the ground too big to loosen by scraping, you scrape the dirt around it."

With the flat side of the trowel, the boys dug carefully, scooping the dirt into their buckets. Damien's mother used the square shovel the same way they used their trowels. When they had a bucketful of dirt from their square, they poured it over the processing screen. Joe and Damien took turns shaking the dirt through the screen.

"Mom! I think we found something!" Damien yelled every time they sifted the dirt. But the "something" always turned out to be just pebbles. Damien decided to save the rocks in a pile.

They dug carefully in N4 E3 all morning. By lunchtime, they had dug down two feet. It took a lot longer than they had thought it would. And as they dug, they noticed changes in the dirt. Under the leaves, the top layer of dirt was the blackest. This was the topsoil formed from years of plants and animals rotting on the ground. Below that was yellow clay. There was a band of sand under the clay. By late afternoon, they hit gravelly dirt.

Working together, it took them all day to dig down five feet. Damien's mother then took pictures of the square's walls. The different colors and textures of dirt made the walls look like waves of ribbons. It was starting to get dark, and everyone was hungry and tired.

"This is harder work than I thought, Damien," Joe said. "I think I'd rather pitch for the O's."

"Yeah," Damien agreed. "But think about how much better it will be when we find something."

"The mayor called last night," Damien's mother said. "He had good news. The City Council supports our dig."

For the rest of the site, they would dig each square in six-inch levels. Everything they found in one level would be recorded before they could begin digging up the next level. Each level of each square would have its own bag for artifacts.

Damien began digging in N1 W1 near the tree. Joe worked next to him in N1 E1. And Damien's mother took N1 W4.

"I bet I find more stuff than you, Joe," Damien said.

"Guys," Damien's mother said, "this is not a contest. We're all in this together. We're a team. We're here to find the Abbotts, not stuff."

"If we find the Abbotts, I'm out of here! Fast!" Damien said. As they started digging, the boys made jokes about finding old Abbott's bones.

leaves

topsoil

clay

sand

gravelly dirt

In their first levels, they found only pebbles and roots. But soon after work began at the second level, Damien was jumping up and down at the processing screen.

"I got something! I got something!" he yelled.

He carefully picked the dirt off it with his fingers. It looked round and tinny, with something red written on it. Damien rubbed the tin hard against his pants.

He held it up to see if he could read it. "Coca-cola . . . Ah, it's just a dumb ol' bottle cap." Damien looked disappointed and started to throw it away.

"Hey, not so fast," his mother said. "When was the last time you had a Coke that wasn't a twist-off cap. Someone sat under this tree years ago and drank a Coke. It's an artifact. Put it in the bag. Everything interesting goes into the bags. When we get into the lab, then we'll decide what's important." The bottle cap went into the second-level paper bag marked, M.A.D. 1, N1 W1, 0.5–1.0 ft. B.S., Damien.

Joe found three cigarette filters and a piece of rusted tin in his second level. He put them in his second-level bag.

There was now a large pile of dirt under the processing screen from the first and second levels. Joe and Damien moved the dirt away to get ready for the third level. Damien's mother took pictures of the boys as they measured levels one and two in their squares.

As they worked level three, Damien's trowel hit something hard. He thought it was probably a rock, so he didn't get excited. As he scraped away the ground around it, though, he saw that it was white. Damien used a whisk broom to brush it clean. As more dirt fell off it, he spotted what looked like a set of teeth.

"Joe," he whispered. "Joe! I think I found Farmer Abbott."

Joe went over and looked. They both stared in silence at the jawbone in the dirt. They were so quiet that Damien's mother got suspicious. She went over and found the boys sitting perfectly still and looking at the ground.

"You boys look like you've seen a ghost," she said. Joe's mouth was open, but he wasn't saying a thing. He pointed to the jawbone jutting up at Damien's knees.

"May I?" she asked, and bent down and began carefully sweeping and troweling the area around the bone until it was completely uncovered. She picked up the bone and studied it. She looked at the teeth and said, "What a pretty set of teeth."

"Mom, that's a disgusting thing to say about the dead!"

"Why? Whose teeth do you think these are?"

"Farmer Abbott's. I bet this is where he died."

"Damien, look at these teeth a little more carefully. Do these look like human teeth? Are they the same size and shape as your teeth? Count them. Hold the bone next to your chin. Do you think this bone came from a human being?" she asked.

Damien looked at it closely and said, "Maybe it came from a real ugly human. . . ."

"A sheep is more likely," his mother said. "We'll find out for sure later. But I'm glad you didn't pry it out of the ground. If you had, it might have broken."

In the notebook she wrote where the bone was found and who found it. Damien put the jawbone back exactly in its place in the pit. He measured how far down it was from the surface and how far it was from the pit's walls. His mother took a picture of it.

"Does anyone know if this jawbone is an artifact?" she asked them.

Both of them said it sure was.

"Why do you say that?"

They knew then it was the wrong answer.

"Did someone make this jawbone or use this jawbone? Just because we're saving it doesn't make it an artifact," Damien's mother said.

"It's not an artifact," Damien tried bluffing. "We meant to say it's a . . . it's a . . ."

". . . a bone!" Joe said for him.

"Archaeological sites have artifacts and non-artifacts," she said. "Artifacts are things people made or used. Non-artifacts are things people didn't make——like seeds, shells, and bones. But non-artifacts can tell us as much as artifacts about the people who made a site. What could this jawbone tell us about Farmer Abbott?"

"That he had a sheep," Joe said right away.

"And our job as archaeologists," she went on, "will be to find out why he had a sheep. Maybe sheep were pretty common on nineteenth-century farms. But, then again, maybe they weren't."

"Yeah. And we have to find out where he put the rest of the sheep," Joe said.

As Damien soon discovered, more of the sheep was buried in his third and fourth levels. Once the bones were measured and photographed in the square, they were bagged for the lab.

From the second level down, everyone was finding interesting things. Joe found the top part of a light blue jar. Damien's mom said it might have come from a canning jar. Then Joe found more glass pieces of the same color. Damien's mother found the handle of a blue and white teacup and part of a leather strap.

As Joe was taking his dirt to the screen, a man came walking through the woods, waving his arms over his head.

"Hello! Are there any archaeologists out here?" he yelled from across the stream.

"It's the mayor. Be nice, Damien," Damien's mother said. She stood up, wiped her hands on her jeans, then crossed the stream to greet the mayor. Damien and Joe couldn't hear them, but they saw her pointing to them. The mayor started waving some more. The mayor and Damien's mother walked over to the site.

"So this is Damien," the mayor said. "It's a pleasure to meet such a nice little boy."

Damien shook the mayor's hand and introduced Joe. When the mayor said Joe was a nice little boy, too, Damien and Joe looked at each other and rolled their eyes.

Damien's mother explained how they were excavating the site and recording their findings. Then she asked the mayor if he'd like to watch Joe work the screen.

133

The mayor asked if he could try it. As he sifted Joe's dirt, he said this reminded him of helping his mother make cakes. He kept shaking the screen and talking about her triple-layer double-dutch chocolate cake that was as light as air. He paid little attention as the little rocks bounced on and off the screen. By Joe's account what happened next wasn't fair. It was Joe's dirt, after all.

After the dirt was shaken off, the screen held about a cup of small rocks. The mayor said, "My, my, that was fun. . . . And what have we here?" He reached over and picked a small coin out of the rocks.

It was the size of a dime, the color of a dime, but it wasn't a dime. On one side was a woman's head with "United States of America" and "1874" written around it. On the other side was the Roman Numeral III. "I found a three-cent piece!" the mayor shouted. "I found a three-cent piece!"

Everyone but Joe was real excited. Damien's mother said this could help them date what they found in their third levels. Unless they found something with a different date on it, the levels 1.0 to 1.5 B.S. were buried around 1874. The mayor kept saying how lucky he was and how much fun archaeology was.

Damien said, "Three cents? Three cents? There's no such thing as a three-cent coin!"

To himself, Joe said that was his three-cent piece, that was his dirt——and that he wanted to go home.

The mayor turned to Damien's mother and told her, "The whole City Council will hear about this." He told her to let him know if they needed anything, anything at all. She thanked him and said they certainly would.

After the mayor left——Damien checked to make sure he left without the coin——Damien's mother went to talk with Joe.

She agreed that it didn't seem fair that the mayor found the coin. But, she told him, "Working a site is a lot like being on a baseball team. Everyone works for the same goal. Whether it's winning the game or digging the best site possible. And that coin did something very special for this site. Since the mayor thinks he found it, we now have the community's support. Thanks, Joe."

Joe felt better. And, anyway, the coin went into the bag marked with his name, not the mayor's.

It had been a long day, but time had passed fast. In less than eight hours they had dug into the nineteenth century.

135

Digging Up the Past

Meet the Author

Carollyn James lives in Takoma Park, Maryland, and is managing editor of *Science and Children* magazine. She is also a freelance writer whose articles have been published in many national magazines.

Meet the Illustrator

Ed Tadiello has completely immersed himself in the study of art. He has been a student at two New York City art schools. He also has held memberships in associations especially for artists and illustrators. The focus of his studies has been the human form. According to Tadiello, one of the biggest challenges in drawing characters is that they have a "natural quality to them." It is when this "natural quality" is achieved that he feels he has created a work of art, one he hopes "will touch and inspire the viewer."

Theme Connections

Think About It

With a small group of classmates, consider what you have learned about the science of archaeology and how an archaeologist thinks and works.

- What did you learn about scientific thinking and methods from this story?
- Can anything worthwhile be learned from common objects that people discard?

Check the Concept/Question Board to see if there are any questions there that you can answer now. If the selection or your discussions about the selection have raised any new questions about ancient civilizations, put the questions on the Board. Maybe the next selection will help answer the questions.

Record Ideas

Would you like to work on a dig with an archaeologist? What site would you like to explore? Record your notes and ideas in your Writing Journal.

Research Ideas

- Study famous archaeologists and how they worked. Find out if any of them had unique methods for acquiring information.
- How do you become an archaeologist? What different subjects do you have to study? Is there anything left to discover about ancient civilizations?

The Search for Early Americans

from *Searches in the American Desert*
by Sheila Cowing

In 1888, the Civil War had been over for twenty years. Thousands of eastern Americans had traveled west in covered wagons, looking for new land to farm, new homes, new ways of life. Roads and railroads were being built across the nation.

In the mountains and on the high desert plateaus, the frantic search for gold and silver was over, too. Most mines were run by big companies digging deep under the earth with heavy machinery.

On the plains, on grassy mountain slopes, and in the desert, wherever grass grew, new settlers drove cattle and sheep, searching constantly for fresh grass and water. The miners and the western settlers clashed with the native Americans. On the Great Plains, the Indians were forced to move onto reservations or to engage in war. In the Rocky Mountains, most native Americans had been killed or driven onto small, isolated reservations where many died of diseases they caught from the white man. Often the Indians found the land set aside for them already occupied by miners or settlers who refused to move. The native Americans were left impoverished and heartsick.

In the Mancos Valley of southern Colorado, which belonged traditionally to the Ute Indians, new ranchers herded their cattle out of the wide treeless valleys up steep, narrow canyons for the winter. There the animals were safe from the terrible icy winds and could be guarded more easily against wolves and mountain lions.

Richard Wetherill and his family had been raising cattle in Mancos for eight years. The Utes were not always friendly toward settlers. But Richard and his family, who were Quakers, had befriended them and had cared for several Indians when they were ill.

Richard was thirty years old, and he and his four younger brothers still lived with their parents. Their married sister lived close by.

Sometimes, during the winter, Richard and his brothers would build a small cabin so they could stay near the cattle. Then they would often ride into the branch canyons looking for ruined cliff dwellings. An old Ute had told them that in the canyons there were the abandoned dwellings of many people——the "ancient ones." One of the dwellings was larger than the others, and the Utes never went there, as it was a sacred place. Richard and his brothers had found only small dwellings.

On December 18, 1888, Richard and his sister's husband, Charlie Mason, rode to the top of Mesa Verde looking for stray cattle and found themselves in a place they had never been before. It was snowing lightly, and they rode close to the edges of the steep cliffs. Thick mesquite underbrush scratched their horses' legs and sometimes snared their hooves.

Cattle ranchers Richard Wetherill and Charlie Mason saw this snowy canyon from the top of Mesa Verde for the first time in December 1888.

Late in the morning, they climbed down to rest the horses and walked out on a point of bare rock. Below them, a snowy canyon opened out. Suddenly, Richard grabbed Charlie's arm and pointed. About a half mile away, across the canyon, was a long, deep cave. Inside, blurred like a mirage in the falling snow, was a man-made wall. It was several stories high, with black window and door holes watching the canyon like eyes. Near the center rose a round, tapered tower.

Keeping their horses as close to the rim as they dared, they started around the canyon. Winding through prickly bushes, they reached a clearing. The cliff dropped away at their feet. Beneath them was the mysterious city in the canyon wall.

Richard climbed down from his horse. He took out his bowie knife and began to slice at the thick branch of a dead piñon tree.

They made a ladder, looping branches with their lariats, and tied it to piñon trunks. When they lowered the ladder over the cliff, it reached the ruins.

There stood a ghost city. This must be the large sacred dwelling the Ute had spoken of. Walls of the rooms had broken, but their remains stood straight, built of stone the red-brown color of oak leaves in winter. Little houses perched one on top of the other. The tower rose near the center, as though uniting the houses. At some point, Richard thought of the name "Cliff Palace" for this place, and the largest ruin at Mesa Verde is still called by that name.

For hours they explored, ducking through low doorways and climbing tumbled walls, searching room after room, leaving footprints in dust perhaps for centuries undisturbed. When they spoke to each other, their voices echoed.

Clay bowls, mugs, and jars for carrying water stood on ledges and floors as though their owners had just put them down and would come back soon to start supper. They found a stone axe, its handle still lashed to its blade. Hundreds of people must have lived here. What had happened to them?

In a back room, they found bones and three skulls. Had there been a battle? No, there would be many more skeletons.

Snow still fell on the mesa and the men were cold, but they were eager to learn whether other large ruins lay close by. Agreeing to camp near where they had first seen Cliff Palace, Richard and Charlie separated. In the late afternoon light, Richard rode north, then across Mesa Verde, following the curve of a deep canyon. There he saw another cliff dwelling rising in places to three stories. He dared not climb down, as it would soon be dark. The walls of this town were protected from the wind by a fringe of spruce trees across the front of the cave. One tall spruce had grown right through a retaining wall. Richard called this ruin Spruce Tree House.

Cliff Palace is the largest cliff dwelling in Mesa Verde National Park in southwestern Colorado. About 400 people lived there at one time.

When morning came and Richard and Charlie tried to find Spruce Tree House again, they rode out to the edge of a different canyon. Curved in a hollow at the base of a cliff lay a third ancient village. It was smaller than Spruce Tree House, built around a square tower four stories high. This ruin they named Square Tower House.

Richard Wetherill and Charlie Mason were not the first to discover cliff dwellings in Mesa Verde. But what they found that December——Cliff Palace——belonged to a prehistoric civilization no one in the United States had dreamed of. Cliff Palace was an important clue in the mystery surrounding the ruins and the people who once had lived there. The towns these people left behind were preserved in the dry desert air. Richard Wetherill would devote the rest of his life to searching for their story. Charlie Mason would never lose interest in his brother-in-law's search although he moved with his family to Creede, Colorado, where he raised trout in a fish hatchery. Sometimes he even accompanied Richard on explorations.

Spruce Tree House, a prehistoric Anasazi dwelling in what is now Mesa Verde National Park, was discovered late one snowy afternoon in 1888 by Richard Wetherill, a cowboy who was so excited by his find that he devoted the rest of his life to archeological exploration.

Richard Wetherill knew that farther south in the open desert, scientists were trying to learn more about the native people who lived in walled adobe villages called pueblos. He felt sure that the Mesa Verde towns belonged to the ancestors of these people, although the walls and towers in the cliffs were more beautiful than any he had seen in pueblos. He wrote to the Smithsonian Institution in Washington, D.C., and the Peabody Museum at Harvard University in Massachusetts, telling them of his discovery. He hoped they would send their scientists to help, or at least sponsor him and his brothers, so that they could hire help for their cattle and be free to explore the canyon dwellings. Both institutions rejected Richard's appeal.

The Smithsonian suggested he ship the artifacts he had found to them. No one would come out to help. They said Richard was not a trained scientist and that he should stop disturbing archeological treasure.

But Richard could not stop. As soon as they moved the cattle out of the summer pasture, he and his brothers climbed back into Mancos Canyon. During the fifteen months after the discovery of Cliff Palace, the Wetherills found one hundred eighty-two large cliff dwellings and many smaller ones. They searched two hundred fifty miles of Mesa Verde's steep cliffs. Richard made maps, marking locations of cliff houses. He drew pictures and took photographs. The men picked up pots, clay figures, and sandals woven from fibers of the yucca plant's long leaves.

When spring came, Richard carried his collection in a ranch cart across the mountains over three hundred sixty miles to Denver, where he sold it to the Historical Society. People did not seem very interested. A few Denver tourists came to the Wetherill ranch to see a cliff dwelling. They told Richard that others thought he was looting graves.

But Baron Gustaf Nordenskiöld, a twenty-three-year-old Swedish archeologist and tourist, saw Richard's collection at the Historical Society and was eager to see more. It took him days to reach the ranch from Denver. First he took a mining train to Durango. Then he bounced all day in a small, rented horsecart, over thirty miles of twisting canyon roads to Mancos. He arrived dirty and tired, but he was still excited. Would Richard allow him to help, he wondered.

It was June. Richard knew that he and his brother Al would be able to explore only a few more days before they would be needed to move the cattle down to the valley. But he was glad to have a scientist interested in his search at last.

They set up camp near an alkali spring below a nine-room cliff house Richard had visited only once before. Baron Nordenskiöld described the water's taste as "nauseous." Was this spring, polluted like many desert springs with soda and salt from the soil, the ancient villagers' only water?

The climb to the ruin was steep and slippery. Loaded with digging tools, they struggled through tangled mesquite and then up the open, stony slope.

They began digging inside the red, broken walls of a circular room. Richard found round rooms in most of the cliff dwellings. Many were dug underground, with firepits and stone benches around the walls. He knew that native people farther south used circular underground rooms for meetings of the tribes' religious clans. The Hopis called the rooms *kivas*.

As Richard, Al, and the baron dug, clouds of red dust clogged their mouths and noses. The three men soaked their bandannas in water and tied them around their faces to make breathing easier.

Richard's shovel scraped on something. He began to dig more slowly, so he wouldn't break anything. It was a piece of pottery, black and white like others he had found.

Quickly the baron stopped him. The baron squatted in the rubble and began to pick and scrape the crusted dirt with a mason's trowel. Gently, patiently, he scraped until the pot stood free. Then the baron picked it up as carefully as he would a newborn baby. The pot had not a single crack.

From then on, Richard used a mason's trowel, too. This was how an archeologist collected artifacts. He watched Nordenskiöld measure, take notes, and draw floor plans in each room, marking locations of every pot, bone, or sandal they found. Richard wanted to learn everything he could about this organized way of searching ruins, called archeology.

All summer, while Richard and Al tended cattle, the baron explored other cliff dwellings with Richard and Al's younger brother, John, in the arm of Mancos Canyon the baron named Wetherill Mesa.

The baron believed the caves had been inhabited for a long time. The walls and towers could not have been built in a few lifetimes. The people had no horses or machines to help them carry or shape the stones and mix the mortar. How long the construction had taken the baron had no way of knowing. How long ago the ruins had been abandoned he could only guess.

Near Spruce Tree House, he cut down the spruce growing through the wall. The tree would not have been allowed to push through the wall of a town people lived in. The baron counted the trunk's growth rings and decided Spruce Tree House must be at least one hundred sixty-two years old. He and Richard believed it was actually much older. They thought the cliff dwellings had been built and left before the Spanish arrived in the 1500s, as there were no white man's tools in any of the ruins.

At the Chicago World's Fair in 1893, Richard Wetherill helped represent Colorado. Fairgoers were amazed at his exhibit. It was hard to believe that at least two hundred years before the United States was a country, children in desert caves played inside three-story red and yellow apartment houses built around graceful, tapered towers. The World's Fair itself was a city of white buildings made to look like ancient Greece and Rome. America did not really have an architectural style of its own. Even the idea of many-storied houses was very new.

In 1889, Baron Nordenskiöld, a Swedish archeologist, worked with the Wetherill brothers excavating prehistoric cave dwellings at Mesa Verde. Here, Richard Wetherill sits on a windowsill of a beautifully made building now called Balcony House.

Others, too, had been discovering the ancient towns in cliffs, on canyon floors, and in the open desert. At the fair, Richard saw photographs of a cliff dwelling near Grand Gulch, Utah, west of Mesa Verde. Seeing them made him long to explore again. Then he met the Hydes, two wealthy brothers who offered to pay him to explore. He was to give everything he found to the American Museum of Natural History in New York City.

At last Richard Wetherill had a chance to prove he could conduct a scientific search. Even though scientists would not come to help him, he wanted his work to meet their standards. Archeology was a new field, and Richard was determined to be accepted within its ranks. He began to plan. He planned a task for each member of his expedition. He planned exactly how he would describe each artifact he found.

Grand Gulch bends and twists for fifty miles, one of the wildest desert canyons in the country. Yet at one time, it must have been a cultural center, for perched high in the steep cliffs are eighty cliff dwellings. At that point the canyon is so narrow that Richard's pack

Richard Wetherill, excavating Pueblo Bonito in Chaco Canyon for the Hyde brothers in 1897, found pottery and baskets at this site.

burros could not pass between its walls. The expedition camped on the cracked white sand wash where once the river flowed among huge rocks shaped like toadstools and dwarves before it entered the canyon.

Each day Richard and his men, carrying heavy packs, climbed the cliffs to the caves on narrow rope-and-branch ladders. Right away, Richard noticed something strange. These people had not used the same articles as the people at Mesa Verde. Digging, he almost never heard the muffled click of his shovel striking pottery. There were not many pottery pieces. Instead, he began to turn up pieces of woven baskets.

Then he found a sandal, woven of yucca fibers like those at Mesa Verde, but much more beautifully. The toe end was round. Mesa Verde sandals were indented at the little toe. He found a spear-throwing stick archeologists called an *atlatl* and spear points, but no bows and arrows. Could these have been different people than those at Mesa Verde?

When he dug into the cave floor, Richard discovered a place where sand had been plastered in a wall around an egg-shaped hole. He knew that Navajos and Utes stored grain this way and began to dig out the hole more carefully, hoping to discover remains of ancient food. Instead, he uncovered a large, finely woven basket. He dug around it until he could lift it out. Underneath lay a man's body.

It was not a skeleton. It was a mummy, a body preserved for centuries by the desert sand's great dryness. With the utmost care, Richard lifted the body out of the hole and laid it on the cave's sand floor two feet above. He cut away the yucca cloth sack and opened the remains of a rabbit-fur blanket.

The man had died in agony. His black-haired head was thrown up and back. His knees were pulled up tightly. He clutched his belly with his right hand, gripping his wrist with the other hand. He had been slashed across his belly and the whole way across his back.

Someone had tried to sew the terrible wound with a one-eighth-inch-thick cord of black, braided human hair. It must have taken a long time to work a deer-bone awl back and forth through the man's flesh. The stitches in the shriveled, leathery skin were half an inch apart. This must have been the only way to try to stop the gushing blood.

Near the man, Richard found a pair of feet and legs cut off at the knees and a pair of hands and arms sliced at the elbows. The rest of the body was missing. There were seven other mummies buried close by, with spear points in their skulls or backbones.

These people had been killed in battle, Richard thought. Their relatives had buried them with care, wrapping each in rabbit fur or in a cloth woven of turkey feathers, and then in yucca-leaf cloth. They had covered each head with a fine new basket holding new sandals, seed jewelry, and stone knives with wooden handles for each to use in his or her new life.

Later Richard found nearly one hundred men, women, and children buried in graves hollowed out in cave floors near Grand Gulch. Most of their skulls had been crushed, or they had been killed with stone spears. In one skeleton, he found a huge, black volcanic glass blade pinning the hip bones together the way a skewer fastens a roasting turkey. How hard someone must have thrown that blade!

Sitting in the sand at the first burial site, Richard looked around at the low walls the cliff dwellers had built in this cave. These walls were not built as well as those in Mesa Verde. Here, there were no graceful towers or many-storied apartment houses. He had found the bodies buried two to five feet below the tumbled walls.

He picked up a piece of a clay pot. It was rough, and he could see the prints of the fingers that shaped it. There were no pots buried with the bodies he had found, not even broken pieces. The people in Grand Gulch had not used pots, even though pots were more efficient than baskets for carrying water and for cooking. Then Richard remembered something.

He and Baron Nordenskiöld had found pots in a trash mound south of a cliff dwelling in Mancos Canyon. They were gray and coiled, not at all strong and polished like the pots the cliff dwellers there had painted black on white with lightning designs. Perhaps, the baron had suggested, the gray pots belonged to an older race of people.

Richard was excited. The heads of these mummies were shaped differently than those of the Mesa Verde people, too. Mesa Verde skulls were short and broad. The baron told Richard that was because they flattened their babies' heads by strapping them to rigid cradleboards, not the padded ones modern native people used. Perhaps the people buried under these cliff dwellings in Grand Gulch belonged to an entirely different, older race of people than the cliff

dwellers who had last lived in these caves. Perhaps the original inhabitants of Grand Gulch had been killed by invaders who wanted to use the caves. Possibly the new people built the walls and made the first pots, pressing river mud around baskets to make the baskets hold water longer.

Richard called the older race the Basket Makers. He sent his field notes to the American Museum of Natural History in New York with the mummies and their sandals and baskets. He did not write well, but a scientist friend wrote an article in *Harper's Monthly*, a popular magazine, using the notes and the photographs.

Other scientists did not believe Richard. Because he had no scientific training, they insisted he was a fraud. At Harvard University, an archeology professor told his students that Richard had invented a new people in order to sell more artifacts. This criticism did not deter Richard. He kept on exploring, because he was so fascinated he couldn't stop. He loved exploring more than anything else.

During the summer of 1895, Mr. and Mrs. Sidney Palmer and their three children, Marietta, Edna, and LaVern, set up camp near Richard's ranch. Richard showed them the cave dwellings at Mesa Verde. That fall, Richard and the Palmers traveled south one hundred fifty miles to see a big ruin they'd heard about called Pueblo Bonito, in the Navajo reservation in northern New Mexico.

Pueblo Bonito, in Chaco Canyon, was the largest ruin Richard Wetherill had ever seen. In A.D. 1100, Chaco Canyon was the hub of a major Anasazi complex of towns connected by hand-built roads. In 1988, it was named a prehistoric archeological site of world importance.

For six days they followed a wheel-rut road. The desert was high and flat with no trees and little grass, and the wind blew constantly. The wagon wheels slipped and dragged in the sand.

When the road turned east through a wide canyon wash where once the Chaco River had flowed, they rode past the ruins of a small pueblo. Soon they saw more tumbled walls. Then, to their left, curved against the dark sandstone mesa, lay a ruin that was larger than anything Richard had ever imagined.

Behind the ruin, he found holes in the cliff face, stairs the ancient pueblo dwellers had chipped with stone tools. Climbing, he stepped out on the mesa top overlooking the wide canyon.

Below him, Pueblo Bonito glowed red in the afternoon sun, spread out like a huge half-moon. The whole of Mesa Verde's Cliff Palace would be lost in one small section.

But that was not all. To the east he could see another great ruin. Across Chaco Canyon he could see mounds where several smaller pueblos might be buried. He might be looking down on an enormous city-state, like Rome or Athens!

Why had this civilization died? Where had all its people gone?

With Mr. Palmer, Richard rode across the northern mesa looking for Navajos who might have some of the answers. In the smoky light

In 1897, Navajo Indians helped Richard Wetherill dig in Pueblo Bonito.

of hogans Wetherill spoke to the Navajos in their own language. The older Indian men all gave him the same answer. The great walls looked exactly the same as they had many generations before, when the Navajos first came to the area. At that time more cedar trees and more grass grew on the mesa. The Chaco Wash had water in it and the stream flowed at the surface of the canyon floor, not far down between the eroded banks of an arroyo. But the ancient ones were gone, and no one knew who they were. *Anasazi*, the people called them, which meant "ancient enemy."

Richard and the Palmers explored for a month. They found eleven large pueblos with over one hundred rooms each, and more than one hundred smaller pueblos. Pueblo Bonito alone had more than six hundred rooms. It covered three acres and in some places rose five stories tall.

After they returned to Mancos, Richard could not stop thinking about Chaco Canyon. At one time thousands of people must have lived there. Could the Navajos, poor, wandering sheepherders, have destroyed so great a city? He did not think so. He knew that answers must lie beneath the piles of rubble inside the walls.

Soon after their visit to Chaco, Richard married Marietta Palmer. They tried to settle down to ranch life, but Richard was too restless. He was so fascinated with the Anasazi that he decided to move to Chaco Canyon. He and Marietta opened a trading post for the Navajos, which Richard hoped would support his family.

The Hyde brothers, who had helped finance the Grand Gulch exploration, agreed to send Richard money to excavate in Chaco Canyon. Richard would again give what he found to the American Museum of Natural History in New York City. The first organized search in Chaco Canyon began in 1896.

Over the next four years, Richard dug out nearly two hundred rooms in Pueblo Bonito. Soon he realized that this pueblo had been built differently than those at Mesa Verde. There, rooms were built as people moved in, with the beautiful towers added. But this huge, horseshoe-shaped pueblo had been designed ahead of time to meet a society's needs.

Some rooms were built of thin, flat rocks, others of large stones and mortar. Such different building methods suggested that the rooms had been built at different times and over many years. Walls in Pueblo Bonito lay twelve feet, or two stories, below the level of the main court and rose five stories above.

Rooms were laid over rooms, with huge pine timber ceilings between. The pine trees grew thirty miles away from the canyon. Traveling by foot, how long had it taken these people to haul pine trunks——thousands of them——to Pueblo Bonito? Construction of the pueblo must have taken a long time.

Richard had no way of knowing how long, or when the pueblo had been started. Years later another searcher, A. E. Douglass, discovered a way to find out. He counted the annual growth rings in the ceiling timbers just as Baron Nordenskiöld had done with the tree at Spruce Tree House. Then he compared those rings to many other pine timbers. Pueblo Bonito, he discovered, was begun around A.D. 950. That was five hundred fifty years before Columbus discovered America. Douglass decided that people had lived in Pueblo Bonito until after A.D. 1300. The Mesa Verde cliff dwellings were built later than the main section of Pueblo Bonito and were inhabited a shorter time.

How could people have grown enough food in the open, hot desert for so long with so little rain? The Chaco River bed was hard, dry sand. When he was digging, Richard found only bitter springs.

Then, in July, it rained almost every day for two weeks. Walls of muddy water swept the wash, flooding ditches that Richard hadn't noticed. On the mesas, rainwater channeled into streams that fell over cliffs into shaded rock pools.

Without measuring instruments, the Anasazi constructed doorways of the same dimensions between Pueblo Bonita's many rooms.

Recent research suggests that the Chaco River once flowed in the wash, flooding its banks each spring the way the Nile River did, watering Egyptian crops in ancient times. Did more rain fall in Anasazi times? Did the cliff pools store enough water for drinking and washing all year around? No one knows. People are still searching for answers in Chaco Canyon.

Not only could the Anasazi feed thousands in desert soil, but they also had time to build the largest city in the desert and to become master artists. Richard found pottery and jewelry more beautiful than any he had ever seen. He found hundreds of jars, many like those he'd found at Mesa Verde, but others painted with intricate designs or encrusted with chunks of turquoise. He found necklaces, pendants, bracelets, and carvings, many inlaid with turquoise or made of abalone shell, which shimmered like pearl in the sunlight.

The nearest turquoise mines were two hundred miles away. The nearest abalone lived in the ocean along the California coast, nearly one thousand miles away. Then Richard found the skeletons of fourteen macaws, large parrots with blue, red, yellow, or green feathers. Parrots live in the western Mexican highlands. These people must have traveled great distances!

Perhaps some of these people had moved to Chaco from the cliff houses at Mesa Verde, but Richard knew now that at Chaco the culture was much more advanced. High on the mesas north and west of Chaco were other ruins that looked similar. Could they have been part of Chaco?

Chaco Canyon was a great center, as Richard had suspected. When modern archeologists looked down on the canyon from the air, they discovered that it was connected to at least seventy-five outlying towns by almost five hundred miles of straight roads. Even though they had no wagons or cars, so many people traveled that the Anasazi dug roads thirty feet wide. In some places, low walls or ledges can still be seen edging the road's shallow depression.

Chaco has been called the greatest archeological ruin north of Mexico. An estimated five thousand people lived in four hundred settlements in and around the canyon, dependent on food grown in desert soil. These prehistoric people developed new building techniques. They watched the seasons change with a kind of solar observatory only recently discovered. They were skilled artists. They traded with people over a thousand miles away.

Why did they leave Chaco? Where did they go? Richard found no evidence of terrible battles as he had at Grand Gulch. Later searchers believe that groups of people moved all over the desert, as Mesa Verde people had moved into Chaco Canyon. They probably moved in search of water.

When the trees in the forest thirty miles away were cut for ceiling timbers, the underground water those roots drew to the surface may have sunk. Then when the seasonal rains fell, the thirsty desert absorbed the water too fast for the people to catch and store it. The Chaco people, archeologists believe, wandered east to the Rio Grande, where the river flowed all year around, or south to Acoma and Zuñi, or west to Oraibi, home of the Hopis.

All over the southwestern desert, searchers have found abandoned cliff and mesa houses. Some are still unexplored, their floors littered with miniature corn cobs and shards of pottery. Since the ancient ones had no written language, people are still searching for clues to their history.

In the open desert south of Phoenix, Arizona, an ancient people archeologists call the Hohokam, ancestors of the Pima and the Papago, played an Aztec ball game in walled courts. They used a process of etching with acid cactus sap to decorate seashells, five hundred years before European artists "discovered" the method. The Hohokam did not build great adobe or stone cities.

Another ancient people, the Mogollon Mimbres in southwest New Mexico, were the first Americans to decorate pottery with animal, bird, and geometric designs. Their artistic abilities were unknown for centuries because they drilled holes in their pots and jugs and buried them with their dead.

In 1910, Richard Wetherill was shot and killed by a Navajo man, after an argument over a horse. Richard was fifty-two years old. Seven years earlier, archeologists, insisting that he was vandalizing Pueblo Bonito, convinced the federal government to stop his search. For many years, his collection lay in a storeroom at the American Museum of Natural History in New York City. In the summer of 1987, however, the results of Richard Wetherill's searches, the artifacts of the Hyde Expeditions, were displayed in a show at the museum.

Because Richard had no training, scientists did not afford him the recognition he deserved. But Richard's search laid a cornerstone for the science that became American Southwestern archeology. In 1914, when Alfred Kidder and S. J. Guernsey discovered in northeastern Arizona the same kind of remains that Richard had described at Grand Gulch, archeologists acknowledged Richard's discovery of the Basket Maker civilization. Another archeologist, John C. McGregor, pointed out in his book that when Richard dug beneath the cliff dwellers' floor and concluded that the graves were those of an older people, he was the first to use the principle of stratigraphy, which teaches that what is buried deeper is older. Above all, Richard is remembered as one of the first Americans to prove that a great civilization existed in the desert long before Europeans settled there.

Years after Richard Wetherill's death, scientists finally credited him with discovering the remains of a great civilization in the American Southwest.

The Search for Early Americans

Meet the Author

Sheila Cowing taught poetry and short-story writing before she began writing for young people. Her poems have been published in literary journals across the country. She is also an editor for *Shoe Tree*, a literary magazine written by and for young writers. Cowing currently lives in New Mexico where she enjoys hiking in and exploring the desert.

Theme Connections

Think About It

With a small group of classmates, consider what the artifacts and buildings discovered in the American Southwest tell us about what that region was like in ancient times.

- What do you know about the Southwest today? Are Native American cultures still an important part of life there?
- What does the archaeological rule "the deeper the older" mean? Is it always true?

Check the Concept/Question Board to see if there are any questions there that you can answer now. If the selection or your discussions about the selection have raised any new questions about ancient civilizations, put the questions on the Board. Maybe the next selection will help answer the questions.

Record Ideas

What did you find to be the most interesting discovery about the Anasazi civilization? Use your Writing Journal to record notes and ideas about the Anasazi and other civilizations.

Research Ideas

- Find out what Native American groups lived where you now live. What happened to them?
- Learn about the Toltecs, another ancient Native American civilization. Compare their civilization and accomplishments with those of the Anasazi.

The Island of Bulls

from *Lost Cities*
by Roy A. Gallant

According to a Greek myth going back more than 2,500 years, there once was a young man named Theseus, son of the king of the great city of Athens, the capital of Greece. At this time there also lived on the nearby island of Crete a king named Minos. Minos was so powerful and so greatly feared that he was able to demand and get whatever he wished, not only from the people of his island-state but also from the people of nearby Athens on the Greek mainland.

Now it happened, according to the myth, that Minos kept on Crete a fierce monster called the Minotaur, a beast that was half bull and half man and ate human flesh. The word "minotaur" is

built out of two words——King Minos's name and the Greek word *tauros,* meaning "bull." The Minotaur was supposedly kept in a labyrinth, a great maze or place of numerous winding corridors that was so complex that it was impossible to find the way out without help.

From time to time, Minos demanded that the king of Athens send him the seven handsomest young men and the seven most beautiful maidens of the land. These fourteen youths were then led into the labyrinth, where one by one they were found and devoured by the Minotaur.

When Theseus came of age he told his father that he wanted to be one of the youths sent to King Minos so that he might slay the Minotaur and once and for all end this terrible sacrifice the people of Athens were forced to make. Although he feared that his son would never return, Theseus's father granted the young man his wish.

On the appointed day the fourteen youths boarded the ship to Crete, a ship that always flew black sails, a sign of the certain death awaiting its passengers. When they arrived the youths were paraded before King Minos, for him to judge whether all were fair enough for the Minotaur. When the king's daughter, Ariadne, saw Theseus, she fell in love with him. She then managed to see him alone before the youths were led off to the labyrinth. Ariadne told Theseus of her love and gave him a small sword and a ball of thread.

As Theseus led the way into the maze he carefully unwound the ball of thread. On hearing the ferocious roars of the Minotaur as it came charging around a corner of the labyrinth to attack him, Theseus dropped the ball of thread and began slashing at the beast with the sword given to him by Ariadne. He managed to weaken the Minotaur and finally cut off its head. He then picked up the thread and followed it out of the labyrinth, leading his thirteen companions to safety and home.

Before he had departed from Athens, Theseus had agreed to change the black sails to white if all had gone well and he had slain the Minotaur. He forgot to do so. When his father, waiting for the ship's return, saw the black sails, he presumed that his son had been killed. He was so stricken with grief that he killed himself before the ship docked. Theseus then became king.

Was there any truth to the account of Minos and his kingdom on the island of Crete? The Greek poet Homer, who lived about 850 B.C., gave us the first known account of the Cretan king Minos and his palace. Later, in 455 B.C., the Greek scholar Thucydides, who lived in Athens, wrote an account of King Minos and his powerful fleet of ships that ruled the Aegean Sea. Still later, the philosopher Aristotle, born in 384 B.C., also wrote of King Minos dominating the whole Aegean area. And there were some who thought that Crete might have been the legendary kingdom of Atlantis, mentioned by the philosopher Plato about 400 B.C.

So Crete must have had a long history, one that stretched back even before Greek scholars wrote about the land. Crete itself did not have a written history until about 2,500 years ago. Even then the Minoans left very little in writing, unlike the neighboring civilizations of Egypt and Babylonia. The Cretans were called Minoans after King Minos. The legend of King Minos and his Minotaur had existed for centuries before the Minoans used writing. It had been handed down orally in story form from one generation to the next. But because it was only a legend, no one could be certain that there had actually ever been such a kingdom.

In his search for Crete's past, Evans came across several seals. The one at left represents the legendary labyrinth. The seal above shows an athlete leaping over a bull's back.

Fascinated by the Minotaur legend and poetic accounts of a highly developed civilization much older than any other known European civilization, an English scholar from Oxford University named Sir Arthur Evans decided to find out if there was any truth to the Minotaur legend and other accounts of an ancient Cretan civilization. The Minoans had ruled supreme from about 3000 to 1450 B.C., although as a civilization they were still older. The Minoan population at its peak was about 80,000, slightly less than the present population of Portland, Maine.

Evans's interest in Crete began during a visit to Athens where he bought a few moonstones from a Greek merchant. The stones, worn by his wife as lucky charms, had strange writing scratched on them. It was the writing that led Evans to Crete in 1894, where he found more of the stones containing the same writing. He first went to the capital of the island, Knossos, where he noted that many of the women were wearing similar round stones of clay around their necks or wrists as lucky charms. Although some of the stones had simple designs carved on them, others had what appeared to be some form of writing. As he traveled around Crete, Evans saw many such stones. They turned out to be very old indeed, and some had been used as personal identity disks by the ancient Cretans. One such stone had the design of a labyrinth. Another had the shape of a creature half human and half bull.

While in Knossos, Evans became curious about several large blocks of carved stone lying about. He decided to dig a few test trenches near the stones to see if anything might lie buried below. Only a few inches beneath the surface one of his thirty workers struck something hard with a spade. Evans's excitement grew as they continued to dig around the hard object. After only a few hours of digging Evans was almost certain that he had stumbled onto the walls of a large and ancient building, possibly the palace of the mighty Minos. In all, he spent more than twenty-five years working in Crete reconstructing the Minoan remains at Knossos. The hard object just beneath the surface indeed turned out to be the palace of King Minos, built some 3,500 years earlier, even earlier than the time of the great rulers of ancient Egypt just across the sea to the south.

Month after month, year after year, the work continued. The palace of Minos turned out to be enormous, sprawling over an area larger than ten city blocks. It was shaped like a large rectangle, in the center of which was a huge courtyard of red cement. Some sections of the building were five stories high. There were twisting corridors and stairways. There were dead-end passageways and a bewildering number of rooms. Indeed, it was a labyrinth. Evans had no doubt that here was the building described in legend as both the home of Minos and of the dreaded Minotaur.

There was great excitement when the workers uncovered the first fresco. Frescoes are paintings done on walls when the walls are being plastered. In this way the plaster and the colors of the painting dry together, a process that preserves the paintings for a long time. One such fresco was a life-size painting of a young man holding a large cone-shaped cup. His skin was a deep reddish color from exposure to the sun. Other frescoes showed Minoan women, who spent most of the time indoors, as white-skinned. Throughout the palace were images of a two-bladed axe, a symbol associated with the Cretan mother-goddess, whom the Greeks called Rhea. At will she was able to enter the double-axe and vanish. An ancient word for this axe was *labrys*, from which the word labyrinth comes.

As the digging continued, Evans realized that the enormous palace had not all been built at the same time. Hallways, rooms, and storage areas were added on century after century. Minos seems to have been the name of the first Cretan king who constructed the original palace. In his honor, each of the future kings of Crete took the name of Minos and added to the palace to suit his own taste. Evans discovered large storerooms with great jars for wine and olive oil. Some of the jars stood as tall as a man and can be seen in place today. There were also containers lined with stone and with fragments of gold leaf. These were probably from the rooms where the Minoan kings kept their stores of gold, silver, and other precious metals. Nearby were apartments for the royal guards who kept watch over the king's wealth.

Evans again became excited when his workers uncovered what is probably the oldest known royal throne. As described by Evans, there "was a short bench, like that of the outer chamber, and then, separated from it by a small interval, a separate seat of honour or throne. It had a high back, like the seat, of gypsum, which was partly imbedded in the stucco of the wall. It was raised on a square base and had a curious moulding below . . . probably painted to harmonize with the fresco at its side."

As the weeks and months passed, many more discoveries were made——the paved courtyard mentioned earlier, stairways with frescoes of olive branches in flower, a wall painting of a monkey gathering flowers in baskets, and a large fresco of a bull with young acrobats. Paintings and impressions of bulls on vases and other objects were so common that it caused Evans to remark: "What a part these creatures play here!"

Like the people of Spain today, the ancient Minoans seem to have loved a sport involving acrobats and bulls. One large fresco shows a bull in full charge and three young acrobats, two girls and a boy. If we read these frescoes correctly, some sport like this may have taken place: Three youths entered a sports arena containing a bull. As the bull charged, one of the youths would grab the animal's horns, leap over the bull's head, and do a handspring off the bull's back, landing upright on his feet and in the arms of one of the other two youths. This sounds like an impossible trick, but so many Cretan artifacts suggest that some such event took place that it is hard to doubt. Is it possible that this type of event inspired the myth of the fourteen Athenian youths, King Minos, and the deadly Minotaur?

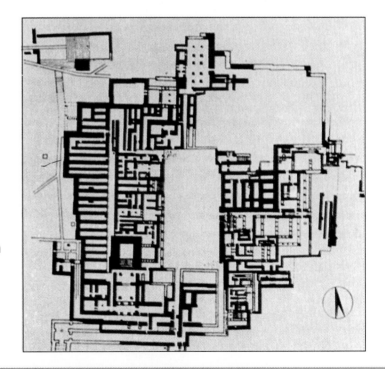

A ground plan reconstruction of the late Minoan palace at Knossos reveals a labyrinth of passageways and hundreds of rooms.

There are frescoes that also show audiences watching the contests in the bull ring. Although in Spain the object of the cruel contest is to kill the bull by plunging a sword into it, in ancient Crete the purpose seemed to be to demonstrate the athletic skills of the acrobats. But surely, from time to time, some of the youths must have been killed during the contests.

With a navy second to none, the Minoan kings ruled the seas. They were wealthy, as suggested by an elaborate game table Evans found, set with crystal, ivory, and gold and silver pieces. And they were enlightened, as evidenced by the modern system of plumbing unearthed at Knossos. Enormous clay pipes, some large enough for a person to stand up in, carried water and sewage away from the palace. There also was a system of pipes for hot and cold water flowing through the palace. After four thousand years, the drainage system at Knossos is still in working order. Nothing equal to it was built in all of Europe

Wall paintings like this one at Knossos suggest that
the Minoans loved a sport in which acrobats vaulted
over the horns and backs of bulls.

until the mid-1800s. Since Evans's time at least three other palaces have been found in other parts of the island, some with as many as 1,500 rooms.

Who were the Minoans, and what happened to bring their splendid civilization down? What they left behind shows them as a people of uncommon grace and elegance who reached an astonishingly high level of craftsmanship. Their vases and bowls of stone and their finely carved gems were unmatched anywhere. And they were apparently a peace-loving people; they had no defense fortifications and none of their art shows scenes of battle, warriors, or weapons, although finely made real weapons of bronze have been found.

Their wealth most likely came from overseas trade. Elegant pottery made by them, and copied by other people, has been unearthed in Egypt, in the Near East, on the Aegean Islands, and in Greece. For many centuries the Minoans enjoyed the good life, but then their civilization collapsed and quickly disappeared.

About the year 1450 B.C. Knossos and other Minoan centers burned. By about 1400 B.C. these cities were completely destroyed. While some scholars have supposed that invaders swept over the island and conquered it, others doubt that this is what happened. They suspect that the catastrophic explosion of the volcanic island of Thera (also called Santorin), 60 miles north of Crete, sent the Minoans and their splendid civilization into oblivion.

The Island of
Bulls

Meet the Author

Roy A. Gallant is a well-known science writer who has written nearly 80 books and more than 200 reviews and articles. Some of the subjects he enjoys writing about are astronomy, fossils, extraterrestrial life, dinosaurs, and astrology. Much of his writing is aimed at young adults and is written in a down-to-earth, easy-to-understand style. Gallant's interests include photography, oil painting, skiing, hiking, and kayaking.

Theme Connections

Think About It

With a small group of classmates, consider what this selection has taught you about distinguishing fact from fiction.

- From what you have read, how much of the Minotaur myth is true? What parts might be true but can't be proved? What parts are almost surely false?
- Imagine the Minoan palaces with as many as 1,500 rooms. Who designed and built these extensive palaces? What were all of the rooms used for? How many servants were needed to run such an estate?

Check the Concept/Question Board to see if there are any questions there that you can answer now. If the selection or your discussions about the selection have raised any new questions about ancient civilizations, put the questions on the Board. Maybe the next selection will help answer the questions.

Record Ideas

Can you think of some other legends or myths that could be based on historical facts? Record your notes and ideas in your Writing Journal.

Research Ideas

- Investigate some of the questions you have raised about life in a 1,500-room palace.
- The Minoans are just one example of the important civilizations of ancient Greece and the surrounding islands. Find out more about some of the others.

FINE Art

Red Figured Amphora. c.490 B.C. **Attributed to the Berlin Painter.** Terra-cotta and paint. The Metropolitan Museum of Art, Fletcher Fund, 1956 (56.171.38). Photograph © 1989 The Metropolitan Museum of Art.

Three Cows and One Horse. Ceiling of the Axial gallery, Lascaux Caves, France. 15,000–13,000 B.C. Photo: © Douglas Mazonowicz/Gallery of Prehistoric Art.

The Great Stupa, part of Sanchi ruins in India. 3rd century B.C.–A.D. 1st Century. Stone. Sanchi, Madhya Prades, India. ©Nari Mahidhar/Dinodia Picture Agency.

Ipuy and His Wife receiving offerings from their children. 1275 B.C. Copy of a wall painting from the Tomb of Ipuy. 47.5 × 74 cm. Egyptian Expedition, The Metropolitan Museum of Art, Rogers Fund, 1930 (30.4.114). Photograph © 1979 The Metropolitan Museum of Art.

169

The People on the Beach

from *The Secrets of Vesuvius*
by Sara C. Bisel
illustrated by Ken Marschall, Laurie McGaw,
Jack McMaster, Margo Stahl

Athens, Greece, June 1982

The telegram lying at my door was marked "Urgent." As I bent down to pick it up, I hoped that it wasn't bad news. After spending a long hot day on my knees in the dusty ruins of an ancient Greek town, I was in no mood for surprises. When I ripped open the envelope I saw that it was from the National Geographic Society in Washington, D.C. They wanted me to telephone them immediately about a special project.

Why are they in such a hurry, I asked myself. As an archaeologist and anthropologist I have been involved in many expeditions. But my jobs are almost never emergencies. If something has been lying in the ground for a few thousand years, another week or two usually doesn't make much difference.

As I shut the door to my tiny apartment, I calculated the time difference between Athens, Greece, and Washington, D.C., and then dialed the long-distance number. My contact at the National Geographic Society wondered if I could spare a few days to examine some human skeletons that had just been found at the town of Herculaneum in Italy. Skeletons in Herculaneum, I thought to myself. Now *that* would be interesting!

Human bones are my specialty. In fact, I'm often called "the bone lady" because most of my work involves examining and reconstructing old skeletons. Believe it or not, bones are fascinating. They can tell you a great deal about someone, even if the person has been dead for thousands of years.

I can examine a skeleton and find out whether a person was male or female. If she was female, for example, I can tell you about how old she was when she died, whether she had children, what kind of work she might have done and what kind of food she ate. I can even glue dozens of small pieces of a skull back together like a jigsaw puzzle and show you what that person looked like.

The editor at *National Geographic* explained that workmen digging a drainage ditch near the ruins of Herculaneum had accidentally discovered some skeletons lying on what had once been the town's beachfront. Nearby, archaeologists had later uncovered some boat storage chambers in the ancient seawall. Much to their surprise, there

My job is to excavate and study the bones of people who lived and died many centuries ago.

were more skeletons inside these cave-like rooms. Here people had found shelter from the terrifying eruption of Mount Vesuvius in A.D. 79. As they lay huddled together in the dark, they were smothered by an enormous surge of scorching gas and ash from the volcano. Flowing hot ash, rock and pumice then buried them. Today, almost two thousand years later, the tangled remains of these ancient Romans lie as they fell, preserved in the wet volcanic earth.

This was an amazing discovery. Although archaeologists have been digging out Herculaneum for centuries, very few bodies had ever been found. As a result, experts had decided that almost all of the Herculaneans must have escaped before the disaster. We now knew that this was not true.

But even more exciting for me was the chance to study the actual skeletons of real ancient Romans. Because the Romans cremated their dead, they left behind plenty of urns full of human ashes but very few complete remains. So these Herculaneans represented the first large group of Roman skeletons ever found.

"I'll book a seat on the next flight to Naples," I said to the *National Geographic* editor and then slammed the receiver down. I quickly rolled up a few T-shirts and several pairs of jeans and stuffed them into my bag. I knew that I had to leave for Italy right away. Now that the skeletons had been exposed to the air, they had to be properly preserved as soon as possible or they would quickly disintegrate and turn to dust. If that was allowed to happen, a priceless opportunity to find out exactly what the ancient Romans had looked like and how they had lived would be lost.

It was strange, I thought grimly, that Vesuvius, the volcano that had caused one of the biggest natural disasters in the world, was now giving me the most exciting assignment any physical anthropologist could ever dream of. I would be the first person to recreate the lives of these men, women and children who had lived and died so long ago. I knew that bones could talk. If I listened carefully, they would whisper their secrets.

What would these skeletons tell me?

Naples, Italy, June 1982

. . . darkness fell, not the dark of a moonless or cloudy night, but as if the lamp had been put out in a closed room. You could hear the shrieks of women, the wailing of infants, and the shouting of men; some were calling their parents, others their children or their wives, trying to recognize them by their voices. People bewailed their own fate or that of their relatives, and there were some who prayed for death in their terror of dying. Many sought the aid of the gods, but still more imagined there were no gods left, and that the universe was plunged into eternal darkness for evermore.

Pliny the Younger
1st century A.D.

I put down my fork and reread the words that described a group of people trying to escape from the fury of Vesuvius on that August day so many years ago. A chill crept up my neck. I was no longer hungry.

I had been hoping to start examining the new skeletons soon after I arrived. But it was late by the time I checked into my hotel, and I knew that not much could be done until morning. You need good light for excavation work. So I'd had a bath, tucked a few books under my arm and gone down to the hotel restaurant where I ordered a plate of pasta. Then I settled down for a crash review lesson on ancient Herculaneum and how the sudden eruption of Vesuvius had changed its fate forever.

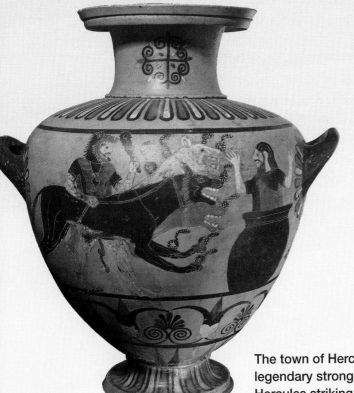

The town of Herculaneum is named after the legendary strongman Hercules. This vase shows Hercules striking Cerebus, the three-headed dog.

The descriptions I was reading had been written by Pliny, a seventeen-year-old student who lived in Misenum, across the Bay of Naples. His uncle had sailed across the bay toward Herculaneum to try to help stranded friends, until his ship was cut off by "bits of pumice and blackened stones, charred and cracked by the flames." Did Pliny's uncle have any idea what he was sailing into, I wondered. Or, when he saw from afar the mountain explode and a column of ash and smoke rise twelve miles into the air, could he simply not believe his eyes until he had taken a closer look?

Pliny's uncle eventually landed at Stabiae, several miles south of Herculaneum. Though "great sheets of flame" were flashing out from the peak of Vesuvius, he actually had a bath and went to sleep. But the people with him sat up in terror all night, while the buildings shook as if they were being torn out of the ground. When the door to the uncle's room became choked by a layer of cinder and ash, they woke him up and fled, tying pillows on their heads as protection against the pumice stones that rained around them.

But Vesuvius eventually caught up with Pliny's uncle. In spite of his calm bravery, he was suffocated by sulphur fumes while trying to get back to his ship.

Meanwhile, about twenty miles across the bay at Misenum, Pliny observed the various stages of the eruption, beginning with the appearance of the mushroom-shaped cloud of ash, followed by falling ash, pumice and stones. He described earth shocks so violent it seemed as if the world was not only being shaken, but turned upside down.

I thought it was amazing that the eyewitness account he wrote had come down through the centuries. Only recently did modern scientists realize how accurate Pliny's description was, after they had studied many other volcanoes themselves. I put down my book. From the window I could see Mount Vesuvius, quiet now, looking more like a gentle slumbering hill than a deadly and still-active volcano.

Pliny's description of panicking crowds had been written about the people at Misenum, who had had to shake the ashes off their bodies so they would not be buried alive.

How much worse must it have been for the Herculaneans, who lived closer to the inferno, hemmed in between the mountain and the sea? Vesuvius's blast was so powerful that ash fell as far away as Africa and Syria.

I know many people who get shivers up their spines at the sight of a big lightning storm, or ten-foot waves crashing onto the seashore. But to have the very earth beneath you suddenly gush ash and fire, to have a glowing avalanche of ash and pumice, hotter than an oven, rip over the land at the speed of a galloping horse. . . .

When Vesuvius erupted, ash and gas came spewing out of the summit, forced straight up into the air by the pressure and heat of the blast. Eventually, this cloud cooled, and some of it collapsed, sending ash and hot gas racing down the slopes at speeds of up to seventy miles per hour, ripping the roofs off houses and overturning ships in the bay. These surges were followed by thick and glowing avalanches of fiery ash, rock and pumice——hot magma that has cooled so quickly that it is still full of volcanic gases, like a hard foamy sponge.

Sulphur fumes caused by the eruption of Mount Vesuvius overcome Pliny's uncle in this painting done in 1813.

Vesuvius had not actually erupted for hundreds of years before A.D. 79, and the people of the area believed the volcano was extinct. But they could remember an earthquake seventeen years earlier that had caused much damage to the town. And in the days before the volcano erupted, occasional rumblings and ground tremors were felt, creating the odd crack in a wall, or causing a statue to tumble off its stand. And other strange things happened: wells and springs mysteriously dried up, flocks of birds flew away, and animals were exceptionally restless.

We know now that the dry wells were caused by the increasing heat and pressure that were building deep in the earth, and that animals are always more sensitive than humans to changes in the earth and the atmosphere. But, I wondered, were the people in Herculaneum aware that something was about to happen? Before the mountain actually erupted, did it occur to anyone that it might be a good idea to leave town? How many waited until the streets were so crowded that escape was almost impossible? Were they spooked by the tremors, their suddenly dry wells, or the nervous actions of their animals? Did they think the gods were showing their anger?

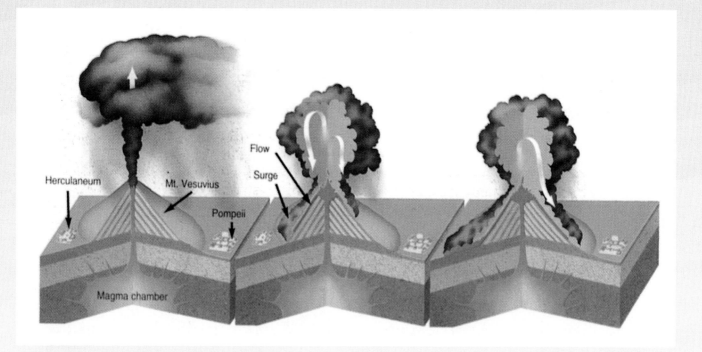

1. At midday on August 24, A.D. 79, Vesuvius erupts, sending a cloud of ash and pumice 12 miles into the air.

2. After midnight, the cloud collapses, sending a surge of ash and hot gas down the mountain, killing the Herculaneans. A flow of hot ash, rock, and pumice eventually buries the town.

3. Early the next morning another surge kills the people of Pompeii. It, too, is followed by a flow of hot debris from the volcano.

We will probably never know exactly what the volcano's victims were thinking in those days before the eruption. We do know that the glowing avalanches that buried Herculaneum and the nearby city of Pompeii created two time capsules of ancient Roman life that have not changed in almost two thousand years.

Sealed by volcanic ash and rock, the buried buildings have been protected from the wind and rain that would have worn down the columns and statues over the centuries. Wooden doors, shutters, stairs, cupboards and tables have not been exposed to the air to rot away, or been destroyed by fire. And unlike other ancient towns, the roads and buildings have not been repaired, or torn down and replaced by something more modern.

Instead, Herculaneum and Pompeii look the way they did so many years ago. The roofs of the houses may be gone, the mosaic floors cracked and the wall paintings faded. But we can still walk down the streets over the same stones that the ancient Romans walked on. We can see a 2,000-year-old loaf of bread, now turned to stone, or eggs still in their shells waiting to be served for lunch.

Although both Herculaneum and Pompeii were buried by the volcano, their fates were quite different. Pompeii, a town of twenty thousand people, lay five miles away from the volcano, but the wind was blowing in its direction when the eruption occurred. Throughout the afternoon and evening of August 24th, ash and pumice rained down on Pompeii. This frightened many people, and some of them fled immediately. But it was not until early the next morning that the first flow of hot gas and ash overwhelmed the town, killing the two thousand people who had failed to escape.

The fallen bodies of the Pompeiians were buried under twelve feet of ash and pumice. When the dead bodies rotted away they left hollow places in the hardened volcanic rock. Archaeologists discovered these cavities in the 1860s and decided to pour in plaster to create lifelike models of the volcano's victims as they lay or crouched in the positions in which they died. Some appear to be gasping or choking in their final moments as they were suffocated by ash so hot that it singed their hair and burned the insides of their mouths. But the plaster also covered up what remained of the skeletons, preventing them from being studied by modern scientists.

Herculaneum, which was less than three miles from Vesuvius, was upwind of the volcano. Most of the falling ash blew in the opposite direction, leaving less than an inch lying over the town by the end of the day. Instead, at about 1:15 early the next morning, a violent surge of ash and hot gas poured over the town. By the time the waves of hot mud followed, everyone was dead. In a few hours, Herculaneum was completely buried under sixty-five feet of hot volcanic matter, which, when it cooled, covered the town like a cement shield.

And so the town lay tightly sealed, for about 1,500 years.

Archaeologists made lifelike models at Pompeii by pouring plaster into the hollow shells of hardened volcanic rock that sealed Vesuvius's victims.

Then in 1709, a well-digger accidentally struck fine polished marble beneath the ground. An Austrian prince who was building a villa in the area realized that the marble was likely just the beginning of a major buried treasure, and he started to dig into the site.

Luckily for the prince, and unhappily for modern archaeologists and historians, the well-digger had found Herculaneum's ancient theater, one of the most luxurious and treasure-filled buildings in the town. The prince wanted art and fine building materials for his villa, so he hired diggers who bored tunnels through the theater, not knowing what it was, and not caring in the least about the damage they were doing to the structure itself.

The prince plundered the building of its bronze and stone statues and vases. Marble was ripped off the walls and pillars, and the treasures were carted off to the prince's own house or those of his rich friends. Before long these valuable artifacts were scattered in museums and private collections all over Europe.

The prince's raiders, burrowing through the site like greedy moles sniffing out treasure, did more damage to Herculaneum than the volcano itself.

More raiding expeditions followed, and it was only in 1860 that serious archaeological work began. But even with many of the most precious objects gone, the excavated town itself told historians a great deal about the ancient Romans and how they lived. Because the ruin had been snugly covered by a wet and heavy layer of earth, Herculaneum was even better preserved than Pompeii (which had suffered more damage under its airy blanket of ash and pumice).

Then just a few years ago came the most amazing discovery of all, when ditch-diggers accidentally found the group of skeletons on the ancient beachfront.

By the time these beach skeletons were found, scientists had discovered that we could learn a great deal about people by examining their bones. We could do much more than make plaster casts. Now we can analyze the bones themselves and reconstruct the skulls to see what the people looked like.

This is where I came in. In the morning, I would help to dig up these bones and begin to study them. For the first time, we would know more about the Romans than what books and paintings and sculptures had shown us. We would be able to see the people themselves.

I would be one of the first modern people to look an ancient Roman in the face.

Herculaneum, June 1982

It was quiet on Herculaneum's ancient beach. Above my head, drying sheets and underwear fluttered from the apartment balconies that now overlook the ruins.

Today this beach is just a narrow dirt corridor that lies several feet below sea level. But thousands of years ago, the waves of the Mediterranean would have lapped where I now stood, and my ears would have been filled with the gentle sound of the surf, rather than the dull roar of midday traffic in modern-day Ercolano, a crowded suburb of Naples.

To one side of me stood the arched entryways of the boat chambers, most of them still plugged by volcanic rock, their secrets locked inside. Only one chamber had been opened so far, and its contents were now hidden behind a padlocked plywood door.

I eyed the wooden door longingly, wishing for a sudden gift of X-ray vision. Dr. Maggi, the director of the excavation and keeper of the key, had been called away to a meeting with some government officials, and would not be back until sometime in the afternoon.

"Dottoressa!"

Ciro Formuola, the foreman of the work crew that was going to help me dig out the skeletons, was calling me from farther down the old beach. He was waving me toward a roped-off area surrounding three ordinary-looking piles of dirt.

I have examined thousands of skeletons in my life, but seeing each one for the first time still fills me with a kind of awe. As I walked over to the mound that Ciro was pointing at, I knew I was about to meet my first Herculanean.

It didn't look like much at first——just a heap of dirt with bits of bone poking out. I knelt down and gently scraped earth off the skeleton, exposing it to the light for the first time in two thousand years. Although the skeleton was badly broken, I had a hunch that it might be female, but I was puzzled by the position of her bones. Her thigh was poking out grotesquely beside a section of skull. It almost looked as if the bones had been carelessly tossed there, they were so broken and tangled.

Then I realized that something dreadful had happened to this woman, and that she had met with a violent death of some kind. Her skull was shattered, her pelvis crushed, and her leg had been thrust up to her neck. Roof tiles were trapped beneath her.

I looked up. Above me was the open terrace where Herculaneans had held sacred ceremonies. Above that was the wall of the town itself, most of the surrounding balustrade now missing.

The beachfront, the ruins of Herculaneum and Vesuvius as they look today.

Had this woman fallen from the wall above? Had some huge force propelled her from the town, perhaps a piece of flying debris, or the blast from the volcano itself, so that she smashed face down onto the ground? What had she been doing on the wall in the first place? Calling down to the people on the beach for help?

I picked up one of the bones and felt its cool smoothness in my hands. Because this was the first Herculanean I got to know, this skeleton was extra special to me. I named her Portia.

By measuring the bones, I could tell that Portia was about 5 feet 1 inch tall. She was about forty-eight when she died——an old woman by Roman standards——and had buck teeth.

Later, after a chemical analysis, we learned that Portia also had very high levels of lead in her bones. Lead is a poison, but in Roman times it was a common substance. It was used in makeup, medicines, paint pigment, pottery glazes, and to line drinking cups and plates. Cheap wine was sweetened with a syrup that had been boiled down in lead pots, so heavy drinkers may have had even more exposure to lead.

I closely examine each bone of a skeleton as I lift it from the wet volcanic earth.

On either side of Portia was a skeleton. One was another female. She lay on her side, almost looking as if she had died in her sleep. As I brushed dirt from her left hand, something shiny caught my eye as it glinted in the sunlight. It was a gold ring.

When we uncovered the rest of the hand, we found a second ring. And in a clump on her hip we found two intricate snakes' head bracelets made of pure gold, a pair of earrings that may have held pearls, and some coins (the cloth purse that had probably once held these valuables had long since rotted away).

We ended up calling her the Ring Lady. She was about forty-five when she died. She was not terribly good-looking; her jaw was large and protruding. There were no cavities in her teeth, but she did have gum disease, which left tiny pits in the bone along her gum line. If she

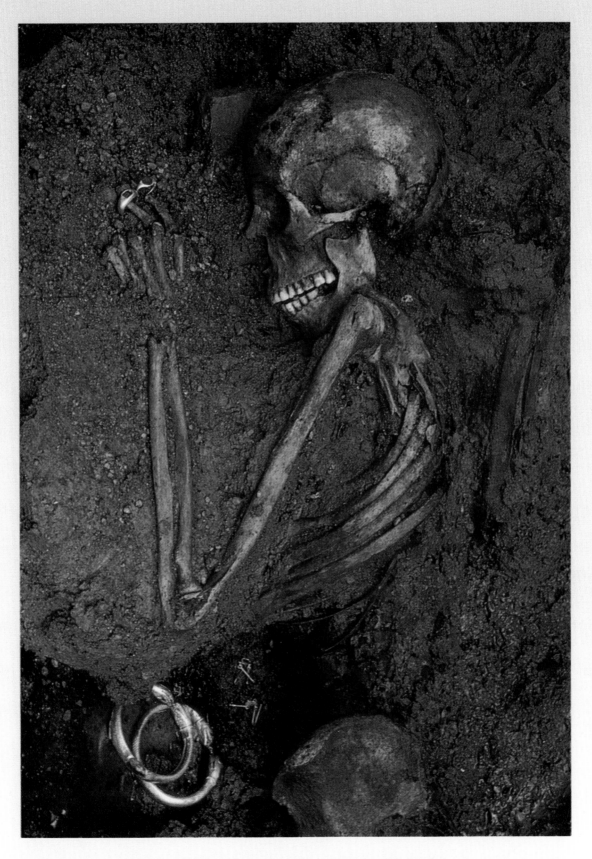

We called this skeleton the Ring Lady because of the two gold rings she wears on her left hand. We also found two bracelets, a pair of earrings and some coins by her side.

had lived today, her dentist probably would have advised her to floss more often!

In fact, most of the Herculaneans I examined had very good teeth, with only about three cavities each. Today, many of us have about sixteen cavities each, in spite of all our fluoride treatments, regular dental checkups and constant nagging to floss and brush! But the Romans had no sugar in their diet. They used honey, but not much, because it was expensive. Instead, the Herculaneans ate a well-balanced diet, including much seafood, which is rich in fluoride. Not only that, but they had strong jaws from chewing and tearing food without using knives and forks. And they did clean their teeth, scrubbing them with the stringy end of a stick rather than using a brush and toothpaste.

On the other side of Portia we dug up the skeleton we called the Soldier. He was found lying down, his hands outstretched, his sword still in his belt. We found carpenter's tools with him, which had perhaps been slung over his back. (Roman soldiers often worked on building projects when they were between wars.) He also had a money belt

An archaeologist carefully brushes dirt away from the
soldier's skeleton. The soldier's sword still lies by his side.

containing three gold coins. He was quite tall for a Roman, about 5 feet 8 inches.

When I examined the man's skull, I could see that he was missing six teeth, including three at the front, and that he'd had a huge nose. And when I examined the bone of his left thigh, I could see a lump where a wound had penetrated the bone and caused a blood clot that eventually had hardened. Near the knee, where the muscle would have been attached, the bone was enlarged slightly. This indicated that he would have had well-developed thighs, possibly due to gripping the sides of a horse with the knees while riding (Romans didn't use saddles).

Had the soldier lost those front teeth in a fight, I wondered. Had he been wounded in the leg during the same fight or another one? His life must have been fairly rough and tumble.

While members of the excavation team poured buckets of water on the three skeletons to loosen the debris, I continued to scrape off the dirt and volcanic matter with a trowel. Later, in the laboratory, each bone and tooth would be washed with a soft brush. Then they would be left to dry before being dipped in an acrylic solution to preserve them. Finally, each bone would be measured, then measured again to prevent errors, and the figures would be carefully recorded.

We found these coins in the soldier's money belt. One of them has the head of the Emperor Nero on it.

By late afternoon my back and knees were stiff from crouching, and the back of my neck was tight with the beginning of a sunburn.

I stood up and stretched. There was still much to do before the three skeletons would be free of their volcanic straitjackets. I started to think about heading back to the hotel for a shower and bite to eat. But a flurry of activity down the beach caught my eye, and suddenly I no longer felt tired.

To my right, Dr. Maggi stood outside the locked wooden door I had seen earlier. He was unbolting the padlock. When he saw me, he waved. I put down my trowel, wiped my hands on my jeans and hurried over. Inside, I knew, was the only group of Roman skeletons that had ever been found——the twelve people who had huddled in the shelter and died together when the volcanic avalanches poured down the mountainside into the sea.

I could hear an odd echo from inside the chamber as Dr. Maggi clicked the padlock open. Behind me, a number of the crew members had gathered. We were all very quiet.

The plywood door seemed flimsy as Dr. Maggi pulled it open. From inside the chamber came the dank smell of damp earth.

A shiver crept up my neck. We were opening a 2,000-year-old grave. What would we find?

As I entered the cave-like boat chamber, I could barely see, even though the sun flooded through the door. Someone handed me a flashlight, but its light cast greenish shadows, making it feel even more spooky.

The light played over the back of the shelter, no bigger than a single garage and still crusted over with volcanic rock. I saw an oddly shaped, lumpy mound halfway back. I took several steps into the chamber and pointed the light at the mound.

The narrow beam found a skull, the pale face a grimace of death. As my eyes grew accustomed to the dim light, I soon realized there were bones and skulls everywhere. They were all tangled together——clinging to each other for comfort in their final moments——and it was hard to distinguish one from another. But I knew that twelve skeletons had been found in all——three men, four women, and five children. One child had an iron house key near him. Did he think he would be going back home?

I took another step into the cave. At my feet was a skeleton that was almost entirely uncovered. From the pelvis I could see it was a female, a girl, lying face down. Beneath her, we could just see the top of another small skull.

It was a baby.

I knelt down and gently touched the tiny skull. My throat felt tight as I thought about this girl, this baby, and what it must have been like for them in this dark cave in the moments before they died.

"Una madre col suo bambino," whispered Ciro behind me.

"I don't think they're a mother and baby," I said. I could see from the pelvis that the girl was not old enough to have had children. I pointed to my own stomach and outlined a beachball tummy with my arms while I shook my head. "This girl has never given birth."

"Allora, é la sorella?"

I frowned, pulled my Italian-English dictionary out of the back pocket of my jeans and flipped through it. I realized Ciro thought these two skeletons belonged to a baby and its older sister.

"We'll see," I murmured. I knew it was important not to jump to conclusions. You have to question everything about bones, especially ones that have been lying around for two thousand years. I've known cases where people thought bone damage was caused by joint disease, when it was in fact caused by rats gnawing at the dead body.

I struggled to free a bronze cupid pin and two little bells from the baby's bones. Whoever the child was, it had been rich enough to wear expensive ornaments. But I knew it would take many more hours of careful study before we knew the real story behind these two skeletons.

Later, in the laboratory, I gained enough information to put together a more likely background for the skeleton of the young girl.

Unlike the baby, she had not come from a wealthy family. She had been about fourteen, and from the shape of her skull I knew she had probably been pretty. When I examined her teeth I could tell that she had been starved or quite ill for a time when she was a baby. She had also had two teeth removed about one or two weeks before she died,

Workers reveal an opening to a partially excavated boat chamber in a row with other chambers sealed tight by volcanic rock.

187

probably giving her a fair bit of pain. And her life had been very hard. She had done a lot of running up and down stairs or hills, as well as having to lift objects too heavy for her delicate frame.

This girl could not have been the child of a wealthy family, like the baby. She had probably been a slave who died trying to protect the baby of the family she worked for.

And there were many others. Near the slave girl lay the skeleton of a seven-year-old girl whose bones also showed that she had done work far too heavy for a child so young.

We found a sixteen-year-old fisherman, his upper body well developed from rowing boats, his teeth worn from holding cord while he repaired his fishing nets.

Particularly heartbreaking were the two pregnant women I examined, for we were also able to recover their tiny unborn babies, their bones as fragile as eggshells. One woman had been only about sixteen years old.

Though it is fascinating to reconstruct the life of a single person by examining his or her bones, for anthropologists and historians the most useful information comes from examining all of the skeletons of one population. This is one reason why Herculaneum is so important.

During the next few months we opened two more boat chambers. In one we discovered forty tangled human skeletons and one of a horse; in another we found twenty-six skeletons creepily lined up like a row of dominoes, as if heading in single file for the back of the chamber.

The skeletons represented a cross-section of the population of a whole town——old people, children and babies, slaves, rich and poor, men and women, the sick and the healthy. By examining all these skeletons, we can get some ideas about how the townspeople lived and what they were like physically.

We found out, for example, that the average Herculanean man was 5 feet 5 inches tall, the average woman about 5 feet 1 inch. In general, they were well nourished. And we have examined enough people to know that although the rich people had easy lives, the slaves often worked so hard that they were in pain much of the time.

Studying these skeletons closely can also help medical researchers and doctors. In ancient times, many diseases could not be cured by surgery or drugs. Instead, people kept getting sicker, until they eventually died. By examining the bones of these people, we can learn a great deal about how certain diseases progress.

By the end of my stay in Herculaneum, I had examined 139 skeletons. Their bones were sorted into yellow plastic vegetable crates that lined the shelves in my laboratory. And each box of bones has a different story to tell.

Even though I can't tell the good guys from the bad, and I can't tell you whether they were happy or not, I know a great deal about these people. I can see each person plainly. I even imagine them dressed as they might have been, lounging on their terraces or in the baths if they were wealthy, toiling in a mine or in a galley if they were the most unfortunate slaves.

Most of all, I feel that these people have become my friends, and that I have been very lucky to have had a part in bringing their stories to the rest of the world.

Here I am cleaning bones at a long table.

The People on the Beach

Meet the Author

Sara C. Bisel is one of the world's leading specialists in ancient bones. She has worked on skeletons in Greece, Turkey, and Israel. Some of her work has been featured in *Discover* and *National Geographic* magazines and on a National Geographic television program.

Meet the Illustrator

Ken Marschall is well known for his wonderful paintings of the *Titanic*, featured in the best-selling book, *Titanic: An Illustrated History*. He has also created illustrations of the *Hindenburg* and of the *Lusitania*.

Theme Connections

Think About It

With a small group of classmates, imagine what it must be like to re-create the lives of ancient people based on their preserved bones.

- How do the remains at Herculaneum compare with the remains of other ancient civilizations you've studied? What can be learned about a society from the skeletons that are left behind?
- Were any other towns buried by volcanic eruptions? Are any modern towns currently threatened by volcanoes?

Check the Concept/Question Board to see if there are any questions there that you can answer now. If the selection or your discussions about the selection have raised any new questions about ancient civilizations, put the questions on the Board. Maybe the next selection will help answer the questions.

Record Ideas

Think about the selections you've read in this unit. Use your Writing Journal to record notes and ideas about the different ways we can learn about ancient peoples and civilizations.

Research Ideas

- Pompeii was another Roman town buried by the eruption of Mount Vesuvius. Much has been learned from its ruins, but there are still many questions to investigate.
- The Roman Empire was the greatest power in Europe for a long time. How did the Romans become so powerful? How did they manage to rule in such distant places as England?

His Majesty, Queen Hatshepsut

Dorothy Sharp Carter
illustrated by Dave Blanchette

In Egypt in about the year 1503 B.C., Queen Hatshepsut, daughter of King Thutmose I, wife of King Thutmose II, ascends the throne at her husband's death. But it is a throne she shares as Queen Regent with her nine-year-old stepson, Prince Thutmose III. Sharing the throne with the prince displeases Queen Hatshepsut. Two years into her reign, she has a dream in which the King of Gods, Amon-Re, tells Hatshepsut's mother that Hatshepsut "shall exercise the excellent kingship of this whole land."

Queen Hatshepsut uses the dream as an excuse to hold a coronation and have herself declared King of Upper and Lower Egypt, a bold and audacious act. How can this be? A woman who is king? Some of the men in her court are angry at her brazen deed, especially the priests who want Prince Thutmose to become king as soon as he comes of age. But King Hatshepsut triumphs and rules Egypt until her death twenty-two years later.

You are about to meet King Hatshepsut and discover what her life was like in a civilization that no longer exists.

"Day 14, month 3 of Sowing . . ." While only three months have passed since my coronation, I date my reign as beginning from the death of my husband. It gives a more settled appearance. And in truth I did begin my rule then, for what use was the presence of a nine-year-old boy?

I, Makare Hatshepsut, am Pharaoh of the whole of Egypt, with no fetters, no restraints to hinder me. I know now how a caged bird feels when at long last the door flaps open and it can escape into the limitless blue of heaven.

It is not that I desire power for its own sake. I am not so vainglorious. But to have the authority to do what I know must be done for my country's good——that is ecstasy. Also——to be completely truthful——I desire to demonstrate to Egypt, to the entire world, that a woman can rule every bit as wisely as a man.

Each morning when Henut wakes me, I lie for a moment not thinking at all, only savoring this enormous bubble of happiness. Arching my neck over the cushioned headrest of my bed, I watch a sliver of sunlight enter the high window and light up the curly frieze border of the ceiling. The chariot of Amon begins its journey across the clear sky just as I am about to begin *my* day.

For another moment I ponder my goals as ruler. I will make Egypt stronger than she has ever been——so strong internally that no country will ever dare challenge her.

I will repair all the temples in the land, in particular those which the vagabond foreign rulers of Egypt, the Hyksos, neglected for so long. In addition, I will construct others to be the most beautiful in the world.

And——an idea lodged in a far corner of my mind——I may in time launch a sailing expedition to Punt, that faraway place we know as God's Land, the source of our indispensable frankincense and myrrh. This can in name be a trading expedition, but in fact a purpose just as important will be to explore, to observe the wonders of the Great Green [the Red Sea], of the manners and customs of the Puntites, of the nature of their land. I may command that expedition myself. For I am immensely inquisitive about foreign peoples, how they live and dress and think. Curiosity may be a queenly rather than kingly trait, but in any case, I intend to indulge it.

"It is the hour, Highness."

Henut stands beside my bed, a fresh linen robe in her hands. I slip into the robe, into my sandals. Henut runs a comb through my hair, adjusts a heavy, elaborate wig. I am ready for the first ritual of the morning.

Outside the door wait two high priestesses of Amon, one wearing the mask of Horus, the other the ibis head of Thoth. They bow. We walk in silence down the hall to the House of the Morning, my main chapel.

Inside, the golden ewers of water stand ready on a marble-topped table. Removing my robe, I lave my body, speaking aloud a prayer.

"Great Father God Amon-Re, as thou bathest in the ocean each morning to begin thy journey across the heavens, so bathes thy daughter. Thus we restore our divine vitality for the day's tasks. Guide me, O my father, to live in *maat* for today and always."

The priestesses anointing me, helping to robe me, are a symbol of triumph. They are the result of my first victory as ruler over Amon's priesthood.

The day I ascended the throne, a chief priest informed me, "Each morning two priestesses will accompany Her Majesty to the House of the Morning. As Her Majesty may know, a king is attended by priests wearing the masks of Horus and Thoth. This would of course be unsuitable in the case of Her Majesty." His voice held an edge of superiority.

"Perhaps my proclamation has not reached your ears, Lord," I replied icily. "My Majesty, being king, is referred to by the whole world as *His* Majesty. Furthermore, the priestesses will naturally don the masks of Horus and Thoth."

Shock and indignation so overcame him that he stammered. "S-such a custom is unheard of in the en-entire h-history of the Two Lands!" He glared at me, suddenly realized who——or what——I was, and gulped.

"I beg Her . . . His Majesty's pardon, but for women . . . priestesses to wear the sacred masks defies the holy tradition of Amon's ritual."

"Then we will change tradition. See that the female Thoth and Horus await My Majesty tomorrow." I dismissed him brusquely. He stumbled away, his face pale even for a priest.

They resent me, the priests, and will yet cause me trouble——I sense it. Despite all I do for Amon. However, for the time all goes well. With use customs come quickly to be accepted, and after three months the priestesses and their masks have become routine.

After my ablutions we proceed to another chapel, already occupied by priests and court officials. Here more prayers are said, and a high priest intones, "May a curse be laid, O Amon, on anyone who offends thee, with or without intention."

Later the same priest feels called on to reassure me. "The curse is aimed at His Majesty's ministers, certainly not at His Majesty himself." But he swiftly adds, "His Majesty takes note, I am sure, of all prayers as a guide to royal conduct."

His tone reminds me of Tutami in the classroom: condescending patronage. At times——many times——the priesthood takes on the all-powerful airs of Amon. It could do with a lesson in humility.

Sacrifice and the reading of the entrails follow: A priest spells out the omens. The day is auspicious for the composing of letters, for the holding of audience, for the visiting of friends. Inauspicious for journeys, either by boat or palanquin or foot. (That I could have forecast myself. There is enough work to keep me occupied at home for some time.)

At last I am escorted back to my quarters. After perfuming my mouth with wine and fruit, I submit to being readied. It is a quiet time to think and plan.

Were I a man, I could confer with my officials while being groomed. However, most of my council would die of embarrassment if called on to witness the plucking of my brows, the massage with unguents, the application of kohl and henna. As a dozen corpses would be of no help to me, I think alone.

One problem is that of Prince Thutmose. How he views my dream of divine birth I do not know. Nor do I care. Deep in my mind this lack of interest concerning Thutmose bothers me. Thorough and careful always in my planning, I do not forget the obstacles, however small, which like sharp stones protrude through the path of my life.

The Prince is such an obstacle. He is more than a stone. Rather, he is a vein of rock that appears treacherously now here, now there, for me to stumble over. One day he may loom before me, a high jagged barrier.

Well. The rock lies there, I am aware of it, and there is nothing to do about it. For the time being.

Yesterday Hapusoneb made a suggestion: Why did I not place the Prince under his care as apprentice priest? It is an honor due a prince to serve the Great God of No-Amon. There he would be under the eye of the entire priesthood.

Under *your* eye, O Hapusoneb, perhaps. The entire priesthood may not be so trustworthy. At all events, the idea has merit and I shall consider it.

While my hair is being dressed, I glance over accounts of palace expenditures. To think I once complained (to be truthful not once but many times) of having to learn to read. How thoughtless children are. True it is they do not know what is good for them.

The palace expenses are revealing. So much waste. No doubt kings seldom pay heed to such petty details, but this is a field I can understand and correct. Not only disbursements of the Great House but those made throughout the government can and shall be curtailed. Some officials act as though the lotuses of the Nile were of gold and have only to be plucked. They shall learn.

As an example, I have cut my immediate toilet staff to twenty. My husband had twice that number, including four barbers to shave him when he surely had beard enough for one alone.

I have limited my attendants to one mat spreader, two manicurists and two pedicurists (all four work at once to save time), three hairdressers, two masseuses, four perfumers (well, one to daub on scent and three others to distill the oils and mix the fragrances), one to prepare my bath, two to dress me, two to apply cosmetics, one to adjust my jewelry (my mother used three such, but to her all jewels were lucky or unlucky depending on the day, and this had to be determined by divination). I do not count laundresses, bleachers, pressers, seamstresses.

Today, with one public appearance, and that an informal one, I will dress as a woman. That means a gown instead of a kilt, a light wig, and crown. What an advantage I have over other pharaohs. I can choose my sex as it pleases me.

A whisper. "Majesty?"

The Keeper of Royal Jewelry stands before me, a tray of gold collars in her hands. They are too heavy, appropriate for formal functions. I shake my head and wave her away to fetch other, lighter necklets.

She returns with a necklace of thin gold wires woven about delicate flowers of pearls and amethysts. And with it my favorite earrings, those the Great God Pharaoh, my father, presented me when I was nine. They are butterflies, their wings of lapis lazuli and garnet, fastened to gold loops. I nod. Why cannot one's officials be as eager and amenable as servants?

A discreet cough disturbs my musing. "Your Majesty."

Only Henut dares interrupt my thoughts. I glance up.

My twenty attendants stand in stiff rows like soldiers, their gaze on the floor. Henut stands before them, her eyes plucking their stance, their hands, their expression, as she would pluck feathers from a goose. If any is found wanting, that one will know shortly.

It appears I am readied for the day.

First is scheduled a conference with Chief Treasurer Nehesi. Nehesi is the newest of my councillors, unearthed by Hapusoneb, my faithful minister of a myriad connections.

The Treasurer is a small man, as shriveled as a dried fig. Son of a Nubian brewer, he completely lacks the elegance and assurance of the average courtier. Far more important, he knows and understands value.

For years he was a middleman at the market, dealing in that unit of commerce called the *shat*. Father once explained to me the meaning of the word.

"As an example, my daughter, let us take the seller of a cow. In exchange for it, he is offered so many bushels of corn or lengths of linen or jars of wine. But, being fond of his cow, he decides the animal is worth more than what is offered. The difference then must be calculated in so many *shat*, and an item of that worth agreed on."

"I should not at all mind doing such work," I told him. "To aid seller and purchaser to find articles of equal value——it is a kind of game."

Father chuckled (I was the cause of many of his smiles and laughs). "A kind of game, yes. Didst thou know, Hatshepsut, that some countries base their unit of value on metal, copper or silver or gold?"

I put my nose in the air. "That would be a clumsy system, metal being so heavy and cumbersome."

Father nodded. "A practice to be expected of foreign lands."

Well, what else? In its ideas and practices my Egypt is years in advance of other nations.

Father would have approved of Nehesi: his careful honesty, his tenacity, his precision, his refusal to be intimidated . . . except by *me*. My Treasurer has yet to figure me out and tends to handle me as gingerly as he would an ostrich egg.

Our conference goes well——better for me than for him. After the usual review of revenue and disbursement, he hesitantly broaches a new subject.

"Your Majesty, the Chief Steward brings to my attention"——he pauses, coughs nervously——"a trivial matter. Of very minor importance." He stops again, struggles to heave up the words he wants. He takes a deep breath, and lo, the words come gushing forth. "Your Majesty, there are complaints from the royal household regarding the inadequate ration of bread." He bows his head. (For me to strike it off?)

I allow my arched brows to arch higher. "How is this possible? Do we not provide fourteen hundred loaves a day?"

"Indeed, your Majesty. Oh, indeed. His Majesty may be unaware that Great God-King Thutmose made provision for *two thousand* loaves daily."

"Treasurer, my staff is much reduced from that era. There is now no harem, and fewer personal attendants."

"True, true. But . . . to maintain His Majesty's residence in the appropriate style for a monarch of His Majesty's glorious status, an adequate household staff is absolutely necessary. The staff has grown, of necessity with His Majesty's tremendous responsibilities, to a somewhat greater size than that of the Great God-King Thutmose II. . . ."

Here he marks my frown at mention of my husband's name and leaps to a happier note. "His Majesty will be most gratified to learn that——this from a memorandum of the Chief Steward——the palace has decreased the amount of beer consumed from 200 to 150 jugs a day. Except, of course, when the amount is augmented for holidays."

Which means ten days out of thirty. My subjects live for feast days.

"My Majesty is well pleased about the beer. But back to the bread. My Majesty detests waste and will not provide for gorging."

The Treasurer is unused to women who argue and is thrown off balance. "Your Highness, could we . . . if I may . . . Your Majesty, with the addition of two hundred loaves more, I believe there would be no waste. And no further complaints."

I ponder. An idea sprouts, leafs out, flowers. It is a good idea and has additional merit: It will flick the priesthood's too-haughty nose.

"Lord Nehesi, the state is making major repairs and improvements on Amon's temple. My Majesty has in mind rich gifts, additions to the temple such as statues, obelisks, fine new ceremonial robes for the priests. In return for these, we will request the temple to supply the Great House with two hundred loaves of bread daily."

My Treasurer smiles thinly. Still overawed by a female sovereign, he cannot believe I am serious in demanding bread from Amon's domain. On discovering that I mean what

201

I say, he wonders if the temple will blame *him* for the proposal, which could have uncomfortable effects; the priesthood can be vindictive in subtle ways.

I have faith in Nehesi's astuteness. Blame can be shared by the Chief Steward, by a dozen other officials. At any rate, I have solved that problem with no increase in my budget. My people will not say of me, "Ah! She flings gold dust about as though it were sand."

Actually Egypt's finances are at present in excellent shape. Our hundreds of granaries in temples and towns are well stocked in the event of a light inundation and the resulting failure of crops. The construction of private buildings is brisk, bringing in good revenue from the state monopoly in brick making; the same is true in papermaking. Fortunately for me, taxation on harvests and ships and property need not be increased this year.

A thought occurs: With my head so full of economies, large and small, I could always find occupation as a simple housewife!

Next on my schedule, I show myself for the first time as Pharaoh at the Window of Appearances. My excuse to the Vizier is that the people adore spectacles of any sort, and a view of Pharaoh is regarded as a grand treat. To be quite honest, I do it for pure pleasure. To distribute largesse in my own name, with no one to nod me permission——ah, I relish that.

Always before, I had stood behind my father or my husband and was handed a small bracelet or two to toss. Today Nefrure alone appears with me. She bounces with anticipation.

"Calm thyself," I chide her.

"Oh, my mother, I do not like to be calm!"

She peers over the railing at the courtyard. It being a hot and windless day, the court is packed with sunshade bearers and fan bearers as well as household officials and relatives of the honorees. A guard marshals the recipients into a queue. On three sides the public, wiping their perspiring faces, strain against the ropes. Even the lowliest wears a clean loincloth for the occasion.

There are seven or eight honorees. As each steps before the balcony and salutes me, I deliver a short speech of praise, ending with "Thou art my faithful servant who hast carried out the orders of My Majesty, who is well pleased with thee. I therefore award thee these gifts with the words 'Thou shalt eat the bread of Pharaoh (Life, Health, Strength!) thy lord, in the temple of Amon.'"

From the tray of gold ornaments I choose necklets, rings, inlaid hatchets, goblets, trinkets in the shapes of bees and lions, to fling to those honored. As the gifts are caught, there are shrieks of delight from the family.

Nefrure is in raptures. She helps to shower "the praise of gold" on her friends Hapusoneb (honored for faithful and meritorious service) and Senmut (for outstanding ideas concerning efficiency and economies in government departments). They will need to grow new necks to wear all the chains she flings to them.

"Senmut needs another bracelet!" Nefrure exclaims, eyes bright with excitement. As I have appointed him her tutor, she sees much of him. They have grown very fond of each other.

"He will not be able to wear so much jewelry or carry it either," I protest. "There will be other opportunities."

"Tomorrow?" she asks hopefully.

I laugh. "Not tomorrow, but very soon."

The last award goes to the Keeper of the Interior Apartments for long and industrious service. "Meritorious" and "outstanding" can certainly not be applied to him, nor I fear, can "faithful." The ceremony will reduce the sting when tomorrow I replace him in office. He is a relic of my husband's rule, disapproves vocally of queen rulers, and treats with no merchant or servant without a fat bribe. His wife is as oily as he, her eyes as shifty as his as she peeps into my face, incredulous that a mere *woman* is capable of filling the throne of the Two Lands. Stupid creature! Ah well, after today I will see little of them. He will be offered the position of Messenger for the Dogs' Food, which he is not likely to accept.

After lunch I escape to my refuge, a chamber furnished with only a long sofa and a small table to hold refreshments. With no other clutter, I can imagine I am on my country estate, the tiles of the floor tinted green as grass, the ceiling molded and painted to resemble a grape arbor, the vines thick with purple fruit.

Here I admit only Henut, to massage my forehead for headache, and my daughter (during those rare moments when she agrees to act like a lady). Today I have invited Senmut——Lord Senmut, as he has been for a month.

Senmut. Ah, Hatshepsut, in spite of thy royal and divine blood and against thy strongest wishes, thou art proved to be all too mortal. To hear the name of Senmut, to glimpse Senmut, to hear Senmut's voice——my breath, my blood cease in their courses, my vision clouds, my ears ring, my head is light.

What does it mean? Surely not that I love him. I have never loved anyone——apart from my dear Egypt——besides my father, and my daughter. I do not allow myself to love anyone. I cannot afford to. Love is weakness. I tell myself that over and over: Love is weakness. Only . . . how do I control my blood, my breath?

I question myself severely. Why do I find this man appealing? He is not handsome, although his face is unique, the features clear cut like his character, mouth thin, eyes both wide and long. The nose is somewhat hooked but not, thanks be to Hathor, as prominent as my own family's nose. The mobility of expression constitutes its charm.

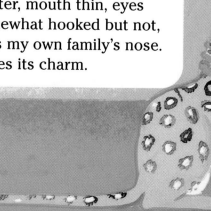

His most significant traits are his boldness of outlook, his self-assurance, his adaptability. As my daughter's tutor he has proved his gentleness, for she can tax one's patience with her teasing.

I say that he is adaptable; already he has adopted the dress, the manners, the carriage, the viewpoint of a nobleman. No. In all frankness he has not done so completely.

With regard to the gods, I have noticed, he is unsophisticated and highly superstitious. And he possesses a peasant's unabashed urge for acquisition. The offices I appoint him to he fulfills without fault. But the titles of those offices he collects and wears as a rustic woman flaunts at one time every string of cheap beads she owns. On all letters, all proclamations, Senmut never fails to include each and every title. Still, modesty is by no means a national characteristic of ours.

Today I confer with Senmut in his new capacity as Controller of Works. We will discuss the reopening of our copper and turquoise mines in the Sinai. (My composure is flawless. No blush, no tremble, no shortness of breath is apparent.)

"The reworking of the mines," I explain, "will require the presence of troops to ensure security from the barbaric sand dwellers. Aside from protection, the project will serve to keep the men occupied. The officers tend to become quickly restless unless they are busy warring and conquering."

Having been at one time a military scribe, Senmut is aware of how the military mind works. He nods.

"The plan is good. The officers will welcome it more than their men."

I look at him inquiringly.

"The common soldiers dislike setting foot on foreign soil. They ask, 'What if we die there? Who will prepare our bodies for burial? Who will recite the ritual over us? Are we to lose eternity because we leave our beloved Egypt?' I fear you must count on some desertions."

An idea comes to mind. These days find me as full of ideas as a palm tree with dates. I make haste to pluck the ideas and put them to work before they rot on the branches. "I will see that a body of priests and two or three embalmers accompany the men. That should allay their fear."

And if I follow Hapusoneb's suggestion of placing the Prince under his supervision as an apprentice priest——which appears most reasonable——then in two or three years' time the boy can himself become part of such an expedition to Sinai. It will provide him training and experience. And it will remove him effectively from the scene of action——for a time.

"That will cheer the men." Senmut's tone approves my decision.

"Have you yourself lived away from Egypt?" I ask.

"At one time. I built a grain warehouse and later the courthouse for the colony that Great Pharaoh Thutmose II"——he bows his head——"established in Cush."

"You engineered those buildings?"

He grimaces slightly. "They were nothing. But seeing them, the general Huy requested me to construct a house in the country for his newly married daughter. *That* I was proud of."

"So you are an architect." Is there no end to this man's talents? "Have you constructed other edifices?"

"A new home for my parents. My tomb and theirs. The deepest joy of life comes from creating a structure——a cottage, a mansion, a palace."

"In which of these did you grow up?"

"The first, Your Majesty. My father is a farmer, and his farm is very small."

"Then you have done doubly well." I contemplate another idea. With deliberation I ask, "Have you ever dreamed of designing a temple? A mortuary temple?"

Senmut draws in a deep breath, holds it for a full minute. His eyes, fixed on my feet, have turned to glass.

The breath pours out in a sigh, and his eyes meet mine. "A dream far beyond hope. Does His Majesty have such a temple in mind?"

Lord Senmut wastes no time in circling a subject. He even takes away *my* breath.

"The place for a temple, yes," I say slowly. "The shape of the temple itself, no." I change my tone to one of indifference. "Should you be interested, you might submit a plan."

He is at once all business. "Indeed, Majesty, I am interested. Would you tell me the site of this temple?"

"Near the tomb of Great Pharaoh Mentuhotep, built some six hundred years ago. As you are aware, it lies close to the valley where my own father is buried."

"It is a magnificent setting. Oh yes. Precisely right for a temple." Already his mind is churning, his eyes bright, his face flushed with the challenge.

To my chagrin I find myself jealous of this challenge. Would his face liven, his eyes glow so fervently if he thought of me as "Hatshepsut" rather than as "His Majesty"? Or——terrible thought——does he use me only to further his ambition? Ah, what a tangle is life! The lowly alone can afford to be direct. I dismiss Lord Senmut with a cool smile.

One further task remains to be done this day. During a short visit to the temple of Amon to view the alterations, I have an interview with my stepson, who has his lessons there. He is not a likable boy. The royal blood in him is so weakened by the common fluid of his mother that he is little better than a peasant. And looks it. Even for eleven years he is thin and knobby. How Egypt would fare under his rule I tremble to think. We will put it off as long as possible. Perhaps forever.

The Third Priest of Amon, Lord Rensonb, is also present. He is a lean, cold, unyielding man with a head like a skull, a fanatic fervor for detail, and a sensitive stomach. According to Hapusoneb, his moods match the state of this organ, which is generally sour.

The story goes that upon learning that I was to ascend the throne, he threw himself on the temple floor before the shrine of Amon and declared that he would die there of starvation rather than see a woman as king. His miserable stomach saved his life; its protest at being denied sustenance was more than he could bear. However, instead of blaming his stomach for his failure, he blamed me.

I nod to Rensonb and address the Prince. "My Majesty has decided to place thee in the Great Temple in order to serve Amon. Would this please thee?"

I sound pompous without meaning to. The boy makes me uncomfortable, he is always so silent and noncommittal.

"I thank thee, yes, gracious Majesty." His voice is shrill, the words are sedate, his glance never lifts from the floor.

"Good. The lord Hapusoneb will oversee thy duties."

He bows, saying nothing.

I turn to the Third Priest.

"Then, Lord, My Majesty leaves the Prince in your hands in the hope he will do honor to the God of Gods."

Never one for humility, the Third Priest must have his say. "His Majesty may rest assured. As the future ruler of the Two Lands, the Prince will be given the best of training."

"For that reason My Majesty places him here." My tone is curt.

"The best of training. And the most intensive. Within three or four years the Prince will be prepared to take his place as king."

209

I am floored by his presumption. My temper, as uncontrollable as Rensonb's stomach, boils up.

"*When* he becomes king is no concern of yours, Lord Rensonb. As director of the temple school you will superintend his education. From First Prophet Hapusoneb My Majesty will receive reports of the Prince's progress—— and of *your* efficiency as educator."

I turn my back on him, nod farewell to Thutmose. For once the boy's face is less impassive than a toad's. The exchange of words has actually upset him; his mouth is wide open as he bows.

It has upset me, also. Were the Third Priest any other man, I would replace him immediately, expel him to some small temple in Cush. But Rensonb's family is as old as my own and was at one time as noble. The manner of ridding myself of him must be subtle. Meanwhile, under Hapusoneb's eye he will hesitate to plant seditious ideas in my stepson's head——I trust.

My conversation with Senmut comes to mind, and a vague scheme grows strong. Very well, little son. Within the year thou wilt journey to the Sinai——well away from Rensonb and from thy mother, Isis——where thy stamina and character will be tested. The desert is an oven and abounds in snakes and poisonous insects, wild and wily tribesmen who resent intrusion. If thou weatherest all these, young Prince, thou mayest acquire worthy blood on thy own. In time——years and years from now——thou mayest even succeed me. *If* no one more suitable appears.

Back at the palace, a scroll is handed me, and my dejection vanishes. It is a sketch, very rough, of Senmut's design for my temple. He has taken the plan of Mentuhotep's shrine but enlarged and improved on it. The longer I study

it, the more I feel it can be worked into a superb model. Mine will be the most beautiful temple, the most magnificent building in all the Two Lands! And justly so, for I wish to be remembered always as a queen who became a king . . . a king greatest of the great.

The location is a kind of amphitheater, and the backdrop of my temple consists of high, rugged, towering cliffs. Instead of a tall, imposing structure that would be lost against the steep cliffs, Senmut has drawn a low but extremely wide building. There are three ascending terraces, like gigantic steps, connected by ramps. Each terrace consists of a huge courtyard leading into a colonnaded hall, the roof of each hall forming the courtyard of the hall above. The complex will be immense; we Egyptians build big, as we think big.

The glory of the plan is in its contrast to the background and in its simplicity. Even the terraces resemble my vision of the myrrh terraces of Punt, the original garden of the gods.

I am too excited by the plan to think. Originally I had thought to require plans from a half dozen of No-Amon's finest architects. Now there is no need. No one in the entire world or in the next thousand years could conceive a design

211

so exactly right. Had I been an artist, I should myself have designed a temple just so. Of course it is still a sketch only, a bare outline——but oh, it has promise.

Tomorrow I will announce my acceptance of the plan to the Great Ones, my council, and give orders to begin work as soon as possible. The embellishment of halls and courtyards can be worked out later. The matter itself is settled.

This means, too, that I will see much of Lord Senmut. Hatshepsut, reel in thy heart before it dies of throbbing! So be it. As I rise, so Senmut shall rise.

He is vital, dynamic . . . almost an extension of myself. I even feel he understands me——which certainly no one else living does. With all my wariness and distrust, I do not mind this. Even a pharaoh needs someone to understand him. But only *one* someone, no more. And this someone I will make to love me. Truly love me.

"Hathor, dear goddess of love, I will have Senmut build thee an altar!" I whisper. "Thanks upon thanks I send thee. Thou hast blessed me with someone to love. . . . I will have the most splendid temple in Egypt. . . . The Prince's future is decided. . . . Above all, I am King of the Two Lands! No, Hathor, thou deservest more than an altar. I will build thee a chapel within my very own temple!"

Even for a pharaoh, joy does not endure. But this day I will forever remember as joyful.

Principal Characters and Gods

Amon——*god of the sun, chief god of No-Amon*
Hapusoneb——*Hatshepsut's Vizier, First Prophet of Amon, and member of her Council of Government*
Hathor——*goddess of love and beauty*
Henut——*Hatshepsut's childhood nurse and later her maid*
Horus——*god of the sun*
Isis——*mother of Thutmose III*
Nefrure——*daughter of Hatshepsut and Thutmose II*
Nehesi——*Chief Treasurer and leader of the expedition to Punt*
Rensonb——*Third Priest of Amon and an ally of Thutmose III*
Senmut——*Hatshepsut's favorite courtier and chief adviser*
Thoth——*god of learning and magic*
Thutmose I——*Pharaoh and father of Hatshepsut*
Thutmose II——*Pharaoh and husband of Hatshepsut*
Thutmose III——*son of Thutmose II and Isis; stepson of Hatshepsut*
Tutami——*tutor of Hatshepsut and her brothers*

His Majesty, Queen Hatshepsut

Meet the Author

Dorothy Sharp Carter spent more than 20 years living in foreign countries, mostly in Latin America. She discovered a love of writing while working on a project for a college class. The project was to collect folktales from Central America and translate them into English. Her professor sent the work to a publishing house and it was published. Carter enjoyed writing so much that she wanted to write more. "Because of the fun I had doing it, I went on to make a similar collection of West Indian folktales." She has also written short stories and articles for several well-known children's publications.

Meet the Illustrator

Dave Blanchette's favorite thing to do has always been drawing. He says, "I don't remember ever being without a pencil in hand." Beginning at age eight, he began to strive to become better at his visual communication by illustrating stories his brother wrote.

Blanchette went on to attend Vesper George School of Art in Boston after returning from Vietnam in 1970. He currently resides in West Wareham, Massachusetts, with his wife Linda.

Theme Connections

Think About It

This selection included many details about daily life in ancient Egypt. With a small group of classmates, think about whether you would have liked to live in this place and time.

- Compare and contrast the ancient Egyptian society with the society in which you live today.
- Do you think Queen Hatshepsut would make a good president? Remember that democracy had not yet been invented when she ruled Egypt.

Check the Concept/Question Board to see if there are any questions there that you can answer now. If the selection or your discussions about the selection have raised any new questions about ancient civilizations, put the questions on the Board. Maybe the next selection will help answer the questions.

Record Ideas

Do you think this selection seems realistic? Use your Writing Journal to record notes and ideas about life in ancient Egypt.

Research Ideas

- What was life like for ordinary people in Queen Hatshepsut's time? Does archaeological evidence provide any clues?
- What was the purpose of the great pyramids and sphinxes in ancient Egypt? How were they built?

Ozymandias

Percy Bysshe Shelley
illustrated by Lane Yerkes

I met a traveller from an antique land
Who said: Two vast and trunkless legs of stone
Stand in the desert. Near them on the sand
Half sunk, a shatter'd visage lies, whose frown
And wrinkled lip and sneer of cold command
Tell that its sculptor well those passions read
Which yet survive, stamp'd on these lifeless things,
The hand that mock'd them and the heart that fed;
   And on the pedestal these words appear:
"My name is Ozymandias, king of kings:
Look on my works, ye Mighty and despair!"
    Nothing beside remains. Round the decay
    Of that colossal wreck, boundless and bare,
    The lone and level sands stretch far away.

To the Not Impossible Him

Edna St. Vincent Millay
illustrated by Lane Yerkes

How shall I know, unless I go
    To Cairo and Cathay,
Whether or not this blessed spot
    Is blest in every way?

Now it may be, the flower for me
    Is this beneath my nose;
How shall I tell, unless I smell
    The Carthaginian rose?

The fabric of my faithful love
    No power shall dim or ravel
Whilst I stay here,——but oh, my dear,
    If I should ever travel!

The Silk Route

7,000 MILES OF HISTORY

John S. Major

illustrated by Stephen Fieser

A.D. 700 . . .

The Roman Empire has fallen. Italy, Spain, and northern Europe are controlled by Germanic tribes. London and Paris are small towns; Rome is a half-deserted city of ruins.

In the eastern Mediterranean, the Roman tradition lives on in the Byzantine Empire, with its capital at the great city of Byzantium (also called Constantinople; now Istanbul).

The Christian rulers of Byzantium face a serious challenge from the rapidly expanding world of Islam. Founded by the Prophet Muhammad in 622, Islam has spread throughout Arabia and now also controls Iraq, Armenia, Persia, and much of North Africa.

Meanwhile, on the other side of the world, China is ruled by the glorious Tang Dynasty (618–906), whose emperors have brought China to a high point of power, territorial control, and cultural brilliance. China's capital, Chang'an, is the largest city in the world.

The great empires of the West and the East are linked by the Silk Route, an ancient trade network of caravan tracks across the steppes and deserts of Central Asia.

Tang Dynasty China, A.D. 700

The Chinese people called their country the Middle Kingdom. But people in the West called China the Land of Silk. Among all of China's many gifts to world civilization——paper, printing, gunpowder, and a great deal more——silk was the most highly prized in the ancient Western world.

Silk cloth was invented in China around 3000 B.C. No one knows who first made silk cloth. Many Chinese people believed that it was invented by the Silkworm Empress. She was the wife of the Yellow Emperor, the mythical founder of Chinese civilization.

On farms all over China men grow grain while women produce silk. They tend groves of mulberry trees and feed the leaves to silkworms. When the silkworms mature, they make cocoons of silk, which the women collect and boil. Then the women unreel the delicate strand of silk from each cocoon, spin it into thread, and weave it into silk cloth. Farmers pay their taxes in grain and silk.

Chang'an

During the Tang Dynasty, bolts of plain white silk cloth of standard width and length were used as a kind of money. The government used silk to pay officials' salaries, and also exported silk along the Silk Route to Central Asia, where it was traded for fine horses for the imperial army.

In the capital city of Chang'an, merchants get a caravan ready to go to the West. Officials watch while workers take bolts of silk from a government warehouse and load them onto camels. The merchants who will join the caravan buy many things in the city market to trade privately along the way. These trade goods include porcelain, dried rhubarb and other herbal medicines, and fancy silk cloth woven in colors and patterns especially designed to suit the tastes of the Islamic and Byzantine worlds.

The Journey Begins

The caravan includes many private merchants as well as Chinese government officials. Like the covered-wagon trains of the American West, members of the caravan travel together to help one another on the long, dangerous journey. Along the way they will face heat, hunger, thirst, and the ever-present possibility of bandit raids.

Few members of the original caravan will travel all the way to the Mediterranean. The silk and other goods that they are bringing from China will change hands several times along the way.

The caravan begins its journey, which will take many months. It is early spring. The caravan must get beyond the fierce western deserts before the heat of summer arrives. Leaving the city walls of Chang'an behind, it passes through rich farmland. A Buddhist temple is on a nearby hillside.

CHINESE: SI
silk, silk thread

Dunhuang

The Buddhist religion came to China from India along the Silk Route around A.D. 100. The oasis town of Dunhuang, for centuries an important trading and supply center for caravans, soon grew into a great religious center as well. Hundreds of Buddhist cave-temples were cut into the soft rock of a nearby cliff. The cave-temples contain Buddhist statues; the walls are decorated with bright religious paintings.

Some of the merchants go to the cave-temples of Dunhuang to pray for a safe journey, while others buy supplies in the town market. Some Chinese officials take charge of a small herd of horses brought from the west by another caravan. They will escort the horses back to the capital; other officials will continue west to purchase still more of them.

Taklamakan

The Taklamakan is one of the world's driest deserts. Its name means "if you go in, you won't come out" in Uighur Turkish, one of the main languages of Central Asia. The caravan skirts the northern edge of the desert, just south of the snow-capped peaks of the Tian Shan Mountains. The route is very rough, passing around sand dunes, across rocky flats, and through tangled willow thickets along dry riverbeds. But the caravan's two-humped Bactrian camels are strong and hardy. They are used to this difficult country.

Many of the camels and camel drivers that set out from Chang'an turned back at Dunhuang. The merchants hired new ones for this stage of the journey, along with extra animals to carry food and water for crossing the desert. Such changes of men and animals will occur several times along the way from China to Damascus.

Kashgar

Hot and tired after their trip across the Taklamakan Desert, the men and animals hurry to reach the oasis city of Kashgar. The pastures near the city are dotted with grazing animals and the camps of herding peoples: Uighurs in round felt yurts, Turkomans and Tibetans in black tents.

Kashgar is famous for its fruit. Dates, melons, and grapes are grown in irrigated fields and vineyards. Everyone in the caravan looks forward to fresh food and water.

Some of the Chinese members of the caravan will end their journey here. They trade silk for dried dates, raisins, jade, and other local products to bring back to China. Others will continue on toward the west, joined by new merchants, guards, and camel drivers with fresh animals from Kashgar.

The Pamirs

The Pamirs are a range of high mountains in eastern Afghanistan. Here the route winds through narrow, high-walled valleys beside rushing rivers. The camel drivers call this section of the Silk Route the "Trail of Bones" because of the many men and animals that have died along the way from falls and from sudden storms in the high, cold passes. The westbound caravan meets a caravan heading for China with luxury goods from Western lands and a herd of fine horses from Ferghana.

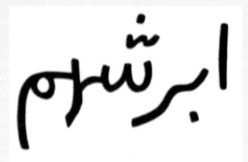

PERSIAN: ABRASHAM
silk

Tashkent, Kingdom of Ferghana

In the central market of Tashkent, the last remaining Chinese officials in the caravan trade bolts of silk for horses that they will take back to China. The horses of Ferghana are considered by Chinese military leaders to be the strongest and toughest in the world.

Tashkent marks the eastern edge of the Persian cultural world. Some private merchants trade Chinese silk, porcelain, and other goods for Persian metalwork, glass, and musical instruments. They too will head back to China from here.

Transoxiana

After making another stop, in the city of Samarkand, the caravan enters the wild country east of the Oxus (Amu Darya) River. No government rules this land; the nomads who live here will rob caravans if they get a chance to.

Suddenly the caravan is attacked by a group of Turkoman bandits on horseback. After a fierce fight with swords and bows and arrows, the bandits are driven off. But some members of the caravan have been killed or wounded, and the bandits escape with a few heavily laden camels.

Herat

In this thriving Persian city, artisans produce fine metalwork, glassware, carpets, and other goods that can be sold for a high price in China. Herat is also, for the moment, on the eastern edge of the rapidly expanding Islamic world. A newly built mosque looms over the city market.

Merchants from the caravan mingle in the market with local merchants and Turkoman nomads, as well as with Arabs from Baghdad and Damascus. Traders from India are here too, selling spices and brightly dyed Indian cloth. Muslim imams, Zoroastrian priests, Nestorian Christian priests, and Buddhist monks tend to the religious needs of the cosmopolitan city.

The caravan will leave its last Bactrian camels in Herat. For the rest of the journey they will use dromedaries, the one-humped camels of Western Asia.

Baghdad

Baghdad is the greatest city of the Islamic world and a hub of world trade. Caravans crowd the roads leading to the city. An Arab merchant leads a group of African slaves bringing ivory, gold, and spices from Zanzibar. Ships coming upriver from the port at Basra bring spices and printed cotton cloth from India, pearls from the Persian Gulf, and precious stones from Ceylon (now Sri Lanka). Some of these goods will soon be heading east to China.

Only a handful of Chinese merchants remained with the caravan, and they will end their journey here. Most of the silk, porcelain, and other products from China have already changed hands several times along the way, increasing in value each time. The last remaining Chinese merchants will sell their goods for a fortune in Baghdad, but then they face a long, difficult, and dangerous trip home again.

Damascus

Arab merchants have brought bolts of silk from Baghdad to Damascus. Only the finest silk cloth has traveled this far; it includes intricately patterned brocades, brilliantly colored satins, and thin gauze to make nightgowns for aristocratic ladies. Wealthy Muslim women, heavily veiled, admire bolts of finished silk cloth in a shop.

Tyre

In the port city of Tyre, on the Mediterranean coast of Lebanon, goods are loaded on ships bound for cities farther to the west. Some of the silk that was traded in the market at Damascus will be sent to Byzantium, the capital of the Eastern Roman Empire.

ΣΕΡΙΚΟΝ

GREEK: SERIKON
silk cloth

Byzantium

In the main hall of a splendid palace, a Byzantine nobleman receives a visit from a bishop of the Orthodox Christian church. Both are dressed in rich garments of silk brocade. The palace women remain in an inner courtyard, out of sight of the men. A visiting prince from Russia, far to the north, awaits his turn to speak to the nobleman. Perhaps he will receive a small present of silk to take back home with him.

The garments worn by the wealthy people of Byzantium are made of silk cloth brought from China, more than 6,000 miles away. Few people in Byzantium have more than a vague idea of where China is or what its people are like, just as few Chinese know anything about the Eastern Roman Empire. Yet Chinese silk is sold in Byzantium, and Byzantine gold coins circulate in the markets of China. The two empires are linked together by trade, thanks to the brave and enterprising merchants of the Silk Route.

A Closer Look

Silk • For thousands of years the painstaking process of raising silkworms and making cloth from their cocoons had been a Chinese monopoly. But around A.D. 550, during the reign of the Eastern Roman Emperor Justinian, two Nestorian Christian monks who had traveled to China returned to Syria, smuggling back with them silkworm eggs hidden in their hollow bamboo walking sticks. This allowed a silk industry to be established in the Middle East, undercutting the market for ordinary-grade Chinese silk. However, high-quality silk textiles, woven in China especially for the Middle Eastern market, continued to bring high prices in Damascus and Byzantium, and trade along the Silk Route therefore continued as before.

Chang'an • Located in the valley of the Wei River, a tributary of the Yellow River, the Tang capital of Chang'an had been the most important city in China for over 1000 years. Located at the eastern end of the Silk Route as well as near the Great Wall that marked the boundary between China and the nomadic tribes of the north, the city guarded China's most important strategic interests. Chang'an, with a population of well over a million people, was famous throughout East Asia for its palaces, parks, temples, schools, and restaurants. The city was a hub of world trade, and it included resident populations of merchants, scholars, and religious leaders from as far away as Korea, Japan, India, Persia, Armenia, and Syria.

China's Door to the West • The rich agricultural lands of China are isolated from the rest of mainland Asia by high mountains, steep valleys, deserts, and grasslands. The corridor formed by the Wei River and the upper reaches of the Yellow River marked a natural highway that pierced the veil of China's natural isolation. During the Tang Dynasty this corridor was carefully kept under Chinese control and guarded against raids by Tibetans to the south and Turkic tribes to the north. A western extension of the Great Wall was marked by guard towers furnished with beacon fires that could bring news of danger to Chang'an in a matter of hours.

Buddhism • Buddhism was founded in northern India by Gautama, the Buddha ("Enlightened One"), around 550 B.C. Buddhists believed that a life of prayer, meditation, and good works could free the soul from attachment to the sinful world. Buddhism soon spread throughout India and into Central Asia, entering China along the Silk Route around A.D. 100. Over the next few centuries it became established in China and was accepted as one of that country's three major religions (along with Confucianism and Taoism). The early Tang Dynasty marked a time of particular power and influence of Buddhism in China. Cave-temples such as those at Dunhuang (also spelled Tun-huang) attracted pilgrims from all over East Asia.

Caravan Life

Caravans were made up of many groups of both private merchants and government officials. The travelers hired professional camel drivers, baggage handlers, camp tenders, and other workers, all of whom typically worked only one relatively short stretch of the entire route. Private merchants hired their own armed guards; the Chinese government officials who traveled between Chang'an and Tashkent had military escorts. The caravans carried supplies of food, water, and animal fodder for crossing the deserts that lay in their path. Depending on the terrain, they might go as few as ten or as many as fifty miles in a day. Each night the travelers pitched tents, hobbled their camels, and set out guards to secure their camp against bandit raids.

Oasis Cities

Within the dry and barren lands between China and the Middle East are a few large oases, isolated pockets of abundant water that make agriculture and urban life possible. Walled cities were surrounded by irrigated fields and pasturelands. Such cities as Kashgar, Bactra (now Balkh), and Samarkand became the capitals of substantial kingdoms as well as great centers of trade along the Silk Route. The Silk Route itself was a network of trails rather than a single highway; branches of the route led from oasis to oasis and to market centers in India, Persia, Russia, and the Middle East.

The oasis cities were surrounded by populations of nomadic herding peoples who traded animal products, such as wool, meat, and hides, for urban goods such as grain and metalware. These nomadic tribes were only loosely under the control of the oasis kingdoms and were feared by townspeople and caravan merchants.

Invasion Routes of Inner Asia

In some sections of Central Asia geography forced the Silk Route trade to flow through narrow and well-defined corridors. Travelers from China to the Middle East could not avoid the dangerous rivers and high mountain passes of the Pamirs; trade between Afghanistan and India had to cross the Khyber Pass. Many times in history these strategic routes carried invading armies as well as peaceful caravans. Alexander the Great's armies reached the Pamirs in the third century B.C.; the Mongol hordes of Genghis Khan rode through them

1500 years later. As late as the nineteenth century Great Britain and Russia competed to control the invasion routes of inner Asia, the meeting point of the great civilizations of China, India, and the Middle East.

Nomad Warfare •

The various nomadic tribes of Central Asia shared a common culture based on tending herds of grazing animals. The men of the tribes were trained from infancy to become expert fighters and hunters from horseback. Their primary duty was to guard the tribe's herds, but they would also raid towns and caravans whenever the opportunity presented itself. Their main weapon was the short, recurved, composite bow, made of wood and horn, with which they could fire volleys of armor-piercing arrows at full gallop: they used lances and swords for close combat. They specialized in lightning-fast attacks, taking their targets by surprise.

The cavalry units of China's imperial army adopted these nomad techniques of warfare to defend the empire's northern frontier. This led to China's almost insatiable demand for the strong, fast, hardy horses of Ferghana, one of the main items of trade along the Silk Route.

The Religions of Central Asia •

Central Asian trading cities such as Herat were multicultural centers that reflected in population, culture, and religious beliefs the diversity of the peoples of Asia. Buddhists from eastern Afghanistan, Turkestan, and as far away as Nepal and China mingled with Hindus from India. Zoroastrianism, the ancient religion of Persia——whose adherents worshipped the forces of light that struggled against Satanic darkness, and maintained temples with sacred fires——was rapidly giving way to the militant, expanding new religion of Islam. Nestorianism, a Syrian form of Christianity, established churches and cathedrals in all the major cities of Central Asia. Pockets of Greek paganism remained among the colonies left behind by Alexander the Great's conquests almost a thousand years earlier. In the surrounding steppelands, nomads worshipped the Great Blue Sky and communicated with gods and spirits through shamans and healers.

Baghdad and World Trade •

Baghdad, together with the port city of Basra at the mouth of the Tigris River, was a focal point of both maritime and caravan trade. Although some caravans from the Silk Route took a northern route from Merv through Armenia to reach Byzantium overland, many others headed south through Herat to Baghdad and Damascus. Arab sailors from the Persian Gulf dominated shipping in the Indian Ocean, trading in cloth from India, gemstones from Ceylon (Sri Lanka), spices from Indonesia, and gold, ivory, and slaves from the eastern coast of Africa. Baghdad grew rich from trade; it soon became a great political center as well. In 751 the Umayyad Caliphate established its capital at Baghdad and claimed the right to rule the entire Islamic world.

The Islamic Expansion •

Islam, founded by Muhammad in the Arabian cities of Mecca and Medina in 622, makes no distinction between religion and civic life. It considers the world to be divided into the *Dar ol'Islam*, the "world submissive to God," and the *Dar ol'Harb*, the "world at war with God." Those who acknowledge the authority of Allah, the one true God according to the teachings of Muhammad, submit to His rule in every aspect of life.

Islamic armies conquered by force but converted by persuasion; believers in other religions were tolerated, but only Muslims had full civil rights in the Islamic world. The Islamic world grew at a phenomenal pace, and by 700 extended from Tunisia to Afghanistan. For about a century before the establishment of the Umayyad Caliphate at Baghdad, Damascus was the center of the Islamic world. To its ancient status as a hub of north–south and east–west caravan routes was added a new status as a city of mosques and universities, a magnet for merchants and scholars.

Byzantium • With the gradual decline of Rome, power in the Roman Empire shifted eastward. An eastern capital was established at Byzantium by the Emperor Constantine in 330. The Germanic invasions of the western portion of the Roman Empire in the sixth century left Byzantium in control of what was left of the empire. The Orthodox Christian Byzantine emperors ruled Greece, western Turkey, the Balkan states, and parts of southern Italy and North Africa, but found their power constantly challenged by Germans in the west, Persians in the east, and, after 622, Arab Muslims in the east and south. Nevertheless, Byzantium itself resisted conquest until it was overrun by the Turks in 1453.

The Eastern Roman Empire was rich and cosmopolitan, and many of the goods that traveled across Asia along the Silk Route were destined for its markets. It was also a transfer center for trade to Europe proper, along maritime routes that extended throughout the Mediterranean and via overland routes along the Danube River to central Europe and up the Volga to Russia and the Baltic Sea. A Frankish nobleman in Paris or a Catholic bishop in Spain might well have worn garments of silk that traveled, via Byzantium, the 7,000 miles from China.

The Silk Route

7,000 MILES OF HISTORY

Meet the Author

John S. Major earned his Ph.D. from Harvard University. He lived in Taiwan and Japan before teaching at Dartmouth College for 13 years. He has written such books as *The Land and People of China* and *The Land and People of Mongolia*. Major is currently a senior editor at the Book-of-the-Month Club, Inc.

Meet the Illustrator

Stephen Fieser earned his M.F.A. from Syracuse University after working for 15 years in graphic design. He specializes in picture books with specific geographic and historical settings, including *The Christmas Sky* and *The Wonder Child*. Fieser also teaches drawing and illustrating at Messiah College and Marywood University.

Theme Connections

Think About It

With a small group of classmates, imagine what it must have been like to set off on a dangerous journey in order to trade for the goods you wanted.

- What would be the greatest hardships and pleasures of traveling the Silk Route?
- Trade today occurs much faster than it did along the Silk Route. How else is it different? Are there any ways in which it is still the same?

Check the Concept/Question Board to see if there are any questions there that you can answer now.

Record Ideas

Why do you think silk was such a valuable commodity? Use your Writing Journal to record notes and ideas about trade and travel in ancient times.

Research Ideas

- Investigate other trade routes from ancient times.
- In addition to the goods that traveled the Silk Route, knowledge was also passed along. Research some of the ideas and inventions that moved from East to West or from West to East in ancient times.

Bibliography

The Ancient Cliff Dwellers of Mesa Verde

by Caroline Arnold. Who were the Anasazi, or "ancient ones," and what happened to their civilization in the southwestern United States? This book will give you clues to the mystery.

The Cricket's Cage

retold by Stefan Czernecki. A clever cricket designs the towers on the buildings in Beijing, China's Forbidden City.

Dig This! How Archaeologists Uncover Our Past

by Michael Avi-Yonah. What do archaeologists do and where do they do it? Find out how archaeologists have helped us learn about ancient civilizations.

Painters of the Caves

by Patricia Lauber. Monet wasn't the only famous French painter! Who drew the mysterious Neanderthal artwork found on cave walls in France?

A Place in the Sun

by Jill Rubalcaba. A cobra bite and the accidental killing of a dove drastically change the life of Senmut, a boy living in 13th-century B.C. Egypt.

Pyramids!

by Avery Hart and Paul Mantell. The hands-on activities in this book help you experience ancient Egypt and all that it had to offer.

Spirit of the Maya: A Boy Explores His People's Mysterious Past

by Guy Garcia. This is the story of the ancient Maya— their everyday lives, history, and customs.

Stones, Bones, and Petroglyphs: Digging into Southwest Archaeology

by Susan Goodman. Join an eighth-grade group of junior archaeologists on their field trip to Crow Canyon Archaeological Center.

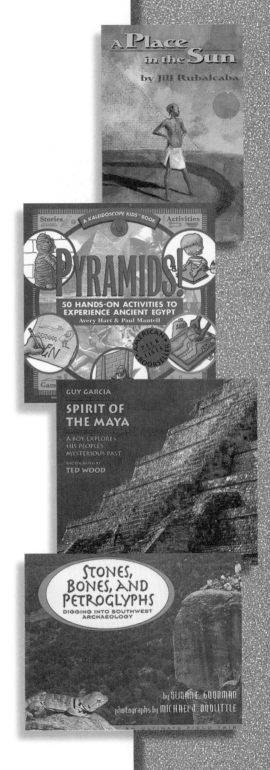

Taking a Stand

What kinds of things are really important to you? What is worth taking a stand for? Each person would answer these questions differently and each answer would tell us much about the person.

The Pretty Pennies Picket

from *Philip Hall Likes Me. I Reckon Maybe.*
Bette Greene
illustrated by Colin Bootman

I no sooner set the ice-cold pitcher of lemonade on the porch when I saw the Blakes' green pickup truck stirring up the dust as it traveled down our rutty road, delivering the members of my girls club. "Ma," I called through the screen door. "Bring out the cookies! The Pretty Pennies are a-coming."

Right away the door opened, but it wasn't Ma. It was my brother Luther wearing a fresh white dress shirt and the blue pants from his Sunday suit. While Susan, Esther, and Bonnie jumped off the truck's back platform, Luther didn't hardly pay no never mind. It wasn't until Ginny the gorgeous climbed down that Luther, wearing a very pleasant expression, took a couple of giant steps toward her and asked, "How y'all getting along, Ginny?"

Ginny didn't get a chance to answer 'cause the one girl who folks say was born into this world talking answered my brother's question. "Fried to a frizzle," said Bonnie Blake. "And that lemonade yonder looks mighty refreshing."

After the lemonade was drunk and the cookies eaten, I performed my duties by rapping on the floor of the porch and saying, "This here meeting of the Pretty Pennies Girls Club is now called to order."

"Trouble with this club," said Bonnie without waiting until we got to new business, "is that we never do nothing but drink lemonade and talk about the boys in the Tiger Hunters' Club."

Heads bobbed up and down in agreement.

Bonnie smiled as though she was onto something big. "What this club needs is somebody with new ideas about things that are fun doing."

Then Ginny did something unusual. She found that one sliver of a moment which Bonnie wasn't cramming with words and said, "We just go from one meeting to the next meeting without ever doing anything. Reckon we could use a new president."

Even before Ginny's words were being applauded, I knew there was some truth to be found in them. We do just sit around gabbing——which is fun——but it was the same amount of fun before I got the idea that we had to become a club. "Philip Hall and the Tiger Hunters ain't the only ones can be a club!" And it was also me that told them how it was a known fact that clubs have more fun than friends. Suddenly I felt ashamed of myself for having promised more than I delivered, but mostly I felt angry with the Pretty Pennies, who were fixing to dump their president without as much as a "begging your pardon."

I looked up at the porch ceiling, looking for something like a good idea waiting to bore through my brain. Well, I looked, but I didn't see nothing but ceiling paint. So I closed my eyes and sure enough something came to me. I waved my hands for quiet. "It so happens that I do have a wonderful idea, but I was waiting to tell y'all about it."

Bonnie began, "Is it fun? 'Cause I got me plenty of chores to do at home so if it's——"

I broke right in. "Quiet! Now next month the Old Rugged Cross Church has their yearly picnic, and I've been thinking that we oughta challenge the Tiger Hunters to a relay race."

"Five of them," said Bonnie. "Five of us."

"Yes siree," I agreed. "But they is going to be something special about our five 'cause we're going to be wearing a special uniform which we ourselves made."

Right away I noticed how all the girls came alive when I mentioned the uniform, so I went on to describe it. "With the money we got in our club treasury, we're going to buy big T-shirts and some different-colored embroidery thread for each Pretty Penny. And then"——my finger traced a crescent across my chest——"we could all embroider the words: THE PRETTY PENNIES GIRLS CLUB OF POCAHONTAS, ARKANSAS." I said, really beginning to feel my presidential powers, "And if we were of a mind to, we could also embroider on the names of all the folks we like."

"You going to embroider on the name of Mister Phil Hall?" asked Bonnie in that cutesy-pooh voice of hers.

I laughed just as though I had nary a worry in this world. Oh, sometimes I think that Philip Hall still likes me, but at other times I think he stopped liking me the moment he stopped being the number-one best everything.

But he wouldn't do that, would he? Stop liking me just because I'm smarter than him? I can't help it and, anyway, my teacher, Miss Johnson, herself said that if I'm going to become a veterinarian I'm going to have to become the best student I know how to be.

On Saturday afternoon all us Pennies went into the Busy Bee Bargain Store for white T-shirts big enough to get lost in. After a lot of discussion, we dropped five T-shirts, fifty skeins of embroidery thread, five embroidery hoops, and five packages of needles onto the wrapping counter in front of Mr. Cyrus J. Putterham.

After taking our money, he pulled one tan sack from the counter and began shoveling everything into it.

"Oh, no, sir," I corrected. "We each need our own bags."

His bushy eyebrows made jumpy little elevator rides up and then down. "Don't you girlies have any feeling? Five sacks cost me five times as much as one."

"But we need them," I explained. " 'Cause we're not even related."

He pulled out four more. "Costs me money, each one does. But you wouldn't care nothing about that. Kids never do!"

As we Pretty Pennies embroidered our shirts on the following Wednesday evening, we drank Bonnie Blake's strawberry soda, ate her potato chips, and gabbed on and on about those Tiger Hunters.

We even sent them a letter saying that they ought to get busy practicing their relay running 'cause we Pretty Pennies were aiming to beat them to pieces.

The next meeting was at Ginny's house, where we all sat in a circle on the linoleum floor and talked about our coming victory over the boys while we munched popcorn from a cast-iron skillet and embroidered away. Then from outside:

Bam . . . bam . . . bam-my . . . bam . . . bam!

Our embroidery dropped to our laps as we grabbed onto one another. Bonnie pointed toward the outside while, for the first time in her life, her mouth opened and closed and closed and opened without a single sound coming out.

Finally, Esther, who almost never had a word to say, said, "Wha——What was that?"

"Let's see," I said, moving cautiously and pulling Esther along with me toward the door. I peeked out just in time to see two figures (both less than man size) race deeper into the halflight before disappearing from sight.

Bonnie, Ginny, and Susan were still sitting like frozen statues.

"It's OK," I told them. "Whoever they were——and I think I know who they were——have already ran away."

Esther followed me out on the porch, where there was a rock the size of a crow's nest and sticking to this rock was a sheet of wide-lined paper. I pulled off the paper, which had been stuck on with a wad of gum, and read aloud:

Dear Pretty Pennies,
You ain't pretty!
You ain't pennies!
And you ain't never going to beat us neither!
> *President Philip Hall*
> *Bravest of all the brave Tiger Hunters*
> *and Lt. Gordon Jennings (also Brave)*

P.S. Why wait for the church picnic to relay race? Meet us at the schoolyard on Saturday and we'll win!

Everybody was really mad and we all began talking at once about those Tiger Hunters who run around scaring the wits out of a person. Bonnie thought we ought to teach them a lesson. "Specially that Phil Hall."

I'd have liked nothing better, but probably for a different reason. It wasn't the scare so much as what he said about not being pretty that ruffled my feathers. Did he mean nobody was pretty? Or was nobody but me pretty? Or . . . or was everybody pretty excepting me? Next thing I knew I was shouting, "We're going to get those low-down polecats!" Then while I had everybody's attention, I gave them their final instructions: "Next Saturday we'll race. Finish embroidering on our club name, front and back. Then everybody wash your shirts so our club name will be clean easy reading. All the folks in Pocahontas is going to know just who it was that beat them Tiger Hunters."

The next morning Philip didn't show up for work at my new business, The Elizabeth Lorraine Lambert & Friend Veg. Stand. Well, he's probably just mad or practicing up his relay running. Or maybe Mr. Hall has him doing chores. But that's the unlikeliest explanation of them all.

Without him there ain't no games or giggles, but today there's not a speck of boredom either 'cause I'm just too busy embroidering my T-shirt and running my business. And with every sale my college money grows. I'm going to become a veterinarian yet.

It was just before bedtime on Friday night that I stitched the last beautiful stitch on my shirt. I held it out for better viewing. Even with the soil from two weeks of handling along with my baby brother Benjamin's mashed-in, smashed-in sweet potato, it was beautiful. Just beautiful!

As I began to draw the wash water, Ma told me to get to bed 'cause I'd be needing my strength for the big race tomorrow. She took the shirt from my hand as she gave me a light shove toward the bedroom. "Reckon I can do the washing if you can do the resting."

When the morning sky came again to Pocahontas, I woke wide awake just as though I hadn't been sleeping at all but only resting up before the big race.

At the kitchen table Ma sat in front of a bowl of peas needing shelling, but her hands sat unmoving in her lap. I tried to remember the last time I had seen my mother just sitting without actually doing anything. All I said was "Morning, Ma," but it was enough to make her look as though she was staring at a spook.

"Reckon I'm going to have to tell you," she said, holding tight to the bowl. "But I don't know how to tell you . . . It's about your shirt. Done shrunk to midget size. Sure did."

As Pa drove down Pocahontas's Main Street, I spotted the rest of the Pennies leaning up against a yellow fireplug. A block away Pa turned his car and angle-parked in front of the E-Z Cash & Carry Market. When the Pennies saw me walking toward them, they all shook their heads just like I was doing something wrong. What does that mean? That I'm not wearing my uniform? No, but I'm carrying it wrapped like a fish in an old newspaper to show them what they'd never believe without seeing. Anyway, they're not wearing theirs either. Too lazy to finish their embroidery probably.

Bonnie began by saying that it was an ordinary washing powder, one of those kinds that they're always talking about over the radio. Then Esther, who would never interrupt anybody, interrupted to say that her water was barely warm.

I was losing patience with everybody talking, everybody understanding but me. "What are you all babbling about mild soap and barely warm water for?"

Suddenly Ginny whipped from a grocery bag a white T-shirt so shrunk that the embroidery's lettering was no longer readable. "We is talking about this."

First we talked about our wasted efforts and then we talked about our wasted money and then we talked about what nobody could understand: what caused the shrinkage.

"Listen here," I said suddenly. "We bought something in good and honest faith that didn't turn out to be a bit of good. Well, if we all go down to the Busy Bee and explain the situation to Mr. Putterham, then he'll give us back our money. Probably even apologize that he can't pay us for our trouble."

"What Mr. Putterham is you talking about?" asked Bonnie, cocking her head like a trained spaniel. "The only Mr. Putterham I know wouldn't apologize to his ma if he ran her down in the broad daylight."

I told her right off. "Trouble with you, Miss Bonnie, is that you ain't got no faith in human nature."

Still, the thought that old bushy eyes ever had a mother was surprising. Reckon I just couldn't see Mr. Putterham having anything that couldn't turn a profit.

Even though I walked into the Busy Bee as slow as I could possibly walk, the others carefully managed to walk even slower. They stayed behind me, pushing me on toward the wrapping counter and the awesome presence of Cyrus J. Putterham. As I watched him tying a piece of string around a shoe box, I got to wishing that one of the other girls had replaced me as president of the Pennies; then they'd be standing here on the firing line instead of me.

The merchant lifted his eyebrows at me, which was a kind of a cheapskate way of asking what I wanted without actually bothering to ask.

"Well, uh . . . Mr. Putterpam——ham! Mr. Putterham, it's uh . . . about what happened two Saturdays ago when we all bought T-shirts from your store. We washed them like we wash anything else," I said, removing the newspaper from my shirt to hold it up. "And they all five shrunk up like this."

He stretched his lips into a hard straight line. "How much you pay for that shirt?"

"Eighty-nine cents."

"See?"

What did he want me to see? "Sir?"

A short blast of air rushed through his nostrils and I came to understand that his patience zipped off on that blast of air. "Something you girls paid only eighty-nine cents for isn't going to last forever. Why, eighty-nine cents for a T-shirt is mighty cheap."

"Oh, no, sir," I corrected him. "Paying eighty-nine cents for something that ain't never been worn is mighty expensive."

He waved his hand as though he was shooing a fly. "All right, I was nice enough to listen to you girls and now y'all get on out of here. I got me a store to run."

"Yes, sir," I said pleasantly. "We appreciate your attention, sure do. But what we really want is for you to refund us our money 'cause a shirt that ain't fit to be washed ain't fit to be sold."

"Get on out of here!" Both his hands went flapping in the air. "Now get!"

We may have left the store like scared chicks, but once outside we became more like mad wet hens. Esther kept saying, "Imagine!" Or sometimes she'd vary it with "Would you imagine that!"

Then, as if we didn't have enough trouble, the Tiger Hunters led by the bravest of all the brave Tiger Hunters came up to say that we were going to be beaten so bad that it would be a long time before we showed our face in Pocahontas again.

"Don't fret about it," I told him. " 'Cause I don't think I want to show my face anymore, anyway." A warm tear had begun to worm its way down my cheek.

Philip looked uncomfortable. What's the matter? Hadn't he ever seen a tear before? "We don't have to relay race today," he was saying. "We can put it off until the Sunday of the Old Rugged Cross Church picnic."

We shook hands on it, but I was not able to say any more. Talking took too much effort. So Bonnie explained while Ginny showed Philip and his Tiger Hunters what happened to our shirts. Right away Philip said, "We don't have to let Mr. Putterham get away with that. That's robbery!"

Philip's comment about its being a robbery struck me like one of God's own revelations!

At the far end of Main Street, sitting on a square of grass, is the old red brick courthouse where Sheriff Nathan Miller has a narrow office and two barred cells. As the Pennies and Hunters strode up the courthouse walk, old men sitting out on sunny park benches looked up.

The sheriff told us all to crowd on in. "I'll never forget what good police work you and Phil did in capturing those fowl thieves. You know, no farmer has reported any livestock missing since they left town."

His words encouraged me to tell him about our "robbery" at the hands of the merchant Putterham. I watched the sheriff's face grow more and more thoughtful. Finally he said, "I'm sorry, but there ain't no way I can help you out."

" . . . But why?"

With his booted feet, the sheriff pushed his chair from his desk. "Follow me," he said, already walking with strong strides from his office.

Outside, the men on the benches now seemed doubly surprised to see us kids half-running in order to keep up with Randolph County's long-legged lawman. A block down Main Street and then two blocks down School Street to the last house at the end of the block. The sheriff walked up the driveway and into the backyard. At a backyard sandpile a little boy dressed in diapers and pullover shirt toddled over, saying, "Dadadadada."

The sheriff picked him up and then asked me, "What do you think of my boy's shirt?"

Surely eleven folks didn't walk all the way over here just to look at a tight-fitting baby shirt. It seemed silly, but he really did want my opinion. "I reckon it's a nice enough baby shirt," I told him.

"Uh-hun!" answered the more than six feet of sheriff as though he had suddenly struck gold. "Uh-hun," he repeated. "For a baby shirt it's mighty fine, but it wasn't bought to be no baby's shirt. No Sir! It was bought for me. Last Saturday I paid eighty-nine cents for that T-shirt at the Busy Bee Bargain Store."

"You too!!——Then why don't you——"

"Because selling bad merchandise," he said, "can get a merchant in trouble with his customers without getting him in trouble with the law."

We Pretty Pennies walked with the Tiger Hunters back toward Main Street like a bunch of beaten soldiers. No reason for hurrying. No good left in the day nohow. Then it struck me like a pie in the face. Why are we defeated? Ten of us and only one of them Putterhams. "Stop!" I said, whirling around like a general of the army. "We ain't giving up this battle!"

"We ain't?" asked Philip.

I was the fightingest president the Pretty Pennies would ever have. "No, we ain't, 'cause if we all stood out in front of the Busy Bee Bargain Store showing off our shrunken shirts, then old Mr. Putterham would be so embarrassed he'd have to refund our money."

I broke into a run, followed by Philip Hall, followed by the rest of them. In front of the Busy Bee, we all formed a loose line——a Penny, a Hunter, a Penny, and so forth. "Pretty Pennies and Tiger Hunters. When we're working together we'll call ourselves the great Penny Hunters," I said.

Since Philip Hall didn't look exactly thrilled by my suggestion, I said, "Well, would you rather be called the Pretty Tigers?" His groan gave me his answer.

When a heavy woman with three chilluns slowly made her way toward the Busy Bee door, Bonnie approached her. A moment later she was spreading out her doll-size shirt across her chest while the woman shook her head and said, "I'm going to do my trading at Logan's."

The very next person who was persuaded not to spend money at the Busy Bee was my sister, Anne. She said she could buy fingernail polish at the dime store just as well.

After Anne, there was our preacher, the Reverend Ross, who was going to buy some white handkerchiefs from Putterham, but the Reverend said he'd "be happy to respect your picket line."

"Respect our what?" I asked.

"Folks who is standing like some of God's own soldiers against the world's injustices is," said the Reverend Ross, "a picket line."

Never before in my whole life had I ever felt so important, but then never before had I been on special assignment for God.

Just then a family of five reached for the Busy Bee's door and I called out, "Don't you folks go buying things in there unless"——I held up my shirt——"you don't object to shrinking."

"Lordy," said the wife, coming right over to get a closer look. "Now ain't that a pity?"

Mr. Putterham stepped outside the door. "What's this? What's going on here?"

I turned to watch Philip Hall 'cause I didn't want to miss seeing him speak right up to that old man merchant. But the only thing I saw was the bravest Tiger Hunter of them all with his mouth flung open, looking for all the world like he would never again be able to speak.

The proprietor's eyes now swept past Philip and were looking down the long picket line. "Don't tell me that all you kids have been struck speechless? Somebody better tell me what's going on!"

I took one step forward. "I reckon you oughta know that we is picketing your store, Mr. Putterdam——ham! Mr. Putterham."

His big, bushy eyebrows jumped up and down as though they were skipping rope. "You is doing WHAT? And to WHOM?"

"We is"——my mouth felt too dry for stamp licking——"picketing you," I said, grateful that the words actually sounded.

"Now you listen here, you," he said. "Nobody pickets Cyrus J. Putterham, Pocahontas's leading merchant. Know that?"

"Yes, sir."

"Good," he said, smiling a pretend smile. "Then y'all get on out of here."

"Uh . . . no, sir," I said, trying to remember the Reverend Ross's words about being one of God's own soldiers.

"What do you mean No, sir?" he asked, allowing his voice to rise into a full shout. "You just got through saying Yes, sir."

"Uh, well, sir, that was my answer to your question." Mr. Putterham blinked as though my words were being spoken in a strange new language. I tried again. "What I was saying, Mr. Putterjam . . . ham! Mr. Putterham, was yes, sir, I know all about you being Pocahontas's leading merchant. But no, sir, we ain't moving from our picket line. Not until we get our money back."

His eyes told me how much he wanted me to understand. "But if I give you folks your money back, then everybody who ever bought bad merchandise from me will be wanting their money back too."

From the picket line a single voice called, "Give back the money!" Then more voices, more Pennies and Hunters together calling, "Give back the money!" And I joined my voice with the Penny Hunters and even some folks on the street who were now chanting, *"Give back the money!"* And taken together the voices sounded as though they were doing a lot more demanding than asking.

The shopkeeper threw up his hands. "All right, all right." He smiled, but it wasn't what you'd call a sincere smile. "Making my customers happy is the only thing that's ever been important to Cyrus J. Putterham. Take your shirts back to the wrapping counter for a full and courteous refund."

After all the shirt money was safely back in the hands of our treasurer, Bonnie Blake, I spoke again to the merchant. "There is one more thing, Mr. Putterpam——ham! Mr. Putterham."

"As long as you girls are satisfied——well, that's thanks enough for me. Why, my very business is built on a foundation of square and fair."

"Yes, sir," I agreed. "Would you mind giving us back our embroidery money?"

"Your what?"

I presented him with the cash register receipt. "Two dollars and fifty cents worth of embroidery thread, ruined when our shirts shrunk."

For a moment I thought his face was growing angry, but then he sighed and placed the additional two-fifty on the counter.

"Thanks, Mr. Putterham."

He smiled and this time it didn't look all that insincere. "You called me Putterham. Finally you did it right."

I smiled back at him. "And finally, Mr. Putterham, so did you."

The Pretty Pennies Picket

Meet the Author

Bette Greene's writing focuses on characters who must learn to stand up for what they know is right. These characters are facing problems that call for moral courage. Greene believes adults need to help young people develop moral courage. Much of her writing is based on memories of growing up in a Jewish family in a small Arkansas town. "My roots, my memories are all Arkansas." She credits much of her success to a teacher who helped her realize she could be anything she wanted to be.

Meet the Illustrator

Colin Bootman is a native of Trinidad who moved to the United States when he was young. He began painting as a child. Bootman still remembers Trinidad, especially the colorful outdoor markets. He now lives in The Bronx, New York, where he works as a freelance artist.

Theme Connections

Think About It

- What issue caused the girls to confront the storekeeper?
- If you were a member of the Pretty Pennies, would you have taken a stand about the shrunken shirts? Why? Why not?

Record Ideas

Pretend you are the storekeeper. What would you have done if a bunch of girls took a stand and demanded a refund for shrunken shirts they bought from your store? Write your ideas in your Writing Journal.

Role-Play

Choose a partner. Pretend one of you is Beth and the other is Mr. Putterham. Beth must try to convince Mr. Putterham to refund her money for the shrunken shirts. Act out this scene using the ideas you recorded in your Writing Journal.

Class Discussion

from *School Spirit*
by Johanna Hurwitz
illustrated by Richard Hull

On Fridays, Mr. Flores brought his guitar to school. The last hour of the day was devoted to singing and talk. It was a relaxed and friendly way to end the week, and Julio and all his classmates looked forward to it. In fact, they were almost sorry when the dismissal bell rang and school was over for the week.

This Friday, however, it didn't look as if Mr. Flores would do any guitar playing. The last hour was going to be devoted to a discussion of the fate of their school. It was nothing to sing about. There had been a lengthy article in the newspaper yesterday explaining the decision before the school board. Cricket Kaufman had cut it out and brought it into class. During the lunch hour, Julio had hardly been aware that he was eating his favorite school lunch: pizza squares with pepperoni, tossed salad, fruit cocktail, and chocolate milk. He carefully studied every word of the article. It gave all the details of why the district was considering the proposed closing, and it explained how much money could be saved.

Now Mr. Flores handed out a flyer on yellow paper to each of the students. It had been prepared by the school for the students to take home to their parents. Much of the information from the newspaper article was repeated on the sheet. It also listed the day and date a month off when the school board would next be meeting to discuss the proposed school closing.

Lucas began to fold his copy of the flyer into a paper airplane. A couple of the other boys noticed and did the same thing. Julio was tempted too. A sheet of paper like this was just begging to be transformed into an airplane. But Julio resisted the urge. He was the class president, and his class was discussing something very serious.

"I don't see why it's our school that has to be closed," Cricket protested. "If they want to close a school, why don't they close one of the other ones?"

"Yeah," agreed several of the other students.

"Well, aside from the fact that this is the building where you go to school, what makes this place so special?" asked Mr. Flores. "Aren't all schools the same?"

"Oh, no," protested Zoe. She was the expert on this subject. "This school is friendlier. There's a nice feeling here. Even though I'm still new in the community, I think it's great that Cricket's mother went to this school."

"My father went here too," said Sara Jane Cushman.

"So did mine," said Arthur Lewis. "Maybe they were in the same class."

"You like the continuity then," said Mr. Flores. He wrote the word CONTINUITY on the chalkboard.

As the teacher turned his back, one of the yellow paper airplanes flew across the room. It was followed by a second one. Mr. Flores turned around and faced the class while the second one was still airborne.

"Now hear this," announced Mr. Flores. "Due to conditions beyond your control the airport is closed and all planes are grounded." He walked over and picked up the two yellow paper planes from the floor. He unfolded them and flattened the sheets out. "This is important information for your parents. If you are missing your notice, I recommend that you come and take one from my desk before you go home."

Julio turned and grinned at Lucas. Mr. Flores was allowing his friend to reclaim his yellow sheet anonymously. No wonder Julio liked their teacher so much.

"I think it's great that this school is old. It's been around here for a long time," said Zoe. "It has a nice old-school smell and feel about it. Not like my last school, which was bright and shiny new and felt more like a hospital than a school."

SENSE OF HISTORY, Mr. Flores wrote on the board.

This time there were no airplanes flying when his back was turned.

"How old is this building anyhow?" asked Arthur.

"It's more than eighty years old," said Cricket before Julio could respond. "It says so in the article."

"Wow. That's how old my great-grandfather is," said Sara Jane.

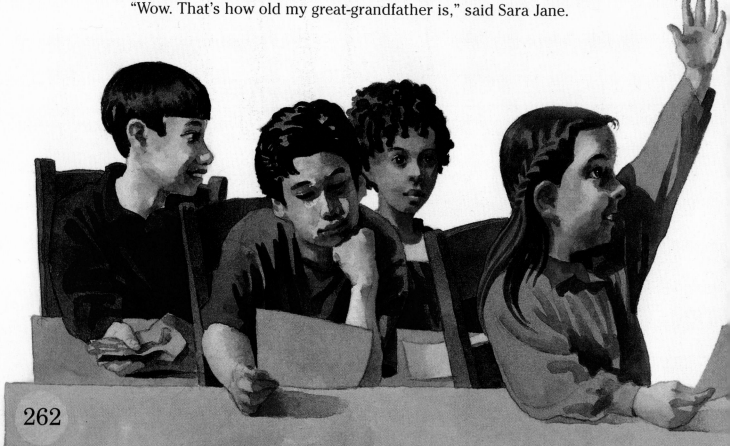

"Maybe Edison went here," suggested Julio. "Maybe that's the way it got his name."

"You could look that up," said the teacher. "And while you're at it, why don't you find out who Armstrong is too."

"I know. I know who that is," shouted Cricket.

Julio looked at Cricket's face. It was red with excitement. She just loved knowing an answer that no one else knew.

"Armstrong is Henrietta Armstrong, who was the first principal of this school. She worked here for forty years. Her picture is in the lobby."

"Oh, right," agreed Julio. He must have passed that picture of the white-haired old lady a hundred thousand times. He saw it and he didn't see it. Now he'd have to make sure to take a good look at it on his way out of the building today. Imagine coming to this building every school day for forty years.

"It doesn't seem nice to honor someone by naming a building after them and then selling the building or tearing it down," said Arthur.

"I sure wouldn't like it if someone did that to me," said Cricket.

"Don't worry, no one is ever going to name a building after you," said Lucas.

"Yes they will," Cricket insisted. "You just wait until I'm the first woman president of the United States. They'll probably want to call this school the Edison-Armstrong-Kaufman School."

"That's too much for anyone to say, and besides, they won't be able to do it if this school is closed," Lucas pointed out.

"I have a suggestion," said Mr. Flores, interrupting Cricket and Lucas. "Who would like to be on a committee to find out what was happening in the world eighty years ago? We can make a time line. Eighty years ago in this community, in the United States, and in the world."

"Ooh, me, me," said Cricket, raising her hand. It was just the type of project she liked.

"Me too," said Zoe.

"Great," said Mr. Flores.

Julio raised his hand.

Mr. Flores nodded in recognition. "Yes, Julio. Do you want to be on the committee too?"

"I want us to do something to rally all the students and to make a difference. Can't we get the school board to change their

minds? How about writing them a letter about how we feel. Maybe all the other classes would write letters too. We should make posters to decorate the halls. Make up a school cheer and a school song. Maybe if we can show the school board that we all have a lot of school spirit, they'll change their minds about sending all of us off to other schools."

Anne Crosby raised her hand. "I want to write a song," she said.

Everyone was surprised by this offer. "Are you a relative of Bing Crosby?" asked Cricket. "I saw him singing in an old movie on TV."

Anne blushed. "No," she said. "But I'd like to make up a song anyway. I like to write poems."

"Great," said Mr. Flores. "If you write a song, I'll accompany you on my guitar." Mr. Flores looked around the room. "Any other ideas?" he asked.

"Maybe we could design T-shirts for everyone in the school," suggested Zoe. "If we all walked around in matching shirts, it would show that we all belong together."

"Blue ones," suggested Cricket.

"No, black," someone else called out.

"It could be like an art project," said Julio. "Maybe the art teacher could help us. If we made a design and everyone brought a plain white shirt to school, we could all make our own shirts in art."

Mr. Flores nodded his head as he wrote TOGETHERNESS on the board.

"I have an idea," offered Sara Jane. "Maybe some of our parents who attended this school would come and tell what it was like in the olden times."

Mr. Flores began a second column of ideas. He wrote LETTER, GUESTS, T-SHIRTS, SONG.

"I think we should plant flowers all around the school yard and do other things to make the school more beautiful," suggested a girl named Joyce Howe. "If we make it look prettier,

Continuity
Sense of History
Togetherness
Letter Song
Guests Cleanup
T-Shirts

they will forget that the building is so old. In the newspaper article it said that this school is very shabby."

"It's the wrong season for planting flowers. They'd all die in the cold. But we should be better about picking up trash," suggested Zoe. "I noticed a lot of papers flying around in the yard, during lunch recess. It doesn't look very nice."

"I saw a couple of soda cans too," said Arthur.

"That's not our garbage," Lucas complained. "People waiting at the bus stop on the corner by the school are the ones who throw a lot of that stuff in the yard."

"We still should clean it up," said Zoe. "If someone from the school board comes by, they don't know whose junk it is. They just see it's in our school yard. It looks like we don't care."

"Sometimes there's garbage inside the school too," said Julio, feeling guilty. Just this morning he had kicked a crumpled ball of paper from one end of the hallway to the other without picking it up.

Mr. Flores added the word CLEANUP to his second list. Before he could write anything more, however, the dismissal bell rang.

"Already?" complained Julio. It seemed too soon for the school day to end.

Mr. Flores turned to face the students. "All these ideas are called brainstorming," he said. "Every time one of you made a suggestion, it gave another one of you an idea. You start working on your ideas, and a week from now we'll pick up at this point. If you want, over the weekend you can write a letter to the school board. Next week we can incorporate everyone's ideas and write a class letter for students to sign."

"All right," said Julio. He felt full of energy and excitement from the class discussion. He couldn't wait to speak with some of the other class presidents and the students in the other rooms. In one of the sixth grades there was a tall and very popular girl named Jennifer Harper who was class president. She always had a group of her classmates around her, and they hung on every word she said. Julio had a feeling she would be a good ally for this cause. He'd have to make a point of speaking to her as soon as possible. For the first time in his life Julio regretted that it was Friday afternoon. Now he'd have to wait until school opened again on Monday morning. What a pain!

Class Discussion

Meet the Author

Johanna Hurwitz was born in New York, New York. It's not surprising that Hurwitz knew from the age of ten that she wanted to be a writer. Her parents met in a bookstore. She grew up in a New York City apartment where the walls were lined with books. Her father was a journalist and bookseller, and her mother was a library assistant.

She began her career with books working at the New York City Public Library while still in high school. She then got two degrees in Library Science. She published her first book while in her thirties and has been writing books for children ever since. In one interview she revealed, "It seems as if all my fiction has grown out of real experiences." She has written books about her children's love of baseball, her own childhood and summer vacations, her mother's childhood, and even her cats and their fleas!

Meet the Illustrator

Richard Hull teaches illustration at Brigham Young University. He was also an art director and graphic designer with a magazine for 15 years. Other books Mr. Hull has illustrated include *The Cat & the Fiddle & More*, *My Sister's Rusty Bike*, and *The Alphabet from Z to A (With Much Confusion on the Way)*. He and his wife currently reside in Orem, Utah.

Theme Connections

Think About It

- What would you do if you thought your school was going to be closed?

Record Ideas

What else might the students have done to keep their school open? Write your ideas in your Writing Journal.

Create a Flyer

Create a flyer in support of keeping your school open. You should include reasons why the school should stay open and any history you wish to use.

The Grimké Sisters

from *Great Lives: Human Rights*
William Jay Jacobs
illustrated by Stephen Harrington

Dignified, serious, dressed simply, with a white handkerchief framing her delicate features, Angelina Grimké stood calmly at the speaker's stand, preparing to address a committee of the Massachusetts State Legislature.

Outside the State House, men shook their fists in anger. Some hooted and jeered. Others hissed, not the hisses heard at today's sports events, but hisses born of genuine hatred.

It was Wednesday, February 21, 1838. Until that day no American woman ever had addressed a legislative body in this country. The visitors' gallery was packed to capacity. Standees jammed the aisles and the lobby outside the hall. Many in the crowd had come out of curiosity, just to see a woman speak in public, something then considered shameful, even indecent.

Yet as Miss Grimké's powerful voice rang out across the audience, boldly, magnetically, her listeners riveted their attention on her, gripped by the intensity of her message. For there at the lectern stood a white southern woman, born to wealth and aristocratic position, delivering a passionate attack on the South's "peculiar institution"——human slavery.

"I stand before you as a southerner," she declared, "exiled from the land of my birth by the sound of the lash and the piteous cry of the slave. I stand before you as a repentant slave holder.

"I stand before you," continued Angelina Grimké, "as a moral being, and as a moral being I feel that I owe it to the suffering slave and to the deluded master . . . to do all that I can to overturn a system . . . built upon the broken hearts and prostrate bodies of my countrymen in chains and cemented by the blood, sweat and tears of my sisters in bonds . . . "

In the audience before her some people openly cried. The chairman of the committee, Miss Grimké later wrote, "was in tears almost the whole time that I was speaking." Sarah, her older sister, was to have been the featured speaker that day. But, ill, she had taken to her bed, persuading young Angelina to substitute for her.

No matter. Before long the names of the two sisters became linked, North and South, as leaders in the forefront of the antislavery movement. Other women, until then hesitant to speak out in public against the curse of slavery, followed their example.

In time the leading women of the age——Lucy Stone, Elizabeth Cady Stanton, Susan B. Anthony——all would express gratitude to the Grimké sisters. It was the Grimkés, they said, who first inspired them to join in battle, crusading for the twin causes of women's rights and the abolition of slavery.

The society into which Sarah and Angelina Grimké had been born could hardly have been a more unlikely setting for the development of social reformers. Charleston, South Carolina, led the South in defending slavery. Wealthy planter aristocrats, including the father of the Grimké sisters, dominated the city's society. The very survival of their gracious and leisurely lifestyle depended on the slave labor system.

It was slaves who planted and harvested their yearly cotton crops——the source of their wealth. It was slaves, too, who built their houses, cooked their meals, cared for their children, stood behind them to fan the flies away as they dined. It was slaves who made possible for the white men their hours of pleasure in hunting and riding, or for the elegant white women the days and evenings filled with tea parties, fancy-dress balls, and an endless round of visits to neighboring plantations.

For young Sarah Grimké, child of the aristocracy, such a life proved, for some reason, not enough to make her happy. Nor did it please the young Angelina, so headstrong, independent, even in childhood, that her mother scarcely could control her. Instead of absorbing the standard school curriculum for girls of the time——music, a touch of French, and gracious manners——the Grimké sisters demanded the right to the same education as their brothers: Latin, Greek, mathematics, philosophy, and law.

Both girls wept at the beatings and other punishments inflicted by slave owners, including even their own parents, to keep blacks humble and obedient. Sometimes Angelina would creep into the slave quarters at night to rub soothing ointment into the open wounds of slaves who had been lashed with the whip.

Sarah, and later Angelina, too, taught the slave girls assigned to them as maids how to read. In most parts of the South such an act was strictly forbidden, but as Angelina admitted with pride in her diary, "The light was put out, the keyhole screened, and flat on our stomachs before the fire, we defied the laws of South Carolina."

In 1819, when Sarah was twenty-seven, her father chose her, instead of his wife or any of her brothers, to travel with him to the North. He was ill and had been advised that a surgeon in Philadelphia might help him, but the illness proved fatal.

The trip was to change Sarah's life. Quakers whom she met in Philadelphia introduced her to their religion. She admired their seriousness of purpose, liked their opposition to slavery. She also approved of the laws passed in Philadelphia to protect free Negroes there.

Although the decision was painful, she decided to leave Charleston and go to live in Philadelphia. Perhaps in the North, she confided to Angelina, a woman might live a life not just of pleasure but of real purpose. In 1829 Angelina, then twenty-four, followed her sister to Philadelphia. Both sisters knew that, hating slavery as they did, the break with their old lives in Charleston could never be healed.

At first the Grimkés tried to live like religious Quakers. They lived simply, dressed simply, and did charity work. But that was not enough for them. Always rebellious, they insisted on speaking aloud in the usually silent Quaker meetings, where they

also made a point of sitting in the sections reserved for black women. To them the Quakers were doing too little, moving too slowly, in putting a stop to slavery in America. Just as they had left the Episcopal Church in South Carolina, they also split from the Quakers.

In 1835 Angelina decided to state publicly that all slaves must be freed. She wrote to William Lloyd Garrison, editor of the *Liberator*, America's angriest antislavery newspaper. Abolition of slavery, she declared in her letter, "is a cause worth dying for." Of Garrison himself, she stated that "The ground upon which you stand is holy ground."

Garrison printed Angelina's letter in the *Liberator*. Overnight Angelina and her sister became heroines of the antislavery movement. Here were the daughters of wealthy slave owners daring to describe the brutal acts they personally had witnessed and demanding that the slaves should be freed at once.

Next Angelina wrote a pamphlet, *An Appeal to the Christian Women of the South*, urging white women to join the fight against slavery——to put an end to "this horrible system of oppression and cruelty . . . and wrong," even if they had to break the law.

In Charleston the postmaster publicly burned copies of the pamphlet in the city's main square. Authorities warned Angelina and Sarah not to return home or they would be arrested.

The threat succeeded in keeping the Grimké sisters away from Charleston, but it could not stop them from speaking out. In 1836 Sarah published "Epistle to the Clergy of the Southern States." In that letter she urged southern ministers at least to stop giving their support to slavery, even if they could not offend their congregations by opposing it publicly.

Well known by then, the Grimkés decided to give their lives totally to the abolitionist movement. They joined the American Anti-Slavery Society and began to speak, as a team, to small meetings of women in New York City.

Soon these so-called parlor meetings became so popular that many ministers opened their churches to the Grimké sisters, usually on the condition that no men be present. But before long men demanded the right to hear the lectures, even though the appearance of women as public speakers was considered unwomanly. Almost everywhere, the Grimkés found themselves facing mixed audiences——larger and larger ones as their popularity grew.

It was during their triumphant tour of New England in 1838 that Angelina delivered her famous address to a session of the Massachusetts Legislature in the State House at Boston.

Angelina, tall, with piercing eyes and a strong voice, enjoyed meeting an audience. Sarah, more reserved, did most of the writing for the Grimké team. The two worked well together.

At first William Lloyd Garrison and other leaders of the abolitionist movement pleaded with them not to endanger the antislavery cause by linking it with questions of women's rights, especially the right of women to speak in public. Garrison changed his mind, however, as did Theodore Dwight Weld, who had coached Angelina in techniques of public speaking when she first joined the American Anti-Slavery Society.

Instead of avoiding the issue of women's rights, the Grimké sisters spoke out more strongly on it. They demanded not only the right to be heard, but also the right of women to vote, to help make laws, and even to serve as elected officials. Finally they demanded that women be given complete legal equality with men in such matters as divorce and ownership of property.

At one of their speeches a gang of boys threw apples at them. Spectators jeered at them. Newspapermen dubbed them "the weird sisters," or "Devilina and Grimalkin."

Nothing stopped the Grimkés. In the spring of 1838 they spoke at the Odeon Theater in Boston to mixed audiences of men and women numbering two thousand to three thousand. Clearly they had taken center stage in the antislavery movement. No other women in the country were so well known or so frequently discussed.

By now it became obvious, too, that Theodore Dwight Weld's interest in Angelina went beyond her ideas. He continued to give her lessons in public speaking. He accompanied the Grimkés on their tours. But he also had fallen in love with Angelina——and she with him.

In May 1838 they were married. The wedding party included, in the words of one guest, "a motley assembly of white and black, high and low." In direct defiance of "the horrible prejudice of slavery" the bride and groom introduced as bridesmaids and groomsmen six former slaves from the Grimké plantation. Two white and two black ministers presented prayers. At the end of the ceremony William Lloyd Garrison read the marriage certificate aloud and then passed it around the room to be signed by each guest.

Theodore and Angelina insisted that the wedding cake be made with sugar grown by free laborers. The cotton for their mattress, they proudly pointed out, had come from a farm in New Jersey, not "the usual slave-grown cotton ticking."

Two days after their wedding Angelina and Theodore left for a honeymoon. As might be expected, they spent it working for the antislavery cause. Along with Sarah, they attended the opening session of the Anti-Slavery Convention of American Women, held in Philadelphia's attractive new Pennsylvania Hall. The hall had been built especially for such occasions, since reformers, even in Quaker-dominated Philadelphia, had experienced difficulty renting space for speeches on such topics as women's rights and abolition.

On the first night of the convention, Angelina Grimké Weld rose to address a mixed audience of more than a thousand blacks and whites. Outside the hall a mob of whites gathered. As Angelina began to speak they shouted and cursed. They stamped their feet. Then they began throwing bricks and stones at the newly opened hall, shattering the windows. Glass fell to the floor, some of it at Angelina's feet.

"What is a mob?" she continued calmly.

What would the breaking of every window be? Any evidence that *we are* wrong, or that slavery is a good and wholesome institution? What if that mob should now burst in upon us, break up our meeting and commit violence on our persons— would this be anything compared with what the slaves endure?

For more than an hour Angelina spoke on as the mob groaned and roared angrily in the background. Nothing could stop her from delivering her message.

Before the meeting could begin on the next night, the mayor of Philadelphia closed the hall, fearing violence. After he left the scene, the mob surged forward. They burst into the offices of the Anti-Slavery Society there and destroyed many precious papers. Then they set fire to the hall, dedicated to free speech, burning it completely to the ground.

In the months that followed the fire Angelina and Theodore Weld did little public speaking. They began to build a family, eventually having three children. Sarah, now alone, came to live with them, first in their home in New Jersey and later in Massachusetts. She took special pleasure in caring for the Weld children.

The three also worked together on an important new collection of documents, *American Slavery As It Is: Testimony of a Thousand Witnesses*. Drawing heavily on advertisements and published accounts in southern newspapers, the study offered powerful evidence against slavery. Included were advertisements for the return of runaway slaves, identified by their owners, for example, as "stamped on the left cheek 'R' and a piece is taken off her left ear, the same letter is branded on the inside of both legs"; or, "branded 'N.E.' on the breast and having both small toes cut off."

Harriet Beecher Stowe relied heavily on the Weld-Grimké evidence in writing *Uncle Tom's Cabin*, the novel that, according to some, became a major emotional cause of the Civil War.

In time, illness and age began to limit the involvement of Sarah, Angelina, and Theodore in the antislavery cause. Still, they continued to circulate petitions against slavery. They also became interested in other reforms of the day, such as less confining clothing for women, sensible diet, and better forms of education.

After the Civil War ended the sisters learned that two of their brother Henry's sons, born of a Negro slave woman, were in the North. Without hesitation they welcomed the boys into their home and paid for their education. One son later became a prominent minister in black churches. The other became a leader in the National Association for the Advancement of Colored People (NAACP).

In 1873 Sarah Grimké died. Six years later Angelina followed her sister to the grave. Both had lived long enough to see the end of slavery in America. And although the women's rights movement had not yet triumphed, the Grimké sisters had been early leaders in drawing the nation's attention to that movement, too.

Women of ability and high character, the Grimkés turned their backs, as young adults, on what surely would have been lives of security, comfort, leisure, and wealth. Instead they chose to live lives of struggle but also of great accomplishment and——through service to others——lives filled with meaning.

The Grimké Sisters

Meet the Author

William Jay Jacobs writes about history for children and young adults. Much of his writing is about important people and events in American history. His family background led him to write about history. "My mother came to America on her own from Austria at the age of twelve. . . . My father escaped from Hungary just before being taken into that country's army. . . . America to me is more than just a place of residence. It is a passion."

Meet the Illustrator

Stephen Harrington began working as an art director for a local advertising agency after graduating from the Rhode Island School of Design in 1983. After four years, he gave it up to become a freelance illustrator, working out of his home. He has now been doing this for the last 11 years. Harrington was able to combine his two loves, art and history, while illustrating *The Grimké Sisters*. Using books from his own collection and those in the local library, he tried to create images that were visually dramatic, as well as historically accurate.

Theme Connections

Think About It

- What did the Grimké sisters give up to take a stand about women's rights?
- How did the Grimké sisters improve life for women?

Record Ideas

 Write about two improvements the Grimké sisters made for others in your Writing Journal.

Write an Article

Write a short editorial article about the Grimkés' struggles. You may write in favor of the sisters or against them in your article.

FINE Art

***Rosa Parks, The Beginning.* Artis Lane.**
Private collection. Photo: Courtesy of the Artist.

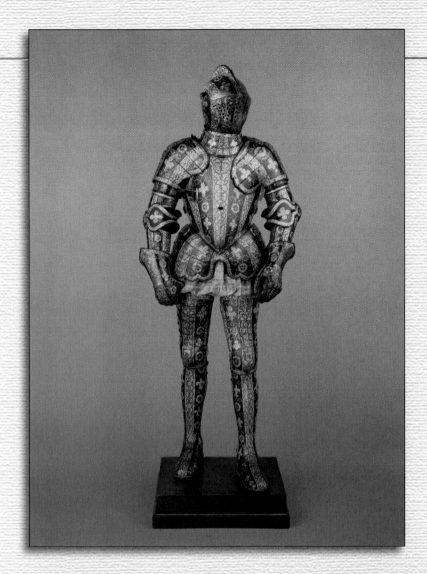

***Armor of George Clifford, third earl
of Cumberland.*** c.1580–1585.
Unknown artist, made in Royal
Workshop at Greenwich. Steel–blue,
etched, and gilded. The Metropolitan
Museum of Art, Munsey Fund, 1932
(32.130.6). Photo: © 1991 The
Metropolitan Museum of Art.

The Uprising. c.1848.
Honoré Daumier. Oil on
canvas. The Phillips
Collection, Washington, DC.

I Have a Dream

from the speech by Martin Luther King, Jr.

Born in 1929, Dr. Martin Luther King, Jr., began his career at the age of twenty-seven as the minister of the Dexter Avenue Baptist Church in Montgomery, Alabama. He later became the leader of the struggle for civil rights for African-Americans. On August 28, 1963, he made his famous "I Have a Dream" speech in Washington, D.C., where more than a quarter-million people were gathered to convince Congress to pass a civil-rights bill. In his speech, Dr. King pleaded for freedom and justice for all people.

So I say to you, my friends, that even though we must face the difficulties of today and tomorrow, I still have a dream. It is a dream deeply rooted in the American dream that one day this nation will rise up and live out the true meaning of its creed——we hold these truths to be self-evident, that all men are created equal.

I have a dream that one day sons of former slaves and sons of former slave-owners will be able to sit down together at the table of brotherhood.

I have a dream my four little children will one day live in a nation where they will not be judged by the color of their skin but by the content of their character. I have a dream today!

I have a dream that one day . . . little black boys and black girls will be able to join hands with little white boys and white girls as sisters and brothers. I have a dream today!

I have a dream that one day every valley shall be exalted, every hill and mountain shall be made low, the rough places shall be made plain, and the crooked places shall be made straight and the glory of the Lord will be revealed and all flesh shall see it together.

This is our hope. This is the faith that I go back to the South with.

With this faith we will be able to hew out of the mountain of despair a stone of hope. With this faith we will be able to transform the jangling discords of our nation into a beautiful symphony of brotherhood.

With this faith we will be able to work together, to pray together, to struggle together, to go to jail together, to stand up for freedom together, knowing that we will be free one day. This will be the day when all of God's children will be able to sing with new meaning——"my country 'tis of thee; sweet land of liberty; of thee I sing; land where my fathers died, land of the pilgrims' pride; from every mountainside, let freedom ring"—— and if America is to be a great nation, this must become true.

So let freedom ring from the prodigious hilltops of New Hampshire.

Let freedom ring from the mighty mountains of New York.

Let freedom ring from the heightening Alleghenies of Pennsylvania.

Let freedom ring from the snow-capped Rockies of Colorado.

Let freedom ring from the curvaceous slopes of California.

But not only that.

Let freedom ring from Stone Mountain of Georgia.

Let freedom ring from Lookout Mountain of Tennessee.

Let freedom ring from every hill and molehill of Mississippi, from every mountainside, let freedom ring.

And when we allow freedom to ring, when we let it ring from every village and hamlet, from every state and city, we will be able to speed up that day when all of God's children——black men and white men, Jews and Gentiles, Catholics and Protestants——will be able to join hands and to sing in the words of the old Negro spiritual, "Free at last, free at last; thank God Almighty, we are free at last."

I Have a Dream

Meet the Author

Martin Luther King, Jr., was a Baptist minister who wanted to end racial segregation in the South. He believed that people should be judged by the "content of their character" and not by their skin color. King worked hard to bring people of all races together, and he believed this could be done without violence. Because of his hard work, he earned the Nobel Peace Prize in 1964. King was the leader of the civil rights movement from the mid-1950s until 1968 when he was assassinated.

Theme Connections

Think About It

Think about the courage it must take to take a stand about something you know a lot of people are against.

Record Ideas

Write a list of words describing Martin Luther King, Jr. Write your list in your Writing Journal.

Write a Paragraph

What was Martin Luther King, Jr.'s, dream? Write a paragraph describing what you think Dr. King was saying in his speech. You should include examples from your daily life of ways Dr. King's dream has come true.

Martin Luther King Jr.

by Gwendolyn Brooks

A man went forth with gifts.

He was a prose poem.
He was a tragic grace.
He was a warm music.

He tried to heal the vivid volcanoes.
His ashes are
    reading the world.

His Dream still wishes to anoint
    the barricades of faith and of control.

His word still burns the center of the sun,
    above the thousands and the
    hundred thousands.

The word was Justice. It was spoken.

So it shall be spoken.
So it shall be done.

A Long Way to Go

Zibby Oneal
illustrated by Michael Dooling

Lila's nanny, Katie Rose, had Saturdays off. On that day, right after lunch, she went home to help her mother. Sometime, she promised, she'd take Lila along, and one Saturday in September that happened.

First thing in the morning, while she was brushing Lila's hair, Katie Rose said, "How would you like to go home with me today?"

Lila forgot how the brush was pulling her long hair. "Really? Today?" she said.

"I asked your mama and she agreed, if we are sure to be home by supper." All morning Lila squirmed with excitement.

Soon after lunch they set off, Katie Rose prim and pretty in her Saturday hat, and Lila wearing her best coat with the beaver collar. They walked to Fourth Avenue and waited for the trolley. Lila had her fare in her pocket.

"You mustn't expect anything grand," Katie said when they were sitting side by side on the trolley's slippery wooden seat. "We're poor and that's a fact. We all have to help. Delia and Sheila help Mama with her sewing from the shirtwaist factory. Mike sells papers and Annie watches the babies."

Lila nodded. Katie Rose had told her many times about her brothers and sisters, but sometimes Lila got mixed up. There were so many of them.

The trolley rattled along Fourth Avenue, sometimes ringing its bell. Lila looked out the windows to the left and right. They rode past rows of shops with striped awnings, past a hotel where a doorman stood holding packages, past a square where fountains were spraying, on and on, starting and stopping. Then the buildings began to look shabbier and the sidewalks became more crowded. Finally Katie stood up. "Next stop's ours." They made their way to the front of the car as the trolley slowed, and climbed down the steep steps when it stopped.

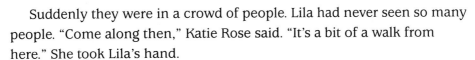

Suddenly they were in a crowd of people. Lila had never seen so many people. "Come along then," Katie Rose said. "It's a bit of a walk from here." She took Lila's hand.

Lila hurried to keep up, trying to look about her as she went. It was like stumbling into a festival or fair. The curbs were lined with pushcarts loaded with every kind of thing for sale——shoelaces and suspenders, bags of potatoes, piles of apples, pillows, pots and pans, barrels of fish. There were huge tin cans full of milk, mounds of shoes, heaps of long underwear. Lila stared. Children were playing in the street, dodging trucks and delivery wagons. Scrawny cats darted under the wheels of carts. Lila had never seen so much going on all at once.

She looked at the tenement buildings along the street and at the fire escapes where laundry was hanging, underwear in plain sight. A woman shook a mop from a window. There was a smell of cooking in the air. The street rang with shouts and laughter. It seemed to Lila that she had never been so far away from home before.

Katie Rose led her across the street toward a dull red building like the others. "Ah, there's Annie," she cried, and Lila saw a girl about her own age on the steps outside the building. She was holding a baby in her arms and watching another, bigger one. "My baby brothers," Katie said as they crossed the street.

Annie lifted the smallest baby onto her shoulder when she saw them coming. She smiled shyly at Lila. "I was hoping Katie Rose would bring you sometime."

Together they went into the building's dark hallway. They climbed a flight of steps and then another. On the third landing, Katie Rose pushed open a door and called, "I'm home! I brought Lila!"

A strong smell of cooking greeted Lila's nose. She blinked, coming in from the darkness of the hallway. In the center of the room was a table where two little girls were sitting with a woman, who Lila guessed, was Katie's mother. All of them were doing something that looked like sewing. "Pulling bastings, are you?" asked Katie Rose. "I told you, Lila, Sheila and Delia help Mama with her sewing. They pull basting threads. And that's Mike over there in the corner."

Before Lila had them sorted out, she was sitting at the table with them, drinking tea. The babies crawled around the legs of the chairs, and the rest of them laughed and told stories. Lila sipped her tea slowly and listened.

"Mike's going to take you out to see the sights, Lila," Katie Rose's mother said.

Lila looked up from her cup. She could see that he didn't want to. "Why doesn't Annie do it?" he muttered.

"You know very well why," said Annie.

"You don't have to take me," Lila said as she followed Mike back down the dark stairway.

"Naw, it's all right." But it didn't sound to Lila as if he really thought so.

"Why couldn't Annie?"

"She's got the babies to mind."

"Can't your mother and Katie do that?"

"Naw, it wouldn't be fair. Mama likes to sit a bit with Katie when she has a chance. Anyway, it's Annie's job, minding them."

"All the time?"

Mike pushed open the outside door and turned to look at her curiously. "After school and weekends," he said, as if he thought anyone would know that.

They stood on the sidewalk in the sunshine. "What d'you want to see?" Mike asked.

"I don't know what there is to see."

"You ever been to the flickers?"

"The what?"

"The motion picture show."

Lila shook her head. Of course she hadn't. Nice people didn't go to places like that, Mama said.

"Want to see one? It costs a nickel."

Lila fingered the change in her pocket. She could feel the smooth edge of a nickel there. All the while she was thinking she shouldn't go, her feet were following Mike down the street.

"Bet you've never seen a nickelodeon," he said. "They're swell. I go there all the time. We could go see a live show. They're swell, too, but they cost more."

The nickelodeon was enough for Lila. At the booth outside the door they paid. Then they went in and found chairs in the darkness. A prickle of excitement ran down Lila's spine as a gray, flickering picture appeared on the screen. Suddenly a train came rushing into view. A cowboy followed on a galloping horse. He waved a gun. The audience yelled. The train went hurtling off a cliff. The audience whistled and stamped on the floor. Then, all at once, nothing. The screen went blank. "Busted," Mike said. "It always happens. But don't worry. You get three reels for a nickel."

Soon the screen flickered again and a picture appeared. A bandit this time. Another chase. Lila stared. She sat without moving until the third reel ended and the lights came on, until Mike said, "It's over."

On the street she stood dazzled by daylight, waiting for whatever would happen next. "I bet you've never been to a penny candy store either," Mike said.

"I haven't."

She had never even imagined one, and she couldn't believe her eyes. In the long glass cases that ran the length of the store, there were gumdrops and jelly beans, jawbreakers, mounds of chocolate-covered cherries, peanuts, and long, thin licorice whips. They walked the whole length of the counter, inspecting the candy, running their fingers along the glass. "Anything costs a penny," Mike said, "but jawbreakers last longest."

Lila felt for pennies in her pocket. She had two, and so she chose a red jawbreaker for herself. Then she chose a green one for Annie because it didn't seem fair that Annie couldn't come.

Mouths full of candy, they wandered out the door. The street was busy as ever, but the slant of the sun had changed. Suddenly Mike's face was serious. "It's time to go get my papers," he said. "I mean the newspapers I sell. It's my job."

"Oh." Lila looked around her, at the alley where a baseball game was going on, at the bunch of boys pitching pennies on the sidewalk, at the horse-drawn ice wagon coming down the street. She sniffed the warm odor of sugar floating through the candy store door. She had never been anyplace that was so exciting. But now it was about to end. Mike was going off to sell his papers. Soon she and Katie Rose would take the trolley home and she would have supper in the nursery and play the next day in the fenced-in park and remember not to dirty her dress.

"You better go stay with Annie now," Mike said. "I'll show you the way."

But she didn't want to go back. She didn't want it all to end. "Can't I come with you?"

"Naw, girls can't."

"Why can't they?"

"Girls don't sell papers."

"Why not?"

"They're too weak." Mike pretended to be holding up the hem of a skirt. "They're too del-i-cate."

Lila stuck out her chin. "I'm not."

"Sure you are. All girls are." He looked at her and grinned.

Lila didn't plan what happened next. It just seemed to happen. One minute Mike was grinning at her, and the next he was holding his jaw.

"What'd you hit me for?" he asked.

"Because of what you said." Lila didn't really know. Maybe she had hit him to show him she wasn't weak.

"What did I say?" He looked puzzled.

"That girls are weak and delicate."

"But it's true." She could see that he really believed it was true, that he hadn't meant to insult her. She didn't care. She was tired of hearing things like that.

"I could sell papers as well as you," she said. "Any girl could."

"You couldn't even carry them."

"I could!"

Mike was stroking his jaw as if it still hurt him. He looked at her. "Yeah?" he said. "Well, come on and try then."

Lila counted more than thirty newsboys waiting to pick up their papers outside the office building where she and Mike stopped. A man was dumping great rope-bound bundles onto the sidewalk. "You wait here," Mike said and hurried into the crowd. In his cloth cap and knickers he looked just like every other boy waiting there. Lila soon lost sight of him.

She stood on the sidewalk, feeling out of place in her Sunday coat and white hair bow——the only girl on the street. Maybe this is a mistake, she thought. But then she thought again. She remembered the yellow chrysanthemum, the flower the suffragists wore, pressed in a book in her room at home. She remembered Grandmama striding off so proudly to speak. Of course she could sell papers!

In a few minutes, Mike was back, carrying a canvas bag on his shoulder. "Go ahead, take some," he said, "since you're so strong." He handed Lila the bag, half full.

Her shoulder sagged under the weight. "Heavy, aren't they?" Mike said. Lila shrugged. "Not very."

She didn't think that he believed her. "Come on, then. I sell on the corner of Tenth Street," he said.

Lila tried to hurry. The strap of the bag cut into her shoulder, and the weight of it bumped against her hip, but she didn't intend to let that slow her down. She walked as fast as she could.

"The headlines aren't much good today," Mike said. "What I like is when there's a murder or the Germans torpedo a ship. That's when you really sell papers. All we got today is some speech about Liberty Bonds

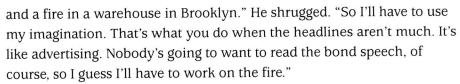

and a fire in a warehouse in Brooklyn." He shrugged. "So I'll have to use my imagination. That's what you do when the headlines aren't much. It's like advertising. Nobody's going to want to read the bond speech, of course, so I guess I'll have to work on the fire."

Lila didn't see how he could talk so much carrying papers. She could hardly breathe. Her shoulder ached and her arm was going numb. But of course she didn't say so. She wouldn't say so if she had to walk another five miles. She bit her lip and kept going.

Then, just when she thought she couldn't carry the papers much longer, when her arm felt dead as a stick of wood, they stopped. "This is it," said Mike. "My corner." He dropped most of his papers onto the sidewalk. Gratefully Lila dropped hers.

"Now let's see you sell," Mike said, but he didn't wait to watch. Instead he began running after customers, waving papers, shouting "Read all about the big fire in Brooklyn! Read about the flames forty feet high!"

Lila pulled a paper from the bag and looked at it. She couldn't see where he was getting all that. The paper didn't say a thing about flames. It didn't really say much about the fire. That was what he meant by imagination, she guessed, but it didn't seem quite fair to fool people that way.

She ran her eyes down the front page. The bond speech. The fire. But then she saw, down at the bottom of the page, not taking much space, a small article headed, SUFFRAGISTS REFUSE TO EAT. Lila read as fast as she could. There were suffragists in jail in Washington who wouldn't eat a bite. They said they'd rather starve than do without the vote. The paper called it a hunger strike.

Lila's eyes widened. This was news. This was something interesting. And, besides, it was true. She pulled a few more papers from her bag and stood herself right in the middle of the sidewalk. "Suffragists starving to death!" she yelled. "Read all about it!"

To her amazement, someone stopped to buy a paper. She tried again. "Read all about the ladies starving to death in Washington!" And, again, someone stopped.

"Crazy women," the man said, but he paid her and didn't seem to think it was strange at all to see a girl selling papers.

Lila felt encouraged. Over and over she waved her papers at people walking past. She shouted her headline until she was hoarse but it felt good to be hoarse, to be shouting and running.

"President making women starve!" she cried. "They won't eat till they get to vote!" Anything she said seemed to work. People bought papers. Maybe they would have bought them anyway, thought Lila. She didn't know, but she didn't care. She was too busy selling. In no time, her bag was empty.

She hadn't had time to think about Mike, but now, bag empty, she turned around to look for him. He was leaning against a lamppost, watching her. "I sold them all," she said breathlessly.

"I noticed."

"Here's the money." She fished the change and a few bills from her pocket.

"You keep it."

"No. Why?"

"You earned it."

"But I didn't do it for that." Lila thought of Annie, minding the babies, of the little girls pulling basting threads all afternoon. "You take the money. I just did it to show you I could."

"Yeah. Well." Mike kicked the lamppost with the toe of his shoe. "I guess you showed me."

There were things that Lila felt like saying, but she decided not to say them. Instead she picked up the empty canvas bag and slung it over her shoulder. Together they started back the way they had come.

It was twilight. The streets were filled with the sounds of horns and engines. Lights blossomed in shop windows. People hurried along the sidewalk. On a corner, leaning against the side of a parked truck, a man was playing a harmonica. "Over There," he played slowly, making the notes sound like a sleepy bugle call. "Over There." It was a tune Katie Rose sometimes sang when she was folding laundry, thinking about her sweetheart overseas. The music sounded soft and sad in the twilight.

The two of them walked on in silence, and the mournful notes of the harmonica followed after them. Lila felt too tired to talk. Her head swam with new things to think about——the candy store with all its treasures, the nickelodeon with its flickering screen, the pushcarts loaded with things to sell, the sounds and smells of this new neighborhood. But most of all it was selling papers that she wanted to remember——running after customers, yelling her headlines. The canvas bag swung against her shoulder. She smiled.

The men who sold goods from the pushcarts were packing up when the two of them turned the corner onto Mike's street. Lila could see Katie Rose standing on the steps at the end of the block, and she knew they should hurry, but instead she slowed down.

"I'm sorry I hit you," she said.

"Yeah, well, I'm sorry for what I said about girls."

"You just didn't know any better."

"I never saw a girl selling papers before." Then he turned to look at her and Lila thought that he looked shy. "You were good at it," he said. "You knew what to do."

Lila smiled and handed him the canvas bag and they went on down the street.

So now it was really over——the wonderful afternoon. Now she would go home with Katie Rose and turn into a proper little girl again. It was like the end of a fairy tale, Lila thought. Except it was sad.

On the trolley she leaned against Katie Rose and closed her eyes. It was over, Lila thought, but she would remember, and a memory, like a jawbreaker, lasted a long, long time.

"And then," said Lila on Sunday morning, bouncing on Grandmama's bed. "And then——"

"And then Katie Rose brought you home."

"Yes."

"Lila, you've told me all about it three times."

She had. She couldn't help it. Saturday afternoon was like a story she didn't want to finish, like a book of beautiful colored pictures that she couldn't bear to close.

"Oh, I liked it all so much, but I'm not going to tell anyone else about it. Just you." Lila looked out the window at the sunlight on the fence around the park. "I wish girls could sell papers," she said a little sadly. "I mean all the time."

"There are more and more things that girls can do. Think of all the jobs women have now that there's a war on. When I was your age we didn't dream of working in offices and factories."

"That's women. I mean girls." And then, "Do you think that if women could vote, they'd let girls sell papers?"

Grandmama laughed. "I don't know. I suppose there'd be a better chance of that happening."

"Then I'm a suffragist," Lila said. "I *thought* I was, but now I'm sure."

"That's fine."

Lila frowned. "But what can I do?"

"Believe that women have rights the same as men."

That wasn't what Lila had in mind. She wanted action. She wanted to shout headlines, run around yelling. "I could give speeches," she said. She imagined herself standing on a wooden box speaking to crowds in the street. It would be a lot like selling papers.

But Grandmama only laughed again. "You're still too young to make speeches."

"But I want to do *something*. It's no use just sitting around believing things."

Grandmama looked thoughtful. "Well, there's a suffragist parade a week or so before the state election. We're going to march up Fifth Avenue all the way from Washington Square to Fifty-ninth Street."

"With signs?" said Lila. "And banners?"

"Oh, yes, and music, too. We're going to make people notice us."

"Would you take me?"

"Well, I was thinking——"

Lila sat up straight. "I'm coming."

"But not without permission you aren't. Not unless your mama and papa agree."

"I'll make them agree," said Lila, though she had no idea how she'd do that.

"Well, I'll try to help you," Grandmama said. "At least I'll mention the parade."

Lila sat quietly in church with her hands in her lap. She played nicely with her brother George until lunchtime, rolling his ball to him over and over though this was the most boring game in the world. She sat straight at the table and ate all her lunch, though that included beets. Really, Lila thought, she was being so perfect it was hard to see how Mama and Papa could say no.

But that was what Papa said. While they were waiting for dessert, Grandmama brought up the parade. She did it in a kind of offhanded way, as if it were something she'd only just remembered. "And I think Lila would like to march, too," she said. Lila looked down at her napkin and crossed her fingers. But Papa said no.

It was such a small word, no, but it seemed to Lila that it was the biggest word in her life. So many nos. She felt tears of disappointment prickling in her eyes. She couldn't look up.

When, after lunch, Papa said, "Come on, Lila, it's time for our Sunday walk," Lila felt like saying, "No!" She didn't want to go for a walk with her father. She felt too mad and disappointed. All the same, she went to get her coat, because a little girl didn't say no to her father.

"Which way shall we walk?" he asked her when they were standing on the pavement.

"I don't care." And she didn't. She didn't care at all.

"What about Fifth Avenue then?"

Lila had known he'd choose that. Papa liked walking along Fifth Avenue, looking at the new motorcars pass by. One day, he said, he thought he might buy one.

And so they walked over to Fifth Avenue. Lila was wearing her best coat again and clean white gloves because Papa liked her to look like a lady when they went walking. But her hands felt crowded in the gloves and her shoulders felt crowded in her coat. She felt crowded all over.

At the corner of Fifth Avenue, they turned and walked north, past banks and office buildings, past shops and department stores. Usually Lila liked looking into the department store windows, but today they didn't seem exciting. She thought of the pushcarts on Katie Rose's street. Fifth Avenue was dull.

"Has the cat got your tongue?" Papa said.

"No. I'm thinking."

"About important things?"

"I was thinking about the parade. It's going to come right up this street."

"Lila, you must forget the parade."

But how could she? She couldn't stop thinking about it, even though the thinking made her sad.

They waited to cross the street while a car passed. "That's a Pierce Arrow," Papa said. "It's really something, isn't it?"

Lila nodded. She supposed so.

"Maybe when George is older we'll buy one like that. He can learn to drive it."

"What about me?"

"Oh, you'll be a beautiful grown lady by then. You can ride in the back and tell George where to take you. You'll have all kinds of pretty clothes to wear. We'll go shopping for things like the dress in that window."

Lila glanced at the dress in the shop window. She had to admit it was pretty. She wondered why she didn't like it more, and then she knew. It looked like the kind of dress that was for sitting around doing nothing.

"I'd rather learn how to drive a motorcar," she said, "I'd rather be *doing* something."

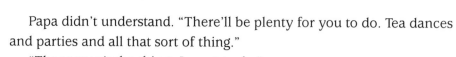

Papa didn't understand. "There'll be plenty for you to do. Tea dances and parties and all that sort of thing."

"Those aren't the things I want to do."

"No? What then?"

"Oh!" Lists of things came tumbling into Lila's head. She wanted to march in the parade, turn cartwheels, walk on her hands, roll her stockings down. She wanted to run and yell, sell papers——but that was not what Papa meant. He meant later, when she was grown-up. What did she want to do *then?* Lila closed her eyes and squeezed them tight. "I want to vote," she said.

The words were out before she knew she was going to say them, but suddenly they seemed just right. "I want to be able to vote same as George."

When she opened her eyes, Papa was looking at her. "That's what you want more than anything?"

Lila nodded. She dug her fists into her pockets and looked up at Papa bravely. "It's what Grandmama says. Girls are people, too. They have rights. It isn't fair the way it is. Billy Ash says he's smarter than me just because he's a boy. But I'm the one who gets all A's, not him. So why should he be allowed to vote and not me? Why should George if I can't? It's not fair, Papa. It's not fair to girls."

Lila paused for breath, but she couldn't stop talking. "When I grow up, I want to be just like Grandmama. I want to make things fair for everyone. That's why I want to march in the parade——to show people that's what I think. And if they put me in jail for marching, then I just won't eat, like the ladies in Washington."

Then Lila stopped. She didn't have anything else to say.

"Well," said Papa, "that was quite a speech."

Lila couldn't tell what he was thinking. His face was very serious. She wondered if he would stop loving her now because of all she'd said. She wondered if he'd already stopped. She waited for him to say something more, but he said nothing at all. He took her hand and they went on walking.

Lila's feet slapped along beside him. It was too late now to take it back, and, anyway, she couldn't take it back without lying. She'd said what she meant. But Papa wasn't saying anything at all. He was looking straight ahead as if he had forgotten all about her, as if he didn't know she was there anymore.

Lila felt hollow in the middle. She bit the insides of her cheeks to keep from crying. On the way home, she counted cracks in the sidewalk.

When they reached the corner of Twenty-first Street and were almost home, Papa said, "How did you happen to know about those women in Washington, the ones who aren't eating? Did Grandmama tell you?"

Lila shook her head, still counting cracks. "No," she said. "I read it in the paper."

"Did you really? For heaven's sake." Lila could have sworn, if she hadn't known better, that he sounded proud of her.

After supper, she had her bath and watched Katie Rose laying out her clothes for school the next day. The same old stockings. The same old dress. Lila sighed. Everything was the same old thing again, except that now it would be different with Papa. She climbed out of the tub and wrapped herself in a towel. She went into her room to put on her nightgown.

And that was when Grandmama came in. She had a funny, puzzled sort of expression. "It looks as if we'll be going to the parade together," she said.

Lila paused. The damp ends of her hair swung against her shoulders. "What?"

"Your father says you may go."

"With you? To the parade?" Lila felt as if she couldn't take it all in so fast.

"That's what he says."

"But why?"

Grandmama shrugged. "I don't know what you said to him on that walk, but you must have said something."

Lila swallowed. He had called it a speech. She had made a speech and he'd listened! A bubble of happiness began to rise inside her. He had listened and it was all right. She grinned at Grandmama. She dropped her towel. And then right there, in the middle of her bedroom, she turned a cartwheel.

There were weeks of waiting before the parade. October crawled by like a snail. Lila imagined marching a hundred times before, at last, the day arrived, the special Saturday.

She woke in a shiver of excitement. She could hardly hold still while Katie Rose braided her hair. "You button your shoes yourself," Katie Rose said. "I can't manage with so much wiggling." And she handed Lila the buttonhook.

"Will you be sure to remember to tell Mike that I'm marching?"

Katie Rose snorted. "Do you think I could forget? You remind me every day."

Lila laughed. She was hoping that maybe——just maybe——Mike would come out to watch the parade.

"And tell Annie I wish she could march, too," Lila said. "Tell her I'm marching for her."

And then she jumped up and started downstairs because she couldn't hold still for more than a minute.

Grandmama was in the parlor, reading the paper. "I'm ready!" Lila cried.

Grandmama looked up. "That's fine, but you'll have a bit of a wait. The parade won't begin for several hours."

Lila twirled on the piano stool. She practiced marching between the parlor windows. Grandmama rattled the paper. "President Wilson has come to his senses, I see. He says he wishes our cause Godspeed."

"What does that mean?" asked Lila.

"It means he wishes us luck. He's changing his spots, I think, just like your papa."

"What does *that* mean?"

"He's changing his mind. It says here he's leaning toward a constitutional amendment."

"So maybe there won't *be* a parade?"

"Of course there'll be a parade. We haven't *got* the amendment yet."

Lila let out her breath, relieved. She wondered how to spend the next few hours.

When at last they set out for the parade, Mama stood in the parlor window waving. Lila skipped and whirled up the sidewalk. They were going to catch a cab at the corner.

The cab dropped them a block from Washington Square. Lila could hear snatches of music as they walked toward it. "Those are the bands warming up," Grandmama said. "There's going to be a lot of music."

Lila trotted along beside her. The music grew louder and louder. And then they were in Washington Square, and Lila's eyes opened round as saucers.

There were women everywhere, hundreds and hundreds of them. Some carried flags, some were unrolling banners with words printed on them. There were women dressed in nurses' uniforms, women in Red Cross costumes, women wearing yellow chrysanthemums in their hats. So many women! There were old women, young women, white women, black women. There was even a woman standing in line propped on crutches.

"How can she march on crutches?" Lila whispered.

"She can if she makes her mind up to do it," Grandmama said. "That's what this is all about."

"Line up! Line up!" someone was shouting. A bass drum boomed. Grandmama took Lila's hand and they slipped quickly into line.

And then the music began. All at once, all the bands were playing and the columns of women began to move. Left, left. Lila was marching. Above her, the yellow banners streamed.

Out of Washington Square they marched and onto Fifth Avenue. Before and behind came the sound of the drums, and the flags snapped in the breeze. Left, left. On they went up the street, marching in time to the music.

From the curbs came the sound of whistles and cheers. Yellow streamers flew from the shop doors. White-gloved policemen held back the crowds as the bands and the marchers passed.

Lila felt she could march forever, her feet in step with the drums. Back straight, chin up. Left, left, left.

Just as they were crossing Tenth Street, it happened. The bands were playing "Over There." People on the sidewalk were shouting. Lila was looking into the crowd——just in case maybe——when something splashed at her feet.

It splashed and then it splattered red pulp and yellow seeds all over her stockings, all over the hem of her coat. "Someone threw a tomato!" she cried. "Someone threw it right at me!" She tugged Grandmama's hand. There were tears in her eyes.

Grandmama looked down. "Never mind. Just keep marching."

"But, Grandmama, a tomato! It's all over my legs!"

"These things happen sometimes, Lila. It is part of doing what we're doing. There are lots of people who don't want us to vote, lots who don't like this parade. Now be a brave girl. Show them they can't stop you. Keep marching."

Lila thought she was going to cry. Her feet kept moving, but she had lost step. She looked down at the red juice all over her white stockings. And then she got mad. She stuck out her chin and looked straight ahead, and her feet began to move in time with the music.

Left, left. A tomato couldn't stop her. She thought about the woman on crutches. She thought of the women who were still in jail in Washington and about the ones who weren't eating. She thought of all the speeches

that Grandmama had made. She thought of her own speech to Papa. She remembered Annie minding the babies and Sheila and Delia pulling bastings all day Saturday. A tomato wasn't much, she thought. A tomato was nothing.

Head up, looking straight ahead, Lila marched on, her feet keeping time with the music.

By the time the parade reached Twenty-first Street, Lila's stockings were dry. The bands were playing "Tipperary." Lila knew the words to that song. She knew they talked about a long way to go. She began to sing to herself as she marched along.

And then Grandmama began singing. And soon women all around them had taken up the song. They sang about what a long way there was to go, and it seemed to Lila that those words meant a lot to them.

Then, suddenly, Grandmama squeezed her hand. "Look, Lila! Look who's waving!"

Lila turned. There on the curb were Mama and Papa, and George in his carriage. Lila waved. Then the parade swept her on. She wondered whether Papa had noticed her stockings.

"Imagine your papa coming out for this parade!" Grandmama leaned over and hugged her. "You know, something tells me we're going to win! One of these days we'll be voting."

They marched on, past the reviewing stand. They marched until Lila's legs felt like stumps. They marched while the sun slid down in the sky and disappeared behind buildings.

It was twilight by the time the parade broke up and Grandmama said, "Let's go home in a cab." Lila was glad to hear that. She didn't feel like walking.

While they waited for a taxi, Lila looked down at her tomato-splattered stockings. She felt proud of them. They were like a badge. She didn't even think of rolling them down.

ABOUT THE WOMEN'S SUFFRAGE MOVEMENT

In 1848, Elizabeth Cady Stanton and Lucretia Mott met at Seneca Falls, New York, to draw up a declaration of women's rights. Now, the idea that women have rights is taken for granted. Then, it was not. Women had few rights and certainly not the right to vote. In their declaration, Mrs. Stanton and Mrs. Mott asked for that.

Both these women were abolitionists who worked before the Civil War for the freeing of slaves. Human rights included women's rights, they thought. If Negroes were freed and allowed to vote, couldn't women expect the same? It didn't work that way. After the Civil War, Congress passed the Fourteenth Amendment to the Constitution, permitting all citizens to vote, providing they were male! The women who had worked so hard for abolition were outraged.

In 1890, they formed the National American Woman Suffrage Association. Mrs. Stanton was its first president and working with her was another important woman in the suffrage movement, Susan B. Anthony. Together they were determined to win votes for women.

For the next thirty years, suffragists worked tirelessly. They collected signatures on petitions, traveled great distances to speak about suffrage, and visited Congress and the president many times with their request. Over and over, they were turned down. Both President Woodrow Wilson and most members of Congress felt that women's suffrage was a matter to be decided by the individual states and not by a change in the Constitution. They were supported by numbers of men——and many women——who opposed women's right to vote at all. Finally, in frustration, the suffragists decided to begin picketing the White House.

This same year, 1917, the United States entered the First World War. American troops were sent to Europe to help England and France in their war with the Germans. Women's suffrage was not the main topic on the minds of the men in government. But the suffragists worked on.

In November 1917, New York finally joined other states in granting women the right to vote. This was a turning point. Members of Congress began to see that pressure for a constitutional amendment was enormous. President Wilson gave it his support, and in 1919 the Senate voted in favor.

In August 1920, the Nineteenth Amendment was finally ratified by two-thirds of the states, and after seventy years of trying, women had won the right to vote.

A Long Way to Go

Meet the Author

Zibby Oneal began telling stories as a young girl. When she learned to write, she began writing down the stories. "While my friends learned to roller skate and jump rope and play jacks, I wrote." As an adult she wrote stories for her young children. As her children grew, so did her characters. "Eventually everyone reached adolescence, but unlike my children, my characters have remained there." Oneal believes writing for young people gives a writer a chance to "make some difference in a reader's life."

Meet the Illustrator

Michael Dooling has illustrated 12 books for children. When he illustrates, he is mostly interested in creating a mood. "I try to make my illustrations convey the spirit, to go beyond just reporting the facts." Dooling lives in Audubon, New Jersey.

Theme Connections

Think About It

- How would you feel if you took a stand about something and people close to you took the opposite stand?

Record Ideas

Would it be worth it to you to be embarrassed about a cause you believed in? Why? Why not? Record your ideas in your Writing Journal.

Write a Sequel

Write a sequel to "A Long Way to Go" portraying Lila as an adult. How do you think her actions as a young person influenced the rest of her life?

GANDHI

Nigel Hunter
illustrated by Richard Hook

MEMORIES OF THE MAHATMA

His face is familiar to people in all parts of the world, but to the people of India, Mahatma Gandhi is part of the landscape itself. In every Indian town and village, you are likely to see his image. It could be a framed portrait in the Post Office or bank or a faded photograph displayed on the crumbling wall of a back street tea shop. It could be a brightly-colored postcard clipped to the side of a street-vendor's stall; or a full-length statue set up in the restful shade of a public park or above the hurly-burly and bustle of the crossroads.

He may be pictured at his spinning wheel, absorbed in concentration, or playing with children, laughing good naturedly. Or perhaps he is drinking tea with the Viceroy. More often, he is portrayed striding purposefully forward, leading the movement for Indian independence; for freedom, peace and friendship. Millions affectionately called him *Bapu,* father of the nation. As a sign of respect he became known as Gandhiji and was also called "Mahatma" (great soul) by one of India's finest poets, Rabindranath Tagore.

People in every part of India remember Gandhi. In the southern town of Madurai, what was once a palace is now a museum dedicated to his memory. Outside, in reconstructed buildings, his modest *ashram* living conditions are shown. Inside, a display of words and pictures portrays the long, painful, triumphant march to freedom from British rule. Behind glass there are relics of Gandhi's life; photographs, letters, documents and books; a pair of spectacles, and a spinning wheel. In one cool and carefully-lit space lies an exhibit that bears witness to his sudden, shocking death: a quantity of simple homespun-cloth, white linen darkened by the stain of blood . . .

Gandhi with his granddaughters in New Delhi.

314

Gandhi's wedding. His head is covered with traditional decorations.

A Hindu Family

When Mohandas Gandhi was born in 1869, the British Empire was at the peak of its power. The British had ruled India for almost three centuries. Certain parts of the country, ruled by princes who were loyal to the British, were allowed to continue as separate princely states. Mohandas' father was the *Diwan,* or Prime Minister, of Porbandar, a small princely state on India's western coast. It was an appointment that passed from father to son.

His first language was Gujarati; his family's religion was Hindu.

When he was thirteen, his parents arranged for him to marry. In later life, he criticized the custom of child-marriage, but at the time he readily accepted it. Mohandas' bride, Kasturbai, was also thirteen, and he soon became devoted to her. He was a very strict husband, and Kasturbai felt he restrained her too much. She was supposed to get his permission before seeing her friends, or visiting the temple. Firmly, she resisted, until he grew to accept her point of view. It was a valuable lesson to Mohandas: he learned that nonviolent persuasion could convince people that they were wrong. Years later, nonviolent resistance would prove to be a powerful weapon in the struggle for social and political reform.

Gandhi's family hoped that he might become a *Diwan*, like his father and grandfather before him. For this, it would be a great advantage for him to study law in England, and so he sailed from Bombay in September 1888. For nearly three years, he would be away from Kasturbai, who had just given birth to a son.

Gandhi was ill at ease in Britain at first. He had very little confidence but studied English manners, dressed expensively, and took dancing lessons, trying to fit into English society as a gentleman. While living in London, Gandhi first read the *Bhagavad Gita,* the greatest holy book of Hinduism. As a boy, he had known some of the Hindu stories, but had not held any particular religious beliefs. He had developed friendships with people of many different religions. This helped him to develop a respect for different religions, but he remained uncommitted to any particular faith. Both the *Bhagavad Gita,* and then the Christian *New Testament,* had a profound effect on him.

As soon as he had qualified in law, Gandhi returned home to India. At first, prospects as a lawyer were uncertain because of his nervousness in public. Then a chance came to work on a business dispute in South Africa. This changed his life.

THE CHALLENGE

Soon after his arrival in South Africa, while traveling to the city of Pretoria, Gandhi was forcibly ejected from a first-class train compartment. This was simply because he was Indian and the South African whites assumed that he had no right to enjoy first-class train travel. He spent the night on the station platform, considering the humiliations that the Indians in South Africa suffered daily.

Ninety thousand Indians lived and worked in South Africa under white British rule, often in appalling conditions, and many were treated almost as slaves. Only a few hundred Indians, who owned a large amount of land, enjoyed the right to vote in the South African government. For all the Indians, government restrictions were a way of life.

Continuing his journey to Pretoria, Gandhi faced more insults. On a stagecoach, he was again shocked that he was not allowed to take a place inside the coach. He was then beaten by the driver for refusing to sit on the footboard, outside the carriage.

Gandhi is ejected from a first-class train seat because he is Indian.

The journey to Pretoria spurred him into action. In the face of this racial injustice, Gandhi lost his public timidity and called a meeting to discuss the Indians' situation. From this, an organization emerged through which Indians could voice their discontent. Within a short time, Gandhi was acknowledged as a leader of the South African Indian community.

Meanwhile, the legal case that had originally brought Gandhi to South Africa was successfully resolved, largely through his own contribution. His method of solving the dispute was to appeal to what he called "the better side of human nature." To Gandhi, the point was not to achieve outright victory for one side over the other, but to bring both sides together in a mutually satisfactory arrangement. Before long, he was a highly successful lawyer.

It was at this time that Gandhi developed a belief that God was "absolute truth" and that the way to reach Him was through the concept of nonviolence.

Over the next twenty years, Gandhi was to lead the Indians of South Africa in their struggle for justice and equality. He developed a form of political struggle based on nonviolent civil disobedience.

In 1894, Gandhi organized a successful petition and newspaper publicity against new anti-Indian laws. He helped to set up the Natal Indian Congress, which aimed to improve life for the Indian community through educational, social and political work. Gandhi returned to his family in India, and there he publicized the injustices in South Africa and sought support to tackle the problems. When he returned to South Africa he was brutally attacked for being a troublemaker by a white mob. As he recovered at a friend's house, a crowd gathered menacingly outside and sang "We'll hang old Gandhi on the sour apple tree . . ." He managed to escape under the cover of night, disguised as a policeman, and said that he forgave his attackers.

During the Boer War (1899–1902) between Britain and the South African Boers, Gandhi formed and led the Indian Ambulance Corps, which worked for the British Army. Since he was demanding rights as a citizen, he felt he owed loyalty to the British Empire; and Britain awarded him a medal. After the war he visited India again, and renewed his contacts with the leaders of the country's growing nationalist movement.

On his return to South Africa in 1903, Gandhi started a magazine for Indians in South Africa. It was called *Indian Opinion,* and it became crucial to the campaign for equality. His lifestyle changed. He decided to give up all his possessions and established a community. Here, he detached himself from his normal family ties. Gandhi believed that to serve others, he must not distract himself with the burden of possessions or involvement with family and the pleasures of family life.

NONVIOLENT REBELS

A new law in South Africa required all Indians over eight years old to register with the authorities, and carry a pass at all times. Failing this, they could be imprisoned, fined, or deported. Under Gandhi's leadership, the Indians resisted this new law. He called their action *satyagraha,* which means "holding to the truth." They would not cooperate with the authorities and their resistance was to be nonviolent. Courageously, they confronted prison, poverty, hunger, and violence against them, peacefully refusing to obey the law.

In 1908, Gandhi visited London to muster support. On his return to South Africa, he was imprisoned. Still wearing prison uniform, he was taken to meet General Jan Christiaan Smuts, the South African leader. Smuts promised that if the Indians registered, he would repeal the registration law. Trusting him, Gandhi called on all Indians to register. But Smuts broke his word. In protest, Gandhi led a public burning of the registration certificates. The campaign continued, with thousands of Indians inviting arrest by refusing to register.

Gandhi spent much of his time in prison reading and writing. He discovered the works of the famous Russian writer Leo Tolstoy, and, inspired by each other's ideas, they began exchanging letters. With the help of a friend, Gandhi founded a new community called *Tolstoy Farm.* The community members grew their own food, made their own clothes and built their own homes. Gandhi himself baked bread and made marmalade, and helped to teach the children.

More new laws, including one that said only Christian marriages were legal, prompted Gandhi to step up his campaigning. Again and again he was jailed, along with thousands of others. Many people were assaulted by the police, and several died. Finally, on the main issues, Smuts gave way. With this vital experience behind him, Gandhi was ready to return to India.

Smuts confronts the prisoner Gandhi.

Gandhi toured India, talking to the people.

An Indian Future

In Bombay in 1915, Gandhi was welcomed as a hero. He no longer wore western clothing, and he chose to speak Gujarati rather than English, as English was the language of the oppressor. For a year, he toured the country, speaking on religious and social matters. He visited the community that had been started by the poet Rabindranath Tagore. Tagore shared many of Gandhi's ideals. He compared Gandhi to Buddha, because like Gandhi, he had also taught the importance of kindness to all living creatures. Outside the city of Ahmedabad, Gandhi founded the *Satyagraha Ashram,* a community committed to nonviolence and service to others.

Gandhi was determined to break down the Hindu "caste" system, which prevented the caste of Hindus who traditionally did the dirtiest work, from ever entering temples. They were called the "untouchables" because their mere touch horrified higher class Hindus. Despite opposition from Kasturbai and others who found it hard to accept, he brought an "untouchable" family into the *Ashram* and renamed them *Harijans,* meaning "Children of God."

Gandhi successfully led the workers of the province of Bihar in a nonviolent campaign against the unjust demands of British landowners. He carried out a fast, threatening to starve himself to death unless his demands were met.

His action resulted in better wages and conditions for mill workers. He also inspired farm workers who were suffering the effects of famine not to pay Government tax demands, and eventually the demands were withdrawn. He always appealed to his opponents' sense of right and wrong. Briefly, during World War I (1914–18), he helped to recruit Indian soldiers for the British Army. This seemed at odds with his belief in nonviolence; but he hoped that service to save the Empire would earn India self-rule after the war. However, Britain passed harsh new laws preventing India from becoming a self-governing country within the Empire.

Turning and Turning

When Gandhi heard about the new British laws, preventing Indian Home Rule, he called on all Indians to suspend business for a day of national, nonviolent protest, including fasting, prayer and public meetings. But troops in Delhi killed nine people, and when Gandhi tried to reach the city, he was arrested and turned back. News of this provoked rioting and violence in several places. It seemed to Gandhi that he had made a grave mistake. People still did not understand that *satyagraha* persuasion should be nonviolent. He punished himself by fasting for three days.

Then came the terrible massacre at Amritsar. On April 13, 1919, about 15,000 people had gathered together to demonstrate peacefully on the day of the Sikh New Year. Suddenly, soldiers of the British Army appeared, under the command of General Reginald Dyer. He gave the order to shoot, and for ten minutes the soldiers fired into the crowd, who were trapped in a square. Nearly 400 men, women and children were killed, and 11,000 wounded. Gandhi was horrified by the brutality of the British Army, directed at unarmed subjects of the Empire. His loyalty to the British was completely shattered. He felt they had clearly lost all right to govern.

In 1920, Gandhi became president of the All-India Home Rule League, which sought independence from the Empire. Following this, he became the leader of the Indian National Congress. He launched a massive program of non-cooperation against the British. Cotton cloth made in Britain was boycotted and clothes made of foreign material were burned on great bonfires. To symbolize getting rid of foreign influences, hand-spinning and weaving were revived throughout the country. To Gandhi, spinning represented economic progress, national unity and independence from the Empire. He himself spun daily.

HIGH IDEALS

The Indian National Congress, led by Gandhi, now called on all Indian soldiers and civilians to quit British Government service. By 1922, 30,000 people, including nearly all the Congress leaders, had been imprisoned for acts of civil disobedience. Then twenty-two policemen who had attacked the stragglers of a protest march were viciously slaughtered. Realizing that even now the nonviolent nature of *satyagraha* was not understood, Gandhi called off the campaign, and fasted again, punishing himself for the violence he felt was his fault. He was then put on trial, accused of stirring up trouble.

In court, Gandhi spoke movingly of the people's misery under British rule and of the absurd laws. He said that perhaps in reality he was innocent, but under these laws, he was guilty,

Gandhi himself enjoyed spinning every day.

322

so he expected the highest penalty. The judge, although he praised Gandhi "as a man of high ideals and a noble and even saintly life," sentenced him to six years' imprisonment.

Two years later, Gandhi was released. For three weeks, he fasted in protest against the increasing conflict between Hindus and Muslims. Then he turned his attention to social reforms, touring the country by train, cart, and on foot, speaking to vast crowds. Many of his followers considered him a saint, and he was showered with gifts, which he turned into funds for the cause. He taught the importance of equality for women and for people of different classes and religions. He encouraged spinning and discouraged taking alcohol or using drugs.

In 1928, a Royal Commission arrived from Britain to review the situation in India. Since it included no Indian members, it was met by protest meetings, which were broken up by the British authorities. The new proposals would have still left the country subject to British control. Now the Indian National Congress decided it could accept nothing less than complete independence.

A Pinch of Salt

The Salt March of 1930 began a new round of nonviolent protest. Gandhi walked 322 km (200 miles) to the coast at Dandi. Thousands joined the march, watched by the world's press. On the beach after morning prayers, Gandhi picked up a lump of sea salt.

Salt was taxed; legally, only the Government could extract it from sea water. Gandhi's signal prompted people all along the coast of India to defy the law by manufacturing salt. In cities and villages, illegal salt was distributed. Following this action, about 100,000 people, including Gandhi and other Congress leaders, were imprisoned. Bravely, without violence, they faced police brutality. Many were badly beaten and some died; but eventually, the campaign succeeded, and salt manufacturing was allowed.

Gandhi discussed India's future at The Round Table conference in London.

Later, Gandhi took part in The Round Table conference in Britain about the future of India. While in London, he chose to stay in an East End hostel for the poor. He visited Lancashire and made friends among the mill workers, even though many were unemployed because of the Indians' boycott of British cloth. He met politicians and celebrities, and went to tea at Buckingham Palace. Everywhere, he impressed people with his sincerity and humor. As for his manner of dress at the Palace, he said, "The King was wearing enough for both of us!"

Only a week later, when he returned to India, he was imprisoned again. Before long, 30,000 others had been arrested too. In prison, Gandhi carried out a prolonged fast against the class divisions among Hindus. He was willing to starve himself to death, if the barriers were not broken down throughout the country. People valued Gandhi's life so greatly that he succeeded in changing traditions that were thousands of years old. For the first time, temples were opened to *Harijans,* and all Hindus could eat together, drink water drawn from the same wells, and even marry each other.

After his release, Gandhi turned to educational and welfare work. He toured rural India, speaking on health care, village industries and reorganization, and about land ownership and justice.

Gandhi opposed Indian involvement in World War II (1939–44), believing now that all war was wholly wrong. Leading members of the Indian Congress, including his close friend Jawaharlal Nehru, disagreed. They were willing to cooperate with the British if they could obtain reforms that would lead to self-government. But Britain would give no promise of independence.

Under Gandhi's direction, people made speeches and signed written protests against taking part in the war. Thousands, including Nehru, were imprisoned for up to a year.

In 1942, Gandhi announced a new *satyagraha* campaign aimed directly at British withdrawal from India. Once again, he was imprisoned. While in prison, he fasted again, coming close to death, in protest against accusations that he had stirred up violence against the British. Kasturbai was one of 100,000 other prisoners. Her health was poor, and in 1944, she died. Feeling her loss keenly, Gandhi himself became ill, recovering only after his release a few months later. With the end of World War II, Indian independence came closer.

Gandhi and Nehru disagreed about Indian involvement in World War II.

Gandhi had always contested religious divisions. Most Indians were either Hindus or Muslims. In the northwest and northeast of the country, Muslims were in the majority. Their leader, Muhammad Ali Jinnah, favored the creation of a separate Muslim state there, to be called Pakistan. Congress, like Gandhi, wanted a united India. Nehru was appointed Prime Minister of a provisional Indian Government, which meant Indian rule by a Hindu for that area. Jinnah announced that the Muslim League would hold a day of action to protest. The result was horrifying violence between Muslims and Hindus, with 20,000 killed or injured.

THE PEACEMAKER

From the rural area of Bengal came reports of Muslim atrocities. Gandhi walked through the villages for four months, seeking desperately to persuade people to end the violence. But soon after, in a neighboring province, there were similar Hindu atrocities to quell.

In 1947, Lord Louis Mountbatten became the last British Viceroy of India. Reluctantly, and against Gandhi's opposition, the Indian National Congress agreed that Pakistan was to become a country in its own right, separate from India. Independence came on August 15, 1947. Gandhi was living in the poorest quarters of Calcutta, where there had been appalling bloodshed, riots and fighting between the Hindu and Muslim communities. While he succeeded in pacifying the people of Bengal, the northwest was in uproar. Millions of people were migrating across the new border separating

A British officer with five Indian soldiers guarding a building burnt by Muslims.

Gandhi's fast brings him near death.

"Muslim" Pakistan from "Hindu" India. Massacres were widespread, causing almost a million deaths. When violence broke out again in Calcutta, Gandhi undertook a fast "to death," refusing food until the northeast was peaceful. Then, in riot-torn Delhi, came his "greatest fast." Dramatically, it brought a pledge of peace among all the community leaders, and throughout India and Pakistan, the violence ceased.

Though millions revered him, and cherished his life so deeply, to some Hindu fanatics, Gandhi was an obstacle. On January 30, 1948, he was murdered——shot three times by an assassin who stepped from the crowd at a prayer meeting. His death caused worldwide shock and sorrow. To countless people, he was a modern-day saint, a teacher of humanity such as the world has rarely seen. As a champion of peace, his influence still remains.

Gandhi walks the streets of Delhi with a welcoming group of residents.

327

GANDHI

Meet the Author

Nigel Hunter's life was greatly influenced by a teacher from New England, Edgar Stillman. Stillman showed Hunter how important imaginative writing was in people's lives, and he made Hunter aware of civil rights leaders like Malcolm X, whose writings were a big influence on Hunter. Because of this, it's no surprise that Hunter's books have focused on politics, including books on Martin Luther King, Jr., the Cold War, and, of course, Gandhi. Hunter now lives with his wife near the beach in Salvador, Brazil, where he teaches English at a university.

Meet the Illustrator

Richard Hook has been a freelance artist since 1966, when he left a job as an illustrator and designer for Harmon Books. He has illustrated more than 50 books on historical topics, such as Anne Frank, Beethoven, and Louis Braille. When he's not illustrating books, Hook is spending time with his wife and three children.

Theme Connections

Think About It

- What did Gandhi give up for his cause?
- What difference did Gandhi make in the lives of the people of India?

Record Ideas

What leaders in the selections in this unit gave up a lot to support their causes? What did they give up? Write your ideas in your Writing Journal.

Role-Play a Problem Related to Taking a Stand

Working in pairs, decide on a taking a stand issue. Ideas can come from your discussions and readings. Role-play the parts with each other, and then role-play for the class. To stimulate interest, ask your classmates to decide what the issue was and how the problem was resolved after the role-playing.

Sweeping Pittsburgh Clean

from *MAKING HEADLINES:*

A BIOGRAPHY OF NELLIE BLY

by Kathy Lynn Emerson

What Elizabeth Cochrane really wanted to do was write. A female writer was not a new idea in 1885; Louisa May Alcott had been earning a living as a novelist for nearly twenty years. Elizabeth had probably read *Little Women.* If she did, she knew that Alcott's character, Jo March, stormed a newspaper office to sell her stories.

Elizabeth may have heard tales of women who were newspaper reporters, too. By 1880, almost every major newspaper in the United States paid women to write feature articles, usually essays in letter form, and send them in through the mail. In New York City, a female writer who used the name Jenny June worked in a newspaper office on a day-to-day basis. Another young woman named Sally Joy had talked herself into a job on the Boston *Post* when she was eighteen. Still, compared to New York, Pittsburgh was a small place, and its people had old-fashioned ideas. Elizabeth might never have become a journalist if it hadn't been for a newspaper column titled "What Girls Are Good For."

This essay expressed ideas held by most men in the 1880s. The writer protested the alarming trend of hiring women to work in shops and offices, and called the employment of women in business a threat to the national welfare.

Other unfair, harshly critical remarks filled the column, too. When Elizabeth Cochrane read them, she became so angry that she sat down and wrote a letter to George A. Madden, managing editor of the Pittsburgh *Dispatch.* She didn't use her name in the letter——that wouldn't have been ladylike. Instead, she signed it "Lonely Orphan Girl" and sent it off.

Elizabeth Cochrane (Nellie Bly) as a young newspaperwoman.

George Madden was so impressed by the letter that he wanted to find the author and hire him to work on the *Dispatch.* It never entered his mind that the writer might be a woman. He pictured the writer as a young man who wanted to work for the *Dispatch,* and had deliberately taken the wrong side of the issue to get attention.

On January 17, 1885, an advertisement appeared in the *Dispatch,* asking "Lonely Orphan Girl" to contact Mr. Madden. Once more Elizabeth addressed a note to the editor, but this time she signed her own name. Mr. Madden may have groaned in dismay, imagining some old "battle-ax" with strong feminist views, but he wrote back anyway. She did, after all, write well. He said that he would be willing to consider publishing an article on "girls and their spheres in life" in the Sunday paper if she would write and submit it.

Elizabeth sent in the article as soon as she could get it written, and Madden liked it. He paid her five dollars, and published her work on January 25 under the title "The Girl Puzzle." Then, throwing caution to the wind, Madden wrote to Elizabeth once more to ask if she had any other suggestions for stories. He had no idea how she would respond, but the last thing he expected was that she would turn up several days later at the Fifth Street offices of the *Dispatch.*

Elizabeth Cochrane appeared fragile for her height of five feet five inches. She wore her chestnut-colored hair in a chignon with bangs, a youthful style in those days, and had a jaunty sailor hat on her head. In spite of the determined gleam in her wide hazel eyes, she had a meek and mild appearance. The *Dispatch's* reporters, who shared the one big city room, didn't know what to think of her.

Newspaper offices in the nineteenth century echoed with the clatter of presses from the floors below. The rooms smelled of printer's ink, gaslights, and tobacco, and were filled with a haze of cigar smoke. Chewing tobacco was popular, too, and the men were often careless when they aimed at the spittoons. The floors were filthy. In Sally Joy's city room in Boston, the more gentlemanly reporters put newspapers down so she wouldn't get her long skirts stained with tobacco juice.

Elizabeth Cochrane looked out of place in this setting. A more timid woman would have turned and fled, but her ladylike appearance masked a will of iron. She informed the gawking reporters, sitting at desks crowded together and piled high with copy paper, that Mr. Madden had sent for her. When they directed her to his desk, she introduced herself and said she had come with her ideas.

In the nineteenth century, newspaper offices such as this one were not considered proper places for a young lady to work.

If George Madden was surprised by Elizabeth Cochrane's sudden appearance in his city room, he was shocked by the subject on which she wanted to write. Divorce, she told him, was an issue that needed to be discussed in the newspaper.

Elizabeth tried hard to persuade Mr. Madden to give her a chance. He protested at first, but finally agreed to let her prove she could do what she said she could. He sent her home to write her article on divorce, and probably thought he would never see her again.

Elizabeth, however, tackled her new project immediately. She had the notes on divorce cases that her father had made during his years as a judge, but she had been doing some research of her own as well. Since she and her mother had spent almost all of their inheritance from her father, they had changed addresses several times, each time selecting a less expensive place. By the time "What Girls Are Good For" was printed, they were living in rundown lodgings in a poor section of the city, where Elizabeth had talked to several women who had suffered because of unfair divorce laws.

All night long, Elizabeth worked on her article, writing and revising, scratching out passages and copying it over. At that time there were no word processors and no portable typewriters to make the work easier. Even in the newspaper offices, articles were composed with pen and ink. Despite the long, slow process, Elizabeth persisted until her story was just the way she wanted it. The next morning she returned to the *Dispatch* office with a final draft that was neat and easy to read. More importantly, the article said something. Mr. Madden was impressed and immediately agreed to publish the story.

George Madden was a businessman. He might have believed, as the article in his paper had said, that respectable women stayed at home until they married, or at worst went into a "woman's profession" such as teaching or nursing. Still, he knew the facts. Since the Civil War, women had been working in mills, factories, and offices. The thought of a woman in politics made him shudder, but a woman had run for president in 1884.

In spite of his doubts, Madden found himself encouraging Elizabeth Cochrane. If one thing could overcome his prejudices, it was the promise of a controversial series for his newspaper. Controversy increased a newspaper's circulation, and that was good business.

He asked for more stories, saying that if the series on divorce were a success, he would give Elizabeth a regular job and pay her five dollars a week. She accepted at once.

Madden had only one problem left. He was worried about allowing Elizabeth to use her own name. What would people say if they knew he had hired an eighteen-year-old girl to write on such a sensitive subject as divorce? What would her family say? She had respectable and old-fashioned older brothers who would not approve of her new career.

Just as Mr. Madden and Elizabeth Cochrane agreed to invent a pen name, Mr. Madden's assistant, Erasmus Wilson, began to hum a popular Stephen Foster song. Everyone knew the words:

Nelly Bly, Nelly Bly,
bring the broom along.
We'll sweep the kitchen clear, my dear,
and have a little song.
Poke the wood, my lady love,
and make the fire burn,
And while I take the banjo down,
just give the mush a turn.
Heigh, Nelly, Ho, Nelly,
listen love, to me;
I'll sing for you, play for you,
a dulcet melody.

From that day on, Elizabeth Cochrane was Nellie Bly, and Madden immediately published her articles on divorce. The subject alone was enough to make people sit up and take notice, but the newspaper-reading public of Pittsburgh was just as intrigued by the author. Who was this Nellie Bly? they wondered.

The *Dispatch* made the most of the mystery surrounding its new reporter's identity. Circulation improved dramatically as Nellie wrote more articles. In time, she came up with an idea that would set the tone for her entire newspaper career——she asked Mr. Madden if she could write about life in the slums and factories of Pittsburgh. As a reporter and a reformer, she would tell the real story of her own experiences visiting these places, from a lady's point of view. She would take an artist with her to sketch what she saw. Mr. Madden saw the circulation of the *Dispatch* going up and up . . . and agreed.

Women working in a Pittsburgh bottling factory in the early 1890s.

Nellie brought the broom along, as the song says, and set out to sweep Pittsburgh clean. It needed it. Under smoke-blackened skies, which glowed flame red at night, workers were little more than slaves to uncaring factory owners. Women in a bottle factory worked fourteen-hour days in an unheated building. Children were endangered by living in dirty, disease-ridden, fire-prone buildings in a slum called the Point.

When Nellie Bly joined the staff of the *Dispatch*, more than 156,000 people lived in Pittsburgh. Many were immigrants, drawn by jobs in the iron and steel industries. Few labor unions protected these unskilled workers, and no social service agencies existed.

Nellie brought her discoveries of social injustices to public attention through the *Dispatch*. She was not content to sit at her hard-won desk in the city room, letting others do the research. Every story was her own, from the first idea, through the investigation and writing, to her byline, or name, on the finished article.

A bottling factory was Nellie's first target. The glass industry was Pittsburgh's third largest business; some seventy factories produced half the nation's glass, and more champagne bottles than there were in France. Accompanied by her artist, she located the factory owner and told him she wanted to write an article for the *Dispatch* about his factory. Deceived by her ladylike manner and pleasant smile, he welcomed her with open arms. He thought she was offering him good, free publicity, so he told her to talk to anyone and look anywhere.

Nellie reported on crowded living conditions in the Point, a Pittsburgh slum.

Nellie talked to the workers as the artist sketched. Some of these women stood on an icy cement floor for fourteen hours at a stretch. To cope with the winter cold that seeped through the factory walls, the workers had to wrap rags around their feet, which kept their toes from freezing. Several hundred workers shared one toilet, along with a family of rats. Worse yet was the daily risk of injury from broken or exploding bottles. Since worker's compensation did not exist, an injury could result in the loss of a person's job and only source of income.

Nellie was shocked by the conditions in the factories, and she channeled all her outrage into print. She held nothing back, including names, dates, and drawings. When her article appeared in the *Dispatch*, every copy of that day's paper sold quickly at the city's newsstands.

The factory owners were enraged when they saw Nellie's articles. Letters flooded the *Dispatch* office. Although Nellie faced protests, and even threats, efforts at reform began which eventually improved conditions in the factories of Pittsburgh.

Nellie attacked the slums next. In the course of her own frequent moves, she had seen how crowded many of the city's tenement buildings were. In the Point she found a family of twelve living in one unheated room. In the rickety wooden shanties along Yellow Row, and the ramshackle cottages on the hill at Skunk Hollow, Nellie Bly asked questions and got answers. When she wrote her story, she named the slumlords, hoping to shame them into repairing their buildings.

The run-down tenement houses of Pittsburgh's Yellow Row were another of Nellie's targets.

The uproar this time was even greater than it had been after her article about the factory. Pittsburgh businessmen began to organize against the threat of Nellie Bly. They claimed she was ruining the city's reputation. Despite fourteen thousand chimneys that polluted the air, they still insisted that Pittsburgh was one of the healthiest cities in the United States. In fact, they said that people worked so hard that they didn't notice the smoke. Pollution had killed the grass and flowers, but a child who complained about the foulness of the air was told she should be "grateful for God's goodness in making work, which made smoke, which made prosperity." With that kind of thinking, no wonder the businessmen threatened George Madden with the loss of all his advertising if he didn't stop those reform-minded articles by Nellie Bly.

George Madden's business sense told him it was time to let things cool down. He gave Nellie a raise to ten dollars a week and made her society editor for the *Dispatch*. Nellie Bly began writing about the upper classes, whose parties, art, drama, and books were part of a world far removed from the city's slums.

Plays, lectures, concerts, and charity balls soon left Nellie bored and restless. "I was too impatient," she wrote, "to work along at the usual duties assigned women on newspapers." Yet nearly a year passed before she could persuade Mr. Madden to let her write serious articles again.

A modern jail, Riverside Penitentiary of Western Pennsylvania, had just been built to replace the old Western Penitentiary. It was the most up-to-date facility of its kind, and Nellie wanted to visit it. Her article would be full of praise, she argued. Why not let her cover its opening? Reluctantly, Madden agreed.

In her article, Nellie praised the new facility's separate cells for inmates and large common work and recreation areas, but she used this praise of one jail as a starting point to criticize the rest. When Madden read her attack on other Pennsylvania jails, he knew trouble lay ahead, but he decided to print the article anyway.

Meanwhile, Nellie wanted to take another look at the factories. This time she went undercover, dressing herself as a poor woman looking for a job. She was hired at the first factory where she applied, though she had no skills. Her job was to hitch cables together in an assembly line with other young women. They could be fined for talking, or even for smiling, but Nellie did manage to learn that they all suffered from headaches.

An aerial view of Pittsburgh in the late nineteenth century.

She soon understood why. The light was so dim that her head began to ache, too. Then her feet started to hurt, because she had to stand. Her hands became raw and started to bleed. Before long, she ached all over. Just like the workers in the bottle factory, these young women kept working in spite of their fear of blindness and the constant discomfort. They had to work to live.

The women's supervisor kept urging them to work faster and faster. He paced back and forth behind them, yelling out threats and foul language. Since Nellie had been brought up to have good manners, she found it difficult to listen to curses and insults for hours on end. Finally, Nellie simply walked away from the assembly line to get a drink of water. The foreman fired her.

When Nellie's two stories appeared in the *Dispatch*, the response was overwhelming. The paper's sales increased, and Nellie was criticized by just about everyone. City law enforcement officials said she wasn't qualified to judge their jails. The clergy called her shameless for visiting a men's prison without a chaperon. Again, the factory owners and businessmen of Pittsburgh threatened to withdraw their advertising. Madden raised Nellie's pay to fifteen dollars a week and sent her back to write the society page.

The other reporters of the *Dispatch* appreciated her, even if the targets of her articles didn't. "Only a few months previous I had become a newspaper woman," she wrote, and in October 1886, she became the first woman invited to join the Pittsburgh Press Club.

Sweeping Pittsburgh Clean

Meet the Author

Kathy Lynn Emerson writes for both children and adults. She credits her interest in writing to her grandfather. "Grandpa penned his memoirs when he was in his eighties, paying special attention to stories from his boyhood . . ." Some of Emerson's writing has been based on her grandfather's boyhood experiences. Her work often involves characters who must learn to be more open-minded. "If there is any single theme running through my work, it concerns the dangers of jumping to conclusions about people."

Theme Connections

Think About It

- How did Nellie take a stand about the poor treatment poeple were getting in factories?

- What did Nellie do when taking a stand?

Record Ideas

How was Nellie's way of taking a stand like Gandhi's? Write your ideas in your Writing Journal.

Write a Diary Entry

Nellie Bly wrote about social injustices in her articles for the newspaper. In your Writing Journal, write a diary entry that Nellie Bly may have written after she witnessed the terrible factory conditions in Pittsburgh.

Taking a Stand

Bibliography

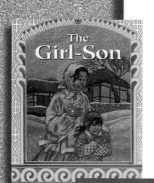

The Girl-Son

by Anne E. Neuberger. What if school were forbidden to you and you had to disguise yourself as the opposite sex to attend? Read about a modern-day Korean educator who had to do just that.

Jane Addams:
Pioneer Social Worker

by Charnan Simon. Jane Addams was a Chicago woman who cared enough about immigrant children to buy a house where they could eat, play, and learn.

Kids At Work: Lewis Hine and the Crusade Against Child Labor

by Russell Freedman. Earlier in this century children as young as three were working in U.S. factories, mines, and fields. Find out how you, as a modern young American, got the right "to play and to dream."

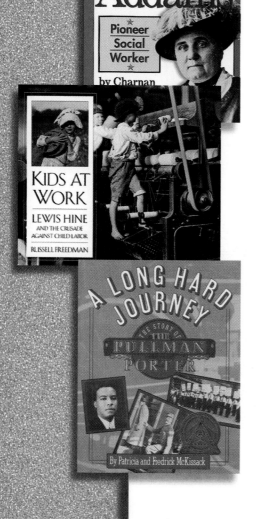

A Long Hard Journey:
The Story of the Pullman Porter

by Patricia and Fredrick McKissack. Read the courageous story of the first black-controlled union, made up of Pullman train porters, and their stand against inequality.

Mandela: From the Life of the South African Statesman

by Floyd Cooper. Nelson Mandela was the world's most famous prisoner who went on to become the President of South Africa. Read about his commitment to his people and his struggles to end apartheid.

Passage to Freedom: The Sugihara Story

by Ken Mochizuki. In 1940, acting against the orders of his government but with the support of his family, Japanese diplomat Chiune Sugihara saved hundreds of Jewish people by writing visas enabling them to leave Lithuania.

Red Scarf Girl: A Memoir of the Cultural Revolution

by Ji-li Jiang. Growing up in Shanghai during the Chinese Cultural Revolution, Ji-li was forced to make decisions that tested her courage and her loyalty to her family.

Run Away Home

by Patricia C. McKissack. When he escapes from the train transporting Geronimo to Alabama, young Sky is helped by an African-American girl and her family.

Beyond the Notes

What is music? What is your favorite music——rock, jazz, classical? Music is all around us and affects each of our lives. Music means different things to different people. What does it mean to you?

The Nightingale

Hans Christian Andersen
translated by Eva Le Gallienne
illustrated by Nancy Ekholm Burkert

In China, you know, the Emperor is Chinese, and all his subjects are Chinese too. This all happened many years ago, but for that very reason the story should be told. It would be a pity if it were forgotten.

The Emperor had the most beautiful palace in all the world. It was built of the finest porcelain and had cost a fortune, but it was so delicate and fragile you had to be very careful how you moved about in it.

The garden was full of exquisite flowers; on the rarest and most beautiful, tiny silver bells were hung, so that people passing by would be sure to notice them. Indeed, everything in the Emperor's garden had been most ingeniously planned, and it was so large that the gardener himself didn't know the full extent of it. If you kept on walking long enough, you came to a wonderful forest with great trees and fathomless lakes. The forest grew all the way down to the deep blue sea; the trees stretched their branches over the water, and large ships could sail right under them. Here lived a nightingale who sang so sweetly that even the poor fisherman——who had so much else to attend to——would stop and listen to her as he drew in his nets at night. "How beautiful that is!" he would say; then he had to get back to his work and forget about the bird. But the next night when he came to tend his nets and heard her singing, he would say again, "How beautiful that is!"

Travelers from all over the world came to the Emperor's city. They were filled with admiration for it, and for the palace and the garden. But when they heard the Nightingale, they all exclaimed, "That's the loveliest thing of all!"

When they returned home the travelers told all about their visits, and the scholars wrote many books describing the city, the palace, and the garden——but not one of them forgot the Nightingale; they kept their highest praise for her. And those who could write poetry wrote exquisite poems about the Nightingale who lived in the forest by the deep blue sea.

These books went all over the world, and at last some of them reached the Emperor. He sat in his gold chair reading and reading, every now and then nodding his head with pleasure when he came to an especially magnificent description of his city, his palace, and his garden. "But the Nightingale is the loveliest thing of all!" the books said.

"What's this?" cried the Emperor. "The Nightingale? I've never heard of her! To think that there is such a bird in my Empire——in my very own garden——and no one has told me about her! I have to read about her in a book! It's positively disgraceful!"

So he sent for his Chamberlain, who was so very haughty that if anyone of inferior rank dared to address him or ask him a question, he only deigned to answer, "Peh!"——which of course means nothing at all!

"I understand there is a highly remarkable bird here called the Nightingale," said the Emperor. "They say she is the loveliest thing in my whole Empire! Why has no one told me about her?"

"I've never heard that name before," answered the Chamberlain. "She's not been presented at Court, I'm sure of that."

"I want her to come here this very evening and sing for me!" said the Emperor. "It seems the whole world knows that I possess this marvel, yet I myself know nothing about her!"

"No! I have never heard that name!" the Chamberlain repeated. "But I shall look for her, and most certainly shall find her!"

But where was he to look?

He ran up and down all the staircases, through all the halls and corridors, asking everyone he met about the Nightingale——but no one knew anything about her. At last he ran back to the Emperor and told him it must be some fantastic story invented by the people who write books. "Your Imperial Majesty shouldn't pay attention to everything that's written down. It's mostly pure imagination."

"But I read this in a book sent me by the High and Mighty Emperor of Japan——therefore it must be true! I insist on hearing the Nightingale. She must be here this very evening! I am graciously inclined toward her——and if you fail to produce her you'll all get your stomachs punched immediately after supper!"

"Tsing-peh!" cried the Chamberlain, and he started running again, up and down the staircases, through all the halls and corridors, and half the Court went with him, for they didn't want to have their stomachs punched——particularly after supper!

They inquired right and left about the marvelous Nightingale, who was known all over the world but had never been heard of by the courtiers in the palace.

At last they found a poor little girl working in the kitchen. She said, "Oh, the Nightingale! I know her well! How beautifully she sings! Every evening I'm allowed to take some scraps of food to my poor sick mother who lives down by the shore. On my way back I feel tired and sit down to rest a moment in the forest, and then I hear the Nightingale! She sounds so beautiful that tears come to my eyes; it's as though Mother were kissing me!"

"Little kitchen maid," said the Chamberlain, "I'll see that you're given a permanent position in the palace kitchen, and you shall even be allowed to watch the Emperor eat his dinner, if only you will lead us to the Nightingale, for we have been ordered to bring her here this evening!"

So, accompanied by half the Court, they set out toward the forest where the Nightingale was usually heard singing. After they had walked some way they heard a cow mooing. "Ah! There she is!" cried the courtiers. "What a powerful voice for such a little creature! But we seem to have heard her before!"

"That's only a cow mooing," said the little kitchen maid. "We still have a good way to go."

Some frogs began croaking in the marshes.

"Lovely!" exclaimed the Court chaplain. "I hear her! She sounds just like little church bells!"

"Those are the frogs croaking," said the kitchen maid. "But we ought to hear her soon."

And then the Nightingale began to sing.

"There she is!" said the little girl. "Listen! Listen! She's up there. Do you see her?" And she pointed to a little gray bird perched high up in the branches.

"Is it possible?" said the Chamberlain. "I never thought she'd look like that! She's so drab and ordinary. . . . But perhaps the sight of so many distinguished people has caused her to lose color!"

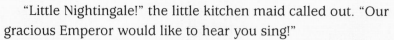

"Little Nightingale!" the little kitchen maid called out. "Our gracious Emperor would like to hear you sing!"

"With pleasure!" said the Nightingale, and sang so that it was a joy to hear her.

"It's like the tinkling of crystal bells," said the Chamberlain. "And look at her little throat——how it throbs! It seems odd that we've never heard her before. She'll have a great success at Court!"

"Shall I sing for the Emperor again?" asked the Nightingale, who thought the Emperor must be present.

"Most excellent little Nightingale!" said the Chamberlain. "It is my pleasure to invite you to appear at Court this evening, where you will delight His Imperial Majesty with your enchanting song!"

"It sounds best out in the forest," replied the Nightingale, but she consented to go willingly since it was the Emperor's wish.

The palace had been scrubbed and polished until the walls and the floors, which were made of porcelain, sparkled in the light of thousands of golden lamps. The finest flowers, those with the silver bells on them, were placed in all the corridors. There was such a coming and going, and such a draft, that all the little bells tinkled so loudly you couldn't hear yourself speak.

In the middle of the Great Presence Chamber, where the Emperor sat on his throne, a golden perch had been placed for the Nightingale. The entire Court was assembled, and the little kitchen maid, who had received the title of Assistant-Cook-to-His-Imperial-Majesty, was allowed to stand behind the door.

The courtiers were dressed in their grandest clothes and they all stared at the little gray bird, to whom the Emperor nodded graciously.

And the Nightingale sang so exquisitely that tears came to the Emperor's eyes and trickled down his cheeks. Then the Nightingale sang even more beautifully——it was enough to melt your heart. The Emperor was so delighted he wanted to give the Nightingale his gold slipper to wear around her neck. But the Nightingale declined the honor with many thanks; she felt she had been sufficiently rewarded.

"I have seen tears in the Emperor's eyes. What could be more precious to me? An Emperor's tears have a mysterious power! I have been amply rewarded!" And she sang again in that sweet, ravishing voice of hers.

"What delightful coquetry!" exclaimed the Court ladies, and they filled their mouths with water and made gurgling sounds in their throats whenever anyone spoke to them. They imagined they were nightingales too! Even the lackeys and the chambermaids admitted to being quite pleased—and that's saying a lot, for they are the most difficult people in the world to satisfy. Yes! The Nightingale was a great success!

From then on she had to remain at Court. She had a cage of her own, and was granted permission to go out twice during the day and once at night; but she had to be accompanied by twelve servants, who each held on tightly to a silk thread fastened to her leg. There wasn't much fun in that kind of an outing!

The whole city talked of nothing but the wonderful bird, and when two people met, one of them had only to say "Nightin" for the other to say "gale"; then they would sigh in perfect understanding. Eleven shopkeepers' children were named after the Nightingale—but not one of them could sing a note, and they were tone-deaf into the bargain.

One day a large parcel arrived for the Emperor, and on it was written, "Nightingale."

"I expect it's a new book about our famous bird!" said the Emperor; but it wasn't a book at all. It was a wonderful example of the jeweler's art, lying in a velvet-lined case——an artificial nightingale that was supposed to be a copy of the real one, only it was encrusted with diamonds, rubies, and sapphires. When you wound it up, it sang one of the real Nightingale's songs and its tail moved up and

351

down and glittered with silver and gold; around its neck was a little ribbon with the inscription, "The Emperor of Japan's nightingale is poor compared with that of the Emperor of China."

"How marvelous!" they all cried; and the messenger who had brought the artificial bird was immediately given the title of Chief-Imperial-Nightingale-Bringer.

"Now let us hear them sing together——what a duet that will be!"

So they sang together, but it didn't turn out very well, for the Nightingale sang in her own free way, while the artificial bird's song was stilted and mechanical. "The new bird is in no way to blame," said the music master. "It keeps perfect time and obeys all the rules of my special method." Then the artificial bird sang by itself and had just as great a success as the real one. And it was so much more beautiful to look at! It sparkled and shimmered like some fantastic jewel.

It sang its one and only tune thirty-three times without ever getting tired. The courtiers would have liked to hear it over and over again, but the Emperor felt it was the real Nightingale's turn to sing a bit. But where was she? No one had noticed, in all the excitement, that she had flown out of the open window, back to her own green forest.

"Here's a nice state of affairs!" cried the Emperor. The courtiers were all furious and accused the Nightingale of rank ingratitude.

"Well! After all, we still have the better of the two birds!" they said. So the artificial nightingale was made to sing again, and though they now heard the tune for the thirty-fourth time, they still hadn't quite caught on to it——for it was very difficult. The music master was loud in his praise of the artificial bird and said it was much better than the real Nightingale, for its outer covering of diamonds concealed the most delicate and intricate of mechanisms.

"You see, ladies and gentlemen——and first and foremost, Your Imperial Majesty!——the real Nightingale is totally unpredictable; she sings on the spur of the moment, and there's no way of knowing what you're going to hear. Whereas with the artificial bird everything has been regulated beforehand. You get just what you expect; there are no surprises! The mechanism can be logically explained. You can

take the bird apart and examine the intricate wheels and cylinders, how one minute cog fits into another, causing it to sing. It's amazing what human skill and ingenuity are able to accomplish!"

"You're absolutely right!" they all agreed, and the very next Sunday the music master was authorized to demonstrate the bird to the common people. "They must hear it sing too," said the Emperor. So they did hear it and were so delighted they seemed quite intoxicated, as though they'd drunk too much tea——for that's what the Chinese drink, you know. They all exclaimed, "Oh!" held up their forefingers, and nodded their heads. But the poor fisherman who had heard the real Nightingale sing said, "Yes! It's pretty enough; it's a fairly good imitation, but there's something lacking——I can't explain just what it is!"

The real Nightingale was banished from the Empire.

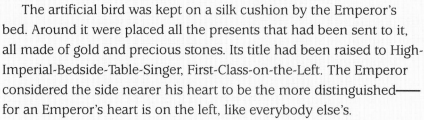

The artificial bird was kept on a silk cushion by the Emperor's bed. Around it were placed all the presents that had been sent to it, all made of gold and precious stones. Its title had been raised to High-Imperial-Bedside-Table-Singer, First-Class-on-the-Left. The Emperor considered the side nearer his heart to be the more distinguished——for an Emperor's heart is on the left, like everybody else's.

The music master wrote five-and-twenty tomes about the artificial bird, so long-winded and so learned and so full of the most complicated phrases that though everybody read them no one could understand a word; but of course they didn't dare admit it——they didn't want to appear stupid, for that would have meant having their stomachs punched, and they didn't like the thought of that!

In this way a whole year passed. By now the Emperor, the Court, and all the Chinese people knew every note and every trill of the artificial bird's song, and they enjoyed it all the more for that; now they were able to join in the singing, which of course they did. Even the street urchins sang, "Zeezee, zee! Gloo, gloo, gloo!" and the Emperor sang it too. It was all perfectly delightful!

But one evening, when the artificial bird was singing away and the Emperor lay on his bed listening to it, something went "crack!" inside the bird——a spring had broken. There was a great whirring of wheels, and the song stopped.

The Emperor leaped out of bed and sent for his personal physician, but there was nothing he could do! So a watchmaker was summoned, and after a great deal of talk and a long and careful examination, he managed to fix the mechanism fairly well, but he said it shouldn't be used too often, as many of the cogs had worn down and would be almost impossible to replace. He couldn't guarantee that the song would ever be the same again. It was a tragic state of affairs! Only once a year was the artificial bird allowed to sing——and even that put quite a strain on it. But the music master made a little speech, full of complicated words, declaring that the song was just as good as ever; and of course that settled it. Everyone agreed it was just as good as ever!

Five more years went by, and the whole country was heavy with grief——for the people were devoted to their Emperor, and now he was sick and the doctors said he hadn't long to live.

A new Emperor had already been chosen, and the people stood outside in the street and asked the Chamberlain if there was any hope of their old Emperor getting well again.

"Peh!" said the Chamberlain, and shook his head.

The Emperor lay in his huge, magnificent bed, so cold and so pale that the courtiers thought him already dead, and they all dashed off to pay court to the new Emperor. The lackeys ran outside to gossip about it, and the chambermaids gave a large tea party. Thick felt had been laid down on the floors of all the halls and corridors to muffle the sound of footsteps; the palace was as quiet as a tomb. But the Emperor wasn't dead yet. He lay there stiff and pale in his magnificent bed with the long velvet hangings and the heavy gold tassels. High up in the wall was an open window through which the moon shone down on him and on the artificial bird by his side.

The poor Emperor could hardly breathe; he felt something heavy weighing on his chest; he opened his eyes and saw that it was Death. He was wearing the Emperor's gold crown, and held the gold sword of state in one hand and the Imperial banner in the other; and from the folds of the heavy velvet hangings strange faces peered out——some hideous and evil, and others mild and gentle. They were the Emperor's good and bad deeds watching him as he lay there with Death weighing on his heart.

"Do you remember this?" they whispered to him one after another. "Do you remember that?" And they reminded him of many, many things——and the sweat stood out on his brow.

"I never knew about all that!" cried the Emperor. "Music! Music!" he shouted. "Strike up the great Chinese gong and drown out their voices!"

But the voices continued, and Death nodded his head, like a real Chinese, in agreement with all that was said.

"Music! Music!" the Emperor cried again. "Precious little golden bird, sing to me! Sing! I implore you, sing! I've showered you with gold and precious jewels. I even hung my gold slipper around your neck with my own hands. Sing to me now! Sing!"

But the bird was silent. It couldn't sing unless it was wound up, but there was no one there to do it. Death kept on staring at the Emperor with his great hollow eyes, and the silence grew more and more terrifying.

Suddenly, through the window, came the sound of an exquisite song. It was the little, living Nightingale perched on a branch outside. She had heard of the Emperor's suffering and had come to bring him hope and comfort with her song. As she sang the phantoms gradually faded away, the blood began to flow more swiftly through the Emperor's feeble body, and Death himself listened and said, "Keep on singing, little Nightingale! Keep on!"

"Yes! If you will give me the golden sword! If you will give me the Imperial banner! If you will give me the Emperor's golden crown!"

And Death gave up the treasures one by one for each song the Nightingale sang. She sang of the peaceful churchyard where the white roses bloom, where the air is sweet with the scent of the elder tree, and where the green grass is moistened by the tears of those who have lost their loved ones. And, as he listened, Death was filled with a great longing to be back in his own garden, and he vanished out of the window like a cold white mist.

"Thank you, thank you!" said the Emperor. "You heavenly little bird——I know you now! I chased you out of my country, out of my Empire. And with your song you have chased the hateful dreams from around my bed; you have driven Death from my heart. How can I ever repay you, lovely bird?"

"You have repaid me," said the Nightingale. "The very first time I sang to you, you gave me your tears——I shall never forget that! Those are the jewels that gladden a singer's heart. But go to sleep now, and wake up well and strong! I'll sing to you!"

The Nightingale sang, and the Emperor fell into a deep sleep; a gentle, refreshing sleep.

When he awoke the next morning the sun was shining through the window, and he felt well and strong again; none of his servants had come back to him, for they thought he was dead, but the Nightingale was still singing.

"You must never leave me!" cried the Emperor. "You need only sing when you feel like singing, and I shall smash the artificial bird into a thousand pieces."

"Don't do that!" said the Nightingale. "It did the best it could! Keep it with you. I can't settle down and live here in the palace, but let me come and go as I like. I'll sit on the branch outside your window and sing to you, so that your thoughts may be serene and joyful; I'll sing of happy people and of those who suffer; I'll sing of the good and evil all around you which is kept hidden from you; for the little songbird flies far and wide——to the poor fisherman, and the peasant in his hut, to all those who are far away from you and from your Court. I love your heart much better than your crown, yet I venerate your crown, for there is an aura of sanctity about it! I shall come and sing for you——but one thing you must promise me!"

"Anything!" said the Emperor, who stood there in his Imperial robes, which he had put on all by himself, holding the heavy golden sword against his heart.

"I ask only one thing of you: Let no one know you have a little bird who tells you everything. It will be much better so!"

And the Nightingale flew away.

The servants and the courtiers came in to attend their dead Emperor. They were struck dumb with amazement when they saw him standing there; and the Emperor said to them, "Good morning!"

The Nightingale

Meet the Author

Hans Christian Andersen was the author of 168 fairy tales. Although best known for writing fairy tales, he also wrote novels, operas, plays, poems, and travel books. *Childlike* seems to be the word that best describes Andersen. He loved to cut animals, castles, goblins, and fairies out of paper while he talked. His story, *The Ugly Duckling*, is said to have been written because he was awkward and unattractive. Andersen must have enjoyed his life, as he once wrote, "My life is a fairy tale."

Meet the Illustrator

Nancy Ekholm Burkert loved to draw and read when she was a child. "As a child I did not see many magazines, and though I remember two or three Disney movies and the 'funnies,' my picture books provided my only source of visual art." She wrote and illustrated her first children's story when she was in the ninth grade. "I illustrate books because I enjoy 'visualizing' a literary work; illustration is like staging a play——designing the sets, the costumes, the lighting, 'casting' the characters."

Theme Connections

Think About It

- Think about what music meant to the characters in "The Nightingale."
- Why did some of the Emperor's subjects prefer the artificial nightingale to the real one?

Record Ideas

In what ways did the real bird prove herself superior to the artificial one? Record your notes and ideas in your Writing Journal.

Research Ideas

- Besides the nightingale, what other birds are common in China? Make a chart showing some different types of birds found in China. Show where they live and write a brief paragraph about the behavior of each bird.

Music

Mary L. O'Neill
illustrated by Janet Montecalvo

Music is a tale told in sounds
Of such infinite reach
All time, all life, all tongues
Are in its speech.
Music is the sound of events
So moving, in its classic or its blue,
The heart nods recognition: "I was there.
And I have felt that, too . . . "

Lady Merida

from ***Stories from the Blue Road***
by Emily Crofford
illustrated by Bill Farnsworth

"Cross over," Josie said.

Her commanding tone aggravated me and I didn't see any reason to walk on the far side of the road just because Mrs. Merida was playing the piano. But which side of the road we walked on didn't seem like a big enough reason to fight with my best friend. I crossed over.

Mrs. Merida lived with Mr. Limon, the plantation owner, and her daughter, the lady from England he had married. Josie remembered the first Mrs. Limon, who had died before my family moved to Arkansas. "It depressed him so bad," Josie had told me, "that he went across the ocean for a vacation——and came back with a new wife."

People didn't say anything in front of Mr. Limon——times were too hard to chance getting put off the plantation——but his mother-in-law made a fine subject for talk behind his back. Some said Mrs. Merida was moonstruck, others came right out with crazy. And she had cancer. They said the cancer and the craziness went together.

Mrs. Merida never visited neighbors or went to the store or to the post office, but some of the kids had seen her walking in the Limons' flower garden. And everybody had heard her playing the piano, which they cited as proof of her madness. Not that we hadn't heard pianos——including the one at school, there were four on the plantation——but none of them sounded anything like Mrs. Merida's. Her music whispered and thundered, stroked and lashed, danced and wept. It made me dream, made me restless, made my heart and my mind yearn for something beyond their ken.

"She's really . . . " Josie traced a little circle by her temple when we were past the house. Set in a grove of oak trees, the Limon house was painted white and had a screened front porch. There were shrubs too, and roses climbing a trellis, and a curving sandy walkway to the front steps. I looked back over my shoulder at the house, walking as slowly as I could so I could hear the piano.

"Mother says she's just eccentric," I said. Mother had never met Mrs. Merida, but she knew Mrs. Limon and liked her.

Josie bounced her hair, which was thick and wavy and the color of a red squirrel. "Well, Papa says she's crazy——and I guess he knows."

Josie's father, Mr. Tomkin, was a ginner, an important position on the plantation. She said that was why he knew all about the lives of the other important people. I liked Mr. Tomkin, but I didn't think it was very nice of him to talk about Mrs. Merida.

Josie put her face so close to mine I could count her freckles. "And furthermore, he says that terrible disease she has is contagious." She bounced her hair again. "That's why she never visits anybody, or even goes to the post office."

Josie's know-it-all attitude and her bossiness really bothered me. Lately it had gotten worse, as if she was trying to see how far she could push me. But I didn't like to argue and I didn't know what to say in Mrs. Merida's defense——for all I knew, maybe Mrs. Merida's disease *was* contagious——so I kept quiet.

After I got home I waited until Bill and Correy went outside to play. Then I told Mother what Mr. Tomkin had said about Mrs. Merida's illness being contagious. Mother was setting up the ironing board and she jerked the legs so hard I thought they would break.

"That's bosh and nonsense!" she exploded. "Cancer is not contagious!" Pulling one of my school dresses over the ironing board, she said, "Meg, would you sweep the kitchen. The clothes have been sprinkled so long they're going to mildew if I don't get them done."

"Sure," I said. I knew she would return to the subject. She only wanted to make the right sentences in her head.

Mother took a flatiron off the stove and touched it with a tongue-moistened finger. The moisture sizzled, she began to iron, and the kitchen filled with a clean, starchy smell.

"People don't mean to be cruel," she said. "It's just that Mrs. Merida and her music are different, so they don't understand them. What they don't understand, they fear; and what they fear, they disparage."

I didn't know the word disparage, but if I asked what it meant she would just tell me to look it up. I had a fair idea about the meaning from the way she had used it, though, so I nodded and reached the broom under the table to sweep out some cornbread crumbs.

"Actually," I told her, "I think Mrs. Merida's music is wonderful, even if you can't clap your hands or sing to it. I don't care what Josie says."

Mother worked the iron around the dress collar. "So do I. Sometimes late at night, when it's still, I can hear it through the bedroom window——so beautiful, so filled with passion." She gave a sad little sigh. "I think Mrs. Merida must play when she's in pain."

"I'd give anything if I could play the piano like that," I said.

"Then why don't you ask her to give you lessons?"

I stopped sweeping and stared at Mother. Even though I didn't believe most of them, considering the number of stories, Mrs. Merida must be at least a wee bit mad. Besides, she was a very important person, and she lived in a very important house. Just thinking about going there was scary . . . and kind of exciting.

Mother set the cooled flatiron back on the stove and picked up the other one. "Meg, believe me——there's nothing to be alarmed about. In fact, the one way Josie's own mother defies her husband is to visit Mrs. Merida."

This time I figured Mother had gotten some wrong information. I couldn't imagine Josie's spiritless, dried-up little mother defying Mr. Tomkin. She could be in the middle of fixing supper and Mr. Tomkin would call from his easy chair in the living room, "Sarah, bring me a glass of water," and without a word she'd stop her work and take him the water. I thought of Mrs. Tomkin as a servant when I thought of her at all.

"Mrs. Tomkin and Mrs. Merida are friends," Mother was saying. "But you must not mention that to anybody——especially not to Josie. Mr. Tomkin pretends he doesn't know, and as long as he thinks no one else knows, it's all right."

I was going to ask her to repeat slowly what she had just said, but the boys charged through the back door, Correy chasing Bill, and ran right through my nice pile of dirt. I threw the broom after them, but I wasn't really all that angry. I knew now how to stand up to Josie! And I would learn to play the piano at the same time.

The next afternoon I left Josie standing on the other side of the road and went up the sandy walkway through the grove of oak trees to the Limon house. Josie had tried to talk me out of it and said she might walk with Peggy's group from now on if I went. That scared me, but it also made me more determined.

It was reassuring to find that the Limons' screened porch creaked just like the porch on our Blue Road house. Mrs. Limon answered my knock. Up close I could see why Mr. Limon had brought her from England. She looked like a movie star, with creamy skin and cornflower-blue eyes.

Clutching my books so tightly that my arm cramped, I stammered, "I——I'm Meg Weston. I wanted to——to talk to your mother about, uh, taking piano lessons."

"Why, yes," she said. "If Mama——that is, nothing like this has happened before."

"Dorothy," a voice behind her said, "will you get out of the doorway so the girl can come in." I liked their accents and wished I could talk that way.

"Hello, Mrs. Merida," I said.

"Lady Merida. Lady Rose Merida."

"Yes, Ma'am, Lady Merida."

She was wearing a soft and shimmery gray dress that went all the way to the floor, but it was only old fashioned, not crazy. She had not torn out hunks of her own hair, as I had heard, and there was no blood dripping from her fingertips either. Her nails were just painted with bright red polish.

Feeling more confident, I continued my inspection. I wanted to be able to describe Lady Merida to Mother. She was terribly thin. Her gray, tightly curled hair topped a small face, and her pale skin was drawn tight over her bones.

Then Lady Merida stepped toward me and my confidence dissolved. Her fierce gaze made the hairs on the back of my neck stand straight out.

"Well, I——I didn't think you would, I mean could, Ma'am. I mean, Lady Merida. I know you're busy." I backed toward the door, ready to run the instant I reached it.

She thrust out a bony hand as if to grab me. "Wait!"

I stopped in my tracks, too terrified to move, and stared at the hand. Blue veins stood out beneath thin white skin, the sinews from her knuckles to her wrists looked like cords, and her red fingernails were filed almost to the quick.

"You want to learn to play. You shall learn!" She pointed her index finger at the piano bench, and on legs more wooden than theirs I moved to it. She sat down beside me. "Put down your books," she said, and added scornfully, "The piano is played with *both* hands."

My hands were shaking so badly, I was sure she'd say something about them, but she didn't, and I quickly forgot my terror during the next thirty minutes as she taught me the connection between the notes on the music sheet, the keys, and my fingers. I was learning fast, I thought. Soon I would be playing like Lady Merida. Once I laughed aloud with the joy of my accomplishment and she smiled a little.

"Did you know I was a concert pianist?" she asked suddenly. She scooted me off the end of the bench and ran her fingers up and down the keyboard. Her hands no longer looked ugly but incredibly graceful. I visualized my own hands moving swiftly over the keys, imagined people around me gasping with admiration.

It started then, the kind of music that made people walk on the other side of the road. "What am I playing?" she demanded.

Drops of sweat crept down from my hairline. Somewhere buried inside all the extra notes I recognized the tune to a song I had heard the older kids singing, but I couldn't remember the title.

"Well, what? They must teach you something at that school."

"It's something about she doesn't love him anymore," I said. "Love has . . ."

Her hands stopped in mid-air; her mouth opened with such horror that it pulled the skin even more tightly over her face.

"That," she said in a quiet, dreadful tone, "is Beethoven's great and immortal Concerto No. 5. The *Emperor* Concerto." She folded her fingers into her palms, then flung them outward. "Blackguards who write asinine tripe to masterpieces should be hanged!" She began to play with the force of her whole body. The piano seemed to be alive, to be breathing its own fury. "Bloody thieves!"

The notes swelled, vibrated, wrapped themselves around me, filled my ears, burst into the space behind my eyes.

Mrs. Limon came in quickly from another room, took my arm, and guided me toward the door. Lady Merida, although she didn't turn to look at me or slow her racing fingers, ordered, "Come back tomorrow. Same time."

The next day I learned to stretch my fingers beyond their reach. When I protested that they wouldn't spread any further, Lady Merida took my hands and showed me that they would. Then she placed my fingers on the keyboard. "Practice!" she said. "Stretch them. Practice!"

Since I didn't have anywhere else to practice playing except at Lady Merida's, she made me spend part of each lesson running up and down scales and playing the same pieces over and over. I didn't mind at first, but after two weeks of the same exercises, it seemed to me that Lady Merida should let me stop doing them. She wouldn't. In fact, when I complained that the exercises were boring she made me practice an extra ten minutes.

But I kept going for the lessons, almost every day except for the times Mrs. Limon met me at the door and told me her mother didn't feel well.

Josie tried everything to get me to quit. I told her playing the piano was important to me and that she might as well give up.

Actually, I was tired of going so often for the lessons. I missed out on a lot of after-school talk. I especially missed standing around in the post office with Josie and the other kids, including boys, while we waited for Miss Hettie, the postmistress, to come back with the mail after meeting the afternoon train.

I had been going for the lessons for a month when I realized that I hadn't really wanted to learn to play the piano. I had wanted to make the piano sound like Lady Merida made it sound. If Josie would stop bullyragging me about going for the lessons, I could quit. I didn't think Lady Merida would mind too much. Sometimes she got a pained expression on her face when I played.

Josie didn't give up, though. She got angry every time I told her good-bye at the Limon house. And finally she said, "I'm going to get myself a new best friend."

I shrugged as if I didn't care, but the truth was that it made me feel sick all over. Josie liked to get her way, she had a quick temper, and she could be mean. But she was more fun than anybody I knew, and she always stuck up for me. There were times when I felt closer to her than to my own family. We could freely tell each other our hurts and dreams, be silly or serious, say we despised somebody without feeling guilty. But even as I told myself that all I had to do was say I wouldn't go anymore, I turned into the Limons' without a word.

Josie kept walking. I stopped before I reached the oak grove to watch her back and the way the sun seemed to set her hair aflame, and she turned around.

"I was," she said——and I heard a quiver in her voice——"going to ask you to stay all night."

"Sure," I said. "If it's all right with Mother. I'd rather spend the night with you than anything." I took a deep breath. "I'm still going for the lesson, though."

"Okay," Josie said. "Come as soon as you can."

I thought about running to hug Josie and talk with her about what we would do that night. School had let out an hour early for a teacher's meeting, and Lady Merida wouldn't be expecting me yet. But Josie had almost caught up with some other kids, so I went on up the walk.

If I hadn't told Lady Merida I would be there, I would have gone home. I had won! I had made Josie understand that my letting her be the leader didn't mean she could bullyrag me. Besides, the air had become light with spring, the sun gifted everything with lazy warmth, and taking a piano lesson inside was the last thing I wanted to do.

Before I reached the porch, I heard the piano and knew immediately that someone other than Lady Merida was playing it. This music was timid and sweet. Starting across the creaky porch, I peered through the partially opened front door. The woman sitting at the piano saw me, jumped up, and darted through the kitchen and out the back way. Mrs. Tomkin, I thought dizzily. Josie's mother! She did visit Lady Merida. She not only visited, she played the piano! She could make music! I realized that Lady Merida was watching me and closed my mouth.

"Since you're here," she said acidly, "come in."

The minute I walked into the living room, she pounced. "You're just like the rest! Insensitive! She"——she pointed a withered arm in the direction Mrs. Tomkin would be taking home through the field——"has the soul of an artist. If she hadn't been deprived as a child, if she wasn't married to that, that . . ."

"He is not either," I said, which surprised me because I never talked back to grown-ups. "Mr. Tomkin is funny——and nice." It was true. Mr. Tomkin had never ignored me like some adults did. He asked me kindly about school and my grades and my favorite subjects.

Her eyes still locked with mine, Lady Merida seemed to be asking herself a question. "Yes," she said. "Yes, I'm going to show you something."

She left the room and returned with a small, framed watercolor. It was so lovely——mountains and sky and sunlit grasses and wildflowers swaying in a breeze——that I sucked in my breath. Since, as Mother told me, I could never win at cards because my face showed everything, Lady Merida knew that I thought the watercolor was beautiful.

"Sarah Tomkin painted this from a childhood memory of her Ozark Mountains," Lady Merida told me. "Up until now I have been the only one on this plantation who knows she has this talent——because she's been ridiculed so often."

We were silent for a minute, and when she spoke again her voice sounded squeezed out. "She can't even read. I don't try to teach her, but she's drawn to the piano like a hungry child."

Instead of giving me my lesson, Lady Merida served us tea in china cups and not-very-sweet cookies that she called biscuits. She talked on and on, sometimes growing bitter about "thieves" who stole not only music but the soul as well. She talked of her childhood, told me about concerts she had played and men who had loved her, and described how the English countryside looked in the spring.

"Meghann," Lady Merida said, and I didn't tell her Meg came from Margaret, "there's nothing wrong with playing church songs and the old familiars, but *listen* to great music, with your senses and with your heart, all the days of your life."

I knew what she was saying, that I would never become a good pianist, and I didn't think it was fair. I had done everything she had told me. Besides, it was one thing for me to think about quitting. It was quite another for Lady Merida to suggest it, and I was certain she was about to.

"You mean you want to stop teaching me?"

She looked into her teacup, which was almost empty, and with a strange little smile said, "No, ducky, I don't want to stop teaching you." She went with me to the door, something she had never done before. "But perhaps not so often, eh? Say——once a week?"

I ran most of the way home, until I got a stitch in my side, and asked Mother if I could spend the night at Josie's. When she said yes, I quickly did my chores, tossed my toothbrush and nightgown and a change of underwear into a pillowcase, and left for Josie's.

The minute I walked into her big, two-story house that had an indoor bathroom, I sensed the excitement and smelled chicken frying. I loved the commotion there, the seven children talking two and three at a time, the laughing and singing, even the arguing.

Mr. Tomkin sat in his easy chair making jokes and asking questions about school. Mrs. Tomkin, as always, moved like a phantom, constantly busy, seldom speaking. I had never really noticed her before, but now I realized that the faded hair she wore in a bun at the nape of her neck had probably once been as lush and red as Josie's. I kept looking for a chance to speak to her in private before supper, but the only time I came close, just as I was about to follow her into the pantry where she stored quarts of fruits and vegetables, Danny and James Lee, Josie's big brothers, came into the kitchen and started teasing me. Danny knelt down in front of me, took both my hands, and said, "Ah, Meggie, hurry and grow up so I can marry you." Then James Lee spun me around and said, "Pay no attention to him, darling, he's fickle. You're *my* girl." My face turned red and I hit them and wished they would keep doing it.

For supper we had fried chicken heaped high on platters at each end of the table, mashed potatoes with milk gravy, two quarts of Mrs. Tomkin's butter beans seasoned with bacon drippings and chopped onion, and watermelon rind preserves. We all said how good it was, Mr. Tomkin first.

"I would like a bit of variety, though," he said, then beamed around the table as if he had a wonderful idea. "I tell you what, let's all save our pennies and buy Mother a cookbook for Christmas."

He had always made remarks like that, and I had credited him with a fine wit, never before seeing below the surface. Knowing as I did now that Mrs. Tomkin couldn't read, I thought that Lady Merida should have gone ahead and called him whatever bad word she'd had in mind. The kids laughed, as they always did when he said something he expected them to laugh at, but this time I understood that some of them——especially Danny and James Lee——laughed out of nervousness. They were afraid to displease Mr. Tomkin. Across from me Danny's biceps jerked after he put his hands in his lap where they wouldn't show. I knew his hands were making fists and that he would like to hit his father.

After supper I got my chance to speak alone with Mrs. Tomkin. Mr. Tomkin and the boys had gone out to slop the pigs. I had drawn scraping the dishes so I'd finished first. The girls were washing and drying and putting away. I heard Mrs. Tomkin going upstairs and quietly followed her. She had her hand on the doorknob to her and Mr. Tomkin's room when I reached the upstairs hall.

"Mrs. Tomkin," I said in a low voice, "Lady Merida showed me the watercolor you did."

She looked around like a frightened deer to see if anybody had heard.

"It's very beautiful," I said.

She blushed and a delicate smile fluttered over her lips.

"Thankee," she said.

When I went to Lady Merida's the next week, I had made up my mind to tell her I couldn't come anymore until fall. After-school softball season had started and I was trying out for sixth-grade pitcher. Josie was trying out for pitcher too, and I really wanted to beat her out. She was not as bossy anymore, but she still had a know-it-all attitude. She said she knew how to slow pitch and fast pitch and how to fake out a batter——that I didn't stand a chance.

Mrs. Limon came to the door. "Mama won't be able to give you lessons anymore, Meg," she said in a shaken voice. "She's very ill."

As I walked toward home, the gravel crunching under my shoes seemed to be saying, "She's dying, she's dying." I looked out over the flat land to where the tree line seemed to cut jagged pieces out of the sky and wondered why I was so upset. Lady Merida had never been patient with me like my teachers at school. She hadn't smiled with pride the way my parents did when I tried hard. We hadn't been friends like Josie and I were. She was not kin I was bound to love whether I liked her or not.

Still trying to figure it out, I turned onto the Blue Road and the crunching changed to a softer, sadder, earthy sound. I went down the grassy bank to the drainage ditch. Violets were growing beside the water. I picked a bouquet and wrapped their stems in a maple leaf I caught as it floated past.

All the way back to Lady Merida's I kept making up speeches, but when Mrs. Limon opened the door, all I said was, "These are for Lady Merida."

"How did you know?" she said. "Violets are her . . . her favorite."

She was going to cry. I glanced away and caught my own reflection in a window glass. My face was streaked with dust and tears.

Nothing had ever stirred the plantation up like what happened when Lady Merida died. She left her piano to Mrs. Tomkin. Not only that, but when Mr. Tomkin tried to sell it, Mrs. Tomkin told him that if he did he'd never get another meal in that house. Now people began to walk on the other side of the road when they passed the Tomkins'. I could sort of see why they did. Take the day Mrs. Tomkin told Josie and me to get our hoes and help weed the garden. She started hoeing and singing like she had a fever. She had changed her hair too. Instead of the bun at the back of her neck, now she plaited it into a crown.

Glowering at me, Josie said, "*You* might have come out all right, but she caught it——at least the crazy part. She's been like this ever since that lady passed on."

Mrs. Tomkin must have heard her, because she leaned her hoe against the garden fence and said, "Come into the house, the both of ye. I'm goin' to play my pieanna. My pie-anna," she said again, wonderingly, "what Lady Merida give me."

She marched into the house. Josie and I trailed behind her, past Mr. Tomkin, who sat forward in his easy chair and asked nervously, "What's the matter, Sarah? It come on you again? You think you better lay down and let the girls fix supper?"

"Hush up," she said.

She sat down at the piano and began to play, at first gentle and timid, like rabbits hopping, then so natural and sweet that it brought a vision of mountain flowers swaying in the wind.

"What's she playing?" Josie whispered.

Josie might have beaten me out for pitcher on the softball team, but she didn't know a thing about music.

"A concerto," I whispered back, and stood there listening with my senses and my heart while the music rose and soared out the window and climbed toward heaven.

Lady Merida

Meet the Author

Emily Crofford grew up in the Arkansas wetlands, where she saw a lot of poverty, prejudice, and sickness. "Although I have spent most of my life in cities, it is the farm country where I grew up that I credit—and sometimes blame—for the part of me that must write." Crofford likes to give hope by writing about humor, beauty, dignity, and caring. She offers this advice to young people who want to write: "Listen. Watch. Feel. Daydream. Read. Then write about what you hear and see and feel and dream." Crofford's other interests include music, watercolor painting, fishing, and camping.

Meet the Illustrator

Bill Farnsworth is an award winning illustrator whose work has been seen on book covers, in magazines, and in children's books for the past nineteen years. His realistic oil paintings have been used in fifteen children's books at the present time. He says of his work, "Every picture I paint has to tell the story 'without words.' "

Theme Connections

Think About It

- What do the Nightingale and Mrs. Tomkin have in common when it comes to music?
- How did Meg's feelings about Lady Merida change and grow over the course of the story?
- How did Josie's mother and Meg change as a result of their friendship with Lady Merida?

Record Ideas

How does being musically gifted affect an individual's life? Record your responses in your Writing Journal.

Write an Ad

Create an ad seeking students for Lady Merida. The ad should list the qualities the ideal student will possess.

Beyond the Notes

FINE Art

Two Young Girls at the Piano. 1892. **Auguste Pierre Renoir.** Oil on canvas. 44 × 34 in. The Metropolitan Museum of Art, Robert Lehman Collection, 1975 (75.1.201). Photograph ©1989 The Metropolitan Museum of Art.

Cycladic Harpest. 2500 B.C. Early Cycladic II. Island marble. 35.8 × 9.5 cm. The J. Paul Getty Museum, Malibu, California.

The Poet Fujiwara no Yasumasa playing the flute by moonlight.
1882. **Tsukioka Yoshitoshi.** Woodblock print. Private collection. Photo:
Art Resource, NY.

The Great Musician

from *Greek Myths*
by Olivia Coolidge
illustrated by Gwen Connelly

In the myth of Orpheus, the Greek love of music found its fullest expression. Orpheus, it is said, could make such heavenly songs that when he sat down to sing, the trees would crowd around to shade him. The ivy and vine stretched out their tendrils. Great oaks would bend their spreading branches over his head. The very rocks would edge down the mountainsides. Wild beasts crouched harmless by him, and nymphs and woodland gods would listen to him enchanted.

Orpheus himself, however, had eyes for no one but the nymph, Eurydice. His love for her was his inspiration, and his power sprang from the passionate longing that he knew in his own heart. All nature rejoiced with him on his bridal day, but on that very morning, as Eurydice went down to the riverside with her maidens to gather flowers for a bridal garland, she was bitten in the foot by a snake, and she died in spite of all attempts to save her.

Orpheus was inconsolable. All day long he mourned his bride, while birds, beasts, and the earth itself sorrowed with him. When at last the shadows of the sun grew long, Orpheus took his lyre and made his way to the yawning cave which leads down into the underworld, where the soul of dead Eurydice had gone.

Even grey Charon, the ferryman of the Styx, forgot to ask his passenger for the price of crossing. The dog, Cerberus, the three-headed monster who guards Hades' gate, stopped full in his tracks and listened motionless until Orpheus had passed. As he entered the land of Hades, the pale ghosts came after him like great, uncounted flocks of silent birds. All the land lay hushed as that marvelous voice resounded across the mud and marshes of its dreadful rivers. In the daffodil fields of Elysium the happy dead sat silent among their flowers. In the farthest corners of the place of punishment, the hissing flames stood still. Accursed Sisyphus, who toils eternally to push a mighty rock uphill, sat down and knew not he was resting. Tantalus, who strains forever after visions of cool water, forgot his thirst and ceased to clutch at the empty air.

The pillared hall of Hades opened before the hero's song. The ranks of long-dead heroes who sit at Hades' board looked up and turned their eyes away from the pitiless form of Hades and his pale, unhappy queen. Grim and unmoving sat the dark king of the dead on his ebony throne, yet the tears shone on his rigid cheeks in the light of his ghastly torches. Even his hard heart, which knew all misery and cared nothing for it, was touched by the love and longing of the music.

At last the minstrel came to an end, and a long sigh like wind in pine trees was heard from the assembled ghosts. Then the king spoke, and his deep voice echoed through his silent land. "Go back to the light of day," he said. "Go quickly while my monsters are stilled by your song. Climb up the steep road to daylight, and never once turn back. The spirit of Eurydice shall follow, but if you look around at her, she will return to me."

Orpheus turned and strode from the hall of Hades, and the flocks of following ghosts made way for him to pass. In vain he searched their ranks for a sight of his lost Eurydice. In vain he listened for the faintest sound behind. The barge of Charon sank to the very gunwales beneath his weight, but no following passenger pressed it lower down. The way from the land of Hades to the upper world is long and hard, far easier to descend than climb. It was dark and misty, full of strange shapes and noises, yet in many places merely black and silent as the tomb. Here Orpheus would stop and listen, but nothing moved behind him. For all he could hear, he was utterly alone. Then he would wonder if the pitiless Hades were deceiving him. Suppose he came up to the light again and Eurydice was not there! Once he had charmed the ferryman and the dreadful monsters, but now they had heard his song. The second time his spell would be less powerful; he could never go again. Perhaps he had lost Eurydice by his readiness to believe.

Every step he took, some instinct told him that he was going farther from his bride. He toiled up the path in reluctance and despair, stopping, listening, sighing, taking a few slow steps, until the dark thinned out into greyness. Up ahead a speck of light showed clearly the entrance to the cavern.

At that final moment Orpheus could bear no more. To go out into the light of day without his love seemed to him impossible. Before he had quite ascended, there was still a moment in which he could

go back. Quick in the greyness he turned and saw a dim shade at his heels, as indistinct as the grey mist behind her. But still he could see the look of sadness on her face as he sprung forward saying, "Eurydice!" and threw his arms about her. The shade dissolved in the circle of his arms like smoke. A little whisper seemed to say, "Farewell," as she scattered into mist and was gone.

The unfortunate lover hastened back again down the steep, dark path. But all was in vain. This time the ghostly ferryman was deaf to his prayers. The very wildness of his mood made it impossible for him to attain the beauty of his former music. At last, his despair was so great that he could not even sing at all. For seven days he sat huddled together on the grey mud banks, listening to the wailing of the terrible river. The flitting ghosts shrank back in a wide circle from the living man, but he paid them no attention. Only he sat with his eyes on Charon, his ears ringing with the dreadful noise of Styx.

Orpheus arose at last and stumbled back along the steep road he knew so well by now. When he came up to earth again, his song was pitiful but more beautiful than ever. Even the nightingale who mourned all night long would hush her voice to listen as Orpheus sat in some hidden place singing of his lost Eurydice. Men and women he could bear no longer, and when they came to hear him, he drove them away. At last the women of Thrace, infuriated by Orpheus' contempt, fell upon him and killed him. It is said that as the body was swept down the river Hebrus, the dead lips still moved faintly and the rocks echoed for the last time, "Eurydice." But the poet's eager spirit was already far down the familiar path.

In the daffodil meadows he met the shade of Eurydice, and there they walk together, or where the path is narrow, the shade of Orpheus goes ahead and looks back at his love.

The Great Musician

Meet the Author

Olivia Coolidge writes books for young people. She has also worked as an English, Latin, and Greek teacher. She was born in London, England, and worked as a teacher in Germany and England. Coolidge moved to the United States in the 1930s, where she continued teaching and writing. She has written many biographies about famous people in history.

Meet the Illustrator

Gwen Connelly has been working as a freelance illustrator and designer since 1980. Before this she worked for several different advertising agencies in the Chicago area. In addition to illustrating children's books, her past work includes creating advertisements and designing merchandising programs. Connelly received her degree in fine art from Montana State University.

Theme Connections

Think About It

Think about how the Nightingale, Lady Merida, and Orpheus used music as a way to express powerful emotions.

Record Ideas

Record in your Writing Journal answers to the following questions.

- Why was Orpheus unable to retrieve Eurydice from Hades?

- Why did Orpheus fail to sing his way into Hades a second time?

Research Ideas

- Compare and contrast the ideas about music and musicians presented in "The Great Musician" with those presented in the previous two stories. Record your ideas in your Writing Journal.

Orpheus with His Lute

William Shakespeare
(KING HENRY VIII, ACT III, SCENE I)
illustrated by Pamela R. Levy

Orpheus with his lute made trees,
And the mountain tops that freeze,
Bow themselves when he did sing.
To his music plants and flowers
Ever sprung, as sun and showers
There had made a lasting spring.

Every thing that heard him play,
Even the billows of the sea,
Hung their heads and then lay by.
In sweet music is such art,
Killing care and grief of heart
Fall asleep, or hearing, die.

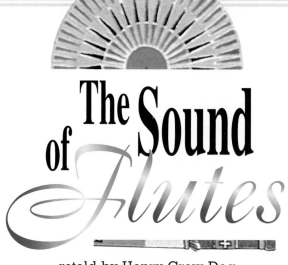

The Sound of Flutes

retold by Henry Crow Dog
illustrated by Paul Goble

Well, you know our flutes, you have heard their sound and seen how beautifully they are made. That flute of ours, the *Siyotanka*, is a very peculiar instrument. It is made for only one kind of music——love music. In the old days, the young men would sit by themselves, maybe lean against a tree in the dark of the night, hidden, unseen. They would make up their own special tunes, their courting songs.

We Indians have always been shy people. A young man hardly could screw up his courage to talk to a *wincincala*——the pretty girl he was in love with——even if he was a brave warrior who had already counted coup upon an enemy.

There was no privacy in the village, which was only a circle of tipis. No privacy in the family tipi either, which was always crowded with people. And, naturally, you couldn't just walk out into the prairie, hand in hand with your girl, to say sweet words to each other. First, because you didn't hold hands——that would be very unmannerly. You didn't show your affection——not by holding hands anyway. Second, you didn't dare take a walk with your wincincala because it wasn't safe. Out there in the tall grass you could be gored by a buffalo, or tomahawked by a Pawnee, or you might run into the U.S. Cavalry.

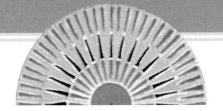

The only chance you had to meet the one you loved was to wait for her at daybreak when the young girls went to the river or brook with their skin bags to fetch water. Doing that was their job. So, when the girl you had your eye on finally came down the water trail, you popped up from behind some bush, and stood so that she could see you——and that was about all you could do to show her that you were interested——stand there grinning foolishly, looking at your moccasins, scratching your ear, humming a tune.

The wincincala didn't do much either, except get very red in the face, giggle, fiddle with her waterbag, or maybe throw you a wild turnip. The only way she could let you know that she liked you, too, was for her to take a long, long while to do her job, looking back over her shoulder a few times, to peek at you.

So the flutes did all the talking. At night, lying on her buffalo robe in her father's tipi, the girl would hear the soulful, haunting sound of the Siyotanka. She would hear the tune made up especially for her alone, and she would know that out there in the dark a young man was thinking about her.

Well, here I am supposed to relate a legend and instead I am telling you a love story. You see, in all tribes, the flute is used as an expression of a young man's love. It has always been so. And whether it is Sioux, or Pawnee, or Cheyenne, or Shoshone, the flute is always made of cedar wood and shaped like the long neck and the head of a bird with an open beak. The sound comes out of the beak. There is a reason for this, and that's where the legend comes in.

Once, untold generations ago, the people did not know how to make flutes. Drums, rattles, bull-roarers, yes——but no flutes. In these long-past days, before the white man came with his horse and firestick, a young hunter went out after game. Meat was scarce, and the people in his village were hungry. He found the tracks of an elk and followed them for a long time. The elk is wise and swift. It is the animal that possesses the love-charm. If a man has elk medicine, he will win the one he loves for his wife. He will also be a lucky hunter.

Our poor young man had no elk medicine. After many hours, he finally sighted his game. The young hunter had a fine new bow and a quiver made of otterskin full of good, straight arrows tipped with points of obsidian——sharp, black, and shiny like glass. The young man knew how to use his weapon——he was the best shot in the village——but the elk always managed to stay just out of range, leading the hunter on and on. The young man was so intent on following his prey that he hardly took notice of where he went.

At dusk the hunter found himself deep inside a dense forest of tall trees. The tracks had disappeared, and so had the elk. The young man had to face the fact that he was lost and that it was now too dark to find his way out of the forest. There was not even a moon to show him the way. Luckily, he found a stream with clear, cold water to quench his thirst. Still more luckily, his sister had given him a rawhide bag to take along, filled with *wasna*——pemmican——dried meat pounded together with berries and kidney fat. Sweet, strong wasna——a handful of it will keep a man going for a day or more. After the young man had drunk and eaten, he rolled himself into his fur robe, propped his back against a tree, and tried to get some rest. But he could not sleep. The forest was full of strange noises——the eerie cries of night animals, the hooting of owls, the groaning of trees in the wind. He had heard all these sounds before, but now it seemed as if he were hearing them for the first time. Suddenly there was an entirely new sound, the kind neither he nor any other man had ever experienced before.

It was very mournful, sad, and ghostlike. In a way it made him afraid, so he drew his robe tightly about him and reached for his bow, to make sure that it was properly strung. On the other hand, this new sound was like a song, beautiful beyond imagination, full of love, hope, and yearning. And then, before he knew it, and with the night more than half gone, he was suddenly asleep. He dreamed that a bird called *Wagnuka*, the redheaded woodpecker, appeared to him, singing the strangely beautiful new song, saying, "Follow me and I will teach you."

When the young hunter awoke, the sun was already high, and on a branch of the tree against which he was leaning was a redheaded woodpecker. The bird flew away to another tree and then to another, but never very far, looking all the time over its shoulder at the young man as if to say "Come on!" Then, once more the hunter heard that wonderful song, and his heart yearned to find the singer. The bird flew toward the sound, leading the young man, its flaming red top flitting through the leaves, making it easy to follow. At last the bird alighted on a cedar tree and began tapping and hammering on a dead branch, making a noise like the fast beating of a small drum. Suddenly there was a gust of wind, and again the hunter heard that beautiful sound right close by and above him.

Then he discovered that the song came from the dead branch which the woodpecker was belaboring with its beak. He found, moreover, that it was the wind which made the sound as it whistled through the holes the bird had drilled into the branch. "*Kola*, friend," said the hunter, "let me take this branch home. You can make yourself another one." He took the branch, a hollow piece of wood about the length of his forearm, and full of holes. The young man walked back to his village. He had no meat to bring to his tribe, but he was happy all the same.

Back in his tipi, he tried to make the dead branch sing for him. He blew on it, he waved it around——but no sound came. It made the young man sad. He wanted so much to hear that wonderful sound. He purified himself in the sweat lodge and climbed to the top of a lonely hill. There, naked, resting with his back against a large rock, he fasted for four days and four nights, crying for a dream, a vision to teach him how to make the branch sing. In the middle of the fourth night, Wagnuka, the bird with the flaming red spot on his head, appeared to him, saying, "Watch me." The bird turned into a man, doing this and that, always saying, "Watch me!" And in his vision the young man watched——very carefully.

When he awoke he found a cedar tree. He broke off a branch, and working many hours hollowed it out delicately with a bowstring drill, just as he had seen Wagnuka do it in his vision. He whittled the branch into a shape of a bird with a long neck and an open beak. He painted the top of the bird's head red with *washasha*, the sacred vermilion color. He prayed. He smoked the branch with incense of burning sage and sweet grass. He fingered the holes as he had watched it done in his dream, all the while blowing softly into the end of his flute. Because this is what he had made——the first flute, the very first *Siyotanka*. And all at once there was the song, ghostlike and beautiful beyond words, and all the people were astounded and joyful.

In the village lived an *itancan,* a big and powerful chief. This itancan had a daughter who was beautiful, but also very haughty. Many young men had tried to win her love, but she had turned them all away. Thinking of her, the young man made up a special song, a song that would make this proud wincincala fall in love with him. Standing near a tall tree a little way from the village, he blew his flute.

All at once the wincincala heard it. She was sitting in her father's, the chief's, tipi, feasting on much good meat. She wanted to remain sitting there, but her feet wanted to go outside; and the feet won. Her head said, "Go slow, slow," but her feet said, "Faster, faster." In no time at all she stood next to the young man. Her mind ordered her lips to stay closed, but her heart commanded them to open. Her heart told her tongue to speak.

"Koshkalaka, washtelake," she said. "Young man, I like you." Then she said, "Let your parents send a gift to my father. No matter how small, it will be accepted. Let your father speak for you to my father. Do it soon, right now!"

And so the old folks agreed according to the wishes of their children, and the chief's daughter became the young hunter's wife. All the other young men had heard and seen how it came about. Soon they, too, began to whittle cedar branches into the shapes of birds' heads with long necks and open beaks, and the beautiful haunting sound of flutes traveled from tribe to tribe until it filled the whole prairie. And that is how Siyotanka the flute came to be—— thanks to the cedar, the woodpecker, the wind, and one young hunter who shot no elk but who knew how to listen.

The Sound of Flutes

Meet the Storyteller

Henry Crow Dog, a Plains Indian, did not write *The Sound of Flutes*. It is a Native American legend that has been handed down through several generations of his people. Henry Crow Dog told this legend and others to a friend who wrote them down. The legends have been collected in a book called *The Sound of Flutes and Other Indian Legends*.

Meet the Illustrator

Paul Goble is a writer and illustrator of Native American books. He was raised in England with a love of the outdoors. As a child Goble enjoyed drawing and hearing stories about pirates, wildlife, and Native Americans. Still interested in Native Americans as an adult, he took his son to the United States to visit Sioux, Crow, and Shoshoni reservations. Goble believes television and movies may give children mistaken ideas about Native Americans. He decided to write and illustrate children's books so he could tell young people what Native American life was really like. Goble now lives in the Black Hills of South Dakota and is an adopted member of the Sioux and Yakima tribes.

Theme Connections

Think About It

Think about how this story and "Lady Merida" describe the difficulty of learning to make music.

Record Ideas

Why is the Siyotanka so important to the Native Americans? Record your notes and ideas in your Writing Journal.

Research Ideas

- Conduct a literature search to locate other Native American legends that deal with music.

On Hearing a Flute at Night from the Wall of Shou-Hsiang

Li Yi

translated by Witter Bynner
illustrated by Cheryl Kirk Noll

The sand below the border-mountain lies like snow,
And the moon like frost beyond the city-wall,
And someone somewhere, playing a flute,
Has made the soldiers homesick all night long.

The Man Who Wrote Messiah

David Berreby

illustrated by Stephen Wells

Barren masts swayed in the wind alongside the mist-covered wharves of Chester, a port in western England. At the steamy, leaded window of the Exchange Coffee House, a large, heavyset man stood anxiously watching idle sailors stomping their feet in the cold. The wind was still unfavorable, and once again no packet boats would be setting out. Yet he had to get to Ireland, and soon.

Once, he had been the toast of Europe, its single most celebrated composer. But by this unpromising day in November 1741, George Frederick Handel was on the verge of financial, and perhaps even artistic, bankruptcy. He was barely one step ahead of his creditors, and his public had abandoned him.

He left the window, settled uneasily on a hard oak chair, and puffed his pipe. It was a day made for glum reflection.

Music had been Handel's passport to the world ever since the day his father, a surgeon in the German town of Halle, had taken him as a youth to the court of Duke Johann Adolf at Weissenfels. His father wanted the boy to be a lawyer.

While the elder Handel attended to business at the court, George Frederick, bored, wandered into the palace chapel and began improvising on the organ. The sound of footsteps made him turn. Standing there, watching, was Duke Johann Adolf.

"Who," the Duke asked, "is this remarkable child?" Handel's father was summoned, and he was told that it would be a crime to make such a prodigy into a lawyer.

George Frederick was a quick study. While still in his teens he left Halle, first for Hamburg, then for Italy, where he mastered the art of composing operas. By his mid-20s, he had set his sights on London, with its lively musical life and money to spare for grand shows.

In 1711, *Rinaldo*, Handel's first opera in Italian for English audiences, played for a remarkable 15 nights to packed houses at the new Haymarket Theatre. It was a success such as the London musical scene had never known, and it launched Handel into society. Dukes and duchesses quit their country estates to hear the opera, and on the city's crowded streets those who had been lucky enough to get tickets whistled its tunes.

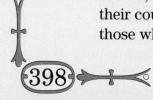

After Handel's "Te Deum" was performed at St. Paul's Cathedral to celebrate a peace treaty in 1713, Queen Anne granted Handel an annual stipend of 200 pounds. With that and his opera receipts, Handel was now probably the best paid composer in the world.

For good measure, Queen Anne's successor, King George I, added 200 pounds to the stipend. And the king also joined the company of many fashionable Londoners by investing thousands in Handel's opera company, the Royal Academy of Music.

The academy was the culmination of Handel's dream. Most musicians depended on handouts from aristocratic patrons. But Handel had learned to be both artist and entrepreneur. Even as he composed, he recruited investors, engaged singers, and performed various administrative duties. As long as his operas pleased the people, they would buy tickets, and the academy would turn a handsome profit.

Investing in Handel seemed a safe bet. At performances of *Amadigi* in 1715, the public kept clamoring to hear arias repeated until finally the theater management banned repetitions so the show could end before dawn. At the opening of *Radamisto* in 1720, unruly crowds fought to get at seats.

Those were the glory days, when all London buzzed with stories of how Handel had refused to be intimidated by patrons or celebrated singers. One tenor had threatened to jump headfirst into a harpsichord if Handel did not alter a tune. "That," the composer replied, "would be vastly more entertaining than your singing." And when a soprano announced she would not sing her part the way he'd instructed, Handel told her she would, or he would drop her out a window. Then he picked her up and headed for the nearest sill.

But by the mid-1720s, Handel's fortunes began fading. Audiences dwindled, and in 1728 the academy had to declare bankruptcy. Also that year, poet John Gay offered *The Beggar's Opera,* a parody of Italian opera, sung in English. It was a huge hit, and spawned a fad for shows with catchy music and English lyrics. The new craze was another nail in the coffin of Handel's Italian repertory.

But he kept on composing and doggedly producing his operas. In 1737 stress and overwork brought on an attack of the "palsy," which took away the use of four fingers of his right hand. Letters expressing concern about his decline flew across England and to the Continent. The future Frederick the Great of Prussia wrote his royal cousins in England, "Handel's great days are over, his inspiration is exhausted and his taste behind the fashion."

It was a desperate Handel who left England that summer for a cure at the famous hot springs of Aachen in Germany. There, he sat each day in the bubbling water. Little trays floated by bearing simple meals and snacks. It was a pleasant place, and it cheered him.

He had not been there long when one afternoon he left the baths and dressed quickly. Several hours later, he had not returned for his next treatment. The nuns who tended the spa grew concerned. Then, from the abbey church, came a burst of glorious music. Habits flying, the nuns ran to investigate. There was Handel, his health unaccountably restored, happily improvising on the organ.

But the return of Handel's health was not accompanied by a return of his operas to public favor. He was deep in debt, and his savings were exhausted by past operatic ventures.

For several years, he barely kept his head above water by giving concerts, as opera after opera failed. By the summer of 1741 Handel, age 56, must have wondered if the time had come to give up the stage altogether.

One morning a servant brought a thick bundle of papers, wrapped in parchment. It was a text assembled by one of Handel's wealthy admirers, a part-time poet named Charles Jennens.

Jennens had been trying for years to interest Handel in setting his words to music. He had already sent Handel a dramatization of the Biblical story of Saul and David. Handel wrote an oratorio, a sort of stripped-down opera performed by singers in ordinary clothes without scenery, but it was not a success. How could it be? No special effects, no grand costumes.

Handel surveyed this new script. Like Jennens's earlier effort, its plot was taken from the Bible. But this was different. The text actually *was* the Bible. Jennens had skillfully assembled Old and New Testament quotations into a stirring narrative of Christ's birth, sacrifice, and resurrection. He had called the piece *Messiah*.

It began with a prophecy from Isaiah, promising deliverance: "Comfort ye, my people." Here were words of solace so simple and familiar that they seemed to draw melody from Handel as easily as he breathed. He was deeply inspired.

The Lord Lieutenant of Ireland had invited Handel to Dublin to present a work for charity. Here was an occasion that would at least benefit those in greater need. Handel set to work.

He composed confidently. He began the *Messiah* on August 22, and 23 days later he was done. This music had given him something more precious than box-office appeal——it had given him hope.

Handel roused himself, paid his bill, and left the Chester coffeehouse. He wandered back to the Golden Falcon Inn. It was a far cry from the palaces and spas to which he had been accustomed. As he entered his small room, he was again fighting despair. After so monumental an effort, was his music to be stopped by the exigencies of wind and tide? He went to bed with a troubled mind, trying to rekindle the hope that the miraculous composition had engendered in him.

The next morning the wind had changed!

Dublin's music-lovers were expecting something extraordinary. Handel had been rehearsing his new work for months, and now the leading newspaper was requesting that at the opening performance ladies not wear hoops in their skirts and "gentlemen come without their swords" to permit an extra 100 people to fit into the theater on Fishamble Street.

It was a hot, noisy crowd that Handel saw as he sat down at the harpsichord on April 13, 1742. He looked at his small force of instrumentalists and nodded. Without further ceremony, on the serene tones of its opening sinfonia, the *Messiah* entered the world.

Before it was over, the music had moved Dubliners to tears. Reviewers were ecstatic.

The next performance was so enthusiastically attended that panes of glass were removed to keep the hall from overheating. Best of all, the work proved a windfall for charity. Four hundred pounds went to hospitals and infirmaries, and 142 prisoners were freed from prison after the *Messiah* paid their debts.

But the London première of the *Messiah* on March 23, 1743, was a different story. Sermons were preached against it. Was the Bible a text to be sung by actors for mere entertainment? And the audience that *did* seek entertainment was disappointed by the lack of action and showy arias. Later, these opera zealots hired thugs to beat people who went to see Handel's works.

No matter, thought Handel. His renewed inspiration extended to other pieces. *Samson*, *Judas Maccabaeus*, and the *Music for the Royal Fireworks* were all successes. He also had failures. But with renewed faith, he went about writing the best music he could. When friends commiserated about the empty seats at a performance of *Theodora*, Handel shrugged and replied, "The music will sound the better."

Through thick and thin, Handel stubbornly clung to his beloved *Messiah*, offering it every year for charity during the last decade of his life. London audiences began to flock to the performances. When King George II heard the oratorio for the first time, the story goes, he could not contain his enthusiasm. As trumpets rang out in the great Hallelujah chorus, he rose to his feet. A stir went through the audience and, in a rustle of silks and clanking of swords, everyone else stood up. To this day, when the joyous strains of this chorus are heard, audiences in the English-speaking world stand.

The mysteriously powerful inspiration that gave birth to the *Messiah* restored Handel's wavering confidence and helped save him from ruin and obscurity. Though late in life he went blind, he still composed and played the organ. It was after the blind composer had conducted a performance of *Messiah* that he fainted and had to be carried home. He lingered through the night of Good Friday, April 13, 1759——17 years to the day after the *Messiah*'s Dublin première. In the early-morning hours, George Frederick Handel died.

But to the delight of listeners of all faiths throughout the world, his *Messiah* lives.

The Man Who Wrote Messiah

Meet the Author

David Berreby writes mostly about science and behavior, linguistics, and social psychology. He has been writing most of his life. "It's just one of those things that I have always done." He was influenced by a writing teacher who taught him "about how to see, how to notice things. He taught us to pay attention." Berreby says that writing isn't "throwing something down on paper" and being content with it. "It's doing it again and again until it's right." To be a good writer, he says you need to be very observant, and you need "persistence, absolute stubborn persistence." He lives in Brooklyn, New York.

Meet the Illustrator

Stephen Wells, a watercolor artist, finds his inspiration in painting the places, things, and people of the Southwest. Working as a professional illustrator and painter, Wells says, "Texas alone provides everything an artist needs, from the life of a working fisherman in the gulf to a dust-covered rancher in west Texas. There is a way of life in paint for others to see." Since graduating from Northwestern University in 1979, Wells has been hired to produce pieces of art for ad agencies, corporations, the U.S. Navy, the Smithsonian Museum, and many others. Wells is married and makes his home in Houston, Texas, but travels the region looking for people and places to "record" with his brush.

Theme Connections

Think About It

Think about what Handel, Mrs. Tomkin, and the Nightingale had in common.

Record Ideas

Research the many different occupations that relate to music. Select one occupation and explore the steps you would have to take to pursue such a career.

Write an Ad

Use your imagination in writing an ad for Handel's newest musical. What would this kind of ad look like?

What Is Jazz?

Mary L. O'Neill
illustrated by Eric Velasquez

Jazz is a swoony
Syncopated beat
In through the eardrums
Out through the feet.
Rackety, coaxie,
Blast that beat
Whop it sassy
Sound it sweet
Clap, stomp, shout,
Blow surprise,
Shoot that trumpet
Till it cries
All the teardrops
In your eyes . . .

The Weary Blues

Langston Hughes • *illustrated by Eric Velasquez*

Droning a drowsy syncopated tune,
Rocking back and forth to a mellow croon,
　I heard a Negro play.
Down on Lenox Avenue the other night
By the pale dull pallor of an old gas light
　He did a lazy sway. . . .
　He did a lazy sway. . . .
To the tune o' those Weary Blues.
With his ebony hands on each ivory key
He made that poor piano moan with melody.
　O Blues!
Swaying to and fro on his rickety stool
He played that sad raggy tune like a musical fool.
　Sweet Blues!
Coming from a black man's soul.
　O Blues!
In a deep song voice with a melancholy tone
I heard that Negro sing, that old piano moan——
　"Ain't got nobody in all this world,
　Ain't got nobody but maself.
　I's gwine to quit ma frownin'
　And put ma troubles on the shelf."
Thump, thump, thump, went his foot on the floor.
He played a few chords then he sang some more——
　"I got the Weary Blues
　And I can't be satisfied.
　Got the Weary Blues
　And can't be satisfied——
　I ain't happy no mo'
　And I wish that I had died."
And far into the night he crooned that tune.
The stars went out and so did the moon.
The singer stopped playing and went to bed
While the Weary Blues echoed through his head.
He slept like a rock or a man that's dead.

Ray and Mr. Pit

from ***Brother Ray: Ray Charles'
Own Story*** by Ray Charles and David Ritz

*Ray Charles was born in Albany, Georgia, in 1930, and spent his
boyhood in the little town of Greensville, Florida. When he was five, he
began to lose his sight. He was blind by the age of seven. Ray Charles has
never let his blindness interfere with his passion for music, and he began
performing while still a teenager. His music is often called rhythm and
blues, but he embraces many forms——from country-and-western to old-
fashioned ballads——fashioning them with his unique style.*

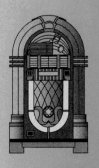

nd then there was music. I heard it early, just as soon as I was seeing or talking or walking. It was always there——all shapes, all kinds, all rhythms. Music was the only thing I was really anxious to get out of bed for.

I was born with music inside me. That's the only explanation I know of, since none of my relatives could sing or play an instrument. Music was one of my parts. Like my ribs, my liver, my kidneys, my heart. Like my blood. It was a force already within me when I arrived on the scene. It was a necessity for me——like food or water. And from the moment I learned that there were piano keys to be mashed, I started mashing 'em, trying to make sounds out of feelings.

Sometimes I'm asked about my biggest musical influence as a kid. I always give one name: Mr. Wylie Pitman. I called him Mr. Pit.

Now you won't find Mr. Pit in any history of jazz . . . but you can take my word for it: Mr. Pit could play some sure-enough boogie-woogie piano. And best of all, he lived down the road from us.

Red Wing Café. I can see the big ol' red sign smack in front of me right now. That was Mr. Pit's place. It was a little general store where he and his wife, Miss Georgia, sold items like soda water, beer, candies, cakes, cigarettes, and kerosene. Mr. Pit also rented out rooms.

Mama and me were always welcome there and, in fact, during one period when we were really down and out, we lived at the Red Wing Café for a while.

Mr. Pit's place was the center of the black community in Greensville, and when you walked into the café you saw two things——right off——which shaped me for the rest of my life.

Talkin' 'bout a piano and a jukebox.

Oh, that piano! It was an old, beat-up upright and the most wonderful contraption I had ever laid eyes on. Boogie-woogie was hot then, and it was the first style I was exposed to. Mr. Pit played with the best of them. He just wasn't interested in a musical career; if he had been, I know he would have made it big. He just wanted to stay in Greensville and lead a simple life.

Well, one day when Mr. Pit started to playing, I waddled on up to the piano and just stared. It astonished and amazed me——his fingers flying, all those chords coming together, the sounds jumping at me and ringing in my ears.

You'd think an older cat would be put off by this young kid hangin' round. Not Mr. Pit. Maybe that's 'cause he and Miss Georgia didn't have children of their own. But for whatever reasons, the man treated me like a son; he lifted me on the stool and put me right there on his lap. Then he let me run my fingers up and down the keyboard. That was a good feeling, and forty-five years later, it *still* feels good.

I tried to figure out how he could make all those notes come together. I was a baby, but I was trying to invent some boogie-woogie licks of my own.

Some days I'd be out in the yard back of the house. If I heard Mr. Pit knocking out some of that good boogie-woogie, I'd drop what I was doing and run over to his place. The man *always* let me play.

"That's it, sonny! That's it!" he'd scream, encouraging me like I was his student or his son.

He saw I was willing to give up my playing time for the piano, so I guess he figured I loved music as much as he did. And all this was happening when I was only three.

I couldn't spend enough time with that gentleman. I was there for hours——sitting on his lap, watching him play or trying to play myself. He was a patient and loving man who never tired of me.

"Come over here, boy, and see what you can do with this pie-ano," he'd say, always helpful, always anxious to teach me something new. And when I look back now, I know he saw something in me, felt something in me, which brought out the teacher in him.

The jukebox was the other wonder. There was a long bench at Mr. Pit's place, and I had my special place, right at the end, smack against the loudspeaker. That's where I would sit for hours, enthralled by the different sounds.

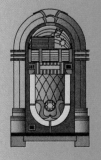

Ray and Mr. Pit

Meet the Authors

Ray Charles is a popular singer, pianist, and songwriter. He was born Ray Charles Robinson, September 30, 1930, in Albany, Georgia. "I was born with music inside me. From the moment I learned that there were piano keys to be mashed, I started mashing them." When he became a performer he dropped his last name because his name was so similar to that of the boxer, Sugar Ray Robinson. Charles is best known for performing soul music, although he has also had success with country-and-western music and rhythm and blues. Charles has said, "I look at music the same as I look at my bloodstream, my respiratory system, my lungs. It's something I have to do."

David Ritz was born in New York City. He is married to Roberta Plitt, a comedienne, and they have twin daughters. Ritz has worked as a copywriter, writer, and teacher.

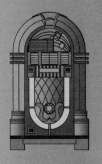

Theme Connections

Think About It

- Why did Ray Charles devote his life to a career in music?

- Why did Ray Charles write the selection "Ray and Mr. Pit"?

Record Ideas

"Ray and Mr. Pit" is a personal narrative in which Ray Charles tells about an influential experience in his life. Think about something that has become important to you—perhaps music or another art form or a sport—and write about an event or incident you experienced as a result of this interest. Record your experience in your Writing Journal.

Create a Blues Time Line

Check for books on rhythm and blues in the library. Create a time line showing where rhythm and blues originated and how it developed. Who are some other famous rhythm-and-blues performers?

What Is Music?

from ***Music Is My Mistress***
by Edward Kennedy Ellington
illustrated by Christine Pratt

*Edward Kennedy Ellington was born in Washington, D. C., in 1899.
Before he was even in high school, a friend decided that Edward should
have an elegant-sounding title. He gave Edward the nickname by which
he was known for the rest of his life: Duke. Until his death in 1974,
Duke Ellington performed music with his band. The music was jazz,
and he transformed it with a special Ellington sound that became
world-famous. For fifty years, Duke Ellington was a major force
in the music world. His influence is still felt.*

What is music to you?
    What would you be without music?

Music is everything.
Nature is music (cicadas in the tropical night).

The sea is music,
The wind is music,
Primitive elements are music, agreeable or discordant.

The rain drumming on the roof,
And the storm raging in the sky are music.

Every country in the world has its own music,
And the music becomes an ambassador;
The tango in Argentina and calypso in Antilles.

Music is the oldest entity.

414

A baby is born, and music puts him to sleep.
He can't read, he can't understand a picture,
But he will listen to music.

Music is marriage.

Music is death.

The scope of music is immense and infinite.
It is the "esperanto" of the world.

Music arouses courage and leads you to war.
The Romans used to have drums rolling before
   they attacked.
We have the bugle to sound reveille and pay homage
   to the brave warrior.

The Marseillaise has led many generations to victories
   or revolutions;
It is a chant of wild excitement, and delirium, and pride.

Music is eternal,
Music is divine.

You pray to your God with music.

Music can dictate moods,
It can ennerve or subdue,
Subjugate, exhaust, astound the heart.

Music is a cedar,
An evergreen tree of fragrant, durable wood.

Music is like honor and pride,
   Free from defect, damage, or decay.

Without music I may feel blind, atrophied,
   incomplete, *inexistent*.

415

Midori
Brilliant Violinist

by Charnan Simon

The crowd at Tanglewood Music Festival was happy. Sitting under the stars on a hot summer night, they were enjoying the music of the Boston Symphony Orchestra. Led by the famous conductor Leonard Bernstein, the orchestra was playing Bernstein's own composition—"Serenade for Violin and String Orchestra."

At the center of the huge concert stage stood a tiny figure—the soloist. She was a Japanese-born violinist named Midori. Just fourteen years old, Midori was a student at the Juilliard School in New York City. But she was playing with all the skill and artistry of a grown-up.

All went well through the first four movements of the Serenade. Then, suddenly, a string snapped on Midori's violin. Unable to play without this E-string, Midori borrowed a violin from a member of the orchestra. A few minutes later, that E-string on that violin snapped, too. Midori had to borrow yet another violin.

When she finished her breathtaking performance, the audience, orchestra, and conductor (Leonard Bernstein) all gave Midori a standing ovation.

The young musician's predicament might have rattled a much more experienced performer. Twice, Midori's concentration had been broken. Twice, she had to stop playing to borrow a violin. To make things worse, each of the borrowed instruments was larger than her own specially made violin. Surely, everyone would have understood if the young violinist had seemed upset or made mistakes.

But Midori was unruffled. She finished playing the difficult serenade flawlessly, as if nothing out of the ordinary had happened. When the music ended, the audience leaped to their feet, cheering. Leonard Bernstein and the entire orchestra joined the audience in giving Midori a standing ovation. Here was a true musician!

After her performance at Tanglewood on July 26, 1986, Midori was famous. Front-page headlines in *The New York Times* announced: "Girl, 14, Conquers Tanglewood with 3 Violins!" Only Midori remained unfazed. "What else could I do?" she asked after the concert. "My strings broke, and I didn't want to stop the music."

Midori has never wanted to stop the music. She was born Mi Dori Goto on October 25, 1971, in Osaka, Japan. Her mother, Setsu Goto, was a well-known violinist. Setsu often

Osaka, Japan, where Midori was born.

took her young daughter with her to rehearsals, where Midori napped while her mother practiced.

One day, when Midori was just two years old, her mother heard her humming. Setsu Goto was astonished. The toddler was humming a difficult Bach concerto——music that Setsu had been rehearsing two days earlier. It was time for Midori to begin music lessons!

Midori was given her own violin on her third birthday. It was tiny, just large enough for her fingers to reach the strings. Every day, Setsu gave Midori a music lesson. Then Midori practiced in the kitchen while her mother made dinner.

By the time she was eight, Midori's talent was impressing many people. A family friend convinced Setsu to make a tape recording of Midori's favorite pieces. The tape was sent to Dorothy DeLay, a famous violin teacher at the Juilliard School of Music in New York.

Dorothy DeLay called Midori's playing "absolutely extraordinary." She immediately invited the young Japanese violinist to attend the Aspen Summer Music Festival in Colorado.

Midori and her mother traveled to the United States in the summer of 1981. Not yet ten years old, Midori amazed everyone who heard her play at the Aspen Festival. The world-famous violinist Pinchas Zukerman described her performance as a "miracle." And, best of all, Dorothy DeLay accepted Midori as her pupil at the Juilliard School.

By the fall of 1982, Midori and her mother had settled into a small studio apartment in New York City. It was hard to leave their home and friends in Osaka, but New York offered more opportunities for Midori and her music.

Eleven-year-old Midori threw herself into her new life. She worked hard to improve her English and made friends with her American classmates. She learned what it was like to take violin lessons from someone other than her mother. She adjusted to the bewildering sights and sounds of bustling New York. "It was very difficult," she admits. "It was the first time I went to a music school, the first time I had a teacher. Also, I had never been around so many kids before!"

The Juilliard School in New York City, where Midori studied music.

And it was an exciting time. Shortly after she moved to New York, the famous conductor Zubin Mehta heard Midori play. He was so impressed that he invited her to perform with the New York Philharmonic Orchestra at its 1982 New Year's Eve concert. Midori received a standing ovation that night——and many invitations to play at other concerts around the world.

Now Midori had to juggle school, music lessons, daily practice sessions, and a growing number of performances. At first, she played at only a few concerts every year. Midori had much to learn about life as a performing artist. She had to learn the simple things, such as the proper way to walk on and off a stage. She also had to learn the complicated things, like how to play with different orchestras led by different conductors on different stages. She had to travel hundreds of miles and then play her violin the very next day. It was hard work for a young girl, but Midori loved it.

"My happiest times are spent playing the violin," she explains. "I just love the feeling of standing on a stage; it's the place I feel safest. And when I'm playing with an orchestra, it's really a magical moment, because then it's a hundred of us joined in producing one thing——music."

After Midori's triumph at Tanglewood in 1986, she received even more invitations to perform. Finally, in 1987,

Midori has performed with the world's greatest orchestras, such as the London Symphony Orchestra.

when she was not yet sixteen years old, Midori left Juilliard. From now on, she would be a full-time professional violinist.

Not everyone agreed with Midori's decision. Some people felt it was too soon for her to stop taking music lessons. They said Midori still needed a teacher to guide her. They said that playing concerts so often would be too hard on such a young girl.

But Midori had always worked hard to get what she wanted. She would continue her regular classes at the Professional Children's School. She would take her schoolwork with her when she traveled to concerts. But she no longer felt she needed violin lessons. She wanted to perform!

And so she has. Since 1987, Midori has appeared on stages all around the world. She has met and played with some of the world's greatest musicians. Many times, she has been the youngest person on stage, but her performances have always been outstanding.

Midori has performed as many as ninety concerts in one year, but she prefers to play only about seventy. That is still more than one performance a week! "This way, I have time to practice and be in the best shape," she says. "I need some time off—and away from the violin—to think about the piece."

Besides performing, Midori likes to record her favorite pieces on albums, tapes, and CDs. She made her first recording in 1986, when she was only fourteen years old. She has also played at the White House and made many television appearances——including one on the 1992 Winter Olympic Games telecast.

Midori has received many awards for her work. In 1991, she was given New York State's Asian American Heritage Month Award. And though Midori now considers herself a New Yorker, she never forgets her Japanese heritage. She makes concert tours in Japan and says, "I like Japan, and I like coming back." Japan likes Midori, too.

She was given Japan's Crystal Award for her contribution to the arts, and in 1988, the Japanese government named her Best Artist of the Year.

People like Midori, who show extraordinary talent as children, are often called "prodigies." Sometimes these highly talented children grow up to be equally talented adults. But sometimes their brilliance seems to fade away. Some people worried that Midori would "burn out" as she grew up.

Fortunately, this has not happened. Now a young adult, Midori is still growing as a musician. Critics still describe her performances as "brilliant," "exquisite," and "breathtaking."

Midori herself is more modest. "I don't know what I'd call myself, but I don't really consider myself a prodigy. I think a lot about music, but it keeps changing because I'm still growing. I go to concerts, opera, ballet, and museums; I adore reading. I never want to finish studying or growing."

When Midori was a teenager, she sometimes wondered what it would be like to have a different career. She considered going to college. She thought she would like to study French or history, or maybe become an archeologist.

But nothing could ever really compete with her music. "The longest I have ever been away from my violin is a day, and I missed it terribly," she told one interviewer. "It's hard to think of anything that brings me such joy as my work."

Midori performs at the Aspen Musical Festival.

Midori has also performed at the world-famous Carnegie Hall in New York City.

Practicing, performing, and traveling leave Midori very little spare time, but she loves to read and shop. She enjoys cooking even though she doesn't like to eat much——except dessert. "That's the only time my mom forces me to do anything," she admits. "She tells me to eat!"

Midori considers herself lucky to have a mother who has always supported her interest in music. She knows that not all children are so fortunate. So, to help make music available to every child, Midori has set up a foundation. The Midori Foundation hopes to offer lecture-demonstrations, produce music videos, and establish musician-in-residence programs in schools around the world. As Midori says, "Music should be an enjoyable and enriching experience that can enhance a child's life."

Certainly music has enriched Midori's life. Those who know her are not surprised that she wants to share her joy in music with others. "I love playing," she says simply. "It isn't like there's me and then there's the violin. The violin is me. I love it so much that I want to share it with other people."

Midori
Brilliant Violinist

Meet the Author

Charnan Simon lived in Ohio, Georgia, Oregon, and Washington while she was growing up. She worked as an editor for *Cricket* magazine before becoming a freelance writer. Simon has written many books and articles for children. She enjoys writing about history and also likes writing biographies and fiction. She now lives in Chicago, Illinois.

Theme Connections

Think About It

Think about how this selection reminds you of any others you have read in this unit.

Midori's schedule is filled with challenge and sacrifice. Discuss with your classmates the personal qualities one must possess to succeed as a professional musician.

Record Ideas

Compare Midori's feelings about music with Ray Charles and Handel's. Record your ideas in your Writing Journal.

Listen to a Recording

From the school or local library, borrow a recording of violin music. Then, with a partner, listen to the music. When you have finished listening, draw a picture of what you visualized while listening. Then share your thoughts and artwork with your classmates.

Mr. Einstein's Violin

Melissa Milich
illustrated by Jim Roldan

In the fall of 1922 Mr. Albert Einstein came to Japan. I was just a little boy then, and people say, "How can you remember?" but I do.

Many guests came to our home during those years and sat in the great wingback chairs in my father's study. But only one bounced me on his knee. That was Mr. Albert Einstein.

There was much cause for celebration when Mr. Albert Einstein decided to visit Japan. Other scientists considered Mr. Einstein the greatest scientist in the world, even when they didn't understand the things he discovered. He had just been awarded the Nobel Prize.

If you were ever to win a Nobel Prize, it would probably change your life enormously, but Mr. Albert Einstein didn't care that he was famous. He had holes in the elbows of his sweaters, and his socks bagged around his ankles. My father called Mr. Einstein's shabby wardrobe his thinking clothes.

Mr. Albert Einstein came in November, when the days had cooled down enough for little boys and girls to sleep well at night, and thus we were put to bed early, perhaps before we were ready. That first night he told long stories to my parents after dinner, and the talk drifted down the hall to my room, where I lay awake, listening. I didn't know the words in the stories he told, but I understood the sadness in them.

Bad dreams. I woke up wanting to cry. Then I realized that a low, mournful weeping sound was already coming from the hallway. I rubbed my eyes, thinking someone had forgotten to turn off the shortwave radio.

But this curious weeping didn't come from the radio. Tiptoeing into the hall, I discovered that it came from the violin of Mr. Albert Einstein.

He sensed that someone was watching him play and turned around to face me. I saw his mouth, eyes, nose, and mustache crinkle together in a big smile, and I knew I would not be in trouble for getting out of bed so late at night.

He tried to speak to me in words, but I could not understand his language. So instead he played the violin, in short, enthusiastic bursts as though telling me something very exciting.

Music and mathematics are the same. He pulled the bow across the strings in a way I had never heard, and the sound made pictures in my head of the moon and the sunlight and my honored grandparents.

This is my latest mathematical equation. I scribbled it just today. The notes burst from his strings in a universal language. I envisioned a lush, green forest with a tiger running through the swaying grass and monkeys playing in the trees.

And now I'm going to have a little fun with relativity. There was an explosion of happiness and light, and the six o'clock commuter train vibrated, shook, jumped its tracks, and took off into the sky, dropping its passengers off on any star they chose.

Here is a man trying to catch a ray of light, and Mr. Albert Einstein played on and on and on.

In the morning I was back in my bed and didn't know how I'd gotten there.

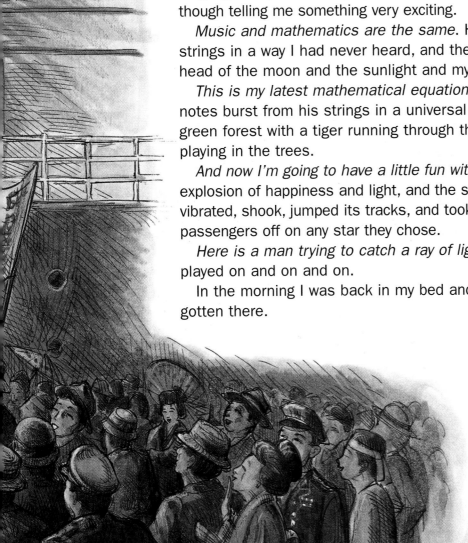

The next night after dinner, as I lay tucked away in my bed, I again heard the adults talking and telling stories. Mr. Albert Einstein told wonderful jokes and made even my mother laugh. Later, when the rest of the house had gone to bed, he played his violin alone in his room——merry tunes, sweet, tangy sounds, the last thing I heard before I fell asleep.

My father asked his houseguest, "Why do you play your violin every night?"

"To clear my head so I can sleep," replied Mr. Albert Einstein.

During the day *Doctor* Einstein would lecture to Japanese scholars at a nearby university. One of these lectures would inspire a young physicist, Hideki Yukawa, who went on to win a Nobel Prize himself several years later.

Mr. Einstein returned from those lectures in a very good mood, for physics was one of his favorite subjects. Then he would pick up the little boy Basho Muramoto and bounce him on his knee. That little boy was *me*.

I do not remember when he left; I only remember the time he stayed with us. Many years passed. A war came to Mr. Albert Einstein's country. A war came to my country. He moved to America and so, eventually, did I.

Mr. Albert Einstein arrived in Princeton, New Jersey, in 1933, his violin in hand. He was even more famous now and just as unconcerned about it as ever. He stopped wearing socks and started smoking a long pipe. Mr. Albert Einstein found New Jersey a good place to think about science. When he had a difficult mathematical problem to solve, he would pick up his violin and play for a while. Then he would stop suddenly, smile, and say, "Now I have it."

When he was not discovering new scientific theories, Mr. Albert Einstein continued to play his violin. And he always enjoyed making friends with children. Once on Halloween, a group of little girls went to his house, intending to play a prank on the famous scientist. But Mr. Einstein seemed to know when children were out to misbehave. When they arrived, he met them at the door with his violin. They probably expected to be spanked with his bow, but instead he proceeded to play. The girls felt ashamed that they had even considered bothering such a great and kind man.

Other children came to his house and asked for help with their arithmetic. There always seemed to be somebody on his doorstep, and then one day it was me.

I was a young man now and I was a little nervous when I knocked at 112 Mercer Street. What if Mr. Albert Einstein didn't remember me? I stood very straight and tall, and it was he who answered the door. I saw the familiar nose and mustache, the familiar wisp of white hair. He was also studying my face, and before I had a chance to introduce myself, Mr. Albert Einstein said, "I used to bounce you on my knee."

I did not come alone. I came with my violin, for Mr. Albert Einstein had inspired me, too.

We played our violins together often in those days, practicing Mozart and Beethoven in the Mercer Street house. Sometimes in between concertos, he would stop and look at me. "You play very well in time," he said.

And what is time? *Time*, said Albert Einstein, *is relative*.

Then we picked up where we had left off, and it was just as though we had never been apart. Because old friends can do that.

Mr. Einstein's Violin

Meet the Author

Melissa Milich decided to study English in college because a writing teacher told her that her spelling and grammar were terrible. Milich decided to look at his criticism as a challenge. As a result, she learned to write well. "It seems everything in my life that has turned out well came as a result of something that was previously a challenge." Milich writes stories for children and adults. She has also worked as an investigative journalist, police reporter, and feature writer for newspapers, magazines, radio, and television. She lives in Watsonville, California.

Meet the Illustrator

Jim Roldan received a box of crayons, his first memorable gift as a child. He drew pictures of cartoon characters, animals, comic book heroes, dinosaurs, and spaceships. He studied art at the Rhode Island School of Design. After a few years of working in a graphic design studio, Roldan started his own business illustrating advertisements, magazines, posters, books, and cartoon characters. He currently lives and works in New Hampshire, where he shares a house with his wife and their two cats.

Theme Connections

Think About It

As Basho Muramonto listened to Einstein play the violin, the music made pictures in his mind. Think about a piece of music that you enjoy and the images it creates in your mind.

Join a group of classmates and discuss the following questions:
- What feelings and ideas about music did Einstein pass on to Muramonto?
- What do Lady Merida, Mr. Pit, and Einstein have in common?

Record Ideas

Summarize what you have learned from your discussion with your classmates. Record your summary in your Writing Journal.

Write a Sequel

Write a paragraph about how a sequel to "Mr. Einstein's Violin" might begin.

Bibliography

Becoming Felix

by Nancy Hope Wilson.   JJ is willing to give up his great love, the clarinet, to save the family dairy farm. Will his sacrifice be enough?

Cecelia and the Blue Mountain Boy

by Ellen Harvey Showell.   When Cecilia finds Blue Mountain, she finds a place where she can share her joy and love of music and dance.

The Jazz Man

by Mary Hays Weik.   The music of a jazz pianist comforts nine-year-old Zeke in his lonely Harlem apartment.

A Mouse Called Wolf

by Dick King-Smith.   "Wolf," short for Wolfgang Amadeus Mouse, is a singing mouse with a lot of talent as well as a lot of heart.

Music

by Angela Shelf Medearis and Michael R. Medearis.
This exploration into African-American music will take you from its roots in rhythm and blues all the way to gospel, rock and roll, and rap.

Play Me a Story: Nine Tales About Musical Instruments

by Naomi Adler and Greta Cencetti. Music is a part of every culture in the world, and this collection of stories features musical tales from places like Australia, Russia, Mongolia, and the American Southwest.

Rubber-Band Banjos and a Java Jive Bass

by Alex Sabbeth. This book contains information on the various types of instruments as well as many projects for homemade instruments.

The Sea King's Daughter: A Russian Legend

retold by Aaron Shepard. A poor musician from the city of Novgorod is faced with a difficult decision when he is asked to play for the Sea King in his underwater palace.

Plants, animals, water, earth, air, people——we are all part of the ecology of the world. How do we affect each other? What can we do to help each other? Why is it important?

Protecting Wildlife

by Malcolm Penny

Introduction

It is dawn in the rain forest of Madagascar. An unearthly howl arises from among the trees. It is joined by another, then several more. Soon a chorus is ringing through the forest, making a weird harmony in the morning mist.

The singers are lemurs, a primitive group of animals related to monkeys. This particular species, called the indri, regularly greets the dawn by calling from the borders of its territory. Soon the indris will begin to feed, pulling branches to their mouths, biting off leaves and fruit.

They are tall, slender animals, covered in dense fur—— brown, with silver-gray arms and legs. They move between the trees in long, athletic leaps in an upright position. When they drop to the ground to cross a clearing, they hop on both feet together, with their arms outstretched.

Indris survive only in a few remaining patches of Madagascar's rain forest.

438

Some of the females have babies riding on their backs. Indri females bear their single babies only every three years: indris are very slow breeders. They are also very rare.

Some time after dawn, other voices are heard in the forest. Soon, there is the sound of chopping, and smoke drifts through the clearings. The local human inhabitants are preparing a new field to grow crops. They have already removed the larger trees for timber and fuel; now they are felling and burning the undergrowth to clear the land. This technique is called slash and burn.

The new vegetable plot will last only for two or three years before the soil becomes sandy and loses all its fertility. Then the people will move on to clear a new area of forest. There are similar situations all over the world, where protecting wildlife has become an urgent problem.

The Malagasy people brought this style of agriculture with them when they came to Madagascar from Malaysia about 1,500 years ago. It worked well in the ancient forests they left behind: fields they abandoned soon recovered, going back to forest within a few years. The forests of Madagascar cannot recover in the same way, and after centuries of this method of agriculture there is little left of them——just bare hills where nothing but cattle can flourish.

The result is that the people are hungry, as the dusty soil is swept from the hills by heavy rain; and the indri, along with the other species of lemurs, are practically homeless. A few small groups of them survive in carefully protected patches of forest.

Habitat Destruction

The destruction of the forests of Madagascar is typical of the loss of wildlife habitat that is going on all over the world. The areas most at risk are rain forests.

The richness of rain forests. Rain forests are moist, warm forests that thrive in tropical parts of South and Central America, Africa, and Southeast Asia. They have existed for

Where once hills were forest covered, only dry grasslands are left.

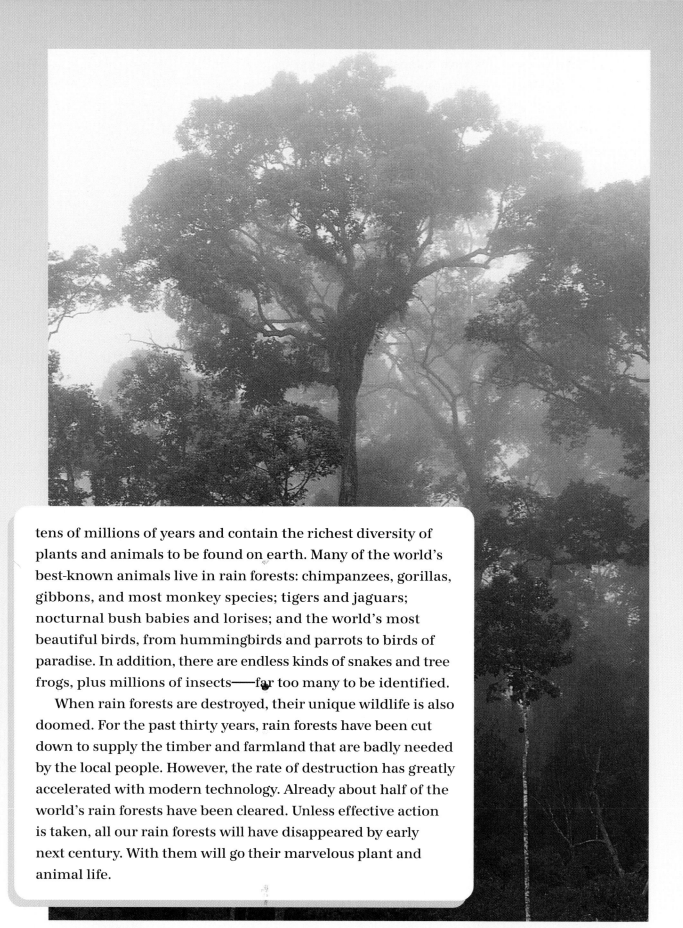

tens of millions of years and contain the richest diversity of plants and animals to be found on earth. Many of the world's best-known animals live in rain forests: chimpanzees, gorillas, gibbons, and most monkey species; tigers and jaguars; nocturnal bush babies and lorises; and the world's most beautiful birds, from hummingbirds and parrots to birds of paradise. In addition, there are endless kinds of snakes and tree frogs, plus millions of insects——far too many to be identified.

When rain forests are destroyed, their unique wildlife is also doomed. For the past thirty years, rain forests have been cut down to supply the timber and farmland that are badly needed by the local people. However, the rate of destruction has greatly accelerated with modern technology. Already about half of the world's rain forests have been cleared. Unless effective action is taken, all our rain forests will have disappeared by early next century. With them will go their marvelous plant and animal life.

Clouds and mist are trapped by trees in the rain forest of Sabah in Malaysia. In this way, the rain forest creates its own climate.

440

Bison once roamed the prairies of North America in vast numbers. Today only a few are left: these grazing bison are protected in Yellowstone National Park, Wyoming.

Floods caused by deforestation in the foothills of the Himalayas make people homeless in Bangladesh, far downstream.

The dangers of erosion. A rain forest is sometimes called "a desert covered with trees." While the trees are standing, their roots hold the soil in place, where it is fed by the leaves and other debris falling from above. When the trees are gone, the soil has nothing to feed it. It becomes loose and sandy, and will soon be eroded, washed away by the heavy tropical rainstorms.

Erosion is one of the most serious threats to all farmland, especially in the tropics. As the rainwater carries the soil away, it forms channels that get deeper and deeper until they reach the underlying rock. The soil is carried down rivers until they reach the sea. As they flow more slowly, the rivers drop the soil in the form of silt. This chokes the riverbed and increases the danger of floods.

The loss of grasslands. Most habitat destruction arises from the need for farmland to feed the world's rapidly increasing human population. Grasslands may be destroyed as a wildlife habitat when they are fenced off and sprayed with weedkillers, in order to raise cattle and grow corn. On the American prairies, for example, large grazing animals, such as deer and buffalo, are no longer able to move freely in search of food. Smaller animals, such as insects, and reptiles and birds that feed on them, are made homeless when the "weeds" are killed.

Other habitats are being destroyed as well. In many parts of the world, wetlands, such as ponds and marshes, are drained to make farmland or commercial forestry plantations. Rivers are dredged, improving the drainage of the surrounding land,

but at the same time destroying the habitat of creatures that live among reedbeds and in shallow streams. Land reclamation, especially beside estuaries, has made farmland out of what were once the feeding and roosting places of millions of birds.

It is vital that sufficient crops are grown to feed people. In developing countries it is hard to grow enough food crops, while in Europe there is a glut of food, leading to surplus grain and milk. Excess food in the U.S. is stored, sold to other countries, or fed to livestock. Many environmentalists agree that, in areas of overproduction, it would be better to reduce farmland and leave areas to become natural grassland and woodland for wild animals.

Hunting and Killing

Humans have always killed other animals to eat. In a few places this is still part of everyday life: Indians in the Amazon jungles, Bushmen in Botswana, and some tribes of Inuit in North America and the Commonwealth of Independent States still hunt in the traditional way for food and raw materials.

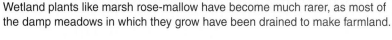
Wetland plants like marsh rose-mallow have become much rarer, as most of the damp meadows in which they grow have been drained to make farmland.

442

Puffins, shags, and kittiwakes nest safely on remote cliffs, but their numbers in the Shetland Islands have been severely reduced by a loss of the sand eels.

Most people no longer have to hunt for food. Nevertheless, hunting still causes the death of many millions of wild animals every year. Many animals are killed by farmers to protect their crops and their livestock. These "enemies" of the farmer range in size from elephants and tigers to beetles and greenflies.

Most of the wild animals killed every year are fish. Because the demand for fish rises as the human population increases, some fisheries are in danger of running out. The fishery around South Georgia, one of the Falkland Islands in the South Atlantic Ocean, is the latest area to be affected by overfishing.

Sand eels——small fish that are collected by trawling in shallow northern waters——have suffered badly from overfishing. This has affected the large bird populations that depend on them for food during their breeding season. Arctic terns, skuas, and puffins in the Shetland Islands, to the north of Scotland, have all fallen sharply in numbers. In 1981, there were 54,000 kittiwakes in the Shetlands; by 1988, there were only a few hundred left.

Hunting for sport. There is another kind of unnecessary hunting. Many people, all over the world, enjoy hunting and killing wild animals as a sport. Not very long ago, it was considered very brave and sporting to go out into the bush of Africa, or the jungles of India, to shoot lions, elephants, or tigers. Today, most people consider this type of hunting barbaric and destructive, and it has almost completely stopped. All the same, especially in North America, the shooting of wild animals is big business, with a whole industry devoted to

443

making and selling guns and special clothing for hunters. The number of animals that may be killed is carefully controlled by the authorities.

Victims of our vanity. The very worst kind of killing is poaching: hunting protected animals because they are worth a lot of money. Spotted cats are protected all over the world, but because there are still some people who like to wear their beautiful skins as coats, there are others who will hunt and kill the rarest leopard or cheetah to supply the market.

In the Far East, rhinoceros horn is regarded as a powerful medicine. In one Arab country, North Yemen, it is used to make the handles of the ceremonial daggers worn by adult men. These people are prepared to pay enormous sums of money for rhino horns. A North Yemeni ceremonial dagger with a rhino horn handle can cost over $50,000. Chinese pharmacists can sell powdered or flaked horn for as much as $5,500 per pound. Knowing this, it is easy to understand why the black rhino is hunted so extensively in Africa north of the Zambezi River.

Surprisingly, there are still people who think it is chic to wear the skins of spotted cats, mainly because they are very expensive. Until such people change their minds, animals like the Asian snow leopard will continue to be very rare because they are hunted for their coats.

Protecting Rhinos

The steam produced by this power station in the U.S. is harmless, but the fumes from the fossil fuels burned at the station cause acid rain.

Pollution

The oldest and most common form of air pollution is smoke. Coal fires and factory chimneys fill the air with soot, blackening buildings and causing thick fog in damp weather. Now burning forests add to the pollution.

All burning fuel releases carbon dioxide. The layer of carbon dioxide in the earth's atmosphere is becoming thicker, so that it traps heat that would otherwise escape into space. This is known as the "greenhouse effect," and scientists suspect it is causing the earth to become warmer. There is a danger that the polar ice caps might start to melt, causing the sea level to rise. If this happens, it will alter the climate, especially the distribution of rainfall. Wildlife as well as people will be in great danger. If the climate changes abruptly, they will be unable to adapt quickly enough to survive.

The fumes from burning fossil fuels contain oxides of sulfur and nitrogen, which react with damp air to make sulfuric and nitric acids. Often, the fumes drift downwind until they come to a place where the air is damp; then they form acids and fall as rain. Acid rain can kill fish in lakes and rivers, and has been

445

blamed for causing the death of trees over large areas of the northern U.S., Canada, Europe, and Scandinavia.

The atmosphere at risk. A very dangerous form of air pollution is caused by CFCs, or chlorofluorocarbons, which are used in some aerosols, refrigerators, and polystyrene fast-food cartons. They drift up into the ozone layer, far above the earth's surface, and break down the ozone molecules. The ozone layer protects the earth from the harmful effects of sunlight. As it becomes thinner, more ultraviolet light will come through. This will help to raise the earth's temperature, already elevated because of the greenhouse effect. It will also increase the risk of skin cancer among people. Its effect on animals and plants is hard to predict.

The radioactive fuel used in nuclear power stations gives off radiation that is extremely dangerous if it escapes into the air. Even small amounts can damage human cells, causing cancer and interfering with the development of unborn babies. The effects of radiation on wildlife are not known, but it seems most likely that they will be very similar to those on human beings. Certainly, large numbers of sheep in Britain, and reindeer in Lapland, are still radioactive following the 1986 accident at the Chernobyl nuclear power station in the Commonwealth of Independent States. This released a dangerous level of radioactivity into the atmosphere, which drifted over much of Europe.

An ocean of chemicals. Water pollution, like air pollution, is made more serious now by the numbers of people involved, and the types of harmful substances that they produce.

Oil pollution has very serious effects on wildlife. It poisons fish and coastal animals like crabs and shellfish, and also clogs the feathers of seabirds. When the birds preen the oil from their feathers, it poisons them. Most oil spills are accidental, but some are deliberate, for example

Oil spilled into the sea kills thousands of birds every year. Only a few are cleaned, like these penguins in South Africa.

Harvest mice flourish in fields of wheat. They suffered in the past from the use of pesticides and from modern harvesting machinery, which cuts the crop very close to the ground and destroys their nests. Now it appears their population is recovering.

when a tanker captain washes out his tanks at sea. Such actions are illegal, but they save time and money, and they can be carried out far at sea, out of sight of land.

The greatest threat to the marine environment is no longer oil pollution. Industrial chemicals have been invented that are far more poisonous and long-lasting. Among them is a group known as PCBs (polychlorinated biphenyls), which are used for various industrial processes. These very strong chemicals can be destroyed by burning, but because this is expensive, they are most often buried in dumps on land, or allowed to pass down rivers into the sea.

PCBs are directly poisonous, but they also weaken the immune system of many animals, so that they become vulnerable to diseases which they would normally resist. The seal plague in the North Sea and the Baltic, first noticed in 1988, was probably made much worse because many of the seals were affected by PCBs.

Poisonous pesticides. Wild animals and plants are also harmed by pesticides and weedkillers, because these substances do not only kill the pests they are intended to, but other creatures, too. The strong chemicals contained in pesticides have harmed many insects, like butterflies, while weedkillers have killed off plants on which caterpillars feed.

Protecting Seals

447

Pesticides can harm many animals because they are passed along the food chain. For example, a field mouse may eat grains of wheat treated with pesticide. The pesticide chemicals are not used up, but stored in the mouse's body. If the mouse is caught by a barn owl, the harmful chemicals will be passed on to the owl. Since barn owls catch many mice, they will in time receive a poisonous dose of pesticides. The accumulated chemicals harm their eggs and the owlets that hatch from them.

Reserves and National Parks

The idea of protecting large areas of wild land was first put into practice in the U.S. in 1872, when Yellowstone National Park was opened. Since then, national parks have been founded in almost every country in the world.

When Yellowstone was founded, wildlife in the Rocky Mountains was not in any danger. The park was set up to protect the extraordinary landscape of geysers and sulfur springs, so that visitors could marvel at it forever. The fact that it was full of wildlife, including buffalo, grizzly bears, and herds of elk, was a secondary consideration.

Later, national parks were established to protect particular species of animals, usually from overhunting. The first of these was in Italy, when in 1922 the king gave his hunting preserve at Gran Paradiso to the nation, to protect the alpine ibex. Since then, most parks have been established to protect the whole environment, including all its animals and plants.

The future of national parks. For a national park to be a success, there must be a balance between the needs of the local people and those of the animals. A good example is Royal Chitwan National Park in Nepal. It is partly forest and partly

Ibex were one of the first animals to be given protection in a national park. The national park of Switzerland not only protects ibex but also provides a safe home for many other alpine animals and plants.

Protecting Bears

The millions of water birds that live in the Everglades National Park include spoonbills, egrets, and herons.

elephant grass over 6 feet tall. Tigers and one-horned rhinoceroses live there, together with two different species of crocodile. However, the park is surrounded by villages, whose people need firewood from the forest and grass from the plain, to build houses and feed cattle.

To save arguments, the local people are allowed into the park at certain times of year to collect grass. The park staff collect dead wood from the forest, and driftwood from the rivers, for the villagers to use as fuel. The villagers are encouraged to plant "firewood forests" around the edge of the park to provide a renewable fuel supply. The park is safe, and the people no longer feel it is taking land that they need.

One of the oldest and largest national parks in the U.S., the Florida Everglades, is suffering from a similar conflict. The park relies on a steady flow of clean water from the north. Unfortunately, the water is also needed for agriculture. More and more people are moving to Florida, and it is necessary to drain land to build houses and to provide people with water. This drainage removes some of the water from the edges of the park. The water that comes from the farmland is often polluted with fertilizer. This polluted water enters the tidal swamp, causing an excessive growth of some green algae.

Eventually the algae will cover the water, removing all oxygen from it. If the problem is not solved soon, the Everglades will be lost, with all its wonderful scenery, and the millions of superb birds, snakes, and alligators that live there.

The Everglades is considered so important that it has been declared a World Heritage Site, a matter of concern to the whole world. Some other World Heritage Sites are Mount Everest, the Grand Canyon, the Serengeti in Africa, and Lake Ichkeul in Tunisia, an important wetland used by migrant birds.

National parks are vital to the whole world, because they will be the only way for future generations to know what the world looked like before farmland and cities took over. Many of them are also the last home of animals that used to be common.

In Africa, the only hope for the black rhinoceros is to be protected in national parks, with armed guards to keep the poachers away. Biologists have discovered ways of making rhinoceroses breed more quickly, by adjusting the numbers in each park.

A black rhinoceros mother and her calf have been rescued from farmland, transported by truck, and released into Etosha National Park, Namibia. Such efforts are often necessary to protect endangered rhinoceroses from poachers.

Changing Our Behavior

The best hope for the black rhino is for people to change their beliefs about the value of its horn, so that the trade in daggers and medicines collapses. Many other changes in beliefs and behavior will be necessary if the natural world is to survive for much longer.

The program to persuade villagers in Nepal to plant trees for firewood is being carried out, not only on the plains near Royal Chitwan National Park, but also in the foothills of the Himalayas. As more trees are planted there, the land will become more stable, instead of being washed away down the rivers, and there will be less danger of flooding in faraway Bangladesh.

Pollution can be reduced as well, for example, by discouraging people from using pesticides and artificial fertilizers on farmland. Today a growing number of people are realizing that soil can be enriched, and pests controlled, by organic methods. Such methods are less suited to large-scale farming, but farmers can use less-harmful chemicals.

The use of CFCs has already been greatly reduced, and there are moves to ban the manufacture and use of most of the PCBs, which have caused so much damage to the environment in the short time since they were invented.

Scientists are working hard to find other ways of providing energy. "Alternative energy sources," as they are called, include wind and water power, and solar energy. Finding alternative energy sources is important for two reasons: they will reduce the pollution from burning fossil fuels, and they will postpone the time when the fossil fuels are used up.

Saving the rain forests. The destruction of rain forests can also be reduced, by changing the way in which people clear the land, and by using the land better when it has been cleared. The main problem with rain forest soil is that it is very soft, made up of leaves that have fallen over thousands of years. If the trees are cleared with heavy machinery, this fragile soil is squashed flat. It quickly becomes waterlogged, and bad for growing plants. If the trees are cleared by people on foot, the soil survives much better.

To help the forests and their animals to survive, it would be better if the clearings were much smaller, leaving "corridors" of forest between them. The animals would still have somewhere to live, and the trees would still be there to produce seeds. Thus the clearings would recover more quickly when the soil was no longer suitable for growing crops.

There are plans to slow down the destruction of rain forests in countries as far apart as Mexico and Madagascar, but at present they are on a small scale. It is important that more areas of rain forest be protected, while there are still some worthwhile areas of forest left.

This patch of Brazilian rain forest was the home of the rare golden lion tamarin.

What You Can Do

There are many organizations that exist to safeguard the environment. By joining and supporting a local group, you can let the authorities know that you, too, are concerned with what is happening to the natural world.

Conservation does not have to be a public matter: it can be personal, too. On a walk in the country, for example, a good motto is "Look, don't touch." In some nature reserves there may be a sign that says "Take only photographs, leave only footprints." If everyone followed this advice, there would be much less damage to the plants and animals that make the countryside such a marvelous place.

Making room for wildlife. If you have a garden or yard, you can make your own nature reserve. To encourage butterflies, for example, you could plant a shrub called Buddleia or "butterfly bush." Butterflies love the nectar from its sweet-scented flower spikes.

You can encourage many butterflies to breed, too, by growing various plants and flowers. Among cultivated annuals, plants that grow for only one season, are alyssum, marigolds, and verbena. Some choices of cultivated perennials, plants that grow for several years, include butterfly weed, daisies, phlox, and primroses. Wild, prickly thistle or nettles are also good choices. Avoid using chemical weedkillers.

In the countryside, ditches and ponds are often drained, or become polluted by fertilizers and weedkillers. By creating a pond in your garden, you can provide an alternative home for frogs and many freshwater insects, including beautiful dragonflies.

You can also help wild birds in winter. Bird feeders and bird baths are especially valuable to birds in winter, when food is scarce and water may be frozen. Once birds know that food and water are available in your garden, or on the terrace of your apartment, many different species may come to feed there. When small birds visit a garden in winter, they help to control pests by eating the eggs of aphids that lie under the bark of trees.

If we successfully conserve the rich wildlife we still have now, the world will be a much nicer place in the future.

Protecting Frogs

Protecting Wildlife

Meet the Author

Malcolm Penny has been on wildlife expeditions and has worked as a producer of wildlife documentaries for television. Penny has written many books about animals and is a successful natural history author.

Theme Connections

Think About It

With a small group of classmates, consider what you have learned about the ways humans endanger wildlife and about the importance of protecting natural habitats.

- Which human threats to wildlife would be the easiest to remedy? Which would be the hardest?
- How would your life and attitude change if you lived within a wildlife habitat?

Check the Concept/Question Board to see if there are any questions there that you can answer now. If the selection or your discussions about the selection have raised any new questions about ecology, put the questions on the Board. Maybe the next selection will help answer the questions.

Record Ideas

Do humans have greater rights to the land, air, and water than do plants and animals? Record your notes and ideas in your Writing Journal.

Research Ideas

- Investigate how recycling, organic farming, selective logging, and alternative energy sources can help to protect wildlife.
- Identify and explore some of the dilemmas that result from the conflicting needs of wildlife and humans.

The Passenger Pigeon

Paul Fleischman
illustrated by Diane Blasius

We were counted not in

nor

but in
billions.

stars

As grains of
sand
at the sea

buffalo

When we burst into flight

that the
sun
was darkened

day

thousands

millions

billions.
We were numerous as the
stars
in the heavens

sand

As the
buffalo
on the plains.

we so filled the sky

sun

and
day
became dusk.

Humblers of the sun
we were!
The world
inconceivable

Yet it's 1914,
and here I am
alone

the last

Humblers of the sun
we were!

inconceivable
without us.

alone
caged in the Cincinnati Zoo,

of the passenger pigeons.

Alejandro's Gift

Richard E. Albert
illustrated by Sylvia Long

Alejandro's small adobe house stood beside a lonely desert road.

Beside the house stood a well, and a windmill to pump water from the well. Water for Alejandro and for his only companion, a burro.

It was a lonely place, and Alejandro welcomed any who stopped by to refresh themselves at the well. But visitors were few, and after they left, Alejandro felt lonelier than before.

To more easily endure the lonely hours, Alejandro planted a garden. A garden filled with carrots, beans, and large brown onions.

Tomatoes and corn.

Melons, squash, and small red peppers.

Most mornings found Alejandro tending the garden, watching it grow. These were times he cherished, and he often stayed for hours, working until driven indoors by the desert heat.

The days went by, one after another with little change, until one morning when there was an unexpected visitor. This visitor came not from the desert road, but from the desert itself.

A ground squirrel crept from the underbrush. Moving warily over the sand, it hesitated and looked around. Alejandro paused, keeping very quiet as the squirrel approached the garden. It ran up to one of the furrows, drank its fill of water, and scampered away. After it left, Alejandro realized that for those few moments his loneliness had been all but forgotten.

And because he felt less lonely, Alejandro found himself hoping the squirrel would come again.

The squirrel did come again, from time to time bringing along small friends.

Wood rats and pocket gophers.

Jackrabbits, kangaroo rats, pocket mice.

Birds, too, became aware of Alejandro's garden.

Roadrunners, gila woodpeckers, thrashers.

Cactus wrens, sage sparrows, mourning doves, and others came in the evening to perch on the branches of a mesquite bush, or to rest on the arms of a lone saguaro, before dropping down for a quick drink before nightfall.

Occasionally, even an old desert tortoise could be seen plodding toward the garden.

Suddenly, Alejandro found that time was passing more quickly. He was rarely lonely. He had only to look up from his hoe, or from wherever he might be at any moment, to find a small friend nearby.

For a while this was all that mattered to Alejandro, but after a time he wasn't so sure. He began asking himself if there was something more important than just making himself less lonely. It took Alejandro little time to see there was.

He began to realize that his tiny desert friends came to his garden not for company, but for water. And he found himself thinking of the other animals in the desert.

Animals like the coyote and the desert gray fox.

The bobcats, the skunks, the badgers, and long-nosed coatis.

The peccaries, sometimes called *javelinas,* the short-tempered wild pigs of the desert.

The antlered mule deer, the does, and the fawns.

Finding enough water was not a problem. With his windmill and well, Alejandro could supply ample water for any and all. Getting it to those who needed it was something else.

The something else, Alejandro decided, was a desert water hole.

Without delay, Alejandro started digging. It was tiring work, taking many days in the hot desert sun. But the thought of giving water to so many thirsty desert dwellers more than made up for the drudgery. And when it was filled, Alejandro was pleased with the gift he had made for his desert friends.

There was good reason to suppose it would take time for the larger animals to discover their new source of water, so Alejandro was patient. He went about as usual, feeding his burro, tending the garden, and doing countless other chores.

Days passed and nothing happened. Still, Alejandro was confident. But the days turned to weeks, and it was still quiet at the water hole. Why, Alejandro wondered, weren't they coming? What could he have done wrong?

461

The absence of the desert folk might have remained a mystery had Alejandro not come out of the house one morning when a skunk was in the clearing beyond the water hole. Seeing Alejandro, the skunk darted to safety in the underbrush.

It suddenly became very clear why Alejandro's gift was being shunned.

Alejandro couldn't believe he had been so thoughtless, but what was important now was to put things right as quickly as possible.

Water hole number two was built far from the house and screened by heavy desert growth. When it was filled and ready, Alejandro waited with mixed emotions. He was hopeful, yet he couldn't forget what had happened the first time.

As it turned out, he was not disappointed.

The animals of the desert did come,
each as it made its own discovery.
Because the water hole was now sheltered
from the small adobe house and the desert
road, the animals were no longer fearful.
And although Alejandro could not see through the desert growth
surrounding the water hole, he had ways of knowing it was no
longer being shunned.

   By the twitter of birds gathering in the dusk.

   By the rustling of mesquite in the quiet desert evening telling of
the approach of a coyote, a badger, or maybe a desert fox.

   By the soft hoofbeats of a mule deer, or the unmistakable sound of
a herd of peccaries charging toward the water hole.

   And in these moments when Alejandro sat quietly listening to the
sounds of his desert neighbors, he knew that the gift was not so
much a gift that he had given, but a gift he had received.

The Southwestern region of the United States is made up of Colorado, Arizona, New Mexico, and Utah. A variety of wildlife can be found in its varied habitats. The following glossary lists some of the animals and plants shown in this book.

The **Arizona Pocket Mouse** eats many kinds of seeds and can hibernate when food cannot be found.

Badgers have distinctive black-and-white "masks" on their faces. They live in family groups in underground burrows. Few animals will attack the badger because of its fierce temperament.

The **Black-Tailed Jackrabbit** has very large ears, which help keep it cool in hot weather. It also has very large feet, which help it run quickly.

Bobcats get their name from their stubby "bobbed" tail. They are found only in North America, where they are the most common wildcat. They eat small mammals, such as rabbits, mice, and squirrels. The bobcat barks hoarsely when threatened.

Botta's Pocket Gopher spends most of its time in underground burrows, some of which can be as long as 150 feet. Botta's Pocket Gophers live by themselves, often fighting other gophers they meet.

The **Cactus Wren** is the largest North American wren—growing up to 9 inches long. It lives in nests in clumps of mesquite on desert hillsides.

Coatis (**kwa**-tees) are short-legged animals that can grow up to two feet long. They eat lizards and insects, but are known for eating fruit, often stripping fruit trees bare. Coatis travel in large groups.

The **Collared Peccary** (**peck**-a-ree) resembles a wild pig but has a snout that points upward. It eats cacti—especially prickly pear, which it devours spines and all. During the midday heat, peccaries often sleep in hollows in the ground.

Costa's Hummingbird is a purple-throated hummingbird no more than $3\frac{1}{2}$ inches long. As it hovers over flowers, its wings beat so fast they make a humming sound. Hummingbirds are the only birds that can hover.

Coyotes can run as fast as 40 miles per hour and leap as far as 14 feet. They run with their tails down, unlike wolves, which run with their tails straight behind them.

The **Curve-Billed Thrasher** is about the size of a robin. It has a long, curved bill and red eyes. It lives in cactus deserts and eats insects.

The **Desert Tortoise** stores water in a pouch beneath its shell. It hibernates underground from October to March. Desert Tortoises can grow up to 15 inches long.

The **Elf Owl** is the smallest American owl and is no bigger than a sparrow. It lives in saguaro deserts and feeds on large insects.

Gambel's Quail lives in desert thickets. The bird has a loud, crackling call, and a large teardrop-shaped feather on its head.

The **Gila Woodpecker** nests in holes in giant saguaro cacti. Its feathers are patterned in black and white stripes. Males have a small red cap, while females and young birds have plain brown heads.

The **Gray Fox** is mostly active at night, but can sometimes be seen during the day looking for food. They are the only canids (the family of wolves, foxes, coyote, and dogs) that can climb, and they often rest in trees.

The **Greater Roadrunner** is a tall bird (20 to 24 inches) that rarely flies, running instead on strong feet. It eats a wide variety of small animals, including snakes, lizards, and scorpions.

Harris's Antelope Squirrel lives in low deserts. Its pale coloring helps it blend with the environment. Antelope Squirrels get most of the water they need from the food they eat.

Merriam's Kangaroo Rat is the smallest kangaroo rat in the United States. It lives in scrublands, feeding mostly on the seeds of mesquite and other desert plants.

Mesquite (mess-**keet**) is a spiny tree that grows in large thickets in the Southwest and Mexico.

The **Mourning Dove's** name comes from its melancholy cooing, which is its mating call. Mourning doves can be found all over North America.

Mule Deer have large ears and are one of the most common animals of the desert. Their diet consists of grasses, twigs, and cactus fruits. Mule Deer can run up to 35 miles per hour, and can jump as far as 25 feet.

The **Phainopepla** (fay-no-**pep**-la) is a tropical bird with an elegant crest on its head. It eats mistletoe berries and insects, which it snatches right out of the air.

Sage Sparrows are small brown birds with white eye rings. They are found in dry foothills and sagebrush.

The **Saguaro** (sah-**gwar**-oh) is a cactus that can grow up to 60 feet tall. It provides fruit for many desert creatures, and bears white flowers.

The **White-Throated Wood Rat** usually lives in the base of a cactus, and it uses the cactus needles to hide the entrance to its home.

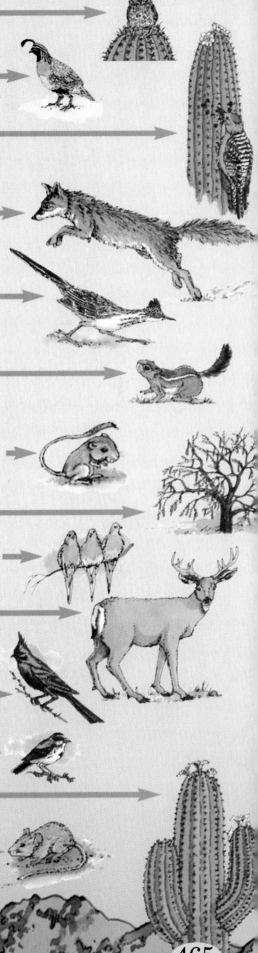

Alejandro's Gift

Meet the Author

Richard E. Albert wrote and sold many "pulp westerns" early in his writing career but spent most of his life working as an engineer. After his retirement he began writing for children. He was 83 when he wrote *Alejandro's Gift*.

Meet the Illustrator

Sylvia Long has recently started illustrating children's books after working several years as a fine artist. Her love of the outdoors and animals has been an inspiration for her wonderful illustrations. Two of the four books she has illustrated have become best sellers, *Fire Race* and *Ten Little Rabbits*.

Theme Connections

Think About It

With a small group of classmates, discuss what you learned about wildlife in the desert.

- Why would animals live in a desert, where water and food are scarce?
- What would have happened to the animals if Alejandro hadn't dug the water hole?

Check the Concept/Question Board to see if there are any questions there that you can answer now. If the selection or your discussions about the selection have raised any new questions about ecology, put the questions on the Board. Maybe the next selection will help answer the questions.

Record Ideas

After reading this selection, do you look at the world around you in a different way? Record your notes and ideas in your Writing Journal.

Research Ideas

- Find out more about animals that live in extreme environments. What adaptations make it possible for them to survive?
- Investigate how animals cooperate with one another.

Windows on Wildlife

by Ginny Johnston and Judy Cutchins

What Are Habitat Exhibits?

The excitement of watching an animal in the wild is unforgettable. What a thrill it is to hear gorillas growl and hoot or watch them care for their young. But few people get a chance to venture into African forests where the great apes live. Many of the world's most fascinating creatures live in habitats too far away or too difficult to visit. However, most people can watch them by visiting a zoo or aquarium.

Until recently, animals in such places were usually caged behind bars, and people walked by to stare at them. The visit held none of the excitement of seeing animals in the wild.

Today, modern zoos, aquariums, and wildlife parks are showing plants and animals in natural-habitat exhibits. These exhibits duplicate a part of an animal's true environment as closely as possible. Since many animals are endangered in their native lands, habitat exhibits may be the only places they can survive.

Building these realistic habitats is not a simple job. It is challenging to build a "river" for hippos or grow a forest indoors. Making rain or snow fall under a roof requires special equipment. Also, before a habitat exhibit can be developed, scientists must spend a great deal of time studying plants, animals, and their natural environment. They watch each species to learn about its way of life and special needs. The scientists then work with exhibit specialists to design a habitat that will be as authentic as they can make it.

Visitors may see more in natural-habitat exhibits than they would see in nature. Windows, for example, allow people to remain warm and dry while watching penguins "fly" under icy water or waddle across snow-covered rocks. Naturalistic exhibits are not only more fun for visitors, but healthier and more comfortable for captive wildlife.

These modern exhibits are much more expensive than cages with bars, but it is worth the money to provide the best possible environment for captive species. The well-being of the plants and animals is the number one goal. Scientists believe that zoo animals live longer and have more babies in naturalistic settings. Raising more young, especially if a species is rare or endangered, will prevent the species from becoming extinct. American zoos no longer take rare animals from the wild for exhibits, so raising these babies is extremely important.

Forest for Gorillas

Slowly the square, white door of the gorilla building slid open. A huge head appeared, and two dark eyes scanned quickly in every direction. It was the gorilla's first look outside in his twenty-seven years at the zoo in Atlanta, Georgia. Captured as a three-year-old in Africa, the male lowland gorilla had lived alone since then in an indoor cage with bars. Now he was about to enter the outdoor area of his new habitat exhibit, the Ford African Rain Forest at Zoo Atlanta. Just outside the gorilla's habitat, the zoo director, exhibit designers, keepers, and news reporters watched anxiously. They wondered what the gorilla's first reaction to the outdoors would be.

After twenty-seven years indoors, this western lowland gorilla explores the Ford African Rain Forest exhibit at Zoo Atlanta.

469

The sloping, grass-covered hillside was designed to look like a clearing in an African rain forest.

The 458-pound gorilla cautiously left the building and moved a few feet away. Hearts beat faster as people watched the powerful ape investigate his new home. He picked up leaves and sniffed them. He felt the grass and looked up at the cloudy sky. The gorilla's old indoor cage of concrete and tile had none of the wonderful smells and sights of the outdoors. A gentle rain began to fall. Confused and startled by the falling drops, the gorilla dashed back inside to safety. Later that day, he ventured out again. Bravely, he ambled farther and investigated every tree and rock on the hillside of the simulated African rain forest. Fallen trees, high grass, and bamboo gave the sloping hillside the appearance of a forest clearing. The curious gorilla seemed to be quite content in his naturalistic home.

Of all the people watching the gorilla that first day, no one was more pleased than his keeper for the past fourteen years. The zookeeper knew the magnificent gorilla would, at last, have a large, interesting place to live. Although the great ape would still go indoors at night, he would spend each day exploring outside.

In just a few weeks, the lone gorilla had next-door neighbors. The Ford African Rain Forest exhibit was designed for several families of lowland gorillas. The four-and-one-half-acre exhibit is divided so that each family has a separate area. A gorilla family is led by an adult male called a silverback. Since silverbacks in captivity are very protective of their families and their territories, they must be kept apart or they will fight. Moats with steep dirt banks separate the families from each other and from zoo visitors. Each moat is twelve feet deep and fifteen feet across. These moats do not have water in them; instead, thick, soft grass grows at the bottom in case a gorilla tumbles in. The silverbacks can see, smell, and hear each other across the moats, but they cannot get too close.

This realistic habitat design, with families near each other, allows the gorillas to behave much as they would in the wild. In an African forest, gorilla families sometimes meet other families as they

The gorilla habitats are separated by steep-sided double moats.

search for food. As they approach each other, one male will beat his chest, slap the ground or trees, and run toward the other silverback. This show of strength usually results in one family's moving away, with no actual fighting between the males. In the zoo exhibit, the gorillas cannot reach each other, but they can still display their feelings across the moats. The gorillas, especially the silverbacks, are alert and aware of the activities of the apes living nearby.

At night and in bad weather, the gorillas are kept inside. The holding building for them is hidden behind a wall of giant artificial rocks at the top of the hillside. Each family has its own sliding door into the building. Inside, the families have large, separate, barred cages. During the day, the gorillas eat fruits and vegetables scattered outside by the keepers. Each evening, they receive their main meal of dried food and milk indoors before they sleep.

The gorilla-habitat exhibit looked nothing like a rain forest before builders got started. Twenty-six thousand tons of soil were moved to build a hillside. More than 3,500 trees, shrubs, and flowers were planted to fill in around several hundred trees already growing in the area. Stands of bamboo were planted to make the area look like a sun-filled opening in an African rain forest. The key to success was finding plants that would simulate the look and feel of a rain forest but would survive in Atlanta's cooler, drier climate. For example, southern magnolias that grow in Atlanta were planted because their wide shiny leaves look very much like the leaves of tropical plants. Some of the exhibit plants must be taken inside a greenhouse for the winter, but most can remain in the exhibit all year round. Rocks and

A young female gorilla, searching for food in the forest clearing, fascinates visitors.

cliffs were made of Gunite, a concrete mixture sprayed over steel wires. The Gunite forms were painted to resemble rocks photographed in Africa. Before the gorillas were released into the exhibit, rock climbers from a nearby university were invited to climb the walls and find any places over which a gorilla might escape.

At Zoo Atlanta, future zookeepers, veterinarians, and scientists will observe gorilla families as part of their training. The Ford African Rain Forest offers close encounters with great apes. Trails wind along outside all four gorilla habitats. At each turn, through the leaves and branches, visitors may spot a gorilla munching bamboo or resting in the sunshine. It is intriguing to watch the delicate and deliberate way apes eat and the gentle way they groom each other. At one place the trail leads through an information building where visitors can learn about gorillas while they watch real ones through a huge window. Gorillas, especially the younger ones, often come close to or even touch the glass. It seems they are curious about people, too.

In western Africa, rain forests have been cut and cleared for farms and lumber. As their habitats disappear, gorillas are becoming very rare. Until recently, zoos have not been very successful in raising young gorillas. Fortunately, as more is learned about the needs of the great apes, American zoos are raising larger numbers of healthy youngsters. Since wild gorillas are never captured for American zoos, in a few years, only those born and raised in captivity will be in exhibits.

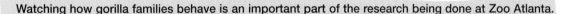

Watching how gorilla families behave is an important part of the research being done at Zoo Atlanta.

Each of the exhibit's two hundred penguins is hand-fed three times a day.

Icy Home for Penguins

It is 9:00 A.M. at SeaWorld's Penguin Encounter in Orlando, Florida. A perky rockhopper penguin, just eighteen inches tall, bounces from one ice-covered rock to another. Around him dozens of gentoo, chinstrap, and crested macaroni penguins waddle by. Tall king penguins strut about with their flipperlike wings outstretched and orange bills pointed up. An exhibit keeper, dressed in warm, waterproof clothes, carries a bucket filled with fresh fish for the penguins' morning feeding. Each fish was stuffed with vitamins before being placed in the bucket. The keeper holds a small herring in front of an Adélie penguin. The hungry bird gulps the fish headfirst.

Visitors to Penguin Encounter travel on a moving sidewalk in front of windows that are ninety-five feet long. Every day thousands of people look into a simulated Antarctic habitat without disturbing the penguins. Each glass window is three inches thick to hold the tremendous amount of water in the sea pool and to maintain the near-feezing temperatures inside the exhibit. The window panels extend below the water so people can watch the penguins swimming in the deep pool. Since the glass is cleaned five times a day, visitors always have a clear view of the penguins.

To duplicate the seasonal changes of sunlight in the Antarctic and to make the penguins feel at home, special lighting is used at Penguin Encounter. When it is summer in North America, it is winter at the South Pole. The sun cannot be seen for several weeks during the Antarctic winter. Imitating this season means keeping the exhibit lights dim from late May until the end of July. The lights are not turned out completely because visitors would not be able to see the penguins. In August, the keepers turn the lights up a little more each morning. By early October, the lights are bright for twenty-four hours a day. This would be like summer at the South Pole, when the sun shines all day and all night.

Simulating the below-zero temperatures of the penguins' natural habitat is not possible at Penguin Encounter, but the birds are kept comfortable by giant air-cooling machines. These machines keep the temperature in the exhibit near freezing all the time. Other machines in the ceiling produce 6,000 pounds of "snow" every twenty-four hours. This finely ground ice falls softly and steadily. Twice a day, keepers shovel it into a smooth layer that melts very slowly. A clear saltwater pool runs the length of the exhibit, and the water is always a chilly 50 degrees. That's about 30 degrees colder than most swimming pools!

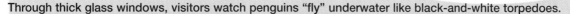

Through thick glass windows, visitors watch penguins "fly" underwater like black-and-white torpedoes.

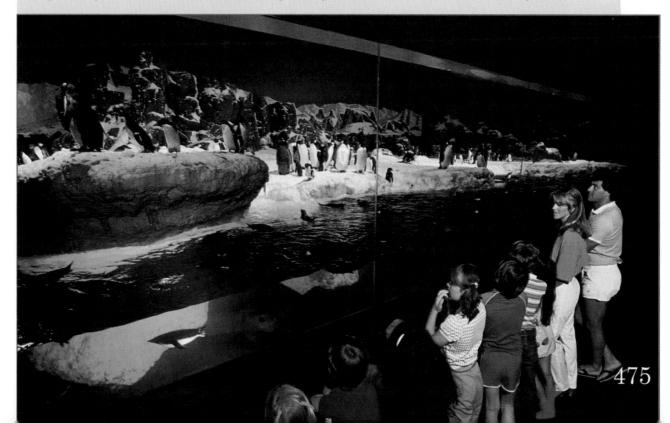

475

A penguin's body is protected by a marvelous feather coat. About seventy shiny, bristly feathers grow from each square inch of skin. These stiff feathers overlap like shingles on a roof. They trap body heat to keep the penguin warm even during Antarctic blizzards, when the temperature can be 100 degrees below zero. Each day, a penguin uses its curved bill to straighten its feathers. The bird also spreads oil over them from a gland near its tail. The oil and tight, overlapping fit of the feathers keep the skin dry even while the penguin is swimming.

Like those of all birds, a penguin's outer feathers wear out in about a year. These old feathers are shed during the molting season. For one month, while a new set of feathers is growing in, a penguin cannot enter the ocean to find food. Without its warm, waterproof layer, a penguin would quickly die in the icy water. In Antarctica, a penguin may lose nearly half of its body weight while waiting for new feathers. At Penguin Encounter, keepers continue to feed the birds during the molting season.

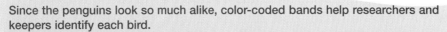
Since the penguins look so much alike, color-coded bands help researchers and keepers identify each bird.

476

The Penguin Encounter at SeaWorld in Orlando, Florida, is not the only Penguin Encounter in the United States. Other exhibits are in California, Ohio, and Texas. Before any were built, teams of scientists studied in Antarctica for six years. They hoped to learn enough about penguins to create suitable habitats for them in America. The scientists watched penguins swim, tumble off rocks into the icy sea, sled across the snow on their bellies, build nests, and raise young. Researchers observed several different species of penguins living close together. They learned that penguins were curious about humans, but not frightened by them.

When the researchers returned to the United States, they worked with a design team to create the first naturalistic exhibit for penguins. It was built at SeaWorld of San Diego, California, in 1983. Adult penguins were brought to San Diego from Antarctica. They seemed to feel comfortable and behaved very naturally in their indoor home. Some mated and produced eggs.

All the penguins in Penguin Encounters in Ohio, Texas, and Florida were hatched from eggs laid in San Diego. No other adults have been taken from the wild. Although penguins are not an endangered species, it is best not to remove animals from their natural habitat or disturb their environment if another way to study them can be found.

Thanks to years of research and careful planning at Penguin Encounters, scientists at last are able to study and raise penguins without traveling thousands of miles to Antarctica. Visitors to the exhibits gain a better understanding of penguins and their unusual, icy habitat.

Indoor Jungle

Stepping inside the huge JungleWorld building at the Bronx Zoo, a visitor enters another world. Not far from the busy streets and bustling crowds of New York City, this simulated Asian rain forest is a jungle adventure. Sounds of birds and insects are everywhere. Splashing waterfalls pour into streams that flow into quiet pools. Tremendous trees, more than fifty feet tall, reach almost out of sight toward skylights in the exhibit ceiling. For the visitor, every sense is awakened because JungleWorld looks, sounds, and even smells like a real rain forest.

This rain forest is completely indoors, so the temperature and amount of moisture in the air can be carefully controlled. Above one of the exhibit's four waterfalls, fog machines spray mist into the air. The moisture forms clouds that drift over the jungle. It is always warm and steamy here, just as it is in a tropical forest. Heating coils hidden beneath the realistic riverbanks at JungleWorld simulate sun-warmed basking areas for monitor lizards and crocodilelike gharials.

To add to the rain forest adventure, sounds of insects, birds, and frogs ring out from speakers hidden around the exhibit. These voices were recorded in faraway forests. Live JungleWorld animals answer with calls of their own. JungleWorld actually includes several rain forest habitats. In a mangrove swamp, playful small-clawed otters grab the tails of proboscis monkeys that perch on low branches; gharials cool themselves in a simulated river; the forest canopy high overhead provides a realistic habitat for troops of monkeys. More than eighty-seven different animal species live under one huge roof at JungleWorld.

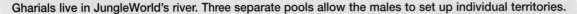

Gharials live in JungleWorld's river. Three separate pools allow the males to set up individual territories.

478

In the exhibit, some animals need to be separated from the visitors and from each other. Instead of traditional cages with bars, exhibit builders cleverly used naturalistic barriers. Visitor trails were placed just a little too far from the trees for the proboscis monkeys to leap onto them. Simulated mudbanks are so steep the gharials cannot climb them. Rocky cliffs extend to the ceiling behind spectacular waterfalls. These cliffs provide barriers to separate the three species of monkeys that would not live so close together in the wild. Sleek clouded leopards stretch lazily and watch monkeys play just a few feet away. A clean, almost invisible glass separates the leopards from the monkeys. Predators are not allowed to hunt living prey as they would in the wild, so the leopards must be separated from other animals.

At night most of the animals enter individual holding shelters hidden behind the plants and rockwork of the exhibit. They move readily into their overnight enclosures because this is where they are fed their big meals of the day. Each animal's diet is carefully planned to contain the necessary vitamins and minerals. Once the animals are secured inside their holding pens, keepers observe each individual closely and act quickly if one needs special attention. Every morning while the animals are still in their holding areas, keepers vacuum the floors of the pools and streams. They rake or wash down the jungle floor. Cleanliness is most important in keeping animals healthy.

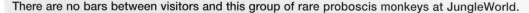

There are no bars between visitors and this group of rare proboscis monkeys at JungleWorld.

Artists at JungleWorld re-created giant rain forest trees.

In the wild, rain forest animals spend much of their time searching for food. To duplicate their natural activities, keepers put some food in the exhibit for the animals to "discover." Fresh leaves, sunflower seeds, and raisins are hidden for the monkeys. This extra food helps keep the leaf eaters from nibbling on the real plants. Crickets are tossed onto the mudbank for the otters. A special "feeding tree" was built for the gibbons. This artificial tree has a secret, bark-covered door in the trunk. Inside, a container is filled with nuts or seeds. Every so often, a device in the tree turns and a few treats fall through pipes and land in openings around the trunk. The quick-learning gibbons search the tree often because they sometimes find a tasty reward. Scientists believe searching for food helps keep the captive animals alert.

Hundreds of exotic ferns, shrubs, and small trees grow throughout the exhibit. But giant rain forest trees could not be brought to JungleWorld. Artificial trees were made with a framework of steel and fiberglass. The "bark" is a layer of hard plastic that was hand carved and painted. Miles of vines wind through the trees of a real rain forest. Gibbons and silvered leaf monkeys use vines to travel quickly through the treetops. Neither of these species spends much time on the ground. But the miles of vines used by the monkeys could not be grown easily in the exhibit. The young, slow-growing vines would constantly be broken by the acrobatic monkeys. So sturdy artificial vines were especially designed for such active climbers.

480

The vines were made by threading thin steel wires through long nylon ropes. Then the ropes were "slimed." Workers spread gooey rubber all over the ropes. Brown and green colors were mixed into the rubber. When the rubber hardened, the vines were shaped and painted to look as though they were covered with mosses and lichens. Then the vines were twisted and hung all through the tree branches. Some were hung near, but not too near, the trails so visitors can enjoy a close view of long-tailed acrobats in action.

JungleWorld is truly a zoo work of art. It is the first exhibit to combine so many different kinds of animals in one complex indoor habitat. Visitors leave knowing and caring more about the beautiful and valuable rain forest environment where tropical plants and wildlife thrive.

Habitat for Tropical Birds

One hundred fifty colorful birds with unusual names such as crested barbet, white-fronted bee-eater, and red-faced mousebird sing and call throughout the R. J. Reynolds Forest Aviary. Part of the North Carolina Zoological Park, the aviary is as big as an auditorium. Glass walls and a transparent roof allow sunlight to warm the aviary, creating a giant greenhouse. This indoor woodland simulates the tropical forests of Africa, Asia, and South America. Exotic birds from around the world share this lush enclosure.

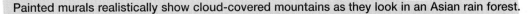

Painted murals realistically show cloud-covered mountains as they look in an Asian rain forest.

481

Visitors do not watch the birds from behind a window. Instead, they can enter the exhibit and walk among the fascinating birds. A booklet with color pictures helps people identify and name them. With thousands of people visiting the aviary, it might seem that some of the quick-flying birds would accidentally escape through the doorways. Yet this almost never happens. The aviary, which is only open during daylight hours, is always brightly lit by the sun. The entrance and exit hallways are dark. Birds will not fly into the dark area. There are two sets of doors in the hallway just in case, but birds rarely leave the lighted aviary.

Inside, a winding pathway takes visitors past trickling streams and rock outcrops that were realistically planned by the zoo's design team. Fig trees from Asia and Africa reach the ceiling to form the forest canopy, or highest level. These tall trees were carefully planted so the soaring birds would have plenty of flying space. Palm, banana, and rubber trees do not grow as tall as the fig trees and so form an understory layer. Canopy and understory trees provide shade and protect the lower levels from the sun's strong rays. Shrubs, vines, and ferns from tropical countries cover the ground. More than 2,000 plants create the multilayered bird habitat. The dense greenery provides hiding places, perches, and nesting materials for fifty-five species of birds.

White African spoonbills and South American scarlet ibises share an artificial stream in the North Carolina Zoo's forest aviary.

482

The green woodhoopoe darts around the understory in search of insects.

The one hundred fifty birds must be observed regularly by the keepers. To make identification of the birds possible, every bird is banded with colored leg bands. No two are alike. Keepers must use binoculars to see the colored bands on tiny lavender finches or scarlet-chested sunbirds. If any bird is not spotted once a month, a serious effort is made to find it. Finding each bird regularly helps the keepers know if one is sick or injured.

The most exciting time of the year in the aviary is nesting season. Each spring, keepers watch for signs of mating and nest building. Bird lovers walking along the curving pathways also search for hidden nests.

When the exhibit was first built, one of the birds gave keepers a special challenge at nesting time. The gray-headed kingfisher from Africa usually digs into mudbanks along creeks and rivers to make its nest. Since the aviary's "mudbanks" are made of wire coated by a layer of rock-hard Gunite, keepers had to give the tunnel nesters a helping hand. They cut a kingfisher-sized hole in the bank and pushed a long plastic tube into it. This duplicated the smooth tunnel made by a kingfisher. It took only a few days for the kingfishers to discover the tunnel and move in to nest. Like most of the aviary birds, they successfully raised young.

Any bird not hatched in the aviary must be introduced to the indoor habitat very carefully. A new arrival is not allowed near the other birds for thirty days in case it has some illness that could spread. During this time, the bird has a complete medical checkup. Before its release, the newcomer is placed in a cage on the floor of the aviary for a few nights. This gives the stranger time to get used to the sights and sounds of its future home. Three or four flight feathers

on each wing are clipped to slow its flying speed. If the bird flies fast at first, it might crash into the clear walls or roof and be seriously hurt. Clipped feathers are shed and replaced by new ones when the bird molts. By that time, the bird is familiar with the aviary and rarely flies into the glass.

Soon after its release, a bird learns where food bowls are placed. Because of the variety of birds, seven different diets are prepared each morning. In addition, some of the nectar feeders drink the sweet juices from orchids and other flowers. Fruit-eating birds gobble up berries as they ripen. Insect eaters catch pests on leaves and flowers. A few birds at the aviary require special diets. For example, the white-fronted bee-eater from Africa eats only insects it catches in the air, so the keepers toss out live insects for the bee-eater to grab.

Since its opening in 1982, the R. J. Reynolds Forest Aviary has become a very successful habitat exhibit. Between forty and fifty baby birds are raised each year. Some of the youngsters are sold to other tropical aviaries. This makes it unnecessary to capture birds in their natural habitats for exhibit purposes.

In the aviary, just as in nature, there is much for visitors to discover. If they look quickly and carefully, they will see brilliantly colored birds fly overhead and disappear into the dense forest. The aviary is what a realistic wildlife exhibit should be——a lifelike home for animals and an educational treat for people.

The bright red of the scarlet ibis from South America makes this bird one of the first to be spotted by a keeper or an aviary visitor.

484

The six-sided aviary building has a clear, domed ceiling four stories high.

Life in the Wild Versus Life in Captivity

Natural-habitat exhibits are exciting places and fun to visit. They are realistic homes away from home for plants and animals, and they let people peek into those fascinating worlds.

But artificial habitats are not perfect. Designers know that nature is far too complex to be duplicated. Some parts of a naturalistic exhibit are very different from the wild. In captivity, for example, plants and animals are tended by keepers specializing in their care. Many exhibit animals are taken indoors at night and during bad weather. Protected from their enemies, zoo animals receive expert medical attention and perfectly balanced meals. Even with such care, zookeepers may not meet every need of a captive species because all of its needs are not yet understood.

Living freely in its own natural environment is, of course, ideal for any living thing. But many wildlife habitats are disappearing. In much of the world people have moved in, cleared the land, and even killed the animals for their own needs. Thousands of plant and animal species are nearing extinction. As conservationists fight to save natural areas, zoos and aquariums have taken on the challenge of protecting some of the rare and endangered species. Natural-habitat exhibits provide safe and healthy places for plants and animals while helping visitors understand their world a little better.

Meet the Authors

Ginny Johnston and Judy Cutchins

write nonfiction science books for children. They started their writing careers by putting together a science newsletter. They realized there was a need for interesting and accurate science books for children, so they started writing books. They have focused on animal books because children like reading about them and the authors like writing about them. Johnston and Cutchins want children to learn the "value of every living thing and an awareness of the environmental concerns that affect them."

Theme Connections

Think About It

With a small group of classmates, discuss what you learned about creating and maintaining realistic habitats at zoos and aquariums.

- Why were zoos first created? Do they provide entertainment for humans or a sanctuary for animals?
- Is it ethical for wild animals to be kept in captivity?

Check the Concept/Question Board to see if there are any questions there that you can answer now. If the selection or your discussions about the selection have raised any new questions about ecology, put the questions on the Board. Maybe the next selection will help answer the questions.

Record Ideas

How do naturalistic wildlife habitats benefit humans as well as animals? Use your Writing Journal to record your notes and ideas.

Research Ideas

- Plan a zoo habitat that would be the ideal environmnent for a particular endangered species.
- Find out about the special dietary needs of some zoo animals and whether their normal foods or substitute diets are provided.

FINE Art

Mount Shuksan and Alpine Lake, North Cascades National Park.
Photo by Alan Kearney/ENP Images.

Dust Bowl. 1933. **Alexander Hogue.** Oil on canvas. National
Museum of American Art, Smithsonian Institution. Photo: Art
Resource, NY.

African Elephants. **Charles Tournemine.** Museé d'Orsay,
Paris. Photo: Giraudon/Art Resource, NY.

A Natural Force

by Laurence Pringle

A lightning bolt flashes in the summer night. It sizzles and spirals down a tree trunk. Wisps of smoke rise from dead pine needles on the forest floor. Flames glow in the night, and a forest fire begins.

The fire spreads quickly. Flames leap up to the crowns of trees, which explode into fireballs. Overhead the fire leaps from tree to tree. A wall of flames moves through the woods, gaining speed. The forest fire seems like a terrible beast with a mind of its own. It roars; it changes direction. It hungrily sucks oxygen from the air and kills almost everything in its path.

Some of the fastest wild animals are able to escape. The unlucky and the less swift perish——burned to death or robbed of oxygen by the fire. Sometimes a dying rabbit becomes an agent of the fire; its fur ablaze, it dashes crazily through the woods, setting fires as it goes.

At last the fire comes to an end. It dies because of rain, or the efforts of fire fighters, or a combination of factors. But the land is blackened, studded with tree skeletons, littered with dead animals. The soil is vulnerable to terrible erosion, and many years pass before the land heals itself with new plant growth and wildlife.

This scene of death and destruction exists in the imaginations of millions of people——*and seldom anywhere else.* Each year there are more than 100,000 forest fires in the United States. Most are started by people, either accidentally or on purpose. Some are started by lightning. Most lightning-caused fires go out, by themselves, after burning less than a quarter acre of land. And most forest fires of any size are beneficial to plants and animals.

Their good effects have been recognized for many years in the Southeastern United States. Each year forest managers there routinely set ablaze two million acres where pine trees grow. In the West, some wildfires are now allowed to burn for months in national parks and forests. This practice upsets people who feel that all forest fires are "bad."

Whether a forest fire is "bad" or "good" depends on many factors. No one advocates that fires be allowed to burn homes or valuable timber. But fire has been a natural force on land for millions of years, not just in forests but on prairies and savannahs (grasslands mixed with trees and shrubs). Fire became part of our planet's environment as soon as there was vegetation dry enough to be lit by lightning. From then on, periodic fires have been as natural as rain over much of the Earth's land surface. Rain can sometimes be destructive. So can fire. But a great deal of the Earth's plant and animal life has been "born and bred" with fire and thrives under its influence.

After many years of suppressing forest fires at all costs, ideas about them are changing. In the past few decades scientists have learned a lot about ecology——the study of relationships between living things and their environment. Now they are learning about ecopyrology——the ecology of fire.

Northwestern foresters deliberately set surface fires in order to help the growth of new trees.

492

The study of fire ecology is complex and fascinating because there are many kinds of forests and many kinds of fires. To understand the natural role of fire, scientists observe current fires and also investigate fires that occurred centuries ago.

They learn about past fires by examining fire scars. When a fire injures a tree's zone of growing cells (the cambium) and the wound heals, a mark that is eventually covered by bark is left. This scar can be seen later, when the tree is cut down. A cross-section near the tree's base reveals many of the fire scars that formed during the tree's life.

Studies of these scars show that fire was a normal occurrence in most of the original forests of North America. In California, scientists discovered that fires have happened about every eight years since the year 1685——as far back as they could date the cedar trees studied. They also found that few fire scars had formed after 1900, when people began preventing forest fires.

Ecologists have concluded that low-intensity fires, burning along the ground, were common in Western forests of ponderosa pine and sequoia. They also occurred frequently in Southeastern pine forests. With the exception of swamps and other year-round wet environments, fire used to be a regular happening in many parts of North America.

Crown fires are inevitable in some Western forests where fuel has accumulated over many years.

493

In many forests of the Pacific Northwest and Northern Rockies, fires were less frequent and usually more intense. Flames reached the crowns of trees, which were often killed or damaged. Forest managers have accepted the idea that crown fires are inevitable in parts of the West. The cool, dry climate prevents much decay of dead leaves and other natural litter on the forest floor. Plenty of fuel is available when ideal fire weather occurs, as it does in these northern forests every fifty to one hundred years or so.

Since fires have been a part of forest environments for many thousands of years, many plants have adapted to survive them. These plants might be called "fire species." Among them are the major forest trees of the Northern Rockies: ponderosa pine, white pine, lodgepole pine, larch, and Douglas fir.

These trees have especially thick bark, which can withstand fire damage better than the bark of other species. Fire species also include such plants as aspen, willow, and pine grass, which send up many sprouts after suffering fire damage.

One group of Western shrubs, known as *Ceanothus,* is especially dependent on fire. It includes redstem, wedgeleaf, snow brush, and deer brush. *Ceanothus* shrubs are three to nine feet tall and thrive where plenty of sunlight reaches the forest floor. Once damaged by fire, the shrubs produce abundant new sprouts. Furthermore, *Ceanothus* seeds must be exposed to high temperatures in order to sprout.

Ordinarily, vital moisture cannot get through the hard seed coat to the embryo plant inside. Heat from the fires causes the seed coat to open permanently. The seedling can then develop when conditions are right. After a forest fire, ecologists have counted as many as 242,000 *Ceanothus* seedlings on an acre of land.

Ceanothus shrubs thrive where fires occur. Western deer and elk feed on the shrubs, especially in wintertime.

The reproduction of jack pine, lodgepole pine, and some other evergreens depends partly on forest fire. These species have sticky resins that hold together the scales of their seed-bearing cones. The cones remain on the trees for many years, storing thousands of pine seeds. In time, a fire releases them. A temperature of about 122 degrees Fahrenheit is needed for the resins to melt so that the seeds can pop out onto the ground.

Fire also burns away all or most of the leaves and other natural litter. Many more seedlings grow from such an exposed seedbed than from a surface covered with a deep layer of leaves.

In a plant community that depends on periodic fire, not all species are well-adapted to it. Some take over if fire is kept out of the forest. Without fire, pines in the Southeast are gradually replaced by such deciduous trees as oaks. If no fire occurs for many years in a lodgepole-pine forest in the Rocky Mountains, the old pines are eventually replaced by Engelmann spruce and fir trees. The entire plant community changes unless a forest fire halts the process. A fire would kill many spruce and fir trees, which are less able to withstand the damage than lodgepole pine. And the fire would help release the seeds that represent a new generation of lodgepole pines.

Ponderosa pine is another fire species. It covers thirty-six million acres of Western land, from Nebraska to the Pacific Ocean and from Mexico to Canada. The large needles of ponderosa pine seem designed to encourage fire. Many needles are dropped each year. Because of their size they do not pack down much, and so they dry quickly. They also contain resins. Thus, the needles decay slowly and burn easily.

Seed pods opening after a fire. A ponderosa pine seedling flourishes on a forest floor where, once, the leaves were burned and seeds fell directly onto the soil.

As long as ponderosa-pine forests have occasional surface fires, the trees thrive and grow in grassy, parklike stands. A ponderosa-pine forest without fire is doomed. When young pines are not thinned out by fire, they grow so close together they are called "dog hair thickets." These thickets are a tremendous crown-fire hazard. Biologists sometimes call these dense stands of trees "biological deserts," because there is so little variety of life in them.

Without fire, white fir and Douglas fir gradually replace the ponderosa pines. The entire forest environment changes. Fir trees have dense crowns, which allow little light to reach the forest floor. Grasses and other surface plants dwindle in numbers and variety—— and so do the animals that depend on them. Ecologists have concluded that fire is vital for the survival of beauty and variety in ponderosa-pine forests.

Fire obviously plays a key role in allowing some major plant communities to thrive. Just as there are plant fire species, there are also animal fire species. Elk and deer rely heavily on *Ceanothus* shrubs for winter food in the West. Their health and numbers depend in part on forest fires, which cause *Ceanothus* to thrive. Periodic fires also affect the availability of aspen, a favorite food of moose.

A lack of occasional fires in pine woods may produce a dog hair thicket of young trees.

The very survival of the endangered Kirtland's warbler seems to depend on fire. About four hundred of these tiny, colorful birds nest in part of Michigan and nowhere else in the world. They are also known as jack-pine birds, because they build nests under or near young jack pines. This species may never have had a very big range. However, its numbers have declined because of fire control in Michigan jack-pine forests. In an attempt to prevent the Kirtland warblers from dying out, foresters now deliberately plan and set some fires to maintain the kind of nesting habitat needed by them.

Forest fires seldom kill wildlife. Most of them do not occur during the season when birds and other animals have young in nests or dens. Many kinds of animals seem able to sense a fire and its direction, and they move out of its way. Even slow-moving creatures like snakes usually escape.

Every forest fire is different and may have different effects. During most of the fire's life it moves slowly. Rain, lack of wind, or lack of fuel may bring the fire almost to a halt for several days. (Some have been known to smolder all winter long, then resume burning in the spring.) Fires have a daily rhythm too, slowing at night when winds usually die down.

Elk in Wyoming feed on willow and cottonwood, plants that produce new sprouts after a fire.

A fire's biography may include a wind-pushed rapid spread when some slow-moving animals are overtaken. It may also burn with great heat in certain areas and suffocate some animals hidden in burrows. Overall, however, wildlife populations are not usually harmed.

Deer, elk, and other large mammals often feed calmly near a surface fire. Usually fire fighters, not flames, are what frighten them away. Foresters working in Southern pine woods report that hawks are attracted by smoke. It may be a signal to them that rodents and other prey are on the move. Eagles and other predatory birds in Africa have also been observed catching insects, lizards, and rodents that are flushed from hiding places by an advancing fire.

Wildlife is attracted to freshly burned land too. Mice and other seed-eating rodents appear in great numbers after a forest fire, sometimes to the dismay of foresters who are concerned about getting a new crop of seedling trees.

For elk, deer, and other plant-eating animals, the end of a forest fire marks the beginning of a period of plentiful and nutritious food. Plants that grow after a fire are usually richer than normal in protein, calcium, phosphate, potash, and other nutrients.

In some ways the burning process is like the process of decay speeded up. As leaves and twigs decay, nutrients are released slowly, over a period of months or years. When leaves and twigs burn, the

Red squirrels and deer mice find abundant seeds after a forest fire. These plentiful seed-eating mammals are hunted by hawks and other predators.

nutrients are released quickly. From the soil they are gradually recycled into the roots of plants. This sudden dose of nutrients shows up in plant tissues for about two years after a forest fire.

Whether the new growth is shrub sprouts, new grasses, or other plants, it is nutritious, tender, and perhaps better-tasting than normal. Elk have been observed eating new sprouts of plants that they usually avoid when the plants are older.

A forest fire also produces a more varied "menu" of plants. The burning away of dead leaves, release of nutrients, and increased sunlight on the forest floor help create an environment in which a great variety of plants can grow. After a forest fire swept through an Idaho Douglas-fir forest, ninety-nine different kinds of plants appeared where only fifty-one species had been found before.

Ecologists suspect that periodic forest fires have other good effects. Woodsmoke seems to inhibit the growth of fungi, which sometimes harm living trees. Fire also affects populations of insects, including some pests, which spend part of their lives in the leafy litter of forest floors.

Forests and forest fires vary a lot. Scientists still have much to learn in order to understand and manage the fires that affect the forested one-third of the United States. There is no doubt, however, that the return of periodic fires will be good for most forests and their wildlife.

This photograph was taken immediately after the Elk Creek Fire in Yellowstone National Park in 1988.

The same place, photographed a year later, is covered by plant growth that was nourished by nutrients from ashes.

A Natural Force

Meet the Author

Laurence Pringle is a freelance writer, editor, and photographer. He taught science and worked for *Nature and Science* magazine before beginning his freelance writing career. Pringle writes science books for children and sometimes illustrates his books with photographs he has taken. He feels that writing is "incredibly hard." He would rather spend his time working on photography. He has contributed to *Highlights for Children* and *Ranger Rick* magazines. His interests include reading, movies, and sports.

Theme Connections

Think About It

With a small group of classmates, discuss what you learned about the positive effects of forest fires.

- How do trees compete with one another?
- Are there positive aspects of other natural events——such as floods, tornados, and earthqakes——that we think of as destructive?

Check the Concept/Question Board to see if there are any questions there that you can answer now. If the selection or your discussions about the selection have raised any new questions about ecology, put the questions on the Board. Maybe the next selection will help answer the questions.

Record Ideas

To what extent should humans intervene during natural events like forest fires? Record your notes and ideas in your Writing Journal.

Research Ideas

- Explore a variety of tree, plant, or flower that grows in a forest. Find out what it needs in order to thrive, how it reproduces, what animals eat it, whether it would survive a forest fire, and so on.

Poem for the Ancient Trees

by Robert Priest

I

am young and
I want to live
to be old
and I don't want to
outlive these trees——this forest.
When my last song is gone
I want these same trees
to be singing on——newer green songs
for generations to come
so let me be old——let me grow
to be ancient
to come as an elder
before these same temple-green sentinels
with my aged limbs
and still know a wonder
that will outlast me.
O I want
long love
long life.
Give me
150 years
of luck.
But don't
let me
outlive
these trees.

502

Saving the Peregrine Falcon

Caroline Arnold
photographs by Richard R. Hewett

High above a tall bank building in downtown Los Angeles, a peregrine falcon soars in the air looking for food below. The peregrine falcon is a wild bird that we do not normally think of as a city dweller. Yet the peregrine is at home among the high-rise buildings, which in many ways are like the cliffs and mountains where peregrines usually live. Window and roof ledges make good places to perch and to lay eggs, and the streets below are filled with pigeons, starlings, sparrows, and other small birds that peregrines like to eat. Today more and more peregrines are becoming part of city life as part of a special program to try to save this beautiful and powerful bird from extinction.

For centuries the peregrine was prized by kings and falconers who used it to hunt. Bird lovers too have always admired the peregrine. Yet a few years ago it was feared that soon there would be no more peregrines. Man's pollution of the environment with the poison DDT had interfered with the birds' ability to produce babies. The total number of peregrines was growing smaller each year. In 1970 there were only two known pairs of nesting peregrines in California. Until the 1940s, when DDT began to be used, there had been nearly two hundred. In the eastern United States the peregrine had already become extinct by 1970. Only with man's help could the peregrine be saved.

Peregrine falcons are found all over the world. The scientific name for those found in the United States is *Falco peregrinus anatum*. Other falcons living in the United States are the gyrfalcon, the prairie falcon, the merlin, and the kestrel. Although the numbers of these other falcons have been reduced by man, none of them were endangered like the peregrine.

Falcons are similar in many ways to birds in the hawk family. When flying, however, a falcon has pointed wings, which are better suited to speed, whereas a hawk has wide-spread wing feathers, which are better suited to soaring.

You can recognize an adult peregrine because it appears to wear a large black moustache. Both males and females have the same color markings but, as with all hawks and

falcons, the female is larger and stronger than the male. A female peregrine is usually about twenty inches long and weighs about thirty ounces. A male is about fifteen inches long and weighs about eighteen ounces. The male is sometimes called a tiercel from the French word meaning "third" because he is about a third smaller than the female peregrine.

Falcons, like hawks, eagles, and owls, catch and eat other animals. They are predators. The peregrine specializes in a diet of birds. In the United States, peregrines used to be called duck hawks because they were seen around marshes and occasionally hunted ducks.

The peregrine's body, like those of other predatory birds, is well adapted for hunting. Its strong feet and sharp talons are ideal for catching and carrying, and its beak is designed for tearing. The peregrine's eyesight is so keen that it has been compared to a person being able to read a newspaper a mile away! A soaring peregrine can see a bird hundreds of feet below.

After spotting a bird, the peregrine points its head down, tucks in its wings and feet, and transforms its body into the shape of a speeding bullet. As it begins to dive, it pumps its wings to increase its speed up to 200 miles per hour! When the peregrine reaches its prey, it grabs it with its feet, then

quickly kills it by breaking its neck. The peregrine then either carries the dead bird to a protected place and eats it, or brings it back to the nest to feed hungry babies.

Baby peregrines are usually called chicks, although a chick in a wild nest is also called an eyas.

Some of the smaller birds that peregrines in the United States eat spend the winter in Central and South America. There they eat grains and insects that have been sprayed with DDT. DDT is a poison used by farmers to kill insects that are harmful to crops. When the birds eat food with DDT on it, the poison is stored in their bodies. Later, when the peregrines eat these birds, they eat the poison too. The more birds the peregrines eat, the more DDT they store.

Scientists in the United States have found that DDT causes birds to lay eggs with shells that are too thin. When they measure the shells of hatched or broken eggs, they find that the thinnest shells are those with the most DDT in them. When parent birds sit on these eggs to keep them warm, the thin shells often break. Thin-shelled eggs also lose moisture faster than thick-shelled eggs. Often the chick growing inside the egg dies because the egg dries out too much. By helping the eggs with thin shells to hatch, scientists can combat some of the effects of DDT.

Most wild peregrines nest on high ledges on rocky cliffs. These nest sites are called eyries. A pair of peregrines makes a nest in an eyrie by scraping clean a small area in the stones or sand. In the scrape the female usually lays three eggs. Scientists carefully watch each peregrine nest. Then if they feel that the eggs are unlikely to hatch without help, they borrow them for a while, but first they let the birds sit on the eggs for five days. This seems to improve the eggs' chances of hatching in the laboratory. To get the eggs to the laboratory, scientists had to find a way to extract the eggs from the nest without scaring off the parent peregrines.

Because the cliffs where peregrines nested were so steep, only a mountain climber could reach a nest. When he approached the nest, the angry parents screeched and swooped at him. The mountain climber quickly and carefully put each speckled egg into a padded box. He then replaced the eggs he had taken with plaster eggs which look just like real peregrine eggs. These fake eggs would fool the parent birds. After the mountain climber left, the parents would return to the nest and sit on the plaster eggs as if they were their own.

It was important to keep the parent birds interested in the nest. After the eggs had hatched, the mountain climber would bring the babies back so that the parents could take care of them.

When the mountain climber returned to the top of the cliff, he put the eggs into a portable incubator. The incubator would keep them safe and warm on their ride back to the laboratory.

During the extinction scare, Brian Walton and the staff of the Santa Cruz Predatory Bird Research Group (SCPBRG) would collect eggs and release birds throughout the western United States. The laboratory at the SCPBRG center was used for hatching eggs and caring for the newly hatched peregrine chicks.

In the laboratory each egg was carefully weighed. Then it was held in front of a bright light in a dark room. This is called candling. When an egg is candled, the shadow of the chick growing inside and a lighter area at the large end of the egg can be seen. The lighter area is called the air pocket.

Then the egg was placed on a rack inside an incubator. The incubator keeps the egg warm and moist. Each day the egg would be weighed and candled again. As the chick grew, water slowly evaporated from the egg, making room for the air pocket to get bigger. The egg's weight shows how much water it is losing. If it was losing water too quickly, the incubator could be made more moist.

Wild birds turn their eggs constantly as they move around in the nest. But in the laboratory, people must carefully turn each egg four or five times each day. This prevents the growing chick from sticking to the inside of the eggshell. If the eggs are not turned, they will not hatch.

Sometimes eggs were found with shells so thin that they had already begun to crack. Then people in the laboratory would try to repair them with glue. Sometimes eggs were also waxed to prevent them from

losing moisture. Everything possible was done to make sure
that each egg hatched into a healthy peregrine chick.

The eggs were kept in the incubator until they were 31½
days old. Then they were carefully watched for the first
signs of hatching.

Each chick has a hard pointed knob on the top of its beak.
This is called an egg tooth. The chick pushes against the
inside of the shell with its egg tooth and breaks the shell.

The first crack in the egg is called the pip. When the pip
appears, the egg is moved to a special hatching chamber.
There the egg will take 24 to 48 hours to hatch. During that
time somebody watched it all the time. Some chicks are too
weak to break out of their shells. Then the scientists were
there to help them.

Often two eggs begin to hatch at about the same time.
Then they were put next to each other in the hatcher. When
a chick is ready to hatch, it begins to peep inside its shell.
The two chicks can hear each other peep. This seems to
encourage them to move around and break their shells.
Sometimes where there was only one egg, the scientists
would make peeping sounds for the chick to hear.

Starting at the pip, the chick slowly turns, pressing its
egg tooth against the shell. Soon the crack becomes a ring
around the shell. Then the chick pushes its head against the
top of the shell, and the shell pops open. After hatching, the
egg tooth is no longer needed, and in a week or so it falls off.

The newly hatched chick is wet and its down feathers are matted together. A cotton swab was used to clean the feathers. If necessary, ointment was put on the chick's navel to prevent infection. In the shell the chick gets nutrients from the yolk through its navel. Normally, by the time a chick hatches, the yolk has been totally absorbed and the navel has closed.

In the wild, a mother bird broods her chicks by sitting on top of them to keep them warm and dry. In the laboratory, the dry chick was placed with one or more other chicks in a small container called a brooder. A heater kept the chicks warm. The chick would rest in the brooder for eight to twelve hours. Then it would be ready for its first meal.

In the wild, the father peregrine hunts birds and brings them back to the nest. Then he and the mother peregrine tear off small bits of meat to feed each chick. The hungry chicks beg for food by peeping and opening their mouths wide.

Bird meat was also used to feed chicks in the laboratory. Usually the chicks were fed quail, although adult birds were also fed pigeon and chicken meat. First the meat was put through a meat grinder to break it into small pieces. The newly hatched chicks were then fed tiny pieces with tweezers. For somewhat older chicks the ground meat could be squeezed through a bag with a nozzle.

Like many birds, falcons have pouches in their necks to store food. These are called crops. Food first goes to the crop and then to the stomach. A bird feeder knew that a chick had had enough when the crop began to bulge.

During the day, young peregrine chicks need to be fed every three to five hours. At night they sleep eight hours between feedings.

Even though the peregrine chicks were cared for by people, it is important that they remain wild. During the first week or so, the chicks cannot see very well. Then it does not matter if people feed them directly. But as they get older, their contact with people must be limited.

Young animals identify with the other animals they see during the first weeks of life. This is called imprinting. Most young animals see only their parents in early life, and they imprint on them.

Peregrines raised in the laboratory that were returned to the wild had to be imprinted on adult peregrines. One way to help them do this was to feed them with a peregrine-shaped puppet. The puppet fooled the peregrine chicks and they behaved as if it were a real bird.

When a peregrine chick was three days to a week old, it was put into the nest of an adult bird that has been imprinted on people. At the SCPBRG center, adult birds were kept in barnlike buildings. Each large, open-air room in these buildings had bars across the top to let in air and light. Each room also has perches and nesting ledges for the birds.

Unfortunately there were not enough adult peregrines at the center to care for all the hatched chicks. Another more common bird, the prairie falcon, is very much like the peregrine, and it was often used as a substitute parent for very young peregrine chicks. During the breeding season, a female prairie falcon would care for adopted peregrine chicks. She would keep them warm and feed them as if they were her own. When the chicks were one to two weeks old, they were put into nests of peregrines which were not imprinted on people. Then, at the age of three weeks, the young peregrines were ready to go back to wild nests.

Before a bird would go back to the wild, a metal band was put on its leg. The band identified the bird and helped people keep track of it as it grew up.

Then the chicks were put into a special wooden pack and taken to the nest site. There the mountain climber put the pack on his back and climbed to the nest. He removed the plaster eggs and put in the young chicks. Then he left as quickly as possible. He did not want to disturb the parent birds any more than necessary.

The parent birds soon returned to the nest. Although they were surprised at first to find healthy chicks instead of eggs in their nest, the parents quickly accepted their new babies. The hungry chicks begged for food, and the parents' natural response was to feed them. The chicks were on their way to growing up as wild peregrines.

Most wild birds do not breed well in captivity. They are easily disturbed by people and by loud noises. At the SCPBRG the birds rarely saw people, although people could see the birds through tiny peepholes.

In the bird buildings a radio was constantly played. The sound blocked out most noises from outside. The radio also helped the birds become used to people's voices. Then they were less likely to be startled when people made noises outside their chambers.

Pairs of peregrine falcons at the SCPBRG center built nests and bred just as birds do in the wild. Their chicks could be released to help increase the number of wild peregrines.

Both in the wild and in captivity, peregrines normally raise only one nest of chicks each year. If the eggs are destroyed, however, the birds will lay a second set. In the wild, peregrine eggs might be eaten by other birds or animals. At the center, scientists purposely took away the first eggs from each pair of breeding falcons and hatched them in an incubator. The birds then laid another set of eggs. In this way each pair of birds could produce twice as many chicks as usual.

During its six weeks in the nest, a peregrine grows from a fluffy chick covered with soft down to a fully feathered bird the size of its parents. These first juvenile feathers are a mottled brown color. The peregrine will get its adult feathers at the beginning of its second year.

Three-week-old peregrine chicks were put into known wild nests that have parent birds on them when possible. But because there were so few peregrines left in the wild, soon all the wild peregrine nests were filled. Some peregrine chicks were put into wild prairie falcon nests. Others were released on their own when they were old enough to fly.

In the wild, a young peregrine is ready to fly at the age of six weeks. Then it leaves the nest and tries to hunt for food. At first it is not a very good hunter. Its parents will help it and continue to feed it. When juvenile peregrines from the laboratory were put into the wild, they had no parents to help them. Then people must help them instead.

Usually the birds were released near cliff tops or mountain ledges far away from where people live. They were placed in a box at the release site when they were about five weeks old. Sometimes the box had to be carried to the release site by a helicopter.

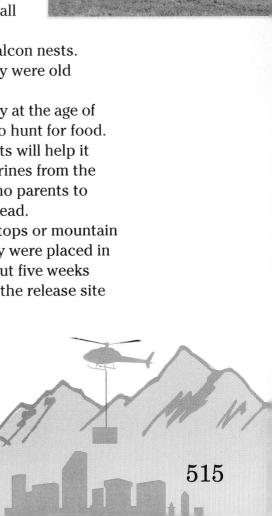

The box had bars across one side, but the people involved tried to stay out of the birds' sight. From behind, they dropped meat into the box for the birds. Then after a week, the box was opened and the birds were allowed to fly free.

People stayed at the site and put food out each day until the birds learn to take care of themselves. This could take four to five weeks. When the birds no longer needed to return to the release site for food, the people's job was finished.

In addition to its identification band, each bird also wore a small radio transmitter. The radio made beeping sounds which could be heard with a radio receiver. During the first few weeks on its own, a bird sometimes got lost or in trouble. Then people could find it by tracking the beeps over the radio receiver. After a few weeks the transmitter would no longer be needed, and it would fall off the bird.

Most birds were set free in wild places where peregrines once lived but are now gone. It was hoped that the new peregrines would stay there, build nests, and bring up chicks of their own.

Some peregrines were released in cities, and they seem to have adapted well to city life. Los Angeles, New York, Washington, Baltimore, Edmonton, London, and Nairobi are just some of the cities around the world where peregrines live. Some live on the ledges of office buildings. Others have built nests on tall bridges. In England peregrines lived for many years in the spire of Salisbury Cathedral.

In cities peregrines were usually released from the tops of tall buildings. As in the wild, people stayed and fed the birds until they could take care of themselves. After a pair of peregrines had claimed a building ledge as a nest site, scientists sometimes built a nest there for the birds. They may even have put a fake egg into the nest. They hoped that this would encourage the birds to begin laying their own eggs.

Peregrines usually do not mate and have young until their third year. In their first breeding years in the wild, peregrines can raise their own chicks. But as the birds get older and store more and more DDT in their bodies, their egg shells will become dangerously thin.

Peregrines must survive many dangers before they are old enough to produce their own chicks. Many hurt themselves when they collide with man-made objects such as fences or telephone and electric wires. Others are shot by unthinking people. Centers like the SCPBRG help sick and wounded peregrines.

The peregrine falcon is a beautiful bird, and it would have been sad to let it become extinct simply through ignorance or carelessness. Many animals that once roamed the earth are now gone because man destroyed or polluted their environments. For the present, the peregrine falcon has been saved from extinction. Through the work of many people around the world its numbers are increasing each year. If you are lucky, maybe where you live, you can see one of these magnificent birds soaring high in the sky.

Saving the Peregrine Falcon

Meet the Author

Caroline Arnold is a well-known writer of nonfiction science and nature books for children. Her books help children learn about the life cycles, habitats, and histories of many amazing animals. She discovered her love of nature at an early age and still remembers how excited she would be when she found a fossil or saw an animal in the wild. "As I write about animals, dinosaur bones, and other scientific subjects, my goal is to convey that same sense of discovery."

Meet the Photographer

Richard Hewett had his own darkroom by the time he was twelve years old. He is best known for his collaboration with Caroline Arnold on a series of children's science books. When Arnold and Hewett work together to create a book, they believe that the text and the photographs are equally important.

Hewett's photograph of a bloodhound named Stretch hangs in the Metropolitan Museum in New York City.

Theme Connections

Think About It

With a small group of classmates, discuss the lengths to which scientists are going to save peregrine falcons.

- Is there a simpler way to help peregrine falcons survive? What are the potential problems with a simpler method?
- Is saving a single endangered species from extinction worth the great amount of effort it requires?

Check the Concept/Question Board to see if there are any questions there that you can answer now. If the selection or your discussions about the selection have raised any new questions about ecology, put the questions on the Board. Maybe the next selection will help answer the questions.

Record Ideas

How can people change their behavior to reverse the harm they have caused to the environment? Record your notes and ideas in your Writing Journal.

Research Ideas

- Investigate other types of wildlife that live in urban areas. Find out whether and how an urban setting changes the lives of wild animals.

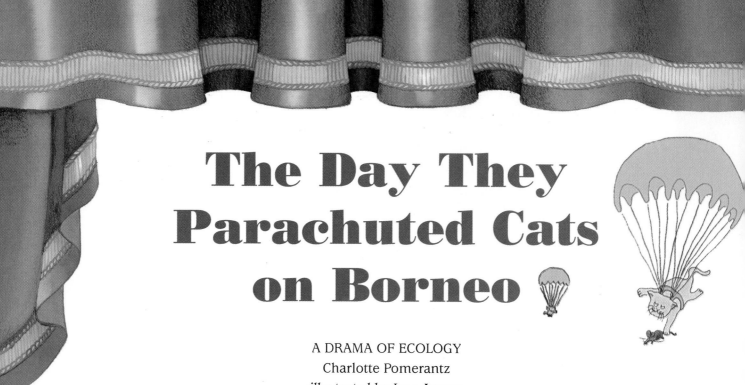

The Day They Parachuted Cats on Borneo

A DRAMA OF ECOLOGY

Charlotte Pomerantz

illustrated by Jose Aruego

This play is based on an actual event reported in the New York Times, *November 13, 1969.*

CAST IN ORDER OF APPEARANCE AND DISAPPEARANCE

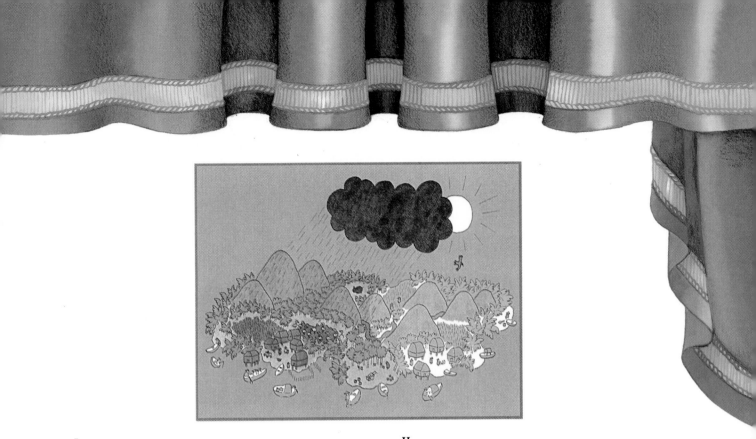

I

I am the island of Borneo,
Where the farmer—poor farmer—bends low,
   bends low.
I have honey bears, rhinos, and tiger cats,
Great falcons, flamingoes, and foxy-faced bats.
I have gold and quicksilver, rubber and rice,
Cane sugar and spice—but not everything nice:
     A land of harsh ridges and savage
       monsoon,
     Of jungles as dark as the dark of the moon.
     Land of thundering rains and earthquakes
       and heat,
     Where the farmer's life is more bitter
       than sweet.
     Land of mosquitoes, which carry with ease
     The dreaded malaria, scourge and disease.

II

I am malaria, dreaded disease.
I cause men to ache and to shake and to freeze.
Three hundred million a year do I seize.
One million I kill with remarkable ease.
But I'm not the big killer I used to be
In the good old days before—ugh!—DDT;
'Cause that stuff kills mosquitoes—one,
   two, three . . .

And the death of them is
  the death of me.

III

My name is dichloro-diphenyl-trichloroethane,
Which you've got to admit is a heck of a name.
But, perhaps, some of you have heard tell of me
By my well-known initials, which are DDT.
An organo-chlorine insecticide,
I come in a powder or liquified.
I'm death to mosquitoes outside or inside.
I was brought here by copter to Borneo,
Where the farmer—now hopeful—bends low,
   bends low.
My job is to kill that cruel killer of man:
A worthy and wise ecological plan.

If you don't know what ecology
means, you'll soon find out.

IV

We are the mosquitoes who roam day
   and night,
Bringing death to the farmer with one
   small bite.
We like the farmer's hut—it buzzes with life.
There's the farmer, of course, his kids and
   his wife.
The caterpillars chew on the roof beams there,
While the geckoes, or lizards, roam everywhere.
There are lots of cockroaches, and always
   some cats
Who pounce on the lizards and scare away rats.
All of us are busy—busy looking for food.
Sometimes we eat each other, which may seem
   rather crude.
But imagine yourself in that hut, and I bet
You would rather eat someone than find
   yourself et.

Now suddenly—zap!—there is no place to hide,
For they sprayed all the huts with insecticide.
That's the end of our tale.

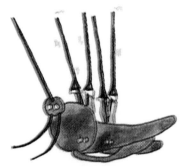

Postscriptum: we died.

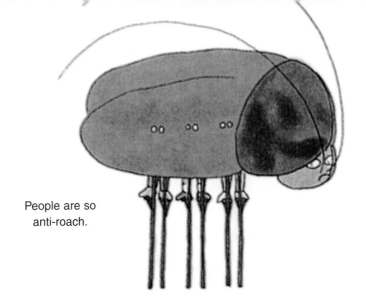

People are so
anti-roach.

V

We are the cockroaches, homeloving pests.
In most people's huts we are unwelcome guests.
When we all got sprayed with that DDT stuff,
The mosquitoes got killed—not us. We're
    too tough.
We just swallowed hard and kept right on
    a-crawling,
Despite the rude comments and vicious
    name-calling.

VI

We're the hungry caterpillars of Borneo,
Where the farmer—also hungry—bends low,
    bends low.
We live on the roof beams, eating and hatching.
We make all our meals out of roof beams and
    thatching.
      Nosh-nosh, nibble-nibble, munch-munch-
        munch,
      For breakfast, supper, high tea and lunch.
Our life is as pleasant as green tea and roses,
Except when the lizards (gulp) poke in their noses
      Then nosh-nosh, nibble-nibble, munch-
        munch-munch,
      The lizards ate half our cousins for lunch.
Those four-legged reptiles ruin our meals . . .

You'd have to be eaten
to know how it feels.

VII

We are the lizards, or geckoes, by name.
To the farmer we're useful, we're charming,
    we're tame.
Over the floors, walls and roof beams we roam,
Of every tropical home sweet home.
For us, cockroaches are scrumptious to eat.
Almost as tasty as caterpillar meat.

At night the caterpillars and the roaches
Walk right up to us and say, *Buenas Noches*.

VIII

Then the copters sprayed, and we lost our
    appetite.
Now we laze away the days, we snooze the
    balmy night.
For every roach we eat, though they *do* taste
    yummy,
Adds DDT to our little lizard tummy.
And makes our tiny nervous system sluggish
    and slow.
We geckoes—leaping lizards!—got no get-up-
    and-go.
    It's true we're not dying of DDT,
    But a slooow gecko ain't nooo gecko,
    As the caterpillars can plainly see.
We watch them eating roof beams like there's
    no tomorrow,
While we lizards hold our tummies in pain
    and sorrow.

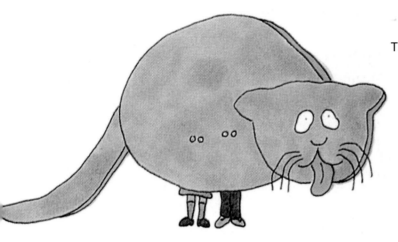

Be careful of the
lizard you eat.
The life you take may
be your own.

IX

We're the cats on the island of Borneo
Where the farmer—who loves us—bends low,
  bends low.
Eating all those lizards, or geckoes, by name,
Is turning out to be (sigh) a dying shame,
'Cause those lizards are poisoned from tail
  to head,
And killing those lizards is killing us dead.
We poor cats got a massive overdose.
What's left to say
(Sob)
Except *adios*.

Whoever thought that little man could affect
us mighty rivers? But the rain has washed
the DDT into our waters, and our tenants, the
friendly fish, are feeling pretty rocky.

X

We're the rivers, the rivers of Borneo.
We watch little man come and go, come and go.
We watched him kill mosquitoes with pesticide.
Saw the roaches poisoned, though not one
  cockroach died
Till . . .
The hungry lizards ate them, one by one
  by one.
Oh what a feast they had—it seemed like good
  clean fun.
But every roach they ate, though they *did* taste
  yummy,
Added DDT to their little lizard tummy.
Then the lizards were filled with deadly
  pesticide.
They felt pretty punchy, though not one
  lizard died
Till . . .
The hungry cats devoured them, one by one
  by one.
Oh what a feast they had—it seemed like good
  clean fun.
But every liz they ate, though they *did* taste
  yummy,
Killed the cats by poisoning their DD Toxic
  tummy.
Now this poor old island is steeped in
  poison air.
Our waters, too, are poisoned. Little man,
  take care!

XI

We're the rats on the island of Borneo,

We never had it so good—heigh—dee—ho.

When the cats who had swallowed the geckoes
lay dying,

We crawled in by thousands from forests outlying.

    When the farmers saw us, they raised an
        anguished cry:

      "Rats bring plague! Fly in help, or we shall
        surely die.

      Help us, men of science, help us kill the rats;

      For the DDT you sprayed has killed off all
        our cats!"

"Borneo for rent," we sang. "Inquire, please,
within.

When the cats die off from DDT, we rats—
move—in."

And then the helicopters came...

XII

We're the copters who've just flown in
    thousands of cats

And chuted them down on the armies of rats,

On the plague-threatened island of Borneo,

A bright green jewel in the blue sea below.

Once we came with DDT; now we come with cats.

Once we sprayed mosquitoes; now we'll fix
    the rats.

Looks like no one really thought the whole
    thing through . . .

Soon all the cats and rats will have a deadly
    rendezvous.

It was, all told,
a rather unusual assignment.

But let the roof beams
tell their own story.

XIII

We're the parapussycats they parachuted down
On every cat-killed, rat-filled little village
    and town
On the dead-cat, dread-rat island of Borneo,
Where the farmer—strictly catless—bends low,
    low, low.

XIV

When we parapussycats were dropped to the
    ground,
What a feast we had—there were rats all around.
Everywhere you looked there were rats and rats
    and rats
Pursued by our élite corps of parapussycats.
We chased the rats for days, till most of them
    had fled,
And those who didn't run fast enough were—
    biff bam!—dead.

It's better than hanging
around fish markets.

XV

The good farmers gave us a ticker-tape parade.
They heaped us with ivory, gold and silk brocade.
They said they would grant us our most
    fantastic wish—
So we asked them for five hundred kettles of fish.
We were wined, we were dined, we slept in
    king-size beds,
Till we heard a strange creaking just over our
    heads . . .
KA-RASH!

XVI

We're the roof beams of thatched huts
    in Borneo,
Where the farmer—enduring—bends low, bends
    low.
If a man, now and then, did some roof patching,
Replaced chewed-up beams and half-eaten
    thatching,

We could keep out the wind, the rain, and
    the sun,
And shelter a man when his labors were done.
Despite caterpillars, we roof beams stayed strong,
And the lizards, by eating them, helped us along.
For the lizard, you see, was the number-one killer
Of the beam-eating (nosh-nosh) cater- (nosh-
    nosh) pillar.

Now we mourn the little lizards—may they rest
    in peace—
While the greedy caterpillars (burp) get more
    and more obese.

XVII

Good day, I'm a farmer in Borneo,
Where the coconut palm and the mango grow.
Here are honey bears, rhinos, and tiger cats.
Great falcons, flamingoes, and foxy-faced bats.
Here are gold and quicksilver, rubber and rice,
Cane sugar and spice—but not everything nice:
    When they sprayed my hut with insecticide,
    My rat-catching cat soon sickened and died.
    When the rats crawled in, I was filled
        with fear:
    The plague can kill more than malaria here.
    When my roof beams caved in, I moved
        next door,
    Until *their* roof beams collapsed to the floor.
But please do not think I wish to offend,
For DDT is the farmer's good friend.
Still, perhaps you'll allow a poor man to say,
He hopes men of science will soon find a way
To kill the mosquitoes till all, all are dead—
But save the roof beams which are over my head,
As well as my most useful rat-catching cat.
How grateful I'd be if you'd only do that!
    Then, men of science, I would not complain.
    But now I must look to my roof—I smell rain!

XVIII

    I am an ecologist. Ecology is the study of
living things in relation to the world around

them—everything around them—air, water, rocks, soil, plants, and animals, including man.

If a tree is cut down, I try to find out what will happen to the birds in the nests, the squirrels in the branches, the insects at the roots. I know that the roots of the tree hold the earth, that the earth holds the rainwater, and that the rainwater keeps the soil moist, so that plants can grow. I am concerned if too many trees are cut down, for then the rain will run off the surface of the soil, making the rivers rise, overflow their banks and flood the land. This is the kind of thing an ecologist thinks about.

Borneo is a huge island in Southeast Asia—the third largest in the world and bigger than all of Texas. It straddles the equator, which is why the climate is hot and steamy. Someone has said that there are two seasons in Borneo— a wet season and a less wet season.

The people are mainly Malays and Dyaks. The

Malays, who live near the coast, are rice farmers and fishermen. Some work on rubber plantations or in the oil fields, for Borneo is rich in oil. Inland are high mountain ranges, where most of the Dyaks live. Until recently, they were headhunters—the wild men of Borneo—and they still hunt with blowguns and poisoned darts. The women grow rice, yams, and sugarcane in tiny forest clearings.

Most of Borneo is part of the Republic of Indonesia. Some of it belongs to Malaysia, and a tiny part is an independent state called Brunei. It is an island of dense tropical forests, where vines grow as high as a thousand feet, where orangutans swing through the trees, and where the giant long-nosed proboscis monkey can grow as tall as a man. There is also a great variety of insects, including the anopheles mosquito. This mosquito carries malaria and is the reason I was sent to Borneo.

Mosquitoes breed in wet places, and there are many

swamps and rain holes in Borneo. In the old days, we used to fight mosquitoes by draining swamps, when possible, and by spraying a thin film of oil on stagnant waters during the breeding season. Those who could afford to, put screens on doors, windows, and openings to keep the mosquitoes out. All this helped to keep malaria down, but millions of people still got sick.

Then, during World War II, a scientist discovered that a certain chemical compound, called dichloro-diphenyl-trichloroethane—DDT for short—was a marvelous insect killer. The discoverer, Dr. Paul Mueller of Switzerland, received the Nobel Prize for his discovery.

In Borneo, we sprayed the walls and insides of the huts with DDT. You know what happened: we killed the mosquitoes—and ended up with no cats. We had not realized how much DDT can accumulate in the fatty tissues of animals. Even a tiny amount of DDT in food or drinking water, with repeated meals, builds up and up until the quantity is large enough to poison a large animal, such as a cat.

As you know, with the cats dead, the rats took over and brought the threat of plague. So cats were flown in to stop the rats. Then, just when matters seemed under control—the roofs fell down. This is but a small example of the complex and subtle connections and balances which exist among all living things.

Because of the poisonous effects of DDT, it has been banned or restricted in the United States, the Commonwealth of Independent States, and other industrial countries. In December, 1969, at a world conference of the Food and Agricultural Organization (a body of the United Nations), an attempt was made to ban the use of DDT all over the world.

But the majority of scientists, representing the nonindustrial countries, refused to go along with the ban. They knew DDT was dangerous to health, but

they needed it to control malaria and other diseases, and to protect food crops from insect destruction. The alternatives to DDT are expensive, and the nonindustrial countries, which contain about eighty percent of the world's population, cannot afford them, for they are very poor.

The wealthy nations pointed out that the danger of pesticides is everyone's responsibility, for when you pollute the atmosphere, and the waters which flow to the oceans, everyone

suffers. Ecologically, the nations of the earth are one.

The poor nations replied that the wealthy nations are not faced with malaria epidemics, wholesale destruction of the food supply, and mass starvation. They can afford to worry about the future of the environment. The poor nations can only think of day-to-day survival. Seventy-five per cent of the people in the world go to bed hungry, and the great majority of them are in the poor, nonindustrial countries.

Ecologists from underdeveloped countries, faced with starvation and disease, can only choose the lesser evil—DDT. But the real answer to their problem is to find new solutions. Work is going forward on drugs for the prevention of malaria. Unfortunately, some of these drugs have bad side effects. Others are not effective for all kinds of malaria. And all drugs are very expensive.

A more fruitful road is for scientists to seek an insecticide that kills mosquitoes and nothing else. Scientists have discovered that under crowded conditions, some mosquitoes release a toxic chemical that kills young mosquitoes. If they can isolate and synthesize that chemical, it would be a great step forward in malaria control.

Another possibility, which shows considerable promise, is to breed a variety of mosquito which leaves seventy-five per cent of the female eggs unfertilized. Released among other mosquitoes, this new strain transmits its infertility to all the offspring. Thus each generation would breed fewer and fewer mosquitoes.

We've been talking about DDT and the farmers of Borneo, but ecological problems are extremely varied and serious, and they cover the whole world. For example, the fumes of automobile exhausts have greatly increased the number of people who get lung diseases. Atomic radiation has increased the incidence of certain types of cancer. The hot water from power plants, when poured into lakes and rivers, kills the fishes.

There is pollution by lumber mills in Lake Baikal in the Commonwealth of Independent States. There is too much sewage in the canals of Amsterdam and Venice. The Danube is no longer blue. One can no longer swim in the Rhine in Germany, or in the Seine in Paris, or in our own Hudson River. Whole stretches of

beaches in Italy, South America, England, and the United States have been polluted with oil slicks from the sea.

This is bad enough, but if the oil spills continue, worse will follow: a thin film of oil will spread over all the oceans. This will cut down the sunlight which very tiny plants, called diatoms, need both to reproduce and to live. These tiny plants, billions and billions of them, are the source of food for all the fishes of the sea. Further, these tiny plants use sunlight to combine with water to form carbon dioxide (used as food by them) and oxygen which is released into the air. Eighty percent of all the oxygen in the world comes from these tiny plants. If sunlight is cut down and the amount of oxygen is reduced, the whole animal kingdom, including man, will suffer.

We need to know these things, so that we can do something to keep the air and water clean for all the people, as well as for all the animals and plants in the world. The ecologist should not protect the farmer against malaria with one hand and bring the roof down on his head with the other. But the answer is not for the ecologist to do nothing, but to be wiser about what he does. This is the moral of Borneo.

The Day They Parachuted Cats on Borneo

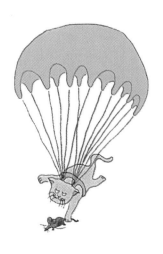

Meet the Author

Charlotte Pomerantz has had articles, poems, and stories published in several magazines for children and adults. As a child she remembers writing stories for enjoyment. "As far back as I can remember, I have liked to write, with no thought of being a writer." Pomerantz continued writing throughout high school and college and found success writing children's stories after her own children were born. They "provided rich, raw material. . . . I started making notes of what they said. . . . I recommend the keeping of a journal to all who would write and remember."

Meet the Illustrator

Jose Aruego is a well-known illustrator of children's books. He was born into a family of lawyers in the Philippines. It was assumed he would also become a lawyer, so he attended law school. After working as a lawyer for three months, Aruego realized he was not happy. He really wanted to go to art school to become a cartoonist, so that is what he did. After graduating, he sold his cartoons to magazines such as *The Saturday Evening Post* and *The New Yorker*. After he married and had a child, he began writing and illustrating books for children. Aruego has written or illustrated more than 60 children's books and has won many awards for his illustrations.

Theme Connections

Think About It

With a small group of classmates, discuss what you have learned about the relationship that exist among the creatures within an ecosysytem.

- Starting with the problem of malaria, how could things have been done differently in Borneo to prevent the chain of reaction of disaster?
- How is a balance maintained in nature? Why don't the stronger, more aggressive species kill off those that are weaker?

Check the Concept/Question Board to see if there are any questions there that you can answer now.

Record Ideas

Why is DDT still being used in poor countries? Record your notes and ideas in your Writing Journal.

Research Ideas

- Investigate natural ways of solving ecological problems as an alternative to using toxic substances.
- Find out more about the food web of the animals native to your community.

Bibliography

The Earth Is Painted Green: A Garden of Poems About Our Planet

edited by Barbara Brenner. The earth is celebrated in this international collection of poems. Join in!

Ecology for Every Kid: Easy Activities That Make Learning Science Fun

by Janice VanCleave. Get closer to ecological issues such as global warming, acid rain, and endangered animals through activities and experiments.

Elephant Woman: Cynthia Moss Explores the World of Elephants

by Laurence Pringle. Cynthia Moss has lived in Africa and studied elephants for many years. Join this world-renowned researcher through her photographs, and meet the elephant families.

Flute's Journey: The Life of a Wood Thrush

by Lynne Cherry. See the migration of a wood thrush from Maryland to Costa Rica, and encounter the natural as well as human-made challenges it faces.

Julie's Wolf Pack

by Jean Craighead George. A gray wolf, Kapu, leads his pack through many challenges in the Arctic wilderness.

Lifetimes

by David L. Rice. Learn about how lifetimes differ in nature. How long does a whale live, how old is a saguaro cactus, and has that star been around forever?

The Most Beautiful Roof in the World: Exploring the Rainforest Canopy

by Kathryn Lasky. Salamanders, spider monkeys, and vipers are just a few of the creatures that call the rainforest canopy *home.* This book looks at their unique world and ecosystem.

Wolf Stalker

by Gloria Skurzynski and Alane Ferguson. Who shot Silver, one of the protected wolves of Yellowstone? Jack and his family are going to try and solve the mystery.

Why are some things worth more than other things? Can things that cost very little money be valuable? What do you consider valuable?

The Miser

Aesop
illustrated by Jean and Mou-sien Tseng

A miser, who never stopped worrying about the safety of his many possessions, sold all his property and converted it into a huge lump of gold. This he buried in a hole in the ground near his garden wall, and every morning he went to visit it and gloat over the size of it.

The miser's strange behavior aroused the curiosity of the town thief. Spying upon the rich man, the thief saw him place the lump of gold back in the hole and cover it up. As soon as the miser's back was turned, the thief went to the spot, dug up the gold and took it away.

The next morning when the miser came to gloat over his treasure he found nothing but an empty hole. He wept and tore his hair, and so loud were his lamentations that a neighbor came running to see what was the trouble. As soon as he had learned the cause of it, he said comfortingly: "You are foolish to distress yourself so over something that was buried in the earth. Take a stone and put it in the hole, and think that it is your lump of gold. You never meant to use it anyway. Therefore it will do you just as much good to fondle a lump of granite as a lump of gold."

*The true value of money is not
in its possession but in its use.*

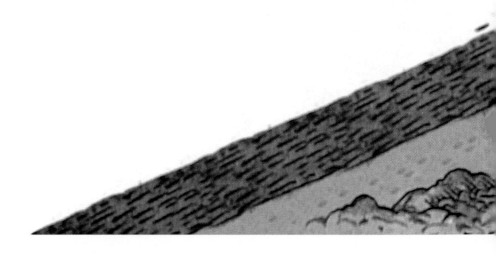

540

The Miser

Meet the Author

Aesop lived, historians believe, sometime during the sixth century B.C. He was born a slave and while working as a slave began telling his stories. Because he was so witty and skillful with words, his master set him free. Many phrases from his stories are now widely used expressions such as, "out of the frying pan into the fire" and "don't count your chickens before they're hatched."

Meet the Illustrators

Jean and Mou-sien Tseng have illustrated many Asian folklore books written by Laurence Yep. Other well-known books they have illustrated are *The Seven Chinese Brothers* by Margaret Mahy and *Why Ducks Sleep on One Leg* by Sherry Garland.

Theme Connections

Think About It

- Think about the question of what gold (money) is really good for in life.

- The true value of money lies in using it, not in just having it. Speculate as to whether the miser's life will really be different without his gold.

Record Ideas

 Record in your Writing Journal specific ideas about how worthwhile values have impacted your life.

Tell a Story

- Working with a partner, plan a modern-day version of "The Miser."

- How did you modernize the story?

- Now tell your version to another pair of students, and ask them how they would have changed the story.

Money Matters

from *Tough Tiffany*
by Belinda Hurmence
illustrated by Michelle Mills

Tiffany Cox——known as Tiff——lives with her parents and five siblings in a small, crowded house in North Carolina. Tiff is forced to share a bed with her twin sisters until the day her mother makes a down payment on two sets of bunk beds. Tiff gets a bunk to herself, and it soon becomes her special, private place.

But the Coxes have trouble making payments on the bunk beds, and a man comes to repossess them. Tiff talks him into waiting one more day. She promises him they will have the money then, but Mama uses some of the bunk-bed money to pay other debts. "When he come around tomorrow, I give him this seventeen dollars and he'll take it and be tickled to get it, you'll see," she assures her children. The man does take the money, but he's angry. He leaves only after Mama promises to pay the remaining balance on her next payday.

Tiff worries when payday arrives and Mama spends her check on new clothes for the family instead of the beds. The Coxes return home that evening to find a note: "Final Notice! Balance Due $76." Tiff wishes that her special bed could be paid for; it is more valuable to her than her new dress.

That weekend, Tiff stays with Granny to help out with a big family reunion. Tiff loves her grandmother and tries to treat her with respect even though the old woman is strict, cranky, and as frugal as Tiff's mother is wasteful.

The next day, Monday, Tiff was to go home. For the time of the reunion, she had postponed thinking about the bunk beds, but on Sunday night when she climbed into the lumpy bed she shared with Granny, she wondered if there would be any bed at all for her to sleep in at home, tomorrow night. She thought about the man she had deceived, coming for his money, and she stirred uncomfortably.

"Settle down there, you girl," Granny said. "Can't nobody get they rest with you threshing around in the bed."

So she lay as still as she could, not moving at all until Granny's snores liberated her; and even then she could not find a smooth place, but kept turning cautiously, lying first on one side and then the other, and thinking longingly of her bunk bed up under the ceiling, her own smooth place, hers alone. When fatigue finally released her into the privacy of sleep, she slept deeply and did not rouse when the old lady arose at dawn, according to her custom.

Sounds from the kitchen mixed in with her dreams, sounds of doors opening and closing and dreams of somebody waiting on the porch; sounds of heavy things being lifted, shifted, quickening sounds of furniture sliding, dreams of her bunk bed sliding down from the ceiling; and a queer little whickering fitted neatly into a dream she managed to shape——Tiny whimpering? herself?—— whickering, whispering——what? The dream lost shape as she felt a presence, something, or somebody hovering. She woke with a small jerk to find Granny beside the bed, fumbling under the mattress. Fumbling, whispering to herself, and that queer little whickering.

"Granny?"

"My money," the grandmother quavered. "I can't find my money."

Tiff said drowsily, "Did you look in your pocketbook?"

"Not that money. My other money, that I keep."

Tiff rolled creakily out of bed and stumbled to the bathroom. When she came back, Granny had the mattress turned back on itself and the sheets and pillows jumbled in a pile on the floor.

The old lady said wildly, pathetically, "It's gone. My money's all gone. Somebody's come and took my money away from me." She began to cry, with hacking, gasping little sobs that horrified Tiff. Granny wasn't the kind of woman who ever cried about anything.

"Don't cry, Granny," she begged. "I'll help you look for your money. Maybe you just forgot where you put it. Where was the last place you saw it?"

The old lady showed her a sort of pocket in the mattress, cleverly sewed, easy to overlook, empty.

Tiff said reasonably, "Did you always keep it there? Maybe you moved it, and forgot." She opened a bureau drawer and searched through an assortment of rolled-up stockings.

"I already looked in there. It's gone, for sure, it's been stole." The old lady showed her a narrow rack, fastened to the back of the bureau drawer, cleverly fashioned out of linoleum scraps, shallow enough that the drawer could be closed, but adequate for holding a sheaf of bills, perhaps; empty.

Tiff moved everything off the shelves of Granny's closet and began searching through boxes.

"I already looked there." The grandmother now wept so uncontrollably that Tiff could not question her further. She searched the house through, moving furniture, groping inside vases, looking under rugs, checking half a dozen or more secret hiding places the grandmother showed her, false floor boards, backs of picture frames, hiding places that would have delighted her if she had not been intent on the more urgent business of soothing the distraught old lady.

"Are you sure you looked in your pocketbook?"

"Yes, but it ain't that money, it's my money that Mr. Honeycutt give for our farm, that was going to last me my days. I never kept it in my pocketbook. It's gone! Oh, help me, Lord, how'm I going to take care of me in my old age?" Tears streamed down her face.

"I'll take care of you, Granny, don't worry. I'll always take care of you. Please don't cry, Granny. Let's look in your pocketbook just to make sure."

The grandmother spread the contents of her pocketbook out on the mattress. There were her handkerchiefs, the lace one for show, the flowered one for blow, her accordion rain bonnet, the door key on a knotted string, her spectacles, her coin purse. Tiff snapped

open the coin purse. Inside were some coins and folded bills with a dusty look to them, smelling faintly of country ham. "Here's money, Granny."

"But my other money——my other——" Her voice broke.

Tiff studied the folded bills and figured. Something. What? "Where did this money, this in your coin purse, where did it come from?"

"Why, I take it, little bits at a time, when I need it, from my other money."

Something more, something more! "Well, your other money, you got all those hiding places you keep it in, and I figure you keep moving it around so nobody will see you going to the same place all the time."

The grandmother nodded.

"Did you ever forget where you put it the last time?"

"Yes, but I kept looking, and then when I found it, I remembered when it was I changed the place."

"Do you ever make up new hiding places to keep it in? You could have made up a new place and forgotten, you know."

Hope struggled with irritation in Granny's face. "You think I forget where I keep my own money?"

"Well, you're always complaining you can't remember anything one minute to the next." Tiff rubbed the bills from the coin purse. Dusty. She was almost sure. "Do you keep your other money in a plastic bag, Granny?"

"In four plastic bags. How you know that?"

"Are they plastic bags that country ham comes in?"

"Yes! Yes! Those good heavy bags that they won't nothing punch a hole in. How you know that, girl? I know you never saw my money." Granny was trembling all over.

Tiff wheeled and ran to the kitchen. The grandmother hurried after her. Saturday, making biscuits, Tiff hadn't been allowed to measure flour out of the big lard can where Granny stored it. Now, she lifted the lid and plunged her bare arm inside, feeling, exploring the dusty white until she touched a packet buried there, just the way she had figured. She fished it out, and after it in quick succession, three more flat important packets, dredged with flour. "All ready for the fry pan, Granny," she teased.

Of course! the old lady said disgustedly; now she remembered. But it had given her a bad time. She sat down at the kitchen table to recover, and to fondle her money.

It was all hundred-dollar bills! Millions of them, it looked like! First time Tiff had ever seen a hundred-dollar bill, let alone millions of them, and she said so.

Granny said gratefully, "Well, you going to look all you want, honey, for one of them hunderd dollars is yours, for a reward, finding my money for me."

"I don't want any reward," said Tiff. "All I did was help you hunt. You'd have found it by yourself, when you used up the flour."

But she might have grieved herself to death, by the time she made that many biscuits, Granny said, smiling now, holding out the reward. "Take it. I want you to have it. You get the look of a hunderd-dollar bill in your mind, and the feel of it in your hand, and you won't never want to break it down, I guarantee you."

Tiff took the bill in her hand for the honor of it, to look at and feel, but not to keep. She could understand how Granny felt, a little. A hundred-dollar bill was an important-looking thing you'd hate to break; but if you didn't break it, what was it good for? She wouldn't say so to Granny, but she'd rather be a spendthrift, like Mama, buying things she couldn't afford and enjoying the spending, than hiding money away for enjoyment. "Granny!" she exclaimed, handing back the bill, "I really truly don't want any reward, but would you lend Mama seventy-six dollars instead?" She explained about the bunk beds and about the man who would almost certainly come to take them back today, and she promised to repay the loan herself, as fast as she could earn the money, or save it from what Mama and Daddy gave her to spend.

Granny snorted. "No, I'll not! Give Flora money for them beds and she'd have it spent on something else before the day's out."

Tiff couldn't argue with that. It had happened too many times before. "Well, anyway, you oughtn't to keep all that money here in your house. It's dangerous. You might get it all stolen."

"I kept it in my house all this time and hasn't nobody stole it off of me."

"That doesn't mean it couldn't happen. You thought it did happen this morning, and look how scared you were. You ought to put your money in a bank."

Granny began telling what was wrong about banks, how your money got mixed up with other people's and the bank people never knew which money was yours and which belonged to somebody else. Tiff didn't know a lot about banks herself, but she knew a whole lot more than Granny did. For an hour she explained the things Ms. Lackey had taught them last year, about checking accounts and deposit slips and passbooks and savings accounts. When she told how the money could earn interest in a savings account, she saw at once that the old lady was intrigued. "Any time you wanted to take your money out, a little bit or all of it, you could just write a check," she urged.

The grandmother fingered her precious hoard and looked sullen. "That's the thing," she admitted. "I don't know how to write but just only my name."

"You can write numbers!" Tiff said. "You're good at numbers. Anybody that can write numbers and their name can write a check." She offered to go with her to the bank and do the talking, and to her satisfaction, the grandmother agreed. When had Granny ever listened to her? It made Tiff feel like she counted for something. Real tough.

"Wait," she said, as Granny put on her hat. "Count your money before you take it to the bank."

"I don't need to count it. I know how much there is of it."

"Well, count it anyway. Ms. Lackey says you ought to always count your money before you do business, so in case you make a mistake, you don't go blaming the other fellow." Granny made her turn her back so Tiff wouldn't find out how much money was in the plastic bags. Listening to the dry shuffle of the floury bills, Tiff felt a twinge of regret that she hadn't accepted Granny's reward. There were so many of those one-hundred-dollar bills, Granny would never miss one. But she went over her reasoning once more and decided she had been right: she was content with her refusal.

"I'm ready," said Granny. She snapped the packets inside her pocketbook and stood up. "Let's go."

The way it happened, Tiff didn't have to do the talking for Granny after all. They arrived at the bank a few minutes before opening time, but they didn't have to wait. A roly-poly man with a fringe of gray hair and a fringe of gray mustache, unlocked the thick glass front door and let them in. "Miss Effie!" he said, hugging Granny and laughing. "I bet I haven't seen you in twenty years!"

He was Mr. Montgomery Todt, president of the bank. Gold letters spelled out his name on the door of his office, where he led them, but Granny called him Gummy, for she had nursed him as a little chap when he couldn't yet say his own name.

"This here's my grandbaby; she the smart one," Granny said, shoving Tiff forward. "Say something girl. Show Mr. Gummy how smart you are."

Mr. Todt saved her by pronouncing roundly, "She already said her smarts, Miss Effie. A girl that could get an old pack rat like you to put her money in the bank just bound to be smart as they come."

Granny giggled at him calling her a pack rat, but Tiff didn't appreciate it one bit. That was her granny he was making fun of, even if she *was* a pack rat.

Mr. Todt asked one of the bank tellers to open a savings and checking account for Granny while she waited in his office. "Where did you get all that money, Miss Effie?" He seemed surprised when Granny told him the money had come from his own mother's father, years ago. "I didn't realize Honeycutt was your homeplace," he said thoughtfully. "No doubt Grandfather told me, and it slipped my mind. I used to listen to him by the hour, back then. Kids today never listen to old folks the way they ought to. I bet a chap as bright as Tiffany here doesn't either."

Granny signed her name in five different places for the bank, and she watched closely when the teller showed the amount deposited. "Wait a minute," she said, and took Tiff aside for a whispered conference. "She says I give her a hunderd dollars more than I did!"

Tiff said, "Ask her to count it again, in front of you."

The grandmother did as she was told. Carefully, slowly, the teller counted the money. "Is that correct?" she inquired.

"If you say so," said Granny. With joy she returned to Tiff. "They giving me a hunderd dollars just for putting my money in here."

"No, they aren't, Granny; you must have made some mistake counting it at home."

"I made a hunderd dollars, just for walking downtown here!" she marveled, not listening.

The old lady was so delighted that Tiff gave up trying to convince her of her mistake. At least it got her banking off to a good start.

Back at the house she set about teaching Granny to write checks. She showed her the place to write in the amount and the line for her signature. "When you get those two lines filled in, any store or person you're paying the money to will write in their own name, if you ask them to," she assured the old lady.

"Let me practice it once," said Granny. "I got a place where I want to pay some money to."

Proudly she wrote her signature, in the round, careful letters she used to sign her social security checks: Effie Turner. Laboriously, in her trembling script, she wrote out the numbers and pushed the check across the table. "You write the rest for me," she directed with a smirk.

Nobody could question the legibility of her handwriting. There stood her name, plain and positive as Granny herself: Effie Turner. Her numbers looked like first grade numbers, but they were equally plain: $76.00.

"Write it, The Outlet Furniture Store," Granny ordered.

"Oh!" was all that Tiff could think to say immediately. She thought of her bunk bed and her private place up at the ceiling, saved. She thought, humbly, that she didn't exactly understand how she felt about money——a little like Mama, a little like Granny, not much like either of them. She would have to figure some more on that one.

She could scarcely see to write the words, but she did write, blinking, as carefully as Granny wrote: Outlet Furniture Store.

"Now you hand that to you mama," said Granny, "and tell her I say she don't have to pay it back, for I already made me a hunderd dollars today."

It was the best reward Granny could have given her, since she still seemed to think Tiff deserved a reward. And it wasn't money loaned that Mama could spend on something else.

"Thank you, Granny," she said meekly.

The old lady clamped her lips tight——her way of showing she was pleased. "Guess you ain't the only one that can figure things." She closed her checkbook importantly. "Now help me find where I'll keep my bank stuff, and after we eat our dinner and clean up around here, I want you to pull that Moody grass out of my flower beds. You done just about half a job last time you was here, and I want you to make it right fore you go home."

Home! Tiff scarcely heard Granny's scolding. She couldn't wait to see their faces at home when she waved that check in front of their noses. What a homecoming it was going to be!

Money Matters

Meet the Author

Belinda Hurmence grew up in the southwestern part of the United States. Her ancestors were pioneers in the Oklahoma Indian Territory. Because of her heritage, she says, "the main characters of my books tend to be pioneers in their own way." While she considers writing a slow process, she continues "to plug along and urge myself, much as I urge struggling writers at all stages, not to give up prematurely."

Meet the Illustrator

Michelle Mills has been drawing since she was three years old. Her dad was also an artist, and if she didn't know how to draw something, he would help her. During the summer, Mills took art classes at The Detroit Institute of Art. In her senior year of high school, she won a scholarship to Parsons School of Design in New York. After receiving her degree in illustration, she moved to upstate New York, where she now has her own studio to work on her illustrations.

Theme Connections

Think About It

- How does Tiffany's grandmother feel about money?

- What is Tiffany's mother's attitude toward money?

- How have these conflicting ideas affected Tiffany's thoughts about money?

Record Ideas

Which character shares your attitude about money? Write your thoughts in your Writing Journal.

Write a Sequel

Write a paragraph as to how a sequel to "Money Matters" might begin.

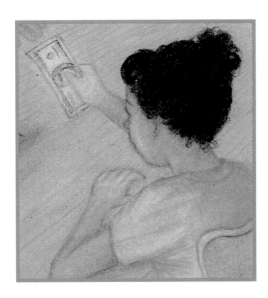

A Gift for a Gift

edited and adapted by Eric Protter
illustrated by David Wenzel

"Honesty is the best policy" is one of the most popular and lasting of all folktale themes. The original version of this story is attributed to Saxony, and it dates from the 17th century. The author is unknown.

A mighty king once lost his way while hunting alone in a forest, and late at night, when he was cold and weary and hungry, he at last reached the hut of a poor miner. The miner was away digging for coal, and his wife didn't realize that the gentleman who rapped on her door and begged for a night's lodging was the king himself.

"We are very poor," she explained, "but if you will be content, as we are, with a plate of potatoes for dinner and a blanket on the floor for a bed, you will be most welcome." The king's stomach was empty; his bones ached; and he knew that on this dark night he would never find his way back to his castle. And so he gratefully accepted the woman's hospitality.

He sat down to dinner with her and greedily ate a generous portion of steaming potatoes baked in an open fire. "These are better than the best beef I've ever eaten," he exclaimed. And still smacking his lips, he stretched out on the floor and quickly fell fast asleep.

Early the next morning the king washed in a nearby brook, and then returned to the hut to thank the miner's wife for her kindness. And for her trouble he gave her a gold piece. Then he was on his way to his palace.

When the miner returned home later that day his wife told him about the courteous, kind and distinguished guest who had stayed overnight in their home. Then she showed her husband the gold piece he had given her. The husband realized at once that the king himself must have been their overnight guest. And because he believed that the king had been far too generous in his payment for their humble fare and lodging, he decided to go at once to present his majesty with a bushel of potatoes——fine, round potatoes, the very kind the king had enjoyed so much.

The palace guards refused at first to let the miner enter. But when he explained that he wanted nothing from the king—— that in fact, he had come only to give the king a bushel of potatoes——they let him pass.

"Kind sire," he said when he finally stood before the king, "last night you paid my wife a gold piece for a hard bed and a

plate of potatoes. Even if you are a great and wealthy ruler, you paid much too much for the little offered you. Therefore, I have brought you a bushel of potatoes, which you said you enjoyed as much as the finest beef. Please accept them. And should you ever pass by our house again, we will be happy to have the opportunity to serve you more."

These proud and honest words pleased the king, and to show his appreciation he ordered that the miner be given a fine house and a three-acre farm. Overjoyed by his good luck the honest miner returned home to share the news with his wife.

Now it so happened that the miner had a brother——a wealthy brother who was shrewd, greedy, and jealous of anyone else's good fortune. When he learned of his brother's luck, he decided that he too would present the king with a gift. Not long before, the king had wanted to buy one of the brother's horses. But because he had been asked to pay an outrageously high price, the king had never bought the animal. Now, thought the avaricious brother, he would go to his sovereign and make him a gift of the horse. *After all*, he reasoned, *if the king gave a three-acre farm and a house to my brother in return for a mere bushel of potatoes, I will probably get a mansion and ten acres for my gift.*

He brushed the horse and polished its harness, and then rode to the palace. Past the sentries he walked, directly into the king's audience chamber.

"Gracious sir," he began, "not long ago you wanted to buy my horse, but I placed a very high price on it. You may have wondered why I did so, great king. Let me explain. I did not want to sell the horse to you. I wanted to *give* it to you, your majesty. And I ask you now to accept it as a gift. If you look out your window you will see the horse in your courtyard. He is, as you know, a magnificent animal, and I am sure that not even you have such a fine stallion in your royal stables."

The king realized at once that this was not an honest gift. He smiled and said, "Thank you, my friend. I accept your kind gift with gratitude. And you shall not go home empty-handed. Do you see that bushel of potatoes there in the corner? Well, those potatoes cost me a three-acre farm and a house. Take them as your reward. I am sure that not even you have a bushel of potatoes in your storeroom with so high a value on them."

What could the greedy brother do? He dared not argue with the king. He simply raised the heavy sack to his shoulders and carried it home, while the king ordered the horse put in his stables.

A Gift for a Gift

Meet the Editor

Eric Protter has lived in four countries. He has written, among other books, *A Treasury of Folk and Fairy Tales*, *Explorers and Explorations*, and *Monster Festival*.

Meet the Illustrator

David Wenzel spent many hours as a child filling up sheet after sheet of paper with sketches and characters. At one point he created a series of illustrations depicting the characters from his two favorite childhood books, Lewis Carroll's *Alice in Wonderland* and *Through the Looking Glass*. He has been working full time as an illustrator since graduating from Hartford Art School in 1975. Wenzel has worked on many projects, rated versions of *Treasure Island* and *The Hobbit*. To this day, he is still inspired by the stories and illustrations he finds in books.

Theme Connections

Think About It

- How did the miner's reasons for giving a gift differ from his brother's reasons?

Record Ideas

 Record in your Writing Journal what you have learned about the negative impact of greed.

Compare Characters

Compare and contrast the values held by three of the characters you encountered in this unit.

- Examine what is most valuable to each character, and note how the character's values are revealed.
- You may choose to list your ideas in your Writing Journal or present them in a chart.

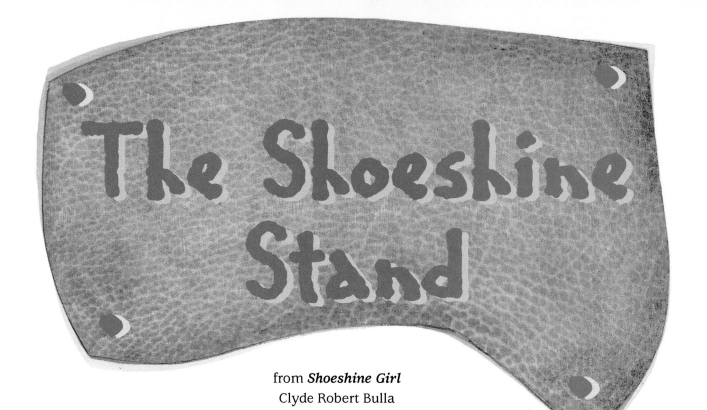

The Shoeshine Stand

from ***Shoeshine Girl***
Clyde Robert Bulla
illustrated by Sally Schaedler

Yesterday Sarah Ida took the train alone to Palmville, where she is to spend the summer with Aunt Claudia. Her parents have sent her away because she was beginning to get into trouble at home. They hope that a change of scenery, and a summer with Aunt Claudia, will give them and Sarah Ida a fresh start. Sarah Ida, however, feels resentful.

In the morning Sarah Ida put on an old shirt and her oldest blue jeans. She went down into the kitchen.

Aunt Claudia was there, frying bacon and eggs. "Good morning," she said. "Did you sleep well?"

"Yes," said Sarah Ida.

"There's apple jelly and plum jam. Which would you like with your toast?"

"Neither one."

They sat down to breakfast. Aunt Claudia said, "You're going to have company."

"Who?" asked Sarah Ida.

"Rossi Wigginhorn."

Sarah Ida frowned. "I don't know any Rossi Wigginhorn."

"She's a neighbor," said Aunt Claudia. "She's been wanting to meet you."

"Why?"

"I told her you were coming. I thought it would be nice if you had a friend your own age."

"Did you ever think," said Sarah Ida, "that I might like to choose my friends?"

"I like to choose my friends, too," said Aunt Claudia. "But when you're in a new place and haven't had a chance to meet anybody——"

"It doesn't matter," said Sarah Ida, "whether I meet anybody or not."

They finished breakfast.

Aunt Claudia asked, "Can you cook?"

"No," said Sarah Ida.

"Would you like to learn?"

"No."

"At least, you'd better learn to make your own breakfast," said Aunt Claudia. "It's something you might need to know. And there are things you can do to help me. I'll teach you to take care of your room, and you can help me with the cleaning and dusting."

"How much do you pay?" asked Sarah Ida.

Aunt Claudia stared at her. "Pay?"

"Money," said Sarah Ida. "How much money?"

Aunt Claudia took the dishes to the sink. She came back to the table and sat down. "I don't like to bring this up," she said, "but I suppose I must. I'm not supposed to pay you anything."

"And why not?" asked Sarah Ida.

"Because your mother asked me
not to. She told me you had borrowed
your allowance for the next two months.
She said you had spent it all and had
nothing to show for it. She asked me not to
give you any money while you're here."

"But I've *got* to have money!" said Sarah Ida. "I'm
going to *need* it!"

"What for?" asked Aunt Claudia.

"Lots of things. Candy and gum. Movies——and popcorn
when I go to the movies. I need it for magazines. And for clothes."

"If you need clothes, I'll buy them," said Aunt Claudia. "We can talk
later about movies. If I buy you a ticket once a week——"

"I want money in my pocket!"

Aunt Claudia sighed. "That seems to be what your mother *doesn't* want.
I think she's trying to teach you the value of money."

"I *know* the value of money, and if you think you can——!"

"All right, Sarah Ida. That's enough."

Sarah Ida ran up to her room. She could feel herself shaking. They didn't
know how she felt about money. They didn't understand, and she didn't
know how to tell them. She *needed* money in her pocket. It didn't have to
be much. But she just didn't feel *right* with none at all!

566

Aunt Claudia was calling her.

Sarah Ida didn't answer.

"Sarah Ida!" Aunt Claudia called again. "Rossi is here."

Sarah Ida lay on the bed and looked out the window.

"Rossi has something for you," said Aunt Claudia. "Is it all right if she brings it up?"

"No!" said Sarah Ida. She went downstairs.

Rossi was waiting in the hall. She had pink cheeks and pale yellow hair. She wore a yellow dress without a spot or a wrinkle.

"I brought some cupcakes," she said. "I made them myself."

"That was sweet of you, Rossi," said Aunt Claudia.

"Yes, that was sweet of you, Rossi," said Sarah Ida.

Aunt Claudia gave her a sharp look. Then she left them alone.

The girls sat on the porch. They each ate a cupcake.

"I think you're awfully brave, coming here all by yourself," said Rossi.

"It was no big thing," said Sarah Ida. "My father put me on the train, and my aunt was here to meet me."

"Well, it's a long trip. I'd have been scared. Are you having a good time in Palmville?"

"I just got here," said Sarah Ida.

"I think you'll like it. There's a lot to see. Come on down the street. I'll show you where I live."

They walked down to Rossi's house. It was old, like Aunt Claudia's. It was half covered with creepy-looking vines.

Sarah Ida met Rossi's mother. Mrs. Wigginhorn was pretty in the same way Rossi was. She had pale hair and a sweet smile.

She said, "I hope you'll enjoy your visit here."

Rossi showed Sarah Ida her room. "My daddy made this shelf for my library. These are all my books. Any time you want to borrow some——"

"I don't read much," said Sarah Ida. She was looking at something else. She was looking at a blue and white pig on the dresser. "What's this?" she asked.

"That's my bank," said Rossi.

"Is there anything in it?"

"About five dollars."

Sarah Ida picked up the pig. It was heavy. She turned it from side to side. She could feel the coins move.

"I need four dollars," she said. "Will you lend it to me?"

"I——I'm saving for a present for my daddy," said Rossi.

"It's just a loan. I'll pay you back."

Rossi looked unhappy. "I'm not supposed to lend money."

"You said I could borrow your books. What's the difference?"

"I just don't think I'd better."

"All right. Forget it." Sarah Ida went to the door.

"No. Wait. You can have it." Rossi was feeling in the top drawer of the dresser. She took out a tiny key on a string. "But don't tell anyone."

"Don't you tell, either," said Sarah Ida.

There was a lock on the underside of the pig. Rossi unlocked it. The coins fell out on the dresser. They were mostly quarters and dimes.

Sarah Ida counted out four dollars. "Are you sure you want to do this?"

"Yes," said Rossi.

"Well, then, good-by," said Sarah Ida.

"Don't you want me to walk back with you?" asked Rossi.

"You don't need to." Sarah Ida left her. She walked out of the house and up the street. The coins jingled in her pocket. She was whistling when she got back to Aunt Claudia's.

She awoke late the next morning. There was sunlight in the room. She looked at the pictures on the walls. For the first time she almost liked them. For the first time in weeks she felt almost happy.

The feeling was quickly gone.

The door opened, and Aunt Claudia came in. Her face was like winter.

She said, "You took money from Rossi yesterday——didn't you?"

Sarah Ida sat up in bed. "How——?"

"Mrs. Wigginhorn called me. She said most of the money was gone from Rossi's bank. She said you would know about it."

"I didn't——" began Sarah Ida.

"What happened? I want to know."

"I borrowed the money. That's what happened. I *borrowed* it."

"You hadn't known poor little Rossi even a day, and already you were borrowing her money."

"Poor little Rossi said I could."

"She's such a friendly child. She didn't know how to say no." Aunt Claudia asked, "Is money so important to you? What do you need it for?"

"I told you. I like to have money in my pocket."

"Do you think that's a good reason?"

"It is to me."

"It isn't to me. Get your clothes on and take that money right back."

Sarah Ida hadn't known Aunt Claudia could sound so fierce. She got up and dressed. The money was in an envelope under her pillow. She stuffed it into her pocket.

She went down the street to the Wigginhorns'. Rossi opened the door. Her eyes and nose were red.

"Sarah Ida——"

"Here." Sarah Ida almost threw the envelope at her. "I might have known I couldn't trust you."

"I couldn't help it," said Rossi. "Mother saw the key on the dresser. She picked up the bank and found out it was almost empty. She kept asking questions till I had to tell her."

"Just forget it," said Sarah Ida coldly. "Forget the whole thing."

She walked away.

Back at Aunt Claudia's, she started up to her room. Aunt Claudia called her. "Your breakfast is ready."

"I don't want any," said Sarah Ida.

"Come here, anyway," said Aunt Claudia.

Sarah Ida stood in the kitchen doorway.

"I shouldn't have lost my temper," said Aunt Claudia, "but you don't seem to understand that what you did was wrong."

"I don't see why it was wrong," said Sarah Ida.

"It's wrong to take advantage of someone. And you took advantage of Rossi."

"If you'd let me have some money, I wouldn't have had to borrow."

Aunt Claudia's lips closed tightly for a moment. She said, "This is a game, isn't it?"

"A game?"

"You're trying me out, to see how far you can go."

"I don't know what you mean."

"I think you do. Money really isn't that important to you, is it? You're just using this whole thing to get what you want. At the same time, you're trying to strike back at me, because——"

"The money *is* important!" cried Sarah Ida. "And if you won't give me any, I'll——I'll go out and get some!"

"How?" asked Aunt Claudia.

"I'll get a job."

"Where?"

"I don't know, but I'll find one. But if I did, you wouldn't let me keep it. You want to keep me under your thumb."

"Sarah Ida, stop this!" said Aunt Claudia. "If you could find work and earn some money, I wouldn't keep you from it. But ask yourself——what could you do? Who would give you a job? I don't want you under my thumb. All I'm trying to do is——"

"I *know* what you're trying to do. And if you think I'm playing a game, I'll show you!"

She rushed out of the house. Aunt Claudia's voice followed her. "Come back! Stop!"

Sarah Ida didn't stop. She cut across the yard and ran up the street.

She came to Grand Avenue. She was out of breath, and there was a pounding in her ears.

She stopped in the doorway of a drugstore and looked up and down the street. People were walking by. Cars were passing. Palmville was bigger than she'd thought. In all these stores there must be someone who would give her some work to do.

There was a dress shop across the street, with girls' dresses in the window. She might try there. But she wasn't even wearing a dress, and she didn't look very neat.

She used the drugstore window as a mirror and tried to comb her hair with her fingers. Inside the store a woman was watching her. She looked friendly. Sarah Ida went in.

"Can I help you?" asked the woman.

"I——" Sarah Ida began, and she couldn't go on. How could she say "I want to work for you"? What kind of work could she do in a drugstore?

"I'm just looking," said Sarah Ida. She looked at the candy, but she couldn't say, "I'll have this and this," because she didn't have any money.

She went outside. She walked past a restaurant, a bank, a hardware store. She came to a pet shop. There were puppies in one window and kittens in the other. She put out her hand to the puppies. One of them came to the window and put his nose against the glass.

She went into the shop. A man and woman were there. All about the shop were animals in cages. There were birds, and in one cage was a green and yellow parrot.

"Do you need help here?" asked Sarah Ida.

The parrot began to squawk. "Polly, Polly! Pretty Polly! My, oh my!"

"What?" asked the woman.

"I said, do you need help!" shouted Sarah Ida.

"Be quiet!" said the woman. "Not you, little girl. I mean that silly bird."

"Silly bird!" said the parrot. "My, oh my!"

The woman threw a cloth over the cage, and the parrot was quiet.

"Now. What was it you wanted?" she asked.

"I wanted to work for you," said Sarah Ida.

"Oh," said the woman.

The man spoke. "What do you know about animals?"

"Not much, but I could learn."

The man said, "Come back when you're a little older."

"How much older?"

"About six years," said the man.

"Do you know where I *could* get work?" she asked.

"What can you do?"

"I——I don't know."

"You might try Al," said the man. "He's got a sign up."

"Yes," said the woman. "He's had it up for a long time."

"He's on the corner." The man pointed. "Why don't you have a look?"

Sarah Ida left the shop. She was sure the man and woman had just been trying to get rid of her. She thought they were probably laughing at her, too.

She went on down the street. And there on the corner she saw the sign. It wasn't very big, and it was stuck to a folding door. It said "Help Wanted."

The folding door was at one end of a shoeshine stand. The stand was a kind of shed with a platform in it. There were four chairs on the platform. Above the chairs was a big sign: "Al's Shoeshine Corner."

A man sat on one of the chairs. His face was hidden behind the newspaper he was reading.

Sarah Ida looked at the "Help Wanted" sign. She looked at the stand. This was the place, she thought. This was just the place!

She would tell Aunt Claudia, "I have a job."

"What kind?" Aunt Claudia would ask.

"Working at a shoeshine stand," Sarah Ida would say. "A shoeshine stand on Grand Avenue."

"Oh, you can't do that!" Aunt Claudia would say.

"You said you wouldn't keep me from earning some money," Sarah Ida would say.

"But you can't be seen working at a shoeshine stand on Grand Avenue," Aunt Claudia would say. "I'll *give* you some money!"

573

Sarah Ida spoke to the man. "Are you Al?"

He put down the newspaper, and she saw his face. He was not young. His hair was thin and gray. His eyes looked like little pieces of coal set far back in his head.

"Yes, I'm Al." He slid down off the chair. His shoulders were stooped. He wasn't much taller than she was. "You want something?"

"I'm Sarah Ida Becker," she said, "and I want to work for you."

"What do you mean, work for me?"

"Your sign says 'Help Wanted.'"

"I put that up so long ago I forgot about it," he said. "Nobody wants to work for me. People don't like to get their hands dirty. They want to do something easy that pays big money."

"Will you give me a job?" she asked.

"You're not a boy."

"The sign doesn't say you wanted a boy."

A man came by.

"Shine?" asked Al.

The man climbed into a chair. Al shined his shoes. The man went on.

Al looked at Sarah Ida. "You still here?"

"If I worked for you, what would I have to do?" she asked.

"Shine shoes, same as I do. Some days I get more work than I can take care of. Then I need help. But whoever heard of a shoeshine girl?"

"Why couldn't a girl shine shoes?"

"Why don't you go on home?"

"You said you needed help. You've got your sign up."

"What do you want to work here for?"

"I need some money."

"You wouldn't get rich here."

"I know that."

He looked her up and down. "I don't think you really want to work."

All at once she was tired of waiting, tired of talking. She started away.

Al said, "What did you say your name was? Sarah what?"

"Sarah Ida Becker."

"You any relation to the lady that used to be in the library? You any relation to Miss Claudia Becker?"

"She's my aunt."

Another man stopped for a shoeshine. When he was gone, Al asked her, "You staying with your aunt?"

"Yes," she said.

"Go tell her you saw Al Winkler. Tell her you want to work for me. Maybe——"

"Maybe what?"

"I don't know yet," he said. "First you see what she says."

Aunt Claudia was waiting on the porch. "Sit down," she said, when Sarah Ida came up the steps. "I want to talk to you."

Sarah Ida sat in the porch swing.

"You must never do this again," said Aunt Claudia. "You must always let me know where you're going. Do you understand?"

"Yes," said Sarah Ida.

"Where have you been?"

"On the avenue."

"What were you doing?"

"Looking for a job. And I found one."

"You found one?"

"Yes, I did."

"Where?"

"On Grand Avenue. Working for the shoeshine man."

"*Who?*"

"Al Winkler, the shoeshine man."

Aunt Claudia looked dazed. "How did you know him?"

"I didn't know him. He had a 'Help Wanted' sign and I stopped."

"Al Winkler," said Aunt Claudia, as if she were talking to herself. "I remember him so well. He came to the library when I worked there. He hadn't gone to school much, and he wanted to learn more. I helped him choose books." She asked, "Does he want you to work at his stand?"

"He said to talk to you about it."

"Do you want to work for him?" asked Aunt Claudia.

"I told you, I want some money of my own."

"This might be a good way to earn some," said Aunt Claudia.

"You *want* me to shine shoes on Grand Avenue?"

"If that's what you want to do."

Sarah Ida was quiet for a while. Things weren't working out the way she'd planned. She'd never thought Aunt Claudia would let her work in the shoeshine stand, and Aunt Claudia didn't seem to care!

Unless——Sarah Ida had another thought. Maybe Aunt Claudia didn't believe she'd go through with it. Maybe she was thinking, *That child is playing another game.*

Sarah Ida said, "You really want me to go tell Al Winkler I'll work for him?"

"If it's what you want to do," said Aunt Claudia.

Sarah Ida started down the steps. Aunt Claudia didn't call her back. There was nothing for her to do but go.

She found Al sitting in one of his chairs.

"What did she say?" he asked.

"She said yes."

"You want to start now?"

"I don't care," she said.

He opened a drawer under the platform and took out an old piece of cloth. "Use this for an apron. Tie it around you."

She tied it around her waist.

A man stopped at the stand. He was a big man with a round face and a black beard. He climbed into a chair and put his feet on the shoe rests.

"How are you, Mr. Naylor?" said Al.

"Not bad," said the man. "Who's the young lady?"

"She's helping me," said Al. "She needs practice. You mind if she practices on you?"

"I don't mind," said Mr. Naylor.

Al said to Sarah Ida, "I'm going to shine one shoe. You watch what I do. Then you shine the other one."

He took two soft brushes and brushed the man's shoe.

"That takes off the dust," he said. "Always start with a clean shoe."

He picked up a jar of water with an old toothbrush in it. With the toothbrush he sprinkled a few drops of water on the shoe.

"That makes a better shine." He opened a round can of brown polish. With his fingers he spread polish on the shoe.

"Now you lay your cloth over the shoe," he said. "Stretch it tight——like this. Pull it back and forth——like this. Rub it hard and fast. First the toe——then the sides——then the back."

When he put down the cloth, the shoe shone like glass. He untied the man's shoelace. He drew it a little tighter and tied it again.

He asked Sarah Ida, "Did you see everything I did?"

"Yes," she said.

"All right. Let's see you do it."

She picked up the brushes. She dropped one. When she bent to pick it up, she dropped the other one. Her face grew hot.

She brushed the shoe. She sprinkled the water.

"Not so much," Al told her. "You don't need much."

She looked at the brown polish. "Do I have to get this on my fingers?"

"You can put it on with a rag, but it's not the best way. You can rub it in better with your fingers."

"I don't want to get it on my hands."

"Your hands will wash."

She put the polish on with her fingers. She shined Mr. Naylor's shoe. She untied his shoelace, pulled it tight, and tried to tie it again.

Al tied it for her. "It's hard to tie someone else's shoe when you never did it before."

Mr. Naylor looked at his shoes. "Best shine I've had all year," he said. He paid Al. He gave Sarah Ida a dollar bill.

After he had gone, she asked Al, "Why did he give me this?"

"That's your tip," said Al. "You didn't earn it. He gave it to you because you're just getting started."

"Will everybody give me a dollar?" she asked.

"No," he said, "and don't be looking for it."

Others stopped at the stand. Sometimes two or three were there at once. Part of the time Sarah Ida put polish on shoes. Part of the time she used the polishing cloth.

Toward the end of the day she grew tired. She tried to hurry. That was when she put black polish on a man's brown shoe.

The man began to shout. "Look what you did!"

"It's not hurt," said Al. "I can take the black polish off. Sarah Ida, hand me the jar of water."

She reached for the jar and knocked it over. All the water ran out.

"Go around the corner to the filling station," Al told her. "There's a drinking fountain outside. Fill the jar and bring it back."

Sarah Ida brought the water. Al washed the man's shoe. All the black polish came off.

"See?" he said. "It's as good as new."

"Well, maybe," said the man, "but I don't want *her* giving me any more shines."

He went away.

Sarah Ida made a face. "He was mean."

"No, he wasn't," said Al. "He just didn't want black polish on his brown shoes."

"Anyone can make a mistake," she said.

"That's right. Just don't make too many." He said, "You can go now." He gave her a dollar. "This is to go with your other dollar."

"Is that all the pay I get?"

"You'll get more when you're worth more," he said. "You can come back tomorrow afternoon. That's my busy time. Come about one."

She didn't answer. She turned her back on him and walked away.

In the morning she told Aunt Claudia, "I'm going to the drugstore."

"Aren't you working for Al?" asked Aunt Claudia.

"Maybe I am, and maybe I'm not," said Sarah Ida.

In the drugstore she looked at magazines. She looked at chewing gum and candy bars. None of them seemed to matter much. Her money was the first she had ever worked for. Somehow she wanted to spend it for something important.

She went home with the two dollars still in her pocket.

She and Aunt Claudia had lunch.

"If you aren't working for Al," said Aunt Claudia, "you can help me."

"I'm going to work," said Sarah Ida. Working for Al was certainly better than helping Aunt Claudia.

She went down to the shoeshine stand.

"So you came back," said Al.

"Yes," she said.

"I didn't know if you would or not."

Customers were coming. Al told Sarah Ida what to do. Once she shined a pair of shoes all by herself.

They were busy most of the afternoon. Her hair fell down into her eyes. Her back hurt from bending over.

Late in the day Al told her, "You've had enough for now. You can go. You got some tips, didn't you?"

"Yes," she said. "Do you want me to count them?"

"No. You can keep them. And here's your pay." He gave her two dollars. "And I want to tell you something. When you get through with a customer, you say 'thank you.'"

"All right," she said.

"One more thing. You didn't say yesterday if you were coming back or not. This time I want to know. Are you coming back tomorrow?"

"Yes," she said.

"Come about the same time," he said. "I'm going to bring you something."

What he brought her was a white canvas apron. It had two pockets. It had straps that went over her shoulders and tied in the back. There were black letters across the front.

"Why does it say 'Lane's Lumber Company'?" she asked. "Why doesn't it say 'Al's Shoeshine Corner'?"

"Because it came from Lane's Lumber Company," he said. "Fred Lane is a friend of mine, and he gave it to me."

It was nothing but a canvas apron. She didn't know why she should be so pleased with it. But it was a long time since anything had pleased her as much. She liked the stiff, new feel of the cloth. The pockets were deep. She liked to put her hands into them.

That night she thought about the apron. She had left it locked up at the stand. She almost told her mother and father about it in the letter she wrote them. She had promised to write twice a week——to make Aunt Claudia happy. But she didn't think they would care about her apron. All she wrote was:

Dear Mother and Father,
I am all right. Everything is all
right here. It was hot today.
Good-by,
Sarah Ida

She didn't tell Aunt Claudia about her apron. She didn't feel too friendly toward Aunt Claudia.

There were times when she didn't even feel too friendly toward Al.

There was the time when she shined an old man's shoes. He paid her and went away. Al said, "I didn't hear you say 'thank you.'"

"He didn't give me any tip," she said. "The old stingy-guts."

They were alone at the stand. Al said, "What did you call him?"

"Old stingy-guts," she said. "That's what he is."

"Don't you ever say a thing like that again," said Al in a cold, hard voice. "He didn't have to give you a tip. Nobody has to. If he wants to give you something extra, that's his business. But if he doesn't, that's his business, too. I want to hear you say 'thank you' whether you get any tip or not."

It scared her a little to see him so angry. She didn't speak to him for quite a while.

But that evening he said, as if nothing had happened, "I could use some help in the morning, too. You want to work here all day?"

"I don't know," she said.

"You can if you want to. Ask your aunt."

She started home. On the way, a boy caught up with her. His arms and legs were long, and he took long steps. He looked ugly, with his lower lip pushed out. He asked, "What are you doing working for Al?"

She walked faster. He kept up with her. "How much is he paying you?"

"I don't see why I should tell you," she said.

"You've got my job, that's why."

The light turned green, and she crossed the street. He didn't follow her.

All evening she thought about what the boy had said. In the morning she asked Al about it.

"Was he a skinny boy?" asked Al. "Did he have light hair?"

"Yes," she said.

"That was Kicker."

"His name is *Kicker?*"

"That's what he called himself when he was little. Now we all call him that. He's my neighbor."

"What did he mean when he said I had his job?"

"I don't know. Once I asked him if he wanted to work for me. He said he did. Then he never came to work. He didn't want the job, but I guess he doesn't want you to have it, either."

"Maybe he changed his mind," she said. "Maybe he wants to work for you now."

"Maybe," said Al. "I'll have a talk with him. I don't think you'll see him anymore."

But later in the week she did see him. He was across the street, watching her.

Every evening, after work, Sarah Ida was tired. But every morning she was ready to go back to Shoeshine Corner. It wasn't that she liked shining shoes, but things *happened* at the shoeshine stand. Every customer was different. Every day she found out something new.

Some things she learned by herself. Like how much polish to use on a shoe. A thin coat gave a better and quicker shine. Some things Al told her. "When a customer comes here, he gets more than a shine," he said. "He gets to rest in a chair. When you rub with the cloth, it feels good on his feet. When you tie his shoelaces a little tighter, it makes his shoes fit better. My customers go away feeling a little better. Anyway, I *hope* they do."

One warm, cloudy afternoon, he said, "We might as well close up."

"Why?" she asked. "It's only three o'clock."

"It's going to rain. Nobody gets a shine on a rainy day."

He began to put away the brushes and shoe polish. She helped him.

"Maybe you can run home before the rain," he said. A few big drops splashed on the sidewalk. "No. Too late now."

They sat under the little roof, out of the rain.

"Hear that sound?" he said. "Every time I hear rain on a tin roof, I get to thinking about when I was a boy. We lived in an old truck with a tin roof over the back."

"You *lived* in a truck?"

"Most of the time. We slept under the tin roof, and when it rained, the sound put me to sleep. We went all over the South in that truck."

"You and your mother and father?"

"My dad and I."

"What were you doing, driving all over the South?"

"My dad sold medicine."

"What kind?"

"Something to make you strong and keep you from getting sick."

"Did you take it?"

"No. I guess it wasn't any good."

She had never heard him talk much about himself before. She wanted him to go on.

"Was it fun living in a truck?"

"Fun? I wouldn't say so. Riding along was all right. Sometimes my dad and I stopped close to the woods, and that was all right, too. But I never liked it when we were in town selling medicine. Dad would play the mouth harp, and he made me sing. He wanted me to dance a jig, too, but I never could."

She tried to imagine Al as a little boy. She couldn't at all. "Why did he want you to sing and dance?" she asked.

"To draw a crowd. When there was a crowd, he sold medicine. We didn't stay anywhere very long. Except once. We stayed in one place six months. My dad did farm work, and I went to school."

He told her about the school. It was just outside a town. The teacher was Miss Miller. The schoolhouse had only one room.

"There was this big stove," he said, "and that winter I kept the fire going. Miss Miller never had to carry coal when I was there."

"Did you like her?" asked Sarah Ida. "Was she a good teacher?"

"Best teacher I ever had. Of course, she was just about the *only* one. I hadn't been to school much, but she took time to show me things. Do teachers still give medals in school?"

"Sometimes. Not very often."

"Miss Miller gave medals. They were all alike. Every one had a star on it. At the end of school you got one if you were the best in reading or spelling or writing or whatever it was. Everybody wanted a medal, but I knew I'd never get one because I wasn't the best in anything. And at the end of school, you know what happened?"

"What?"

"She called my name. The others all thought it was a joke. But she wasn't laughing. She said, 'Al wins a medal for building the best fires.'"

"And it *wasn't* a joke?" asked Sarah Ida.

"No. She gave me the medal. One of the big boys said, 'You better keep that, Al, because it's the only one you'll ever get.'"

"And did you keep it?"

He held up his watch chain. Something was hanging from it——something that looked like a worn, old coin.

"That's what you won?" asked Sarah Ida.

He nodded.

"That's a medal?" she said. "That little old piece of tin?"

She shouldn't have said it. As soon as the words were out, she was sorry.

Al sat very still. He looked into the street. A moment before, he had been a friend. Now he was a stranger.

He said, "Rain's stopped. For a while, anyway."

He slid out of his chair. She got up, too. "I——" she began.

He dragged the folding door across the stand and locked up.

"Go on. Run," he said. "Maybe you can get home before the rain starts again."

She stood there. "I didn't mean what you think I did," she said. "That medal——it doesn't matter if it's tin or silver or gold. It doesn't matter *what* it's made of, if it's something you like. I said the wrong thing, but it wasn't what I *meant*. I——" He had his back to her. She didn't think he was listening. She said, "*Listen* to me!"

He turned around. "You like ice cream?"

"Yes," she said.

"Come on. I'll buy you a cone."

She went with him, around the corner to Pearl's Ice Cream Shack.

"What kind?" he asked.

"Chocolate," she said.

They sat on a bench inside the Shack and ate their chocolate cones.

"It's raining again," he said.

"Yes," she said.

Then they were quiet, while they listened to the rain. And she was happy because the stranger was gone and Al was back.

The Shoeshine Stand

Meet the Author

Clyde Robert Bulla knew he wanted to be a writer by age seven. His family did not encourage his writing; he could only write and read after he finished his farm chores. When Bulla became an adult he began writing children's stories after a friend suggested he try it. Some of the things he likes to write about are monsters, Native Americans, animals, and friendship.

Meet the Illustrator

Sally Schaedler majored in illustration at Washington University in Missouri and also attended the School of Visual Arts in New York. Schaedler has won several awards for her work, but it was the award for a portrait she did in high school that led her to become an artist. She enjoys developing the interaction between characters in a story and making them "become real people."

Theme Connections

Think About It

- If you have any kind of job, paid or unpaid, think about what the rewards of having a job are for you.

- What argument would you use to convince someone of the value of hard work?

Record Ideas

Record your ideas in your Writing Journal as to the pros and cons of a particular point of view with respect to the value of working hard.

Write an Ad

Use your imagination in writing an ad looking for a person who values the rewards of work. What would this kind of ad look like?

The Gold Coin

Alma Flor Ada

translated by Bernice Randall ● *illustrated by Neil Waldman*

Juan had been a thief for many years. Because he did his stealing by night, his skin had become pale and sickly. Because he spent his time either hiding or sneaking about, his body had become shriveled and bent. And because he had neither friend nor relative to make him smile, his face was always twisted into an angry frown.

One night, drawn by a light shining through the trees, Juan came upon a hut. He crept up to the door and through a crack saw an old woman sitting at a plain, wooden table.

What was that shining in her hand? Juan wondered. He could not believe his eyes. It was a gold coin. Then he heard the woman say to herself, "I must be the richest person in the world."

Juan decided instantly that all the woman's gold must be his. He thought that the easiest thing to do was to watch until the woman left. Juan hid in the bushes and huddled under his poncho, waiting for the right moment to enter the hut.

Juan was half asleep when he heard knocking at the door and the sound of insistent voices. A few minutes later, he saw the woman, wrapped in a black cloak, leave the hut with two men at her side.

Here's my chance! Juan thought. And, forcing open a window, he climbed into the empty hut.

He looked about eagerly for the gold. He looked under the bed. It wasn't there. He looked in the cupboard. It wasn't there, either. Where could it be? Close to despair, Juan tore away some beams supporting the thatch roof.

Finally, he gave up. There was simply no gold in the hut.

All I can do, he thought, is to find the old woman and make her tell me where she's hidden it.

So he set out along the path that she and her two companions had taken.

It was daylight by the time Juan reached the river. The countryside had been deserted, but here, along the riverbank, were two huts. Nearby, a man and his son were hard at work, hoeing potatoes.

It had been a long, long time since Juan had spoken to another human being. Yet his desire to find the woman was so strong that he went up to the farmers and asked, in a hoarse, raspy voice, "Have you seen a short, gray-haired woman, wearing a black cloak?"

"Oh, you must be looking for Doña Josefa," the young boy said. "Yes, we've seen her. We went to fetch her this morning, because my grandfather had another attack of——"

"Where is she now?" Juan broke in.

"She is long gone," said the father with a smile. "Some people from across the river came looking for her, because someone in their family is sick."

"How can I get across the river?" Juan asked anxiously.

"Only by boat," the boy answered. "We'll row you across later, if you'd like." Then turning back to his work, he added, "But first we must finish digging up the potatoes."

The thief muttered, "Thanks." But he quickly grew impatient. He grabbed a hoe and began to help the pair of farmers. The sooner we finish, the sooner we'll get across the river, he thought. And the sooner I'll get to my gold!

It was dusk when they finally laid down their hoes. The soil had been turned, and the wicker baskets were brimming with potatoes.

"Now can you row me across?" Juan asked the father anxiously.

"Certainly," the man said. "But let's eat supper first."

Juan had forgotten the taste of a home-cooked meal and the pleasure that comes from sharing it with others. As he sopped up the last of the stew with a chunk of dark bread, memories of other meals came back to him from far away and long ago.

By the light of the moon, father and son guided their boat across the river.

"What a wonderful healer Doña Josefa is!" the boy told Juan. "All she had to do to make Abuelo better was give him a cup of her special tea."

"Yes, and not only that," his father added, "she brought him a gold coin."

Juan was stunned. It was one thing for Doña Josefa to go around helping people. But how could she go around handing out gold coins—— *his gold coins?*

When the threesome finally reached the other side of the river, they saw a young man sitting outside his hut.

"This fellow is looking for Doña Josefa," the father said, pointing to Juan.

"Oh, she left some time ago," the young man said.

"Where to?" Juan asked tensely.

"Over to the other side of the mountain," the young man replied, pointing to the vague outline of mountains in the night sky.

"How did she get there?" Juan asked, trying to hide his impatience.

"By horse," the young man answered. "They came on horseback to get her because someone had broken his leg."

"Well, then, I need a horse, too," Juan said urgently.

"Tomorrow," the young man replied softly. "Perhaps I can take you tomorrow, maybe the next day. First I must finish harvesting the corn."

So Juan spent the next day in the fields, bathed in sweat from sunup to sundown.

Yet each ear of corn that he picked seemed to bring him closer to his treasure. And later that evening, when he helped the young man husk

several ears so they could boil them for supper, the yellow kernels glittered like gold coins.

While they were eating, Juan thought about Doña Josefa. Why, he wondered, would someone who said she was the world's richest woman spend her time taking care of every sick person for miles around?

The following day, the two set off at dawn. Juan could not recall when he last had noticed the beauty of the sunrise. He felt strangely moved by the sight of the mountains, barely lit by the faint rays of the morning sun.

As they neared the foothills, the young man said, "I'm not surprised you're looking for Doña Josefa. The whole countryside needs her. I went for her because my wife had been running a high fever. In no time at all, Doña Josefa had her on the road to recovery. And what's more, my friend, she brought her a gold coin!"

Juan groaned inwardly. To think that someone could hand out gold so freely! What a strange woman Doña Josefa is, Juan thought. Not only is she willing to help one person after another, but she doesn't mind traveling all over the countryside to do it!

"Well, my friend," said the young man finally, "this is where I must leave you. But you don't have far to walk. See that house over there? It belongs to the man who broke his leg."

The young man stretched out his hand to say good-bye. Juan stared at it for a moment. It had been a long, long time since the thief had shaken hands with anyone. Slowly, he pulled out a hand from under his poncho. When his companion grasped it firmly in his own, Juan felt suddenly warmed, as if by the rays of the sun.

But after he thanked the young man, Juan ran down the road. He was still eager to catch up with Doña Josefa. When he reached the house, a woman and a child were stepping down from a wagon.

"Have you seen Doña Josefa?" Juan asked.

"We've just taken her to Don Teodosio's," the woman said. "His wife is sick, you know——"

"How do I get there?" Juan broke in. "I've got to see her."

"It's too far to walk," the woman said amiably. "If you'd like, I'll take you there tomorrow. But first I must gather my squash and beans."

So Juan spent yet another long day in the fields. Working beneath the summer sun, Juan noticed that his skin had begun to tan. And although he had to stoop down to pick the squash, he found that he could now stretch his body. His back had begun to straighten, too.

Later, when the little girl took him by the hand to show him a family of rabbits burrowed under a fallen tree, Juan's face broke into a smile. It had been a long, long time since Juan had smiled.

Yet his thoughts kept coming back to the gold.

The following day, the wagon carrying Juan and the woman lumbered along a road lined with coffee fields.

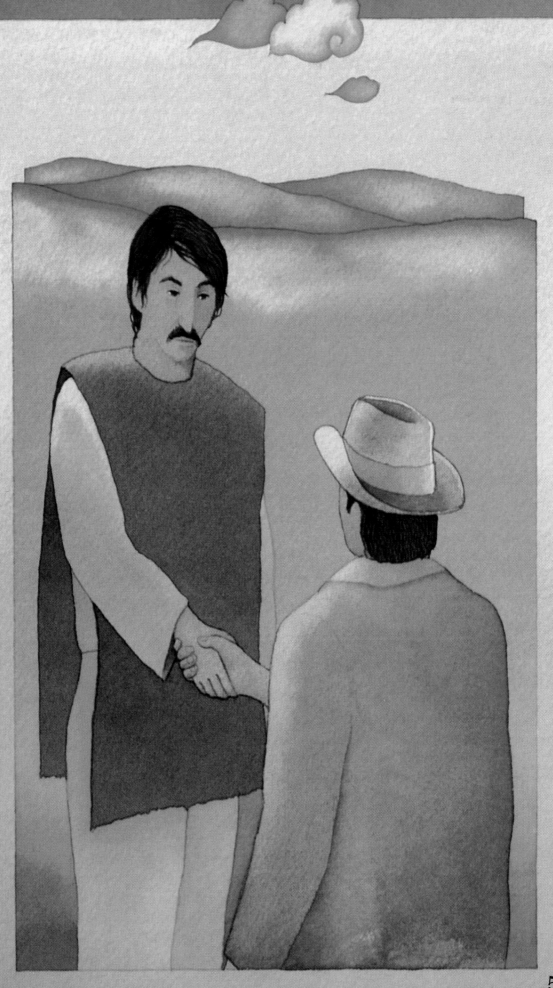

The woman said, "I don't know what we would have done without Doña Josefa. I sent my daughter to our neighbor's house, who then brought Doña Josefa on horseback. She set my husband's leg and then showed me how to brew a special tea to lessen the pain."

Getting no reply, she went on. "And, as if that weren't enough, she brought him a gold coin. Can you imagine such a thing?"

Juan could only sigh. No doubt about it, he thought, Doña Josefa is someone special. But Juan didn't know whether to be happy that Doña Josefa had so much gold she could freely hand it out, or angry for her having already given so much of it away.

When they finally reached Don Teodosio's house, Doña Josefa was already gone. But here, too, there was work that needed to be done . . .

Juan stayed to help with the coffee harvest. As he picked the red berries, he gazed up from time to time at the trees that grew, row upon row, along the hillsides. What a calm, peaceful place this is! he thought.

The next morning, Juan was up at daybreak. Bathed in the soft, dawn light, the mountains seemed to smile at him. When Don Teodosio offered him a lift on horseback, Juan found it difficult to have to say good-bye.

"What a good woman Doña Josefa is!" Don Teodosio said, as they rode down the hill toward the sugarcane fields. "The minute she heard about my wife being sick, she came with her special herbs. And as if that weren't enough, she brought my wife a gold coin!"

In the stifling heat, the kind that often signals the approach of a storm, Juan simply sighed and mopped his brow. The pair continued riding for several hours in silence.

Juan then realized he was back in familiar territory, for they were now on the stretch of road he had traveled only a week ago—though how much longer it now seemed to him. He jumped off Don Teodosio's horse and broke into a run.

This time the gold would not escape him! But he had to move quickly, so he could find shelter before the storm broke.

Out of breath, Juan finally reached Doña Josefa's hut. She was standing by the door, shaking her head slowly as she surveyed the ransacked house.

"So I've caught up with you at last!" Juan shouted, startling the old woman. "Where's the gold?"

"The gold coin?" Doña Josefa said, surprised and looking at Juan intently. "Have you come for the gold coin? I've been trying hard to give it to someone who might need it," Doña Josefa said. "First to an old man who had just gotten over a bad attack. Then to a young woman who had been running a fever. Then to a man with a broken leg. And finally to Don Teodosio's wife. But none of them would take it. They all said, 'Keep it. There must be someone who needs it more.'"

Juan did not say a word.

"You must be the one who needs it," Doña Josefa said.

She took the coin out of her pocket and handed it to him. Juan stared at the coin, speechless.

At that moment a young girl appeared, her long braid bouncing as she ran. "Hurry, Doña Josefa, please!" she said breathlessly. "My mother is all alone, and the baby is due any minute."

"Of course, dear," Doña Josefa replied. But as she glanced up at the sky, she saw nothing but black clouds. The storm was nearly upon them. Doña Josefa sighed deeply.

"But how can I leave now? Look at my house! I don't know what has happened to the roof. The storm will wash the whole place away!"

And there was a deep sadness in her voice.

Juan took in the child's frightened eyes, Doña Josefa's sad, distressed face, and the ransacked hut.

"Go ahead, Doña Josefa," he said. "Don't worry about your house. I'll see that the roof is back in shape, good as new."

The woman nodded gratefully, drew her cloak about her shoulders, and took the child by the hand. As she turned to leave, Juan held out his hand.

"Here, take this," he said, giving her the gold coin. "I'm sure the newborn will need it more than I."

The Gold Coin

Meet the Author

Alma Flor Ada credits her family with giving her a love of stories. "My father told me stories he invented to explain to me all that he knew about the history of the world." Ada has written many textbooks and children's stories and enjoys translating stories, written by other authors, from English to Spanish.

Meet the Translator

Bernice Randall is editorial director of Santillana Publishing Company. She has worked for several other publishing companies in the past. She also teaches a workshop at Stanford Publishing Course.

Meet the Illustrator

Neil Waldman illustrates children's books. He always wanted to paint and draw as a child. "I sensed, as a small child, that finger paints and coloring books were more than just fun. They were important tools that lead to a road of joy, discovery, and fulfillment."

Theme Connections

Think About It

- How was Juan affected by the farming experiences?
- Why did Doña Josefa call herself the richest woman in the world?

Record Ideas

To reflect the episodic nature of this folktale, record your ideas as episodes.

Write a Sequel

Write a paragraph as to how a sequel to "The Gold Coin" might begin.

FINE Art

El Pan Nuestro. **Diego Rivera.** Mural. Education Secretariat, Mexico.
Photo: ET Archive, London/Superstock.

Mrs. James Smith and Grandson. 1776.
Charles Wilson Peale. Oil on canvas.
National Museum of American Art,
Washington, DC. Photo: Art Resource, NY.

The Gleaners. 1857.
**Jean-François
Millet.** Oil on canvas.
33 × 44 in. Musée
d'Orsay, Paris. Photo:
Scala/Art Resource,
NY.

President Cleveland, Where Are You?

Robert Cormier
illustrated by Mary Beth Schwark and Bob Kuester

That was the autumn of the cowboy cards——Buck Jones and Tom Tyler and Hoot Gibson and especially Ken Maynard. The cards were available in those five-cent packages of gum: pink sticks, three together, covered with a sweet white powder. You couldn't blow bubbles with that particular gum, but it couldn't have mattered less. The cowboy cards were important——the pictures of those rock-faced men with eyes of blue steel.

On those wind-swept, leaf-tumbling afternoons we gathered after school on the sidewalk in front of Lemire's Drugstore, across from St. Jude's Parochial School, and we swapped and bargained and matched for the cards. Because a Ken Maynard serial was playing at the Globe every Saturday afternoon, he was the most popular cowboy of all, and one of his cards was worth at least ten of any other kind. Rollie Tremaine had a treasure of thirty or so, and he guarded them jealously. He'd match you for the other cards, but he risked his Ken Maynards only when the other kids threatened to leave him out of the competition altogether.

You could almost hate Rollie Tremaine. In the first place, he was the only son of Auguste Tremaine, who operated the Uptown Dry Goods Store, and he did not live in a tenement but in a big white birthday cake of a house on Laurel Street. He was too fat to be effective in the football games between the Frenchtown Tigers and

602

the North Side Knights, and he made us constantly aware of the jingle of coins in his pockets. He was able to stroll into Lemire's and casually select a quarter's worth of cowboy cards while the rest of us watched, aching with envy.

Once in a while I earned a nickel or dime by running errands or washing windows for blind old Mrs. Belander, or by finding pieces of copper, brass, and other valuable metals at the dump and selling them to the junkman. The coins clutched in my hand, I would race to Lemire's to buy a cowboy card or two, hoping that Ken Maynard would stare boldly out at me as I opened the pack. At one time, before a disastrous matching session with Roger Lussier (my best friend, except where the cards were involved), I owned five Ken Maynards and considered myself a millionaire, of sorts.

One week I was particularly lucky; I had spent two afternoons washing floors for Mrs. Belander and received a quarter. Because my father had worked a full week at the shop, where a rush order for fancy combs had been received, he allotted my brothers and sisters and me an extra dime along with the usual ten cents for the Saturday-afternoon movie. Setting aside the movie fare, I found myself with a bonus of thirty-five cents, and I then planned to put Rollie Tremaine to shame the following Monday afternoon.

Monday was the best day to buy the cards because the candy man stopped at Lemire's every Monday morning to deliver the new assortments. There was nothing more exciting in the world than a fresh batch of card boxes. I rushed home from school that day and hurriedly changed my clothes, eager to set off for the store. As I burst through the doorway, letting the screen door slam behind me, my brother Armand blocked my way.

He was fourteen, three years older than I, and a freshman at Monument High School. He had recently become a stranger to me in many ways——indifferent to such matters as cowboy cards and the Frenchtown Tigers——and he carried himself with a mysterious dignity that was fractured now and then when his voice began shooting off in all directions like some kind of vocal fireworks.

"Wait a minute, Jerry," he said. "I want to talk to you." He motioned me out of earshot of my mother, who was busy supervising the usual after-school skirmish in the kitchen.

I sighed with impatience. In recent months Armand had become a figure of authority, siding with my father and mother occasionally. As the oldest son he sometimes took advantage of his age and experience to issue rules and regulations.

"How much money have you got?" he whispered.

"You in some kind of trouble?" I asked, excitement rising in me as I remembered the blackmail plot of a movie at the Globe a month before.

He shook his head in annoyance. "Look," he said, "it's Pa's birthday tomorrow. I think we ought to chip in and buy him something . . ."

I reached into my pocket and caressed the coins. "Here," I said carefully, pulling out a nickel. "If we all give a nickel we should have enough to buy him something pretty nice."

He regarded me with contempt. "Rita already gave me fifteen cents, and I'm throwing in a quarter. Albert handed over a dime——all that's left of his birthday money. Is that all you can do——a nickel?"

"Aw, come on," I protested. "I haven't got a single Ken Maynard left, and I was going to buy some cards this afternoon."

"Ken Maynard!" he snorted. "Who's more important——him or your father?"

His question was unfair because he knew that there was no possible choice——"my father" had to be the only answer. My father was a huge man who believed in the things of the spirit. He had worked at the Monument Comb Shop since the age of fourteen; his booming laugh—— or grumble——greeted us each night when he returned from the factory. A steady worker when the shop had enough work, he quickened with gaiety on Friday nights and weekends, and he was fond of making long speeches about the good things in life. In the middle of the Depression, for instance, he paid cash for a piano, of all things, and insisted that my twin sisters, Yolande and Yvette, take lessons once a week.

I took a dime from my pocket and handed it to Armand.

"Thanks, Jerry," he said. "I hate to take your last cent."

"That's all right," I replied, turning away and consoling myself with the thought that twenty cents was better than nothing at all.

When I arrived at Lemire's I sensed disaster in the air. Roger Lussier was kicking disconsolately at a tin can in the gutter, and Rollie Tremaine sat sullenly on the steps in front of the store.

"Save your money," Roger said. He had known about my plans to splurge on the cards.

"What's the matter?" I asked.

"There's no more cowboy cards," Rollie Tremaine said. "The company's not making any more."

"They're going to have President cards," Roger said, his face twisting with disgust. He pointed to the store window. "Look!"

A placard in the window announced: "Attention, Boys. Watch for the New Series. Presidents of the United States. Free in Each 5-Cent Package of Caramel Chew."

"President cards?" I asked, dismayed.

I read on: "Collect a Complete Set and Receive an Official Imitation Major League Baseball Glove, Embossed with Lefty Grove's Autograph."

Glove or no glove, who could become excited about Presidents, of all things?

Rollie Tremaine stared at the sign. "Benjamin Harrison, for crying out loud," he said. "Why would I want Benjamin Harrison when I've got twenty-two Ken Maynards?"

I felt the warmth of guilt creep over me. I jingled the coins in my pocket, but the sound was hollow. No more Ken Maynards to buy.

"I'm going to buy a Mr. Goodbar," Rollie Tremaine decided.

I was without appetite, indifferent even to a Baby Ruth, which was my favorite. I thought of how I had betrayed Armand and, worst of all, my father.

"I'll see you after supper," I called over my shoulder to Roger as I hurried away toward home. I took the shortcut behind the church, although it involved leaping over a tall wooden fence, and I zigzagged recklessly through Mr. Thibodeau's garden, trying to outrace my guilt. I pounded up the steps and into the house, only to learn that Armand had already taken Yolande and Yvette uptown to shop for the birthday present.

I pedaled my bike furiously through the streets, ignoring the indignant horns of automobiles as I sliced through the traffic. Finally I saw Armand and my sisters emerge from the Monument Men's Shop. My heart sank when I spied the long, slim package that Armand was holding.

606

"Did you buy the present yet?" I asked, although I knew it was too late.

"Just now. A blue tie," Armand said. "What's the matter?"

"Nothing," I replied, my chest hurting.

He looked at me for a long moment. At first his eyes were hard, but then they softened. He smiled at me, almost sadly, and touched my arm. I turned away from him because I felt naked and exposed.

"It's all right," he said gently. "Maybe you've learned something." The words were gentle, but they held a curious dignity, the dignity remaining even when his voice suddenly cracked on the last syllable.

I wondered what was happening to me, because I did not know whether to laugh or cry.

Sister Angela was amazed when, a week before Christmas vacation, everybody in the class submitted a history essay worthy of a high mark——in some cases as high as A-minus. (Sister Angela did not believe that anyone in the world ever deserved an A.) She never learned——or at least she never let on that she knew——we all had become experts on the Presidents because of the cards we purchased at Lemire's. Each card contained a picture of a President,

and on the reverse side, a summary of his career. We looked at those cards so often that the biographies imprinted themselves on our minds without effort. Even our street-corner conversations were filled with such information as the fact that James Madison was called "The Father of the Constitution," or that John Adams had intended to become a minister.

The President cards were a roaring success and the cowboy cards were quickly forgotten. In the first place we did not receive gum with the cards, but a kind of chewy caramel. The caramel could be tucked into a corner of your mouth, bulging your cheek in much the same manner as wads of tobacco bulged the mouths of baseball stars. In the second place the competition for collecting the cards was fierce and frustrating——fierce because everyone was intent on being the first to send away for a baseball glove and frustrating because although there were only thirty-two Presidents, including Franklin Delano Roosevelt, the variety at Lemire's was at a minimum. When the deliveryman left the boxes of cards at the store each Monday, we often discovered that one entire box was devoted to a

single President——two weeks in a row the boxes contained nothing but Abraham Lincolns. One week Roger Lussier and I were the heroes of Frenchtown. We journeyed on our bicycles to the North Side, engaged three boys in a matching bout and returned with five new Presidents, including Chester Alan Arthur, who up to that time had been missing.

Perhaps to sharpen our desire, the card company sent a sample glove to Mr. Lemire, and it dangled, orange and sleek, in the window. I was half sick with longing, thinking of my old glove at home, which I had inherited from Armand. But Rollie Tremaine's desire for the glove outdistanced my own. He even got Mr. Lemire to agree to give the glove in the window to the first person to get a complete set of cards, so that precious time wouldn't be wasted waiting for the postman.

We were delighted at Rollie Tremaine's frustration, especially since he was only a substitute player for the Tigers. Once after spending fifty cents on cards——all of which turned out to be Calvin Coolidge ——he threw them to the ground, pulled some dollar bills out of his pocket and said, "The heck with it. I'm going to buy a glove!"

609

"Not that glove," Roger Lussier said. "Not a glove with Lefty Grove's autograph. Look what it says at the bottom of the sign."

We all looked, although we knew the words by heart: "This Glove Is Not For Sale Anywhere."

Rollie Tremaine scrambled to pick up the cards from the sidewalk, pouting more than ever. After that he was quietly obsessed with the Presidents, hugging the cards close to his chest and refusing to tell us how many more he needed to complete his set.

I too was obsessed with the cards, because they had become things of comfort in a world that had suddenly grown dismal. After Christmas a layoff at the shop had thrown my father out of work. He received no paycheck for four weeks, and the only income we had was from Armand's after-school job at the Blue and White Grocery Store——a job he lost finally when business dwindled as the layoff continued.

Although we had enough food and clothing——my father's credit had always been good, a matter of pride with him——the inactivity made my father restless and irritable. The twins fell sick and went to the hospital to have their tonsils removed. My father was confident that he would return to work eventually and pay off his debts, but he seemed to age before our eyes.

When orders again were received at the comb shop and he returned to work, another disaster occurred, although I was the only one aware of it. Armand fell in love.

I discovered his situation by accident, when I happened to pick up a piece of paper that had fallen to the floor in the bedroom he and I shared. I frowned at the paper, puzzled.

"Dear Sally, When I look into your eyes the world stands still . . ."

The letter was snatched from my hands before I finished reading it.

"What's the big idea, snooping around?" Armand asked, his face crimson. "Can't a guy have any privacy?"

He had never mentioned privacy before. "It was on the floor," I said. "I didn't know it was a letter. Who's Sally?"

He flung himself across the bed. "You tell anybody and I'll

muckalize you," he threatened. "Sally Knowlton."

Nobody in Frenchtown had a name like Knowlton.

"A girl from the North Side?" I asked, incredulous.

He rolled over and faced me, anger in his eyes, and a kind of despair too.

"What's the matter with that? Think she's too good for me?" he asked. "I'm warning you, Jerry, if you tell anybody . . ."

"Don't worry," I said. Love had no particular place in my life; it seemed an unnecessary waste of time. And a girl from the North Side was so remote that for all practical purposes she did not exist. But I was curious. "What are you writing her a letter for? Did she leave town, or something?"

"She hasn't left town," he answered. "I wasn't going to send it. I just felt like writing to her." I was glad that I had never become involved with love——love that brought desperation to your eyes, that caused you to write letters you did not plan to send. Shrugging with indifference, I began to search in the closet for the old baseball glove. I found it on the shelf, under some old sneakers. The webbing was torn and the padding gone. I thought of the sting I would feel when a sharp grounder slapped into the glove, and I winced.

"You tell anybody about me and Sally and I'll——"

"I know. You'll muckalize me."

I did not divulge his secret and often shared his agony, particularly when he sat at the supper table and left my mother's special butterscotch pie untouched. I had never realized before how terrible love could be. But my compassion was short-lived because I had other things to worry about: report cards due at Eastertime; the loss of income from old Mrs. Belander, who had gone to live with a daughter in Boston; and, of course, the Presidents.

Because a stalemate had been reached, the President cards were the dominant force in our lives——mine, Roger Lussier's and Rollie Tremaine's. For three weeks, as the baseball season approached, each of us had a complete set——complete except for one President, Grover Cleveland. Each time a box of cards arrived at the store we hurriedly bought them (as hurriedly as our funds allowed) and tore off the wrappers, only to be confronted by James Monroe or Martin Van Buren or someone else. But never Grover Cleveland, never the man who had been the twenty-second and the twenty-fourth President of the United States. We argued about Grover Cleveland. Should he be placed between Chester Alan Arthur and Benjamin Harrison as the twenty-second President or did he belong between Benjamin Harrison

and William McKinley as the twenty-fourth President? Was the card company playing fair? Roger Lussier brought up a horrifying possibility——did we need *two* Grover Clevelands to complete the set?

Indignant, we stormed Lemire's and protested to the harassed storeowner, who had long since vowed never to stock a new series. Muttering angrily, he searched his bills and receipts for a list of rules.

"All right," he announced. "Says here you only need one Grover Cleveland to finish the set. Now get out, all of you, unless you've got money to spend."

Outside the store, Rollie Tremaine picked up an empty tobacco tin and scaled it across the street. "Boy," he said. "I'd give five dollars for a Grover Cleveland."

When I returned home I found Armand sitting on the piazza steps, his chin in his hands. His mood of dejection mirrored my own, and I sat down beside him. We did not say anything for a while.

"Want to throw the ball around?" I asked.

He sighed, not bothering to answer.

"You sick?" I asked.

He stood up and hitched up his trousers, pulled at his ear and finally told me what the matter was——there was a big dance next week at the high school, the Spring Promenade, and Sally had asked him to be her escort.

I shook my head at the folly of love. "Well, what's so bad about that?"

"How can I take Sally to a fancy dance?" he asked desperately. "I'd have to buy her a corsage . . . And my shoes are practically falling apart. Pa's got too many worries now to buy me new shoes or give me money for flowers for a girl."

I nodded in sympathy. "Yeah," I said. "Look at me. Baseball time is almost here, and all I've got is that old glove. And no Grover Cleveland card yet . . ."

"Grover Cleveland?" he asked. "They've got some of those up on the North Side. Some kid was telling me there's a store that's got them. He says they're looking for Warren G. Harding."

"Holy Smoke!" I said. "I've got an extra Warren G. Harding!" Pure joy sang in my veins. I ran to my bicycle, swung into the seat——and found that the front tire was flat.

613

"I'll help you fix it," Armand said.

Within half an hour I was at the North Side Drugstore, where several boys were matching cards on the sidewalk. Silently but blissfully I shouted: President Grover Cleveland, here I come!

After Armand had left for the dance, all dressed up as if it were Sunday, the small green box containing the corsage under his arm, I sat on the railing of the piazza, letting my feet dangle. The neighborhood was quiet because the Frenchtown Tigers were at Daggett's Field, practicing for the first baseball game of the season.

I thought of Armand and the ridiculous expression on his face when he'd stood before the mirror in the bedroom. I'd avoided looking at his new black shoes. "Love," I muttered.

Spring had arrived in a sudden stampede of apple blossoms and fragrant breezes. Windows had been thrown open and dust mops had banged on the sills all day long as the women busied themselves with housecleaning. I was puzzled by my lethargy. Wasn't spring supposed to make everything bright and gay?

I turned at the sound of footsteps on the stairs. Roger Lussier greeted me with a sour face.

"I thought you were practicing with the Tigers," I said.

"Rollie Tremaine," he said. "I just couldn't stand him." He slammed his fist against the railing. "Jeez, why did *he* have to be the one to get a Grover Cleveland? You should see him showing off. He won't let anybody even touch that glove . . ."

I felt like Benedict Arnold and knew that I had to confess what I had done.

"Roger," I said, "I got a Grover Cleveland card up on the North Side. I sold it to Rollie Tremaine for five dollars."

"Are you crazy?" he asked.

"I needed that five dollars. It was an——an emergency."

"Boy!" he said, looking down at the ground and shaking his head. "What did you have to do a thing like that for?"

I watched him as he turned away and began walking down the stairs.

"Hey, Roger!" I called.

He squinted up at me as if I were a stranger, someone he'd never seen before.

"What?" he asked, his voice flat.

"I had to do it," I said. "Honest."

He didn't answer. He headed toward the fence, searching for the board we had loosened to give us a secret passage.

I thought of my father and Armand and Rollie Tremaine and Grover Cleveland and wished that I could go away someplace far away. But there was no place to go.

Roger found the loose slat in the fence and slipped through. I felt betrayed: weren't you supposed to feel good when you did something fine and noble?

A moment later two hands gripped the top of the fence and Roger's face appeared. "Was it a real emergency?" he yelled.

"A real one!" I called. "Something important!"

His face dropped from sight and his voice reached me across the yard: "All right."

"See you tomorrow!" I yelled.

I swung my legs over the railing again. The gathering dusk began to soften the sharp edges of the fence, the rooftops, the distant church steeple. I sat there a long time, waiting for the good feeling to come.

President Cleveland, Where Are You?

Meet the Author

Robert Cormier writes suspenseful fiction stories for young adults. He was greatly influenced by three books when he was young. They were *The Adventures of Tom Sawyer* by Mark Twain, *The Web and the Rock* by Thomas Wolfe, and *The Daring Young Man on the Flying Trapeze* by William Saroyan.

Meet the Illustrators

Mary Beth Schwark and Bob Kuester Mary Beth Schwark is a freelance illustrator. Two of the works she has illustrated are *Your Former Friend, Matthew* and *The Kid with the Red Suspenders*, both by LouAnn Gaeddert. In addition to illustrating, Schwark enjoys playing the drums and the keyboard. Bob Kuester met Schwark while they were doing commercial art for an advertising agency, and they both worked as freelance illustrators. Although Schwark is still a freelance artist, Kuester returned to commercial art.

Theme Connections

Think About It

- Think about how values apply to perhaps your own collecting. Are there certain collectibles that are valued today by your age group?

- Have you ever been in a position where you had to consider someone else who needed help and as a result could not get a collectible or some other treasured item?

Record Ideas

Record in your Writing Journal one highlight of this unit. What really changed or impacted your way of thinking?

Bring in a Collectible

Look for examples of the various gimmicks that manufacturers today use to turn their products into collectors' items. For example, makers of porcelain figurines often break their molds after a certain number of the figurines are produced.

- Bring in two examples of advertisements for collectibles, and share them with the class.

- Discuss why you think some items will become valuable collectors' items and why others will not.

The No-Guitar Blues

from *Baseball in April and Other Stories*
by Gary Soto
illustrated by José Miralles

T he moment Fausto saw the group Los Lobos on
"American Bandstand," he knew exactly what he wanted
to do with his life——play guitar. His eyes grew large with
excitement as Los Lobos ground out a song while teenagers
bounced off each other on the crowded dance floor.

He had watched "American Bandstand" for years and had
heard Ray Camacho and the Teardrops at Romain Playground,
but it had never occurred to him that he too might become a
musician. That afternoon Fausto knew his mission in life: to play
guitar in his own band; to sweat out his songs and prance
around the stage; to make money and dress weird.

Fausto turned off the television set and walked outside,
wondering how he could get enough money to buy a guitar. He
couldn't ask his parents because they would just say, "Money
doesn't grow on trees" or "What do you think we are, bankers?"
And besides, they hated rock music. They were into the conjunto
music of Lydia Mendoza, Flaco Jimenez, and Little Joe and La
Familia. And, as Fausto recalled, the last album they bought was
The Chipmunks Sing Christmas Favorites.

But what the heck, he'd give it a try. He returned inside and
watched his mother make tortillas. He leaned against the kitchen
counter, trying to work up the nerve to ask her for a guitar.
Finally, he couldn't hold back any longer.

"Mom," he said, "I want a guitar for Christmas."

She looked up from rolling tortillas. "Honey, a guitar costs a lot of money."

"How 'bout for my birthday next year," he tried again.

"I can't promise," she said, turning back to her tortillas, "but we'll see."

Fausto walked back outside with a buttered tortilla. He knew his mother was right. His father was a warehouseman at Berven Rugs, where he made good money but not enough to buy everything his children wanted. Fausto decided to mow lawns to earn money, and was pushing the mower down the street before he realized it was winter and no one would hire him. He returned the mower and picked up a rake. He hopped onto his sister's bike (his had two flat tires) and rode north to the nicer section of Fresno in search of work. He went door-to-door, but after three hours he managed to get only one job, and not to rake leaves. He was asked to hurry down to the store to buy a loaf of bread, for which he received a grimy, dirt-caked quarter.

He also got an orange, which he ate sitting at the curb. While he was eating, a dog walked up and sniffed his leg. Fausto pushed him away and threw an orange peel skyward. The dog

caught it and ate it in one gulp. The dog looked at Fausto and wagged his tail for more. Fausto tossed him a slice of orange, and the dog snapped it up and licked his lips.

"How come you like oranges, dog?"

The dog blinked a pair of sad eyes and whined.

"What's the matter? Cat got your tongue?" Fausto laughed at his joke and offered the dog another slice.

At that moment a dim light came on inside Fausto's head. He saw that it was sort of a fancy dog, a terrier or something, with dog tags and a shiny collar. And it looked well fed and healthy. In his neighborhood, the dogs were never licensed, and if they got sick they were placed near the water heater until they got well.

This dog looked like he belonged to rich people. Fausto cleaned his juice-sticky hands on his pants and got to his feet. The light in his head grew brighter. It just might work. He called the dog, patted its muscular back, and bent down to check the license.

"Great," he said. "There's an address."

The dog's name was Roger, which struck Fausto as weird because he'd never heard of a dog with a human name. Dogs should have names like Bomber, Freckles, Queenie, Killer, and Zero.

Fausto planned to take the dog home and collect a reward. He would say he had found Roger near the freeway. That would scare the daylights out of the owners, who would be so happy that they would probably give him a reward. He felt bad about lying, but the dog was loose. And it might even really be lost, because the address was six blocks away.

Fausto stashed the rake and his sister's bike behind a bush, and, tossing an orange peel every time Roger became distracted, walked the dog to his house. He hesitated on the porch until Roger began to scratch the door with a muddy paw. Fausto had come this far, so he figured he might as well go through with it.

He knocked softly. When no one answered, he rang the doorbell. A man in a silky bathrobe and slippers opened the door and seemed confused by the sight of his dog and the boy.

"Sir," Fausto said, gripping Roger by the collar. "I found your dog by the freeway. His dog license says he lives here." Fausto looked down at the dog, then up to the man. "He does, doesn't he?"

The man stared at Fausto a long time before saying in a pleasant voice, "That's right." He pulled his robe tighter around him because of the cold and asked Fausto to come in. "So he was by the freeway?"

"Uh-huh."

"You bad, snoopy dog," said the man, wagging his finger. "You probably knocked over some trash cans, too, didn't you?"

Fausto didn't say anything. He looked around, amazed by this house with its shiny furniture and a television as large as the front window at home. Warm bread smells filled the air and music full of soft tinkling floated in from another room.

"Helen," the man called to the kitchen. "We have a visitor." His wife came into the living room wiping her hands on a dish towel and smiling. "And who have we here?" she asked in one of the softest voices Fausto had ever heard.

"This young man said he found Roger near the freeway."

Fausto repeated his story to her while staring at a perpetual clock with a bell-shaped glass, the kind his aunt got when she celebrated her twenty-fifth anniversary. The lady frowned and said, wagging a finger at Roger, "Oh, you're a bad boy."

"It was very nice of you to bring Roger home," the man said. "Where do you live?"

"By that vacant lot on Olive," he said. "You know, by Brownie's Flower Place."

The wife looked at her husband, then Fausto. Her eyes twinkled triangles of light as she said, "Well, young man, you're probably hungry. How about a turnover?"

"What do I have to turn over?" Fausto asked, thinking she was talking about yard work or something like turning trays of dried raisins.

"No, no, dear, it's a pastry." She took him by the elbow and guided him to a kitchen that sparkled with copper pans and bright yellow wallpaper. She guided him to the kitchen table and gave him a tall glass of milk and something that looked like an *empanada*. Steamy waves of heat escaped when he tore it in two. He ate with both eyes on the man and woman who stood arm-in-arm smiling at him. They were strange, he thought. But nice.

"That was good," he said after he finished the turnover. "Did you make it, ma'am?"

"Yes, I did. Would you like another?"

"No, thank you. I have to go home now."

As Fausto walked to the door, the man opened his wallet and took out a bill. "This is for you," he said. "Roger is special to us, almost like a son."

Fausto looked at the bill and knew he was in trouble. Not with these nice folks or with his parents but with himself. How could he have been so deceitful? The dog wasn't lost. It was just having a fun Saturday walking around.

"I can't take that."

"You have to. You deserve it, believe me," the man said.

"No, I don't."

"Now don't be silly," said the lady. She took the bill from her husband and stuffed it into Fausto's shirt pocket. "You're a lovely child. Your parents are lucky to have you. Be good. And come see us again, please."

Fausto went out, and the lady closed the door. Fausto clutched the bill through his shirt pocket. He felt like ringing the doorbell and begging them to please take the money back, but he knew they would refuse. He hurried away, and at the end of the block, pulled the bill from his shirt pocket: it was a crisp twenty-dollar bill.

"Oh, man, I shouldn't have lied," he said under his breath as he started up the street like a zombie. He wanted to run to church for Saturday confession, but it was past four-thirty, when confession stopped.

He returned to the bush where he had hidden the rake and his sister's bike and rode home slowly, not daring to touch the money in his pocket. At home, in the privacy of his room, he examined the twenty-dollar bill. He had never had so much money. It was probably enough to buy a secondhand guitar. But he felt bad, like the time he stole a dollar from the secret fold inside his older brother's wallet.

Fausto went outside and sat on the fence. "Yeah," he said. "I can probably get a guitar for twenty. Maybe at a yard sale——things are cheaper."

His mother called him to dinner.

The next day he dressed for church without anyone telling him. He was going to go to eight o'clock mass.

"I'm going to church, Mom," he said. His mother was in the kitchen cooking *papas* and *chorizo con huevos*. A pile of tortillas lay warm under a dishtowel.

"Oh, I'm so proud of you, Son." She beamed, turning over the crackling *papas*.

His older brother, Lawrence, who was at the table reading the funnies, mimicked, "Oh, I'm so proud of you, my son," under his breath.

At Saint Theresa's he sat near the front. When Father Jerry began by saying that we are all sinners, Fausto thought he looked right at him. Could he know? Fausto fidgeted with guilt. No, he thought. I only did it yesterday.

Fausto knelt, prayed, and sang. But he couldn't forget the man and the lady, whose names he didn't even know, and the *empanada* they had given him. It had a strange name but tasted really good. He wondered how they got rich. And how that dome clock worked. He had asked his mother once how his aunt's clock worked. She said it just worked, the way the refrigerator works. It just did.

Fausto caught his mind wandering and tried to concentrate on his sins. He said a Hail Mary and sang, and when the wicker basket came his way, he stuck a hand reluctantly in his pocket and pulled out the twenty-dollar bill. He ironed it between his palms, and dropped it into the basket. The grown-ups stared. Here was a kid dropping twenty dollars in the basket while they gave just three or four dollars.

There would be a second collection for Saint Vincent de Paul, the lector announced. The wicker baskets again floated in the pews, and this time the adults around him, given a second chance to show their charity, dug deep into their wallets and purses and dropped in fives and tens. This time Fausto tossed in the grimy quarter.

Fausto felt better after church. He went home and played football in the front yard with his brother and some neighbor kids. He felt cleared of wrongdoing and was so happy that he played one of his best games of football ever. On one play, he tore his good pants, which he knew he shouldn't have been wearing. For a second, while he examined the hole, he wished he hadn't given the twenty dollars away.

Man, I coulda bought me some Levi's, he thought. He pictured his twenty dollars being spent to buy church candles. He pictured a priest buying an armful of flowers with his money.

Fausto had to forget about getting a guitar. He spent the next day playing soccer in his good pants, which were now his old pants. But that night during dinner, his mother said she remembered seeing an old bass guitarron the last time she cleaned out her father's garage.

"It's a little dusty," his mom said, serving his favorite enchiladas, "but I think it works. Grandpa says it works."

Fausto's ears perked up. That was the same kind the guy in Los Lobos played. Instead of asking for the guitar, he waited for his mother to offer it to him. And she did, while gathering the dishes from the table.

"No, Mom, I'll do it," he said, hugging her. "I'll do the dishes forever if you want."

It was the happiest day of his life. No, it was the second-happiest day of his life. The happiest was when his grandfather Lupe placed the guitarron, which was nearly as huge as a washtub, in his arms. Fausto ran a thumb down the strings, which vibrated in his throat and chest. It sounded beautiful, deep and eerie. A pumpkin smile widened on his face.

"OK, *hijo*, now you put your fingers like this," said his grandfather, smelling of tobacco and aftershave. He took Fausto's fingers and placed them on the strings. Fausto strummed a chord on the guitarron, and the bass resounded in their chests.

The guitarron was more complicated than Fausto imagined. But he was confident that after a few more lessons he could start a band that would someday play on "American Bandstand" for the dancing crowds.

The No-Guitar Blues

Meet the Author

Gary Soto wasn't interested in books or school as a child. While he was in school, he read a poem that expressed emotions he also felt. Soto realized he wanted to express his feelings by writing. He now writes poetry, essays, and fiction and produces short 16mm films.

Meet the Illustrator

José Miralles was born in Barcelona during the Spanish Civil War. He always wanted to be an artist, and at sixteen years old he published his first illustrations in a Barcelona newspaper. After completing his studies in art, Miralles went on to illustrate for many other publications. His work has appeared in magazines and books worldwide. Some of his favorite subjects are history, religion, and children.

Theme Connections

Think About It

Characterization through dialogue rather than strict description is often a more powerful way to depict characters. Do you agree or disagree with this statement?

Record Ideas

Record your comparisons as well as those from your classmates that you found interesting.

Current Article or Music

Bring in a current article from a newspaper or magazine or a contemporary song that highlights personal integrity. Share with your classmates why you picked this article or music and how it may change or impact your life.

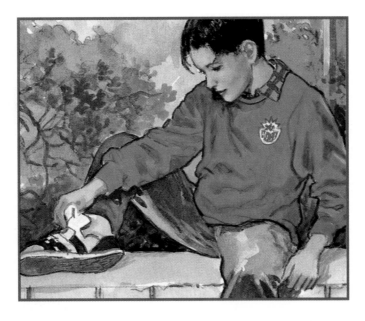

The Courage That My Mother Had

by Edna St. Vincent Millay

The courage that my mother had
Went with her, and is with her still:
Rock from New England quarried;
Now granite in a granite hill.

The golden brooch my mother wore
She left behind for me to wear;
I have no thing I treasure more:
Yet, it is something I could spare.

Oh, if instead she'd left to me
The thing she took to the grave!—
That courage like a rock, which she
Has no more need of, and I have.

The Coin

by Sara Teasdale

Into my heart's treasury
I slipped a coin
That time cannot take
Nor a thief purloin——
Oh, better than the minting
Of a gold-crowned king
Is the safe-kept memory
Of a lovely thing.

The Hundred Penny Box

Sharon Bell Mathis
illustrated by Leo and Diane Dillon

Michael sat down on the bed that used to be his and watched his great-great-aunt, Aunt Dew, rocking in the rocking chair.

He wanted to play with the hundred penny box——especially since it was raining outside——but Aunt Dew was singing that long song again. Sometimes when she sang it she would forget who he was for a whole day.

Then she would call him John.

John was his father's name. Then his mother would say, "He's Mike, Aunt Dew. His name is Michael. John's name is John. His name is Michael." But if his father was home, Aunt Dew would just say "Where's my boy?" Then it was hard to tell whether she meant him or his father. And he would have to wait until she said something more before he knew which one she meant.

Aunt Dew didn't call his mother any name at all.

Michael had heard his father and mother talking in bed late one night. It was soon after they had come from going to Atlanta to bring back Aunt Dew. "She won't even look at me——won't call my name, nothing," his mother had said, and Michael could tell she had been crying. "She doesn't like me. I know it. I can tell. I do everything I can to make her comfortable——" His mother was crying hard. "I rode half the way across this city——all the way to Mama Dee's——to get some homemade ice cream, some decent ice cream. Mama Dee said, 'The ice cream be melted fore you get home.' So I took a cab back and made her lunch and gave her the ice cream. I sat down at the table and tried to drink my coffee——I mean, I wanted to talk to her, say something. But she sat there and ate that ice cream and looked straight ahead at the wall and never said nothing to me. She talks to Mike and if I come around she even stops talking sometime." His mother didn't say anything for a while and then he heard her say, "I care about her. But she's making me miserable in my own house."

Michael heard his father say the same thing he always said about Aunt Dew. "She's a one-hundred-year-old lady, baby." Sometimes his father would add, "And when I didn't have nobody, she was there. Look here——after Big John and Junie drowned, she gave me a home. I didn't have one. I didn't have nothing. No mother, no father, no nobody. Nobody but her. I've loved her all my life. Like I love you. And that tough beautiful

boy we made——standing right outside the door and listening for all he's worth——and he's supposed to be in his room sleep."

Michael remembered he had run back to his room and gotten back into bed and gotten up again and tiptoed over to the bedroom door to close it a little and shut off some of the light shining from the bathroom onto Aunt Dew's face. Then he looked at Aunt Dew and wished she'd wake up and talk to him like she did when she felt like talking and telling him all kinds of stories about people.

"Hold tight, Ruth," he had heard his father say that night. "She knows we want her. She knows it. And baby, baby——sweet woman, you doing fine. Everything you doing is right." Then Michael could hear the covers moving where his mother and father were and he knew his father was putting his arms around his mother because sometimes he saw them still asleep in the morning and that's the way they looked.

But he was tired of remembering now and he was tired of Aunt Dew singing and singing and singing.

"Aunt Dew," Michael whispered close to his great-great-aunt's wrinkled face. "Can we play with the hundred penny box?"

"Precious Lord——"

"Aunt Dew! Let's count the pennies out."

"Take my hand——"

"Aunt Dew!"

"Lead me on——"

Michael thought for a moment. He knew the large scratched wooden box was down beside the dresser, on the floor where he could easily get it.

Except it was no fun to count the pennies alone.

It was better when Aunt Dew whacked him a little and said, "Stop right there, boy. You know what that penny means?" And he'd say, "You tell me," and she would tell him.

But when she started singing it was hard to stop her. At least when she was dancing what she called "moving to the music," she'd get tired after a while. Then she would tell him about the pennies and help count them too.

Michael cupped his large hands——everybody talked about how large his hands were for his age——around his great-great-aunt's ear. "Aunt Dew!" he said loudly.

Aunt Dew stopped rocking hard and turned and looked at him. But he didn't say anything and she didn't say anything.

Aunt Dew turned her head and began to sing again. Exactly where she had left off. *"Let me stand——"*

Michael moved away from the rocking chair and sat back down on the bed. Then he got up and went to the dresser. He reached down and picked up the heavy, scratched-up hundred penny box from the floor, walked to the bedroom door, and stood there for a moment before he went out.

There was no way to stop Aunt Dew once she started singing that long song.

Michael walked down the hall and held the huge box against his stomach. He could still hear Aunt Dew's high voice.

"I am weak. I am worn."

"What's wrong?" his mother asked when he walked into the kitchen and sat down on a chair and stared at the floor.

He didn't want to answer.

"Oh," his mother said and reached for the hundred penny box in his arms. "Give me that thing," she said. "That goes today! Soon as Aunt Dew's sleep, that goes in the furnace."

Michael almost jumped out of the chair. He wouldn't let go of the big, heavy box. He could hear his great-great-aunt's voice. She was singing louder. *"Lead me through the night, precious Lord. Take my hand."*

"You can't take the hundred penny box," Michael cried. "I'll tell Daddy if you take it and burn it up in the furnace like you burned up all the rest of Aunt Dew's stuff!" Then Michael thought of all the things he and Aunt Dew had hidden in his closet, and almost told his mother.

His mother walked closer to him and stood there but he wasn't afraid. Nobody was going to take Aunt Dew's hundred penny box. Nobody. Nobody. Nobody.

"Aunt Dew's like a child," his mother said quietly. "She's like you. Thinks she needs a whole lot of stuff she really doesn't. I'm not taking her pennies——you know I wouldn't take her pennies. I'm just getting rid of that big old ugly wooden box always under foot!"

Michael stood up. "No," he said.

"Mike, did you say no to me?" his mother asked. She put her hands on her hips.

"I mean," Michael said and tried to think fast. "Aunt Dew won't go to sleep if she doesn't see her box in the corner. Can I take it back and then you can let her see it? And when she goes to sleep, you can take it."

"Go put it back in her room then," his mother said. "I'll get it later."

"Okay," Michael said and held the heavy box tighter and walked slowly back down the hall to the small bedroom that used to be his. He opened the door and went in, put the hundred penny box down on the floor and sat down on it, staring at his aunt. She wasn't singing, just sitting. "John-boy," she said.

"Yes, Aunt Dew," Michael answered and didn't care this time that she was calling him John again. He was trying to think.

"Put my music on."

The music wasn't going to help him think because the first thing she was going to do was to make him "move" too.

But Michael got off the hundred penny box and reached under his bed and pulled out his blue record player that he had got for his birthday. He had already plugged it in the wall when he heard her say, "Get mine. My own Victrola, the one your father give me."

"Momma threw it out," Michael said and knew he had told her already, a lot of times. "It was broken."

636

Aunt Dew squeezed her lips real tight together. "Your momma gonna throw me out soon," she said.

Michael stood still and stared at his great-great-aunt. "Momma can't throw *people* out," he said.

"Put my music on, boy," Aunt Dew said again. "And be quick about it."

"Okay," Michael said and turned the record player on and got the record, Aunt Dew's favorite, that they had saved and hidden in the bottom drawer.

The dusty, chipped record was of a lady singing that long song, *"Precious Lord, Take My Hand."* Michael turned it down low.

Aunt Dew started humming and Michael sat down on the bed and tried to think about what he'd do with the hundred penny box.

Aunt Dew got up from her rocking chair and stood up. She kept her arms down by her sides and made her thin hands into fists and clenched her lips tight and moved real slow in one spot. Her small shoulders just went up and down and up and down. "Get up, John-boy," she said, "and move with me. Move with Dewbet Thomas!"

"I don't feel like dancing," Michael said and kept sitting on the bed. But he watched his great-great-aunt move both her thin arms to one side and then to the other and hover her hands about and hold her dress. Then she stopped and started all of a sudden again, just swinging her arms and moving her shoulders up and down and singing some more. Every time the record ended, he'd start it again.

When he was playing it for the third time, he said, "Aunt Dew, where will you put your hundred pennies if you lose your hundred penny box?"

"When I lose my hundred penny box, I lose me," she said and kept moving herself from side to side and humming.

"I mean maybe you need something better than an old cracked-up, wacky-dacky box with the top broken."

"It's *my* old cracked-up, wacky-dacky box with the top broken," Aunt Dew said. And Michael saw her move her shoulders real high that time. "Them's my years in that box," she said. "That's me in that box."

"Can I hide the hundred penny box, Aunt Dew," Michael asked, hoping she'd say yes and not ask him why. He'd hide it like the other stuff she had asked him to and had even told him where to hide it most of the time.

"No, don't hide my hundred penny box!" Aunt Dew said out loud. "Leave my hundred penny box right alone. Anybody takes my hundred penny box takes me!"

"Just in case," Michael said impatiently and wished his great-great-aunt would sit back down in her chair so he could talk to her. "Just in case Momma puts it in the furnace when you go to sleep like she puts all your stuff in the furnace in the basement."

"What your momma name?"

"Oh, no," Michael said. "You keep *on* forgetting Momma's name!" That was the only thing bad about being a hundred years old like Aunt Dew——you kept *on* forgetting things that were important.

"Hush, John-boy," Aunt Dew said and stopped dancing and humming and sat back down in the chair and put the quilt back over her legs.

"You keep on forgetting."

"I don't."

"You do, you keep on forgetting!"

"Do I forget to play with you when you worry me to death to play?"

Michael didn't answer.

"Do I forget to play when you want?"

"No."

"Okay. What your momma name? Who's that in my kitchen?"

"Momma's name is Ruth, but this isn't your house. Your house is in Atlanta. We went to get you and now you live with us."

"Ruth."

Michael saw Aunt Dew staring at him again. Whenever she stared at him like that, he never knew what she'd say next. Sometimes it had nothing to do with what they had been talking about.

"You John's baby," she said, still staring at him. "Look like John just spit you out."

"That's my father."

"My great-nephew," Aunt Dew said. "Only one ever care about me." Aunt Dew rocked hard in her chair then and Michael watched her. He got off the bed and turned off the record player and put the record back into the bottom drawer. Then he sat down on the hundred penny box again.

"See that tree out there?" Aunt Dew said and pointed her finger straight toward the window with the large tree pressed up against it. Michael knew exactly what she'd say.

"Didn't have no puny-looking trees like that near my house," she said. "Dewbet Thomas——that's me, and Henry Thomas—— that was my late husband, had the biggest, tallest, prettiest trees and the widest yard in all Atlanta. And John, that was your daddy, liked it most because he was city and my five sons, Henry, Jr., and Truke and Latt and the twins——Booker and Jay——well, it didn't make them no never mind because it was always there. But when my oldest niece Junie and her husband——we called him Big John——brought your daddy down to visit every summer, they couldn't get the suitcase in the

house good before he was climbing up and falling out the trees. We almost had to feed him up them trees!"

"Aunt Dew, we have to hide the box."

"Junie and Big John went out on that water and I was feeling funny all day. Didn't know what. Just feeling funny. I told Big John, I said, 'Big John, that boat old. Nothing but a piece a junk.' But he fooled around and said, 'We taking it out.' I looked and saw him and Junie on that water. Then it wasn't nothing. Both gone. And the boat turned over, going downstream. Your daddy, brand-new little britches on, just standing there looking, wasn't saying nothing. No hollering. I try to give him a big hunk of potato pie. But he just looking at me, just looking and standing. Wouldn't eat none of that pie. Then I said, 'Run get Henry Thomas and the boys.' He looked at me and then he looked at that water. He turned round real slow and walked toward the west field. He never run. All you could see was them stiff little britches——red they was——moving through the corn. Bare-waisted, he was. When we found the boat later, he took it clean apart——what was left of it——every plank, and pushed it back in that water. I watched him. Wasn't a piece left of that boat. Not a splinter."

"Aunt Dew, where can we hide the box!"

"What box?"

"The hundred penny box."

"We can't hide the hundred penny box and if she got to take my hundred penny box——she might as well take me!"

"We have to hide it!"

"No——'we' don't. It's *my* box!"

"It's *my* house. And I said we have to hide it!"

"How you going to hide a house, John?"

"Not the house! Our hundred penny box!"

"It's *my* box!"

Michael was beginning to feel desperate. But he couldn't tell her what his mother had said. "Suppose Momma takes it when you go to sleep?"

Aunt Dew stopped rocking and stared at him again. "Like John just spit you out," she said. "Go on count them pennies, boy. Less you worry me in my grave if you don't. Dewbet Thomas's hundred penny box. Dewbet Thomas a hundred years old and I got a penny to prove it——each year!"

Michael got off the hundred penny box and sat on the floor by his great-great-aunt's skinny feet stuck down inside his father's old slippers. He pulled the big wooden box toward him and lifted the lid and reached in and took out the small cloth roseprint sack filled with pennies. He dumped the pennies out into the box.

He was about to pick up one penny and put it in the sack, the way they played, and say "One," when his great-great-aunt spoke.

"Why you want to hide my hundred penny box?"

"To play," Michael said, after he thought for a moment.

"Play now," she said. "Don't hide my hundred penny box. I got to keep looking at my box and when I don't see my box I won't see me neither."

"One!" Michael said and dropped the penny back into the old print sack.

"18 and 74," Aunt Dew said. "Year I was born. Slavery over! Black men in Congress running things. They was in charge. It was the Reconstruction."

Michael counted twenty-seven pennies back into the old print sack before she stopped talking about Reconstruction. "19 and 01," Aunt Dew said. "I was twenty-seven years. Birthed my twin boys. Hattie said, 'Dewbet, you got two babies.' I asked Henry Thomas, I said 'Henry Thomas, what them boys look like?'"

By the time Michael had counted fifty-six pennies, his mother was standing at the door.

"19 and 30," Aunt Dew said. "Depression. Henry Thomas, that was my late husband, died. Died after he put the fifty-six penny in my box. He had the double pneumonia and no decent shoes and he worked too hard. Said he was going to sweat the trouble out his lungs. Couldn't do it. Same year I sewed that fancy dress for Rena Coles. She want a hundred bows all over that dress. I was sewing bows and tieing bows and twisting bows and cursing all the time. Was her *fourth* husband and she want a dress full of bow-ribbons. Henry the one started that box, you know. Put the first thirty-one pennies in it for me and it was my birthday. After fifty-six, I put them all in myself."

"Aunt Dew, time to go to bed," his mother said, standing at the door.

"Now, I'm not sleepy," Aunt Dew said. "John-boy and me just talking. Why you don't call him John? Look like John just spit him out. Why you got to call that boy something different from his daddy?"

Michael watched his mother walk over and open the window wide. "We'll get some fresh air in here," she said. "And then, Aunt Dew, you can take your nap better and feel good when you wake up." Michael wouldn't let his mother take the sack of pennies out of his hand. He held tight and then she let go.

"I'm not sleepy," Aunt Dew said again. "This child and me just talking."

"I know," his mother said, pointing her finger at him a little. "But we're just going to take our nap anyway."

"I got a long time to sleep and I ain't ready now. Just leave me sit here in this little narrow piece a room. I'm not bothering nobody."

"Nobody said you're bothering anyone but as soon as I start making that meat loaf, you're going to go to sleep in your chair and fall out again and hurt yourself and John'll wonder where I was and say I was on the telephone and that'll be something all over again."

"Well, I'll sit on the floor and if I fall, I'll be there already and it won't be nobody's business but my own."

"Michael," his mother said and took the sack of pennies out of his hand and laid it on the dresser. Then she reached down and closed the lid of the hundred penny box and pushed it against the wall. "Go out the room, honey, and let Momma help Aunt Dew into bed."

"I been putting Dewbet Thomas to bed a long time and I can still do it," Aunt Dew said.

"I'll just help you a little," Michael heard his mother say through the closed door.

As soon as his mother left the room, he'd go in and sneak out the hundred penny box.

But where would he hide it?

Michael went into the bathroom to think, but his mother came in to get Aunt Dew's washcloth. "Why are you looking like that?" she asked. "If you want to play go in my room. Play there, or in the living room. And don't go bothering Aunt Dew. She needs her rest."

Michael went into his father's and his mother's room and lay down on the big king bed and tried to think of a place to hide the box.

He had an idea!

He'd hide it down in the furnace room and sneak Aunt Dew downstairs to see it so she'd know where it was. Then maybe they could sit on the basement steps inside and play with it sometimes. His mother would never know. And his father wouldn't care as long as Aunt Dew was happy. He could even show Aunt Dew the big pipes and the little pipes.

Michael heard his mother close his bedroom door and walk down the hall toward the kitchen.

He'd tell Aunt Dew right now that they had a good place to hide the hundred penny box. The best place of all.

Michael got down from the huge bed and walked quietly back down the hall to his door and knocked on it very lightly. Too lightly for his mother to hear.

Aunt Dew didn't answer.

"Aunt Dew," he whispered after he'd opened the door and tiptoed up to the bed. "It's me. Michael."

Aunt Dew was crying.

Michael looked at his great-great-aunt and tried to say something but she just kept crying. She looked extra small in his bed and the covers were too close about her neck. He moved

them down a little and then her face didn't look so small. He waited to see if she'd stop crying but she didn't. He went out of the room and down the hall and stood near his mother. She was chopping up celery. "Aunt Dew's crying," he said.

"That's all right," his mother said. "Aunt Dew's all right."

"She's crying real hard."

"When you live long as Aunt Dew's lived, honey—sometimes you just cry. She'll be all right."

"She's not sleepy. You shouldn't make her go to sleep if she doesn't want to. Daddy never makes her go to sleep."

"You say you're not sleepy either, but you always go to sleep."

"Aunt Dew's bigger than me!"

"She needs her naps."

"Why?"

"Michael, go play please," his mother said. "I'm tired and I'm busy and she'll hear your noise and never go to sleep."

"She doesn't have to if she doesn't want!" Michael yelled and didn't care if he did get smacked. "We were just playing and then you had to come and make her cry!"

"Without a nap, she's irritable and won't eat. She has to eat. She'll get sick if she doesn't eat."

"You made her cry!" Michael yelled.

"Michael John Jefferson," his mother said too quietly. "If you don't get away from me and stop that yelling and stop that screaming and leave me alone——!"

Michael stood there a long time before he walked away.

"Mike," his mother called but he didn't answer. All he did was stop walking.

His mother came down the hall and put her arm about him and hugged him a little and walked him back into the kitchen.

Michael walked very stiffly. He didn't feel like any hugging. He wanted to go back to Aunt Dew.

"Mike," his mother said, leaning against the counter and still holding him.

Michael let his mother hold him but he didn't hold her back. All he did was watch the pile of chopped celery.

"Mike, I'm going to give Aunt Dew that tiny mahogany chest your daddy made in a woodshop class when he was a teen-ager. It's really perfect for that little sack of pennies and when she sees it on that pretty dresser scarf she made——the one I keep on her dresser——she'll like it just as well as that big old clumsy box. She won't even miss that big old ugly thing!"

"The hundred penny box isn't even *bothering* you!"

His mother didn't answer. But Michael heard her sigh. "You don't even care about Aunt Dew's stuff," Michael yelled a little. He even pulled away from his mother. He didn't care at all about her hugging him. Sometimes it seemed to him that grown-ups never cared about anything unless it was theirs and nobody else's. He wasn't going to be like that when he grew up and could work and could do anything he wanted to do.

"Mike," his mother said quietly. "Do you remember that teddy bear you had? The one with the crooked head? We could never sit him up quite right because of the way you kept him bent all the time. You'd bend him up while you slept with him at night and bend him up when you hugged him, played with him. Do you remember that, Mike?"

Why did she have to talk about a dumb old teddy bear!

"You wouldn't let us touch that teddy bear. I mean it was all torn up and losing its stuffing all over the place. And your daddy

647

wanted to get rid of it and I said, 'No. Mike will let us know when he doesn't need that teddy bear anymore.' So you held onto that teddy bear and protected it from all kinds of monsters and people. Then, one day, you didn't play with it anymore. I think it was when little Corky moved next door."

"Corky's not little!"

"I'm sorry. Yes——Corky's big. He's a very big boy. But Corky wasn't around when you and I cleaned up your room a little while back. We got rid of a lot of things so that Aunt Dew could come and be more comfortable. That day, you just tossed that crooked teddy bear on top of the heap and never even thought about it——"

"I *did* think about it," Michael said.

"But you knew you didn't need it anymore," his mother whispered and rubbed his shoulder softly. "But it's not the same with Aunt Dew. She will hold onto everything that is hers——just to hold onto them! She will hold them tighter and tighter and she will not go forward and try to have a new life. This is a new life for her, Mike. You must help her have this new life and not just let her go backward to something she can never go back to. Aunt Dew does *not* need that huge, broken, half-rotten wooden box that you stumble all over the house with——just to hold one tiny little sack of pennies!"

"I don't stumble around with it!"

His mother reached down then and kissed the top of his head. "You're the one that loves that big old box, Mike. I think that's it."

Michael felt the kiss in his hair and he felt her arms about him and he saw the pile of celery. His mother didn't understand. She didn't understand what a hundred penny box meant. She didn't understand that a new life wasn't very good if you had to have everything old taken away from you——just for a dumb little stupid old funny-looking ugly little red box, a shiny ugly nothing box that didn't even look like it was big enough to hold a sack of one hundred pennies!

Mike put his arms around his mother. Maybe he could make her understand. He hugged her hard. That's what she had done—— hugged him. "All Aunt Dew wants is her hundred penny box," Michael said. "That's the only thing——"

"And all you wanted was that teddy bear," his mother answered.

648

"You can't burn it," Michael said and moved away from his mother. "You can't burn any more of Aunt Dew's stuff. You can't take the hundred penny box. I said you can't take it!"

"Okay," his mother said.

Michael went down the hall and opened the door to his room.

"No, Mike," his mother said and hurried after him. "Don't go in there now."

"I am," Michael said.

His mother snatched him and shut the door and pulled him into the living room and practically threw him into the stuffed velvet chair. "You're as stubborn as your father," she said. "Everything your way or else!" She was really angry. "Just sit there," she said. "And don't move until I tell you!"

As soon as Michael heard his mother chopping celery again, he got up from the chair.

He tiptoed into his room and shut the door without a sound.

Aunt Dew was staring at the ceiling. There was perspiration on her forehead and there was water in the dug-in places around her eyes.

"Aunt Dew?"

"What you want, John-boy?"

"I'm sorry Momma's mean to you."

"Ain't nobody mean to Dewbet Thomas——cause Dewbet Thomas ain't mean to nobody," Aunt Dew said, and reached her hand out from under the cover and patted Michael's face. "Your Momma Ruth. She move around and do what she got to do. First time I see her——I say, 'John, she look frail but she ain't.' He said, 'No, she ain't frail.' I make out like I don't see her all the time," Aunt Dew said, and winked her eye. "But she know I see her. If she think I don't like her that ain't the truth. Dewbet Thomas like everybody. But me and her can't talk like me and John talk——cause she don't know all what me and John know."

"I closed the door," Michael said. "You don't have to sleep if you don't want to."

"I been sleep all day, John," Aunt Dew said.

Michael leaned over his bed and looked at his great-great-aunt. "You haven't been sleep all day," he said. "You've been sitting in your chair and talking to me and then you were dancing to your record and then we were counting pennies and we got to fifty-six and then Momma came."

"Where my hundred penny box?"

"I got it," Michael answered.

"Where you got it?"

"Right here by the bed."

"Watch out while I sleep."

He'd tell her about the good hiding place later. "Okay," he said.

Aunt Dew was staring at him. "Look like John just spit you out," she said.

Michael moved away from her. He turned his back and leaned against the bed and stared at the hundred penny box. All of a sudden it looked real *real* old and beat up.

"Turn round. Let me look at you."

Michael turned around slowly and looked at his great-great-aunt.

"John!"

"It's me," Michael said. "Michael."

He went and sat down on the hundred penny box.

"Come here so I can see you," Aunt Dew said.

Michael didn't move.

"Stubborn like your daddy. Don't pay your Aunt Dew no never mind!"

Michael still didn't get up.

"Go on back and do your counting out my pennies. Start with fifty-seven——where you left off. 19 and 31. Latt married that schoolteacher. We roasted three pigs. Just acting the fool, everybody. Latt give her a pair of yellow shoes for her birthday. Walked off down the road one evening just like you please, she did. Had on them yellow shoes. Rode a freight train clean up to Chicago. Left his food on the table and all his clothes ironed. Six times she come back and stay for a while and then go again. Truke used to say, 'Wouldn't be *my* wife.' But Truke never did marry nobody. Only thing he care about was that car. He would covered it with a raincoat when it rained, if he could."

"First you know me, then you don't," Michael said.

"Michael John Jefferson what your name is," Aunt Dew said. "Should be plain John like your daddy and your daddy's daddy—— stead of all this new stuff. Name John and everybody saying 'Michael.'" Aunt Dew was smiling. "Come here, boy," she said. "Come here close. Let me look at you. Got a head full of hair."

Michael got up from the hundred penny box and stood at the foot of the bed.

"Get closer," Aunt Dew said.

Michael did.

"Turn these covers back little more. This little narrow piece a room don't have the air the way my big house did."

"I took a picture of your house," Michael said and turned the covers back some more.

"My house bigger than your picture," Aunt Dew said. "Way bigger."

Michael leaned close to her on his bed and propped his elbows up on the large pillow under her small head. "Tell me about the barn again," he said.

"Dewbet and Henry Thomas had the biggest, reddest barn in all Atlanta, G–A!"

"And the swing Daddy broke," Michael asked and put his head down on the covers. Her chest was so thin under the thick quilt that he hardly felt it. He reached up and pushed a few wispy strands of her hair away from her closed eyes.

"Did more pulling it down than he did swinging."

"Tell me about the swimming pool," Michael said. He touched Aunt Dew's chin and covered it up with only three fingers.

It was a long time before Aunt Dew answered. "Wasn't no swimming pool," she said. "I done told you was a creek. Plain old creek. And your daddy like to got bit by a cottonmouth."

"Don't go to sleep, Aunt Dew," Michael said. "Let's talk."

"I'm tired, John."

"I can count the pennies all the way to the end if you want me to."

"Go head and count."

"When your hundred and one birthday comes, I'm going to put in the new penny like you said."

"Yes, John."

Michael reached up and touched Aunt Dew's eyes. "I have a good place for the hundred penny box, Aunt Dew," he said quietly.

"Go way. Let me sleep," she said.

"You wish you were back in your own house, Aunt Dew?"

"I'm going back," Aunt Dew said.

"You sad?"

"Hush, boy!"

Michael climbed all the way up on the bed and put his whole self alongside his great-great-aunt. He touched her arms. "Are your arms a hundred years old?" he asked. It was their favorite question game.

"Um-hm," Aunt Dew murmured and turned a little away from him.

Michael touched her face. "Is your face and your eyes and fingers a hundred years old too?"

"John, I'm tired," Aunt Dew said. "Don't talk so."

"How do you get to be a hundred years old?" Michael asked and raised up from the bed on one elbow and waited for his great-great-aunt to answer.

"First you have to have a hundred penny box," his great-great-aunt finally said.

"Where you get it from?" Michael asked.

"Somebody special got to give it to you," Aunt Dew said. "And soon as they give it to you, you got to be careful less it disappear."

"Aunt Dew——"

"Precious Lord——"

"Aunt Dew?"

"Take my hand——"

Michael put his head down on Aunt Dew's thin chest beneath the heavy quilt and listened to her sing her long song.

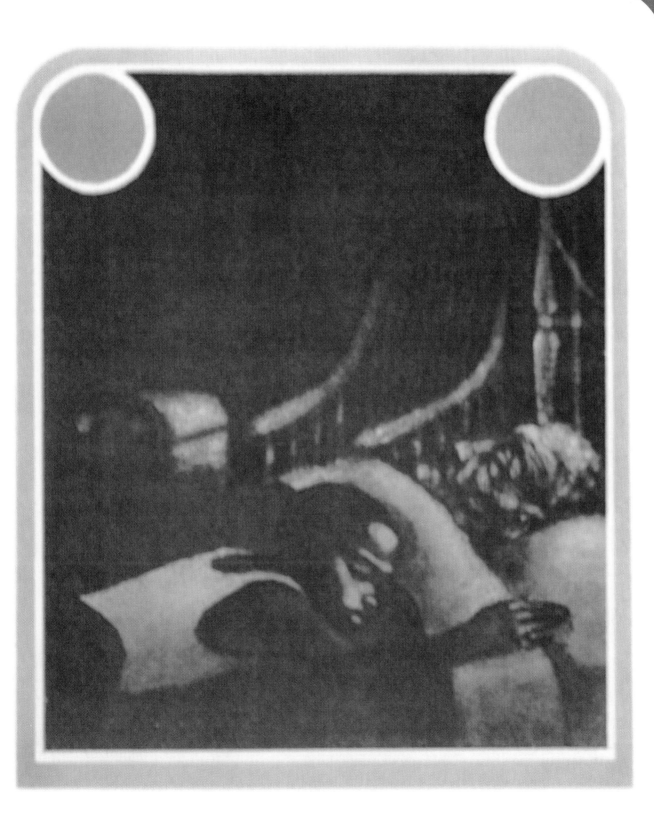

The Hundred Penny Box

Meet the Author

Sharon Bell Mathis's stories are about the lives many children lead——lives where children are responsible for themselves and others. Her stories are tough and real but full of hope that things will get better. She graduated Magna Cum Laude from Morgan State before becoming the writer-in-residence at Howard University from 1972–1974. To this day Sharon Bell Mathis's stories are starkly realistic, and she writes for those children whose lives are anything but carefree.

Meet the Illustrators

Leo and Diane Dillon

work so interdependently when they are illustrating a book that, after the project is finished, they can't be sure who painted what. Illustrating *The Hundred Penny Box* presented a special challenge to the artistic team. The story is told through dialogue rather than action scenes. The Dillons were concerned with preserving the sense of intimacy created by the words. "We wanted to . . . give the reader the feeling he was looking through an old family photo album," Diane says. Their illustrations were done in brown watercolor, using water and bleach to lighten tones, thus creating the look and feel of old photographs.

Theme Connections

Think About It

- Are all values worthwhile? How would you prioritize the values in the selections in the unit—from most to least important to you?

- The author chose to tell the story from Michael's point of view. How might the story have been different from Aunt Dew's or Michael's mother's vantage point?

Record Ideas

 How does this selection remind you of others you have read in this unit? Record your ideas in your Writing Journal.

Make a Questionnaire

Think of at least five questions you would like to ask one of the characters in the selection, and write them in your Writing Journal.

- Have a classmate ask you the questions.

- Answer the questions, pretending that you are the character in the selection.

- Then write the answers in your Writing Journal.

- Share your questions and answers with the class.

Bibliography

Abuelita's Heart

by Amy Cordova. This special grandmother spends a night with her granddaughter in the high desert of the Southwest and teaches her about the treasures of the earth and of the heart.

The Black Pearl

by Scott O'Dell. Ramon and his father harvest a priceless treasure from the cave of the monster devilfish and reap the consequences.

Gold and Silver, Silver and Gold

by Alvin Schwartz. Here is a collection of legends, true stories, and tall tales all about treasure: hunting it, finding it, losing it, and the good and bad luck it can bring.

The Golden Bracelet

retold by David Kherdian. What is a Golden Bracelet? When Prince Haig learns the answer, he learns about the things that have true value.

Lily's Crossing

by Patricia Reilly Giff. Have you ever gotten into trouble because of your imagination? Lily's overactive imagination leads her and her new friend Albert to adventure and secrets to be uncovered.

The Monkey Thief

by Aileen Kilgore Henderson. Steve Hanson's life as a couch potato changes dramatically when he spends eight months with his uncle in Costa Rica and discovers a whole new world filled with nature and ancient treasures.

To See With the Heart: The Life of Sitting Bull

by Judith St. George. Chief Sitting Bull was a great Native American warrior chief, but more importantly, he was a leader and a man of vision who shared wisdom, heart, and courage with his people.

Wringer

by Jerry Spinelli. Palmer dreads turning ten and having to participate as a "wringer" at the town's Family Fest. What he values is different from that of many of the people in the town, and he wonders if he has the courage to stand up for his own beliefs.

Writer's Handbook

Grammar, Mechanics, and Usage

Table of Contents

Grammar, Mechanics, and Usage

Writer's Handbook

Grammar, Mechanics, and Usage

Study Skills

Writing and Technology

Writer's Handbook

Grammar, Mechanics, and Usage

Complete and Incomplete Sentences

Rule: A **sentence** is a group of words that expresses a complete thought.

A complete sentence must have a subject and a predicate. The **subject** of a sentence tells *who* or *what*.

> **Subjects:** The vegetable garden has been planted. (What? The vegetable garden)
> Many vegetables can be harvested in sixty days. (What? Many vegetables)

The **predicate** of a sentence tells *what happens* or *happened*.

> **Predicates:** The tomatoes have ripened nicely.
> (What happened? have ripened nicely)
> The corn has grown as high as our fence.
> (What happened? has grown as high as our fence)

A sentence is incomplete if its subject or its predicate is missing.

> **Incomplete:** Needs to be watered. (What needs to be watered?)
> Several different kinds of flowers. (What happened to several different kinds of flowers?)

An incomplete sentence, a sentence that is missing one of its parts, is called a **sentence fragment**.

> **Fragment:** Just last summer.

> **Complete Sentence:** Just last summer we planted
> that tree.

Writer's Handbook

Grammar, Mechanics, and Usage

Compound Subject and Predicate

Rule: A subject of a sentence that has two or more parts is called a **compound subject**. A predicate of a sentence that has two or more parts is called a **compound predicate**.

The conjunctions *and, but,* or *or* are used to connect compound subjects and predicates.

Subjects with One Part:
Chickadees gather in the schoolyard.
Wrens gather in the schoolyard.

Compound Subject:
Chickadees and wrens gather in the schoolyard.

A compound predicate has two or more parts. The parts are usually connected with the conjunction *and* or *or.*

Predicates with One Part: The birds get up early.
The birds search for food.

Compound Predicate:
The birds get up early *and* search for food.

If a compound subject or compound predicate has three or more parts, use commas to separate the parts. Put the conjunction just before the last part.

Compound Subject:
Twigs, leaves, *or* bits of grass make good materials for a bird's nest.

Writer's Handbook

Grammar, Mechanics, and Usage

Compound Sentences

Rule: A conjunction such as *and, but, or, yet,* or *so* can be used to combine two sentences expressing related ideas. A semicolon can also be used to link two related sentences. The combined form is called a **compound sentence**.

Follow these rules to form compound sentences:

You can use conjunctions—such as *and, but, or, yet,* or *so*—to combine sentences that express closely related thoughts. Place a comma before the conjunction.

Two sentences:
It was Karen's birthday. She had a sleepover party.

Compound sentence
It was Karen's birthday, so she had a sleepover party.

You can use a semicolon to combine two closely related sentences. The semicolon takes the place of the comma and conjunction.

Two sentences:
It was Karen's birthday. She had a sleepover party.

Compound sentence
It was Karen's birthday; she had a sleepover party.

Do not combine sentences that are not closely related. For example, do not combine these sentences:

Two sentences:
Karen's friends brought sleeping bags. They played games and talked.

Writer's Handbook

Grammar, Mechanics, and Usage

Phrases and Clauses

Rule: A **phrase** is a group of words that does not contain a subject and a verb. A **clause** is a group of words containing a subject and predicate.

Phrases and clauses help you show relationships and connections between ideas. Follow these guidelines to use them:

Using Phrases

A **preposition** shows how one word is **related** to another word in the sentence. A **prepositional phrase** always begins with a preposition and is followed by a noun or a pronoun and any of its modifiers. Prepositional phrases are used to add details.

The prepositional phrases are underlined in the following sentences:

> We went <u>through the gate</u> and <u>up the hill.</u>
> <u>Into the brisk wind</u> we rode our bikes.
> <u>Over the ridge</u> Charlie could see the foothills <u>of the Rocky Mountains.</u>

In your writing, place a phrase as close as possible to the word the phrase relates to. Study these two examples:

> **Misleading:** The girl watched the clown in the blue dress. (Who wears the blue dress?)

> **Clearer:** <u>The girl in the blue dress</u> watched the clown.

Writers use two types of **clauses**, independent and dependent.

Using Clauses

An **independent clause** can stand by itself as a sentence. A **dependent clause** has a subject and a predicate, but it cannot stand by itself. It usually begins with a connecting word. It depends on the independent, or main, clause. Often, a dependent clause tells *when*, *where*, *how*, or *why* the action in the independent, or main, clause takes place.

dependent clause	independent clause
When I juggle,	people watch closely.

independent clause	dependent clause
They all laughed	when I told a funny story.

Grammar, Mechanics, and Usage

Phrases and Clauses (continued)

Here are some connecting words that are used to introduce a dependent clause:

after	although	as	because	before
if	since	that	though	until
when	where	which	while	who

Some dependent clauses are not necessary to the meaning of the sentence. In that case, use a comma to separate the clauses.

Examples: Last night I saw Dave, who lives on our block.
He drove his 1946 car, which he works on a lot.

Sometimes a dependent clause is necessary to the meaning of the sentence. In that case, do not put a comma between the clauses.

Examples: Dave has friends who like old cars, too.
They buy the parts that the old cars need.

Use a comma after a dependent clause that begins a sentence.

Examples: When there is a classic car show, Dave is there.
If you get a chance, you should see Dave's car.

Writer's Handbook

Grammar, Mechanics, and Usage

Using Commas

Rule: In a series of three words or phrases, use a **comma** after each word or phrase that comes before *and* or *or*. Use a comma when you write **dates** and **addresses**, in **direct address**, and in certain **letter parts**.

In a **series** of three or more **nouns**, **adjectives**, **verbs**, or **phrases**, use a comma after each noun, adjective, verb, or phrase that comes before *and* or *or*.

Nouns:	Lava, rocks, and gas erupted from the volcano.
Adjectives:	The volcano was high, steaming, and cone-shaped.
Verbs:	Pumice, a volcanic rock, can be used to scour, scrub, or polish.
Phrases:	Eruptions occur on islands, along cracks in the ocean, and around the Pacific Ring of Fire.

Follow these guidelines when you use commas in other places:

Use a comma to separate the day from the year. When you write a date in a sentence, use a comma after the year (unless it comes at the end of a sentence) to separate it **from the rest of the sentence**.

Dates: The railroad came to our town on March 17, 1893. A canal was started on June 28, 1887, at a site near the lake.

Use a comma to separate each part of a **place name**. When you write a place name within a sentence, use a comma after the last word in the place name (unless it comes at the end of a sentence) to separate it from the rest of the sentence.

Place Name: Many trains pass through Milwaukee, Wisconsin. Near Erie, Pennsylvania, there is a famous canal.

Grammar, Mechanics, and Usage

Using Commas (continued)

When you **address the person you're speaking to** by name, use one or two commas, as necessary, to separate the person's name from the rest of the sentence.

Address a Person: Have you ever flown in a jet, Carlos?

Yes, Mrs. Jones, I enjoy flying.

Use a comma after the **greeting** and after the **closing** of a friendly letter.

Friendly Letter: My Dear Friend,   Your cousin,

Use a comma after the closing of a business letter. Note that the greeting of a business letter ends with a colon, not a comma. For examples, see page 670, Using Colons and Semicolons.

Business Letter: Very truly yours,   Sincerely,

Writer's Handbook

Grammar, Mechanics, and Usage

Using Parentheses, Dashes, and Ellipses

Rule: Parentheses, dashes, and ellipses are special kinds of punctuation marks. Use **parentheses** to set off extra information within a sentence. Use **dashes** to show an interruption. Use **ellipses** to show a pause in speech, an unfinished sentence, or a place where words are left out of a quotation.

Follow these guidelines when you use them:

Put **parentheses** around extra information in a sentence. The information may tell what one of the words in the sentence means.

> **Anglers (people who fish for fun) often try to catch a specific kind of fish.**

The words in **parentheses** may give the reader more information.

> **The flag of Great Britain (also called the Union Jack) was adopted in 1801.**

You may also use **dashes** to set off a phrase that breaks the even flow of a sentence.

> **The colors of the rainbow—red, orange, yellow, green, blue, indigo, and violet—are not difficult to remember.**

In dialogue, you can use a **dash** to show that a sentence was interrupted before it could be finished.

> **"You're about to spill your —" Robert shouted as I knocked over my milk.**

Use **ellipses** to show a pause in speech.

> **"I love pineapples . . . in fact, they are my favorite fruit," said Jeff.**

Use **ellipses** to show that a sentence was not finished. A period is placed after the sentence, followed by three dots.

> **Some animals that are marsupials are kangaroos, koalas, opossums, wombats. . . .**

Use **ellipses** to show that one or more words from a quotation have been left out.

> **The dictionary says a flamingo is a "large aquatic bird . . . with rosy-white plumage."**

Grammar, Mechanics, and Usage

Using Colons and Semicolons

Rule: Colons and semicolons are punctuation marks. A **semicolon (;)** is used to separate two connected and complete thoughts in one sentence. A **colon (:)** shows that something more is to follow.

Colons and semicolons look similar but serve different purposes.

Follow these rules when you use them:

Use a **semicolon (;)** to separate two connected and complete thoughts in one sentence. Use a semicolon instead of a comma and a conjunction such as *and, but, or,* or *so.*

> **My little brother likes to collect trading cards; my sister collects cards, too.**

Notice that a semicolon separates a sentence into two parts. Each part is a complete thought with a subject and a predicate. A semicolon is used to separate two thoughts that would otherwise be separated by a comma and a conjunction.

Use a **colon (:)** in a sentence to show that something is to follow. What follows might be a list of items or names, or it might be a complete thought that explains the first part of a sentence. If what follows is a complete thought, begin the sentence with a capital letter.

> **List follows colon:**
> She collects all kinds of cards: baseball cards, football cards, even dinosaur cards.

> **Explanation follows colon:**
> My brother's card collection is different: He only collects trading cards of famous inventors.

Use a colon between hours and minutes when you write a time. Use a colon after the greeting in a business letter.

> **11:30 A.M.   5:15 P.M.   Dear Mr. Edison: Dear Ms. Lee:**

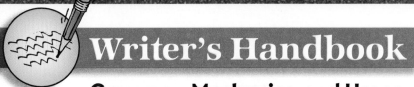

Grammar, Mechanics, and Usage

Parts of Speech

Rule: All words can be classified into groups called parts of speech. They include **nouns**, **pronouns**, **verbs**, **adjectives**, **adverbs**, **prepositions**, **conjunctions**, and **interjections**.

A **noun** names a person, place, thing, or idea.

> Chicago offers many attractions for visitors.

A **pronoun** takes the place of a noun.

> Chicago offers many attractions for visitors. It is a beautiful city.

A **verb** names an action or tells what someone or something is, was, or will be.

> Visitors often walk along the lakefront. They see a beautiful view. They will take pictures.

An **adjective** describes a noun or a pronoun.

> The skyline of the city is a beautiful sight. The graceful skyscrapers soar upward.

An **adverb** describes a verb, an adjective, or another adverb. An adverb may answer the question *How? How often? When?* or *Where?*

> Elevated trains rumble noisily above the streets. People usually walk quickly to their nearby office buildings.

A **preposition** shows the relationship between a noun or pronoun and a verb, an adjective, or another noun in a sentence.

> The Adler Planetarium sits beside Lake Michigan. Lake Shore Drive runs along the lake.

A **conjunction** is used to connect words, phrases, or sentences.

> Chicago has many museums and art galleries.
> A breeze usually blows by the lake, but Chicago isn't really a windy city.

An **interjection** is a word or phrase that expresses strong emotion.

> Wow! The view from the Sears Tower is incredible.
> Hooray! We are going to get some deep-dish pizza.

Writer's Handbook

Grammar, Mechanics, and Usage

Using Possessive Nouns

Rule: A **possessive noun** is used to show ownership. Possessive nouns can be singular or plural.

Follow these rules to form possessive nouns:

Form the possessive of a **singular noun** by adding an apostrophe and *s* (*'s*).

Singular noun: San Francisco is a city in California.

Possessive form: San Francisco's hills are well known.

Form the possessive of a **plural noun** that ends in *s* by adding an apostrophe after the *s* (*s'*).

Plural noun ending with *s:*
Cable cars travel up and down the hills of San Francisco.

Possessive form:
The cars' bells clang as they move along.

Form the possessive of a **plural noun** that does not end in *s* by adding an apostrophe and *s* (*'s*).

Plural noun not ending with *s:*
People flocked to San Francisco during the gold rush.

Possessive form:
People's efforts made San Francisco an important mining supply center.

Writer's Handbook

Grammar, Mechanics, and Usage

Using the Right Pronoun for the Right Noun

Rule: **Pronouns** are words that take the place of nouns. Pronouns must agree in number, gender, and person with the nouns that they replace.

Use **singular pronouns** to take the place of singular nouns. Singular pronouns, such as *I*, *you*, *he*, *she*, or *it*, stand for one person or thing.

> **Singular nouns and pronouns:** Dan built a great rocket. He made it in his backyard.

Use **plural pronouns** to take the place of plural nouns. Plural pronouns, such as *we*, *you*, or *they*, stand for more than one person or thing.

> **Plural nouns and pronouns:** The sixth-graders are having an art fair. They asked our class to help.

Use **subject pronouns** to take the place of subject nouns. The subject noun of a sentence tells who or what the sentence is about. Subject pronouns include *I*, *you*, *he*, *she*, *it*, *we*, and *they*.

> **Subject nouns and pronouns:** Dan built a rocket. He made it to impress his teacher and friends.

Use **object pronouns** to take the place of object nouns. The object noun of the sentence follows the verb and shows what the subject does or did. Sometimes an object pronoun follows words such as *to*, *for*, *with*, *at*, or *from*. Object pronouns include *me*, *you*, *him*, *her*, *it*, *us*, and *them*.

> **Object pronoun:** Dan built a rocket. He made it to impress his teacher and friends.

Grammar, Mechanics, and Usage

Using the Right Pronoun for the Right Noun (continued)

Use **possessive pronouns** to take the place of possessive nouns. Possessive pronouns show who owns or has something. Such possessive pronouns as *my, your, his, her, its, our,* or *their* appear before a noun. Other possessive pronouns, such as *mine, yours, his, hers, its, ours,* or *theirs,* stand alone.

> **Possessive nouns and pronouns:** Dan's father is an engineer. His father knows more about rockets than ours does.

Always be sure your readers know exactly to *whom* or *what* each pronoun refers. If it is not clear to which noun your pronoun refers, use the noun again.

> **Not clear:** Ann took Jill to see a movie. She thought the movie was very funny.

> **Clear:** Ann took Jill to see a movie. Jill thought the movie was very funny.

Writer's Handbook

Grammar, Mechanics, and Usage

Using Present-Tense Verbs

Rule: A **verb tense** is a form of a verb that tells the time an action takes place—in the present, in the past, or in the future. **Present-tense verbs** show action that happens now or action that happens again and again.

A **verb** is a word that tells what the subject does. It tells about an action or a state of being.

When you use present-tense verbs, follow these rules:

If the subject of a sentence is singular except for the words *I* or *you*, add -*s* or -*es* to verbs to form the present tense. For most verbs, add -*s* to the end of the verb. With some verbs, you add -*es*. For example, if the verb ends with *ch*, *sh*, *s*, *x*, or *z*, add -*es*. If the verb ends with a consonant followed by *y*, change the *y* to *i* and add -*es*.

Ending added: Marla plants a vegetable garden each summer. She weeds the garden every week. She fixes the fence and worries about rainfall. She finally picks lettuce and tomatoes.

If the subject of a sentence is plural, do not add an ending to the verb. Also, do not add an ending to the verb if the subject of the sentence is *I* or *you*.

No ending: Marla and her family bring me fresh beans and squash. I make salads with green peppers. The homegrown vegetables taste delicious.

Irregular verbs have special present-tense forms that you must remember. Here are some examples:

Irregular Verbs	Present-Tense Forms
be	I am. You are. We are. They are. He is. She is. It is.
do	I do. We do. You do. They do. He does. She does. It does.
have	I have. We have. You have. They have. He has. She has. It has.

Writer's Handbook

Grammar, Mechanics, and Usage

Using Past-Tense Verbs

Rule: A **verb tense** is a form of a verb that tells the time an action takes place. A verb in the **past-tense** form shows action that has already happened.

A **verb** is a word that tells what the subject does. It tells about an action or a state of being.

When you use past-tense verbs, follow these rules:

- Add *-ed* to form the past tense of most verbs.
  Add *-ed:* Jack helped his father. They washed the windows. They painted the garage. Jack carried leaves to the curb. He saved money for a computer. He planned for the future.

For some verbs you need to change the spelling before you add *-ed*.

- If the verb ends with *e*, drop *e* when you add *-ed*.
  Drop *e*: save   saved

- If the verb ends with a consonant plus *y*, change the *y* to *i* and add *-ed*.
  Change *y* to *i* and add *-ed:*   carry   carried

- For most verbs that have one syllable, one short vowel, and one final consonant, double that final consonant before adding *-ed*.
  Double Final Consonant: plan   planned

Irregular verbs have special forms in the past tense.

Irregular Verbs	Past-Tense Forms
be	I was. He was. She was. It was. You were. We were. They were.
do	did
have	had
go	went
come	came
say	said
give	gave

Writer's Handbook

Grammar, Mechanics, and Usage

Making Subject and Verb Agree

Rule: In a sentence, the verb must **agree** with the subject. A singular subject takes a singular verb. A plural subject takes a plural verb.

The **subject** of a sentence is the word or words that refer to the person(s) or thing(s) that performs or receives the action of the verb. The **verb** is the word that refers to the action.

Most verbs follow this pattern in the present tense.

Present Tense	
Singular	**Plural**
I walk.	We walk.
You walk.	You walk.
He, she, it walks.	They walk.

- If the subject is a singular noun or *he*, *she*, or *it*, add *-s* to the verb.

  Takes *-s* ending: Suwana plays ice hockey.
  She plays ice hockey.

- Verbs that end in *-s*, *-x*, *-ch*, or *-sh* take the ending *-es*. In verbs that end in a consonant plus *y*, the *y* changes to *i* before the *-es* ending.

  Takes *-es* ending: The goalie touches the ball with his hands.

  Final *y* changes to *i* before *-es*: Everyone tries his or her best.

Grammar, Mechanics, and Usage

Making Subject and Verb Agree (continued)

Some common verbs, such as *be* and *have*, are irregular. They have special patterns that you must memorize.

Be: Present Tense	
I am.	We are.
You are.	You are.
He, she, it is.	They are.

Have: Present Tense	
I have.	They have.
You have.	You have.
He, she, it has.	They have.

- The words *anyone, everyone, somebody, nobody, either,* and *each* are singular and take a singular verb.

  Everyone tries his or her best for the leading role.

- A subject consisting of two singular words connected by *and* is usually plural and takes a plural verb.

  Maria and Russel practice outside.

- A subject consisting of two singular words connected by *or* or *nor* takes a singular verb.

  Either Rochelle or Jason takes the lead part.

- A subject consisting of a singular word and a plural word connected by *or* or *nor* takes a verb that agrees with the word nearer the verb.

  The principal or the students talk at the assembly.

- Sometimes other words come between the subject and the verb. Make sure that the verb agrees with the subject.

  One of the English teachers is in charge of the play.

Writer's Handbook

Grammar, Mechanics, and Usage

Using Adjectives and Adverbs to Make Comparisons

Rule: **Adjectives** and **adverbs** are used in making comparisons.

An **adjective** modifies a noun or a pronoun. An **adverb** modifies a verb, an adjective, or another adverb.

- To adjectives of one syllable and to most adjectives of two syllables, add the ending *-er* when comparing two persons, places, or things. Add the ending *-est* when comparing more than two.

wild	**wilder**	**(the) wildest**
lovely	**lovelier**	**(the) loveliest**

  The flowers in that vase are <u>lovely</u>. Those in Mr. Yu's garden are even <u>lovelier</u>. Emily's flower shop has the <u>loveliest</u> flowers in town.

- With adjectives of more than two syllables and with some adjectives of two syllables, use *more* when comparing two persons, places, or things. Use *most* to compare more than two. With *more* or *most*, do not use an *-er* or *-est* ending.

helpful	**more helpful**	**(the) most helpful**

- For some adjectives, either form of the comparative or superlative may be used.

wicked	**wickeder**	**wickedest**
wicked	**more wicked**	**(the) most wicked**

- Most adverbs end in *-ly*. With adverbs that end in *-ly*, use *more* when comparing two actions. Use *most* when comparing more than two.

rapidly	**more rapidly**	**(the) most rapidly**

- A few adverbs do not end in *-ly*. To adverbs that do not end in *-ly*, add the ending *-er* when comparing two actions. Add the ending *-est* when comparing more than two.

- Spelling changes may occur in adjectives and adverbs before an *-er* or *-est* ending.

pretty	**prettier**	**(the) prettiest**
far	**farther**	**(the) farthest**

Writer's Handbook

Grammar, Mechanics, and Usage

Using and Punctuating Dialogue

Rule: In a story, what characters say to each other is called **dialogue**. A speaker's exact words are called a **quotation**. These words are put inside **quotation marks** (" ").

Place quotation marks (" ") around a speaker's exact words.

Quotation marks: Sara said, "My gerbil escaped."

Begin the first word of a quotation with a capital letter, even if it is not at the beginning of a sentence.

Capital letter: Rob said, "He just ran under the bed."

In most cases, use a comma to separate a quotation from the speaker tag.

Comma: Rob said, "He just ran under the bed."

Put the end punctuation mark for the quotation inside the closing quotation marks.

End marks: Sara asked, "Are you sure?"
"No, he's disappeared!" exclaimed Rob.

Use two sets of quotation marks when a speaker tag interrupts a quotation. Separate the speaker tag from the quotation with commas. Do not capitalize the first word after the speaker tag because it is part of the first sentence of the quotation.

"You know," said Rob, "he runs as fast as a flash."

If the interrupted quote contains two complete sentences, use a period and a capital letter.

Two sentences: "Sara!" shouted Rob. "He's heading for the door."

Always start a new paragraph when the speaker changes.

Example: "Oh, Rob, grab him!" shouted Sara.
"I don't think I can run as fast as he can," complained Rob.

Don't use quotation marks with an indirect quotation. An indirect quotation reports what someone said or asked but does not show the exact words of the speaker.

Indirect quotation: Sara said the gerbil had escaped before.

Writer's Handbook

Grammar, Mechanics, and Usage

Using *-ing* Verbs As Nouns

Rule: A verb form ending in *-ing* can be used as a noun in a sentence. Verb forms ending in *-ing* that are used as nouns are called **gerunds**.

Like a noun, an *-ing* verb can be used as a subject, a predicate nominative, a direct object, or the object of a preposition. Look at this example:

Skiing is a popular sport.

Here, *skiing* is used as the subject. Notice that the ending *-ing* is added to a verb to use it as a noun.

These guidelines can help you use *-ing* verbs as nouns:

An *-ing* verb can be used by itself in place of a noun.

Subject:	Dancing can be a lot of fun.
Predicate Nominative:	My favorite sport is bicycling.
Direct Object:	Dr. Maxwell has finished her shopping.
Object of Preposition:	Is this a good stream for fishing?

An *-ing* verb can also form part of a phrase. Then, the entire phrase can be used as a subject, a predicate nominative, a direct object, or the object of a preposition.

Subject:	Catching a cold is a problem in the winter.
Predicate Nominative:	A composer's job is writing music.
Direct Object:	She enjoys making pizzas.
Object of Preposition:	After raking leaves, I was tired.

Writer's Handbook

Study Skills

Parts of a Book

Books are divided into several parts. All books do not have the same number of parts, but each part is usually found in the same place in every book. Many fiction books may have only a **title page** and a **copyright page**, but some will also have a **table of contents** and a **glossary**. Nonfiction books have a title page and a copyright page and often a **table of contents, glossary, bibliography,** and **index**.

When you look for information about a story, subject, or question, you will usually use several books. However, you will not have time to read every page of every book. Instead, use the parts of a book to help you find the information you need.

The title page, copyright page, and table of contents are at the front of the book.

- The **title page** gives the title of the book, the name of the author or editor, and the name of the publisher.

- The **copyright page** comes after the title page. It gives the publisher's name and the place and year in which the book was published.

- The **table of contents** is a list, in order of appearance, of the units, chapters, or stories in the book, with the page number on which each item begins.

The glossary, bibliography, and index are at the back of the book. Sometimes a bibliography is found, instead, at the end of each chapter or unit.

- The **glossary** is an alphabetical listing of new or special words that are used in the book along with their definitions.

- The **bibliography** is an alphabetical listing of books in which the author of the book found information about the subject. It may also include other writings that the author thinks would interest the reader.

- The **index** is an alphabetical listing of names, places, and topics covered in the book, with the numbers of the pages on which they are mentioned or discussed.

Writer's Handbook

Study Skills

Using the Card Catalog

Each library has a **card catalog**—a list of all the books in a library. Some libraries list the books on cards found in small file drawers. Other libraries have the card catalog on computers. In both systems, you can find books listed on three types of cards: author, title, and subject.

The catalog is a good place to start your research about a subject. The following information can help you get the most out of it:

- The **author** card lists the author's name at the top of the card. A **title** card lists the book's title at the top. A **subject** card lists the subject of the book at the top. On a computer, you can look up either an author's name, a book title, or a subject.

- A book entry may contain a **call number**. On a card, this number is in the upper left-hand corner. This number matches the numbers and letters on the spine of the book. The call number also tells you on which shelf you can find the book. An *R* means that a book is in the reference section. A *J* or *JUV* before the number means that the book is in the juvenile section. If there is no letter identification, the book is in the adult section.

- Every card shows the year in which the book was **published**. Make sure you check the publication date if you need to obtain recent information.

- If the book has **illustrations**, the abbreviation *ill.* is shown.

- The entry includes a **summary** of the book. The summary tells what the book is about.

- The card tells if the book includes an index, a glossary, or bibliography. An index will help you locate pages that have information about your subject. A glossary will give you definitions of key terms used in the book. A bibliography might lead you to other books.

- **Cross-references** are at the bottom of each card. They give all the headings under which the book is listed in the card catalog. If you look under the other headings, you may find more books on your subject.

Writer's Handbook

Study Skills

Using a Dictionary, Glossary, or Thesaurus

A **dictionary** is a book that tells the meanings of most of the words that people use when they speak, read, and write. A **glossary** is the section in the back of a book that gives the meaning of words that appear in that book. A **thesaurus** is a dictionary of synonyms and antonyms. Words in it may be organized in alphabetical order or by subject. In that case, check the index to see how to find a certain word.

- Each word listed in a dictionary, glossary, or thesaurus is called an **entry word**. All entry words are listed in alphabetical order and are printed in boldface type.

- **Guide words** are at the top of each dictionary, thesaurus, or glossary page. These words are usually in boldface type. The word on the left indicates the first entry word listed on the page. The word on the right indicates the last entry word listed on the page. All other words on the page fall in alphabetical order between the two guide words. (A thesaurus may use guide numbers instead of words. In this case, you use the index to find a certain word.) Guide words can help you find the page on which the word you are looking for is listed.

- A **dictionary** or **glossary entry** gives the word's spelling, pronunciation, part of speech, and meaning or meanings. The part of speech is abbreviated; for example, *v.* stands for *verb*. Entries may also give synonyms for the word, spellings of the word with endings added, and the word's history or etymology.

> **in•dulge** (in dulj´) *v.* **indulged, indulging**.
> 1. Give in to. 2. Give in to the wishes of.
> [Latin indulgēre, to be tolerant, give as a favor.]
> **syn** *pamper, satisfy, gratify, humor*

Study Skills

Using a Dictionary, Glossary, or Thesaurus (continued)

- A **pronunciation key** is found at the beginning of a dictionary or glossary. The key has symbols that stand for vowel and consonant sounds. The symbols are shown with example words. Pronounce these to hear the sounds. Then use the symbols to pronounce unfamiliar words.

- In a **thesaurus entry**, you will find synonyms and related words and perhaps an antonym or two.

    happy, adj. gladly, merry, cheerful, joyful, delighted, pleased. Antonym—see SAD, CHEERLESS, MELANCHOLY

- From the list, select the word that best conveys your meaning. Remember that synonyms have meanings that are similar but not identical. If you are unsure which word best expresses your meaning, cross-check the meaning of the word in a dictionary.

Writer's Handbook

Study Skills

Using an Encyclopedia

Encyclopedias are basic reference books that contain articles on a wide variety of subjects. The articles in them are usually arranged in alphabetical order (a few are thematic). Today, some encyclopedias are also available on CD-ROM.

Use an encyclopedia to help you gather basic information when you begin researching an unfamiliar subject.

These guidelines can help:

- Locate the encyclopedia's index. It is usually at the back of a one-volume encyclopedia or a separate volume of a multivolume set. The index is an alphabetical list of all the articles and subjects in an encyclopedia.

- Decide what the key word or words in your research question or problem are. Look up those words in the index of an encyclopedia. For a question about Hans Christian Andersen's role in children's literature, you might look under *Andersen, Hans Christian* and *Children's Literature* in the index.

- In the index, after each main article's title, you will see a volume number or letter, then a page number. Other articles that have information might also be listed. Make a list of the titles, volume numbers or letters, and page numbers of articles that might have information about your topic.

  Children's literature 3:445; 12:567
  Fairy tales 5:147
  Folktales 5:596

- Look at your list and select the encyclopedia volumes that you think will be most helpful. Turn to the given pages to locate the articles.

- Read any headings or subheadings within each article. Headings tell you what information you will find in the article's sections. They might give you some idea of how to narrow your topic or arrange the information in your own report.

Study Skills

■ Throughout the article and at its end, look for suggestions of other places in the encyclopedia where you might find more information about your topic. These suggestions are called cross-references.

(See **Danish literature***) See also* **Storytelling**

Also, a list of books with more information about your topic may be given at the end of an article.

Andersen, Hans Christian. *The Complete Fairy Tales and Stories*

Cote, Elizabeth. *Hans Christian Andersen: A Fairy Tale Life*

Study Skills

Using Primary Sources

Primary sources give firsthand information about people or events. Primary sources can include personal diaries, journals, letters, legal papers, photographs, or other documents of an individual or a time period. Works of art and other original objects produced during the time period being researched can also be considered primary sources, as well as films, tapes, recordings, and personal interviews.

Primary sources can make your report factual and interesting. For example, if you were researching slavery in America, a written interview with a former slave who described how it felt to be a slave would be more reliable and emotionally involving than a book in which another researcher described a slave's feelings. The interview is a primary source; the book written by someone else is called a secondary source.

Follow these guidelines when you use primary sources:

■ Find out what primary sources are available for the time period or subject you are researching. For example, if you are researching France in the late nineteenth century, you might want to visit an art museum, or at least study reproductions of French Impressionist paintings. If you are studying American history, you might want to look at *The Annals of American History*. This multivolume set includes accurate reproductions of letters and speeches of such leaders as Thomas Jefferson and Martin Luther King, Jr., and legal documents such as the Constitution of the United States. These are primary sources; a librarian can help you find others.

■ Study each primary source carefully. What conclusions or interpretations can you draw from it? Is the information useful to your report? Will using it help your audience better understand what you are trying to say?

■ Can you conduct personal interviews that will improve your report? When you talk to someone directly, that person becomes a primary source.

■ Always check your research information in a number of sources.

Writer's Handbook

Study Skills

Note Taking

Researchers take notes to help them remember important information about their research. They organize the information under headings and list below them important supporting facts or details.

Follow these guidelines when you take notes:

- When possible, use key phrases; abbreviate words and condense sentences.

  Peasants lvd in huts; slept on straw

- Organize your notes so that main ideas are easy to find. Leave space between a main idea and the facts below it or highlight main ideas with a colored marker.

  Peasants in the Middle Ages Led Hard Lives
  lived in huts; slept on straw
  had few rights
  worked for lords
  paid lords rent and taxes

- Take notes on only the most important facts about a main idea. Not all facts are important enough to include.

- If the author uses especially interesting language to express an idea, you may want to quote her or his words exactly. If so, put quotation marks around the words. Also record the author's name, the book title (or magazine name and article title), and the page number of the quotation.

  "Peasants in the Middle Ages had to work hard to grow food, not only for their own families but also for their lord." Fiona Macdonald, *The Middle Ages*, page 30.

- Use spacing well. Leave plenty of space along the margins of the paper so that you can add questions or comments about the text or add references to related material.

- Review your notes and add information from other sources you have read and from your own experience. Include your opinions about how the information fits in with other information you have gathered on the subject.

Writer's Handbook

Study Skills

Using Graphic Organizers

Graphic organizers, such as time lines, charts, and diagrams, can present a great deal of information in a small amount of space. They help organize information so that readers can understand it more easily.

When you choose a graphic organizer, follow these guidelines:

Use a **time line** to show the sequence of important events over a particular period of time and the relative amount of time between them. A time line may cover any chosen length of time, from the lifetime of a person, for example, to a historical period of hundreds or thousands of years.

The First Hundred Years of Baseball

believed invented	rules written	first World Series	National Baseball Hall of Fame founded
1839	1845	1903	1939

- To make a time line, choose a title and make a list of the main events and the time of each. Use concise, descriptive phrases. Then draw a line across a sheet of paper. Make a dot for the time of each event. Vary the space between the dots, according to the length of time between events. Below each dot, write a time. Above each dot, write an event.

Use a **diagram** to show the parts of an object or show how something works. Labels on a diagram help explain the parts or steps in the illustration. Diagrams often help readers visualize information that is mechanical or scientific.

Include the following features when you make a diagram:

- a title, which tells what the diagram is about
- labels that tell about the parts of an object or the steps in a process
- lines that connect each label with the part or step it describes
- arrows that show the order of steps in a process or the stages in a cycle (They can also show movement or directions.)

Study Skills
Using Graphic Organizers (continued)

Parts of a Trumpet

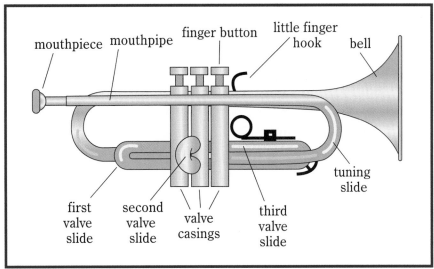

Use a **chart** when you are presenting similar information about several items. Charting information will help you see relationships between different items. It can also help you present research results.

Road Signs			
Sign	*Shape*	*Color*	*Type*
Stop	octagon	red	regulatory
Yield	triangle	yellow	regulatory
Milepost	rectangle	green	guide sign
Railroad Crossing	round	yellow	warning

Include the following features when you make a chart:

- a title that tells what the chart is about

- row heading down the left side of the chart (These are the items you will give information about.)

- column heading across the top of the chart (These tell the kinds of information the chart will show about each item.)

- words, phrases, or numbers rather than complete sentences

Writer's Handbook

Study Skills

Outlining

An **outline** is a written plan that writers use to organize their notes and ideas before they begin to write a first draft. An outline arranges information into main topics and subtopics.

When you are doing research, you can be sure your report or project is organized logically if you put your ideas into outline form before you begin to write.

Follow these guidelines:

- On a sheet of paper, write the **title** for your outline. This title will be the title of your paper or project.

- Check the headings on your note cards. Then separate the cards into piles by their headings. The large, obvious divisions will be **main topics**.

- Next, check your note cards to see how each main topic can be divided. These divisions will be **subtopics** and must relate to the main topic. In the outline here, the two main topics are "Kinds of balloons" and "Uses of balloons."

- Number each main topic with a Roman numeral (I, II, III, and so on) followed by a period. Your completed outline should include at least two main topics.

- Under each main topic, indent and number each subtopic with a capital letter followed by a period, as shown in the sample outline. Include at least two subtopics under each main topic—or none at all.

- If subtopics need to be divided further, under each subtopic indent again as shown and number each subtopic with an Arabic numeral (1, 2, 3, and so on) followed by a period. If you use **sub-subtopics**, you should have at least two—or none at all.

Study Skills
Outlining (continued)

BALLOONS

I. Kinds of balloons

    A. Gas balloons

        1. Sport balloons

        2. Expandable balloons

        3. Super-pressure balloons

        4. Zero-pressure balloons

    B. Hot-air balloons

II. Uses of balloons

    A. Recreational uses

    B. Scientific uses

        1. Forecasting weather

        2. Other uses

Study Skills

Making a Bibliography

A **bibliography** is a list of writings and other material about a particular subject. It may include books and other written material in which the author found information to use in a book, an article, or a report. A bibliography is also a list of books in which the reader can find more information about the subject.

A bibliography tells readers where the writer got her or his information. It also tells readers where they can read more about the subject. When you write about your research, provide a bibliography for your readers.

- Make a separate note or card for each book you use in your research. On the card, put the author's full name with the last name first, the title of the book, the publisher's name, and the date of publication. The publisher's name is found at the bottom of the title page; the date of publication is found on the back of the title page.

  Put the information in this form:

  Moreland, Jennifer. Industrial Revolution of the 19th Century 1760–1900. Tucson, Arizona: Zephyr Press AZ, 1992.

- Note the form and punctuation: the first and last names are inverted; a comma is placed after the last name and a period after the first name. The title is underlined or italicized and followed by a period. A colon is placed after the city of publication. A comma is placed after the name of the publisher. A period is placed after the date of publication.

- Place the title *Bibliography* in the center of the line at the top of the page. Leave a line space between the title and the first entry. List your entries in alphabetical order by the last name of the author. If a source does not have an author's name, list the work alphabetically by its title (ignore the initial word *a, an,* or *the*). Leave a space between entries.

Bibliography

Industry. Broomall, Pennsylvania: Chelsea House, 1996.

Moreland, Jennifer. Industrial Revolution of the 19th Century 1760–1900. Tucson, Arizona: Zephyr Press AZ, 1992.

Writer's Handbook

Writing and Technology

Understanding and Using URLs

The World Wide Web is a huge collection of information that you can reach through your computer. To reach it, you use a **browser**. Your browser can connect you to many different **Websites**. Websites are all over the world. To reach a site, you must first find it. You need its address, which is called a **URL**. (URL is short for "uniform resource locator.")

Every URL has three different parts. Each part is necessary, and each must be entered correctly into a browser. Here is a typical Internet address:

http://www.nameofplace.gov/index

The first part of a URL tells the browser how the information will travel to your computer. Usually, the method will be HyperText Transfer Protocol. Luckily, you do not have to remember that name. Instead, you use the abbreviation http followed by a colon (:) and two forward slashes (//).

The next part of the URL tells where the file is actually located. That part of the URL is called the **domain** name. In the address above, the domain name is this part:

www.nameofplace.gov

A domain name usually gives you some clues about the site itself. It may contain a familiar name, such as the name of a company or a company's initials. It usually ends in one of the following three-letter abbreviations:

com
edu
gov
mil
net
org

The four most common abbreviations are **.com**, **.edu**, **.gov**, and **.org**. Sites ending in .com are commercial sites; those ending in .edu are educational; those ending in .gov are governmental; and those ending in .org are sponsored by nonprofit organizations.

Writing and Technology

Understanding and Using URLs (continued)

A domain name may also contain a state or country abbreviation. You may see abbreviations that look like these:

au (Australia)
ca (Canada)
fr (France)
il (Illinois)
tx (Texas)

Sometimes the domain name completes the URL. At other times, though, it may be followed by a single slash and then more information. This information tells the browser exactly what document you want. Sometimes this is just a single word, like *index*. However, the address could also contain a collection of letters, hyphens, numbers, and tildes (~).

When you know the URL of a site, you can find the site by typing the URL into your browser. However, you must type it correctly. These guidelines can help:

■ Do not add any spaces or final punctuation.

■ Make sure that you type every letter and mark correctly.

■ Do not type lowercase letters where capitals belong.

■ Do not confuse the number *1* with the letter *l*.

■ Do not mix up hyphens (-) and underscores (_).

If you leave out one letter or mark, your browser will not find the site you seek. Can you see the difference between these two URLs?

http://www.nameofplace.gov/list-of-names1.html
http://www.Nameofplace.gov/List_of_names.htm

If you are writing a URL onto paper, copy it correctly. Put it between pointed brackets, so you or another reader will know where the URL begins and ends.

< http://www.Nameofplace.gov/List_of_names.htm>

Writer's Handbook

Writing and Technology

Using Different Search Tools to Find Information

You can use your computer to find information on many different topics. To find what you want, you will probably use either a **search tool** or a **directory**.

A **search tool** allows you to search for particular words, names, or phrases. Suppose you want to find information on Sharon Bell Mathis, an author. If you use a search tool, you must type her name into a box.

How you type her name will determine your success. Search tools work in different ways. With some, if you type in "Sharon Bell Mathis" you will be flooded with information about the town of Sharon, Alexander Graham Bell, and singer Johnny Mathis.

Follow these guidelines to improve your chances of success:

- See if the search tool has a link to search tips. This might be called "advanced search" or "help." Read these tips.

- Try typing the name inside quotation marks, like this: "Sharon Bell Mathis." Many search tools will then search for that phrase instead of the individual names in it.

- Try typing the name with the word AND between the names, like this: Sharon AND Bell AND Mathis. Many search tools will then only search for entries that contain all three names.

- Try typing the name with a plus sign before each name, like this: +Sharon +Bell +Mathis. Some search tools will then look only for sites that contain all three names.

A **directory** allows you to browse through categories of related sites. When you use a directory, such as Yahoo, you are shown categories, such as Cities, Literature, and Entertainers. You can then browse within the correct category to find increasingly narrower subcategories.

Writer's Handbook

Writing and Technology

On-Line Safety Tips

Even though you use computers in a safe place, such as a home, school, or library, remember that computers connect you to people who are often strangers. You can look at Websites that were created in other places, and you can post and read messages on bulletin boards that are read throughout the world. You can communicate with people directly by e-mail.

Computers can offer you new ways to connect with people. Meeting people on-line can be fun and exciting. However, remember to follow general safety rules, just as you do when you meet any stranger. When you go on-line, keep these tips in mind:

- Never believe everything that you read on-line. Some people make up special on-line personalities, either for fun or for deception. They might pretend to be older or younger than they really are, or they might pretend to have another name.

- Never give out personal information on-line, unless you know that you are dealing with someone that you and your family know well. Do not post personal information on bulletin boards, for example. Do not give out any of the following information:

  your full name or address
  your school's name or location
  your phone number
  your Social Security number
  your parent or guardian's name
  where your parent or guardian works

- Never reply when someone asks for personal information. If you receive any message that makes you feel uncomfortable or scared, do not write back. Instead, print out the troubling message and give it to an adult.

- Never give out your password. Do not even tell it to your friends.

Writing and Technology

On-Line Safety Tips (continued)

- Never agree to meet anyone in person unless you first tell a responsible adult and get that person's permission. Any meetings should be in a public place, not in a car or private home. Do not go alone.

- Never send pictures of yourself to someone you have never met. If someone asks for a picture, check with an adult. Remember that the person may not be honest about who he or she really is.

- Never download a file from an unknown source. The file might contain a virus that will harm your computer. It might also contain a secret program that can damage your computer or gather information about you.

Glossary

A

ablution (ə blo͞o´ shən) *n.* A cleansing.

abolition (ab´ ə lish´ ən) *n.* The termination, or ending, of something.

abolitionist (ab´ ə lish´ ən ist) *n.* A person who wanted to end slavery.

abrupt (ə brupt´) *adj.* Sudden; without warning.

accelerate (ak sel´ ə rāt´) *v.* To increase speed.

access (ak´ ses´) *n.* Permission or ability to enter, approach, communicate with, or pass to and from.

accumulate (ə kyo͞o´ myə lāt´) *v.* To gather more and more; to pile up.

accursed (ə kûr´ sid) *adj.* Affected by a curse or a spell.

acrylic (ə kril´ ik) *n.* A synthetic, or human-made, liquid that dries clear and hard like plastic.

adapt (ə dapt´) *v.* To adjust to new or different conditions.

adherent (ad hir´ ənt) *n.* One who believes or follows.

adobe (ə dō´ bē) *n.* Sun-dried brick.

advance (əd vans´) *v.* To bring or move forward.

advocate (ad´ və kāt´) *v.* To speak in favor of; to support.

aerosol (âr´ ə sôl´) *n.* A liquid sealed under pressure in a can with a gas. When a button on the can is pressed, the liquid sprays out.

aggravate (ag´ rə vāt´) *v.* To annoy.

alkali (al´ kə lī´) *n.* A chemical compound or element that forms salts and neutralizes acids.

ally (a´ lī´) *n.* Someone who works with another as a helper.

alpine ibex (al´ pīn ī´ beks) *n.* A wild mountain goat from a high mountain area.

alter (ôl´ tər) *v.* To change; to make different.

ambassador (am bas´ ə dər) *n.* A representative; one who represents something.

701

ambrosia (am brō´ zhə) *n.* Something
delicious to smell.

amethyst (am´ ə thist) *n.* A purple or
violet gem.

amphitheater (am´ fə thē´ ə tər) *n.* An area
with flat ground surrounded by rising hills
or cliffs.

ample (am´ pəl) *adj.* More than enough; plenty.

amply (am´ plē) *adv.* Sufficiently; plentifully;
enough.

anoint (ə noint´) *v.* To apply oil or ointment
as part of a religious ceremony; to make
sacred in a ceremony.

anonymously (ə no´ nə məs lē) *adv.* Without
being identified or named.

anthropologist (an´ thrə pol´ ə jist) *n.*
A scientist who studies the various
physical aspects or cultural features of
human beings.

antislavery (an´ tē slā´ və rē) *adj.*
Against slavery.

anvil (an´ vil) *n.* The iron block on which a
blacksmith hammers and shapes metal.

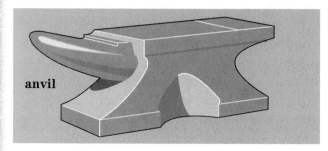

anvil

aria (är´ ē ə) *n.* A song that is sung by one
person in an opera.

aristocracy (ar´ ə stok´ rə sē) *n.* The
upper class.

aristocrat (ə ris´ tə krat´) *n.* An upper-
class person.

armor (är´ mər) *n.* A covering that protects
the body during fighting.

arroyo (ə roi´ ō) *n.* A small gulch or gulley.

ascent (ə sent´) *n.* The act of rising or
moving upward; climb.

asinine (as´ ə nīn´) *adj.* Silly; stupid.

astuteness (ə stōot´ nəs) *n.* Cleverness;
shrewdness.

attain (ə tān´) *v.* To reach; to gain;
to accomplish.

audacious (ô dā´ shəs) *adj.* Extremely
daring; recklessly brave.

augment (ôg ment´) *v.* To add to; to
increase; to enlarge.

Word History

The word **augment** comes from the
French word *augmenter.* This French
word goes back to a Latin word meaning
"to increase."

aura (or´ ə) *n.* A certain quality; an
atmosphere surrounding something.

authorize (ô´ thə rīz´) *v.* To make legal; to
give legal power to.

Word Derivations

Below are some words derived from the
word *authorize.*

authorized	authorizing
unauthorized	authorization

avaricious (av´ ə rish´ əs) *adj.* Greedy.

avert (ə vûrt´) *v.* To prevent or change the
probable outcome of; to ward off.

aviary (ā´ vē er´ ē) *n.* A place where birds
are kept.

awl (ôl) *n.* A pointed tool for poking holes
in things.

B

bade (bād) *v.* A past tense of **bid:**
To command.

balustrade (bal´ ə strād´) *n.* A railing with
upright supports.

barge (bärj) *n.* A flat-bottomed boat used for carrying freight.

barren (bar´ ən) *adj.* Bare.

bass (bās) *n.* The lowest part in the musical range; the lowest range of the male singing voice.

bastings (bā´ stingz) *n.* Long, loose stitches that are usually removed when final stitches are put in.

beacon (bē´ kən) *adj.* Used to signal.

belabor (bi lā´ bər) *v.* To beat; to hit.

bewildering (bi wil də ring) *adj.* Confusing and overwhelming; puzzling.

biceps (bī´ seps) *n.* A muscle in the upper arm.

biologist (bī ol´ ə jist´) *n.* A scientist who studies living things, both plant and animal.

blackguard (blag´ ärd) *n.* A scoundrel; a bad person.

blackmail (blak´ māl´) *n.* A payment received by threatening to tell a secret unless paid.

bolt (bōlt) *n.* A roll of fabric.

boogie-woogie (boog´ ē woog´ ē) *n.* A type of jazz played on the piano.

boycott (boi´ kot) *v.* To refuse to do business with someone.

Word History

The term **boycott** originated in 1880 when Irish tenants refused to do business with Charles C. Boycott, an English land agent who would not reduce rents and who tried to have these tenants evicted.

---

brandish (bran´ dish) *v.* To shake; to wave.

bridal garland (brīd´ l gär´ lənd) *n.* A wreath of flowers for a wedding ceremony.

brimstone (brim´ stōn´) *n.* Sulfur, a yellow mineral substance with a sharp odor.

brooch (brōch) *n.* A pin that is highly decorated, worn as jewelry.

brood (brood) *v.* To sit on eggs in order to hatch them.

buckle (buk´ əl) *n.* A bend or bulge.

Buddhist (boo´ dist) *n.* One who follows the teachings of Gautama Buddha.

buenos noches (bwe´ nōs nō´ ches) *n. Spanish.* Good night.

bull-roarer (bool´ ror´ ər) *n.* A strip of wood on a string that is twirled around one's head to make a roaring sound.

bush baby (boosh´ bā´ bē) *n.* A primate of Africa with large eyes and ears, woolly fur, and a bushy tail.

C

calculation (kal´ kyə lā´ shən) *n.* The result of counting, computing, or gauging something.

calypso (kə lip´ sō) *n.* A style of jazz from the West Indies.

canister (ka´ nə stər) *n.* A tank that holds compressed gas.

caravan (câr´ ə van´) *n.* A group of people traveling together through a desert or hostile region.

carbide (kär´ bīd) *n.* A compound made with carbon and another element.

Carthaginian (kär´ thə ji´ nē ən) *adj.* Relating to or having to do with Carthage, which was an ancient city and state of North Africa near present-day Tunis.

chamber (chām´ bər) *n.* 1. A room in a royal palace, especially a bedroom. 2. An enclosed space.

chamberlain (chām´ bər lin) *n.* An important official in a royal court.

champion (cham´ pē ən) *n.* One who defends others.

chaperon (shap´ ə rōn´) *n.* A person who stays with a young, unmarried woman in public.

chaplain (chap´ lin) *n.* A religious leader in a royal court.

cherish (châr´ ish) *v.* To value and enjoy; to hold dear.

chignon (shēn´ yon) *n.* A twist or knot of hair worn at the nape of the neck.

chimney (chim´ nē) *n.* A narrow crack in rock or ice.

chorizo con huevos (chō rē´ sō kōn we´ vōs) *n. Spanish.* Sausage with eggs.

cicada (si kā´ də) *n.* A large insect that makes a shrill sound.

Pronunciation Key: **a**t; l**ā**te; c**â**re; f**ä**ther; s**e**t; m**ē**; **i**t; k**ī**te; **o**x; r**ō**se; **ô** in b**ou**ght; c**oi**n; b**oo**k; t**oo**; f**o**rm; **out**; **u**p; **ū**se; t**û**rn; **ə** sound in **a**bout, chick**e**n, penc**i**l, cann**o**n, circ**u**s; **ch**air; **hw** in **wh**ich; ri**ng**; **sh**op; **th**in; **th**ere; **zh** in trea**s**ure.

circulation (sûr´ kyə lā´ shən) *n.* The number of newspapers sold to readers.

cite (sīt) *v.* To state as proof or as an example.

civil disobedience (siv´ əl dis´ ə bē´ dē əns) *n.* The refusal to obey certain laws in order to eventually change those laws.

civilization (siv´ ə lə zā´ shən) *n.* A culture, society, or group of human beings who have developed education, agriculture, trade, science, art, government, and so on.

cog (kog) *n.* The part of a gear that sticks out like a tooth; a tiny part of a machine.

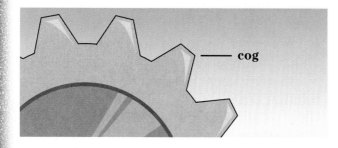

cog

colossal (kə lo´ səl) *adj.* Of incredible size or power; great.

concept (kon´ sept) *n.* An idea.

condescending (kon´ də sen´ ding) *adj.* Acting as if one is coming down to the level of a person thought of as inferior.

conjunto (kōn hoon´ tō) *n. Spanish.* A set; an ensemble.

conserve (kən sûrv´) *v.* To preserve; to keep.

Word History

The word **conserve** is a French word that comes from two Latin terms: *com-*, which means "with" or "together," and *servare*, which means "to keep."

constitutional amendment (kon´ sti too´ shə nl ə mend´ mənt) *n.* A change added to the Constitution of the United States.

contagious (kən tā´ jəs) *adj.* Spreading by touch or by contact.

contempt (kən tempt´) *n.* Scorn; disdain.

contest (kən test´) *v.* To struggle against.

continuity (kon´ tən oo´ ə tē) *n.* Something that exists without interruption.

controversy (kon´ trə vûr´ sē) *n.* Disagreement; strife.

convert (kən vûrt´) *v.* To change.

coquetry (kō´ ki trē) *n.* Flirting.

corps (kor) *n.* A group of individuals working together under a common direction.

corridor (cor´ ə dōr) *n.* A narrow strip of land; passageway.

corsage (kor säzh´) *n.* A bouquet to be worn on a woman's dress.

cosmopolitan (koz´ mə po´ lə tən) *adj.* Having people, ideas, and elements from many parts of the world.

cosmos (koz´ məs) *n.* The world or universe.

cottonmouth (kot´ n mouth´) *n.* A type of poisonous snake known as a pit viper because above each nostril it has a pit that is sensitive to heat; also called a water moccasin.

couch (kouch) *v.* To lower a weapon and hold it ready for attack.

coup (koo) *n.* A daring deed in battle, especially touching an enemy without being harmed.

courtier (kor´ tē ər) *n.* A person in attendance at a royal court.

cradleboard (krād´ l bord´) *n.* A wooden frame that Native American women wore on their backs to carry their babies.

crayfish (krā´ fish´) *n.* A freshwater shellfish like a small lobster.

credit (kred´ it) *n.* A person's reputation for paying bills.

Word Derivations

Below are some words derived from the word *credit*.

credited	creditor
creditable	discredit

creditor (kred´ i tər) *n.* One to whom money is owed.

creed (krēd) *n.* A statement of belief.

cremate (krē´ māt) *v.* To burn to ashes.

crescent (kres´ ənt) *n.* A curved shape like a new moon.

croon (kro̅o̅n) *v.* To sing in a low, moaning tone.

crown (kroun) *n.* The leaves and the live branches of a tree.

crown

culmination (kul´ mə nā´ shən) *n.* The end; the finish.

curious (kyo̅o̅r´ ē əs) *adj.* 1. Strange. 2. Interesting. 3. Prying; inquisitive; wanting to know.

curtail (kər tāl´) *v.* To cut short; to put a stop to.

curvaceous (kûr vā´ shəs) *adj.* Having curves.

D

dank (dangk) *adj.* Damp; moist.

DDT **D**ichlorodiphenyl-trichloroethane: An insecticide; a substance used to kill insects.

deceitful (di sēt´ fəl) *adj.* Misleading; cheating.

deciduous (di sij´ o̅o̅ əs) *adj.* Falling off or shedding yearly. Deciduous trees shed their leaves every year.

deign (dān) *v.* To lower oneself.

delirium (di lēr´ ē əm) *n.* A state of excitability; a madness.

delude (di lo̅o̅d´) *v.* To mislead; to deceive.

deport (di port´) *v.* To banish; to expel from a country.

Word Derivations

Below are some words derived from the word *deport*.

deported	deportation
deportable	deportee

depression (di presh´ ən) *n.* 1. A shallow hole or a dent. 2. **Depression:** A period from 1929 through the 1930s when people made and spent very little money; also called the Great Depression.

descent (di sent´) *n.* The act of inclining downward or moving from higher to lower.

desperation (des´ pə rā´ shən) *n.* Rashness; recklessness; hopelessness.

despise (di spīz´) *v.* To look down on; to scorn.

deter (di tûr´) *v.* To hold back; to prevent.

dictate (dik´ tāt) *v.* To prescribe; to command.

disbursement (dis bûrs´ mənt) *n.* Money spent.

discern (di sûrn´) *v.* To understand differences by using one's intellect or senses.

disconsolately (dis kon´ sə lit lē) *adv.* Unhappily; cheerlessly.

discord (dis´ kord) *n.* Disagreement.

discordant (dis kor´ dnt) *adj.* Harsh; jarring.

dismal (diz´ məl) *adj.* Dreary; cheerless; sad.

disparage (di spar´ ij) *v.* To belittle; to run down.

dispel (di spel´) *v.* To drive away; to banish.

distract (di strakt´) *v.* To draw one's attention away.

Word History

The word **distract** comes from two Latin terms: *dis-*, which means "apart," and *tract*, which means "to draw."

Pronunciation Key: at; l**ā**te; c**â**re; f**ä**ther; s**e**t; m**ē**; **i**t; k**ī**te; **o**x; r**ō**se; **ô** in b**ou**ght; c**oi**n; b**oo**k; t**oo**; f**o**rm; **ou**t; **u**p; **ū**se; t**û**rn; **ə** sound in **a**bout, chick**e**n, penc**i**l, cann**o**n, circ**u**s; **ch**air; **hw** in **wh**ich; ri**ng**; **sh**op; **th**in; **th**ere; **zh** in trea**s**ure.

divulge (di vulj´) *v.* To tell; to reveal.

document (dok´ yə mənt) *n.* A written proof or testimony.

dominant (dom´ ə nənt) *adj.* Important; controlling.

down (doun) *n.* Very soft or fine feathers.

dredge (drej) *v.* 1. To coat with a powder. 2. To scoop mud from a channel.

drudgery (dru´ jə rē) *n.* Work that is boring and tiring.

dulcet (dul´ sit) *adj.* Pleasant; soothing.

dumb (dum) *adj.* Unable to talk.

durable (door´ ə bəl) *adj.* Lasting; long-wearing.

dwindle (dwin´ dəl) *v.* To become less.

E

ebony (eb´ ə nē) *n.* A dark, heavy wood from Africa.

eccentric (ik sen´ trik) *adj.* Odd; peculiar.

ecstatic (ek stat´ ik) *adj.* Extremely joyful; intensely happy.

elated (i lā´ tid) *adj.* Joyfully excited.

elder (el´ dər) *n.* An older, respected member of a group.

elevator (el´ ə vā´ tər) *n.* A flap on a wing of an airplane that is raised or lowered to raise or lower the plane's nose.

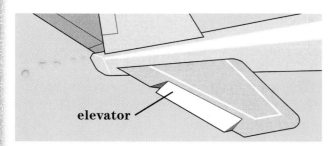

elevator

élite (i lēt´) *adj.* The best.

Elysium (i lizh´ ē əm) *n.* The place where the good go after death, according to ancient Greek religious ideas.

embalmer (em bäm´ ər) *n.* A person who preserves dead bodies.

emboss (em bôs´) *v.* To write in letters that stand out from the surface; to decorate in a raised pattern.

encrusted (en krust´ id) *adj.* Covered with.

endangered (en dān´ jərd) *adj.* At risk of becoming extinct; in danger of being killed off.

endure (in door´) *v.* To tolerate; to get through something without giving up.

engage (en gāj´) *v.* To employ; to hire.

engender (en jen´ dər) *v.* To produce; to cause.

enhance (in hans´) *v.* To improve the quality of.

enlightened (en līt´ nd) *adj.* Informed; educated.

enterprising (en´ tər prī zing) *adj.* Willing to try something new or that requires an energetic, problem-solving attitude; creative.

enthralled (en thrôld´) *adj.* Charmed; fascinated.

entity (en´ ti tē) *n.* Something that exists on its own.

entrails (en´ trālz) *n.* The organs inside the body.

entrepreneur (än´ trə prə nûr´) *n.* A person who starts a business that usually involves risk.

Word History

Entrepreneur is a French word that comes from another French word, *entreprendre*, which means "to take on."

envision (en vizh´ ən) *v.* To see in one's mind, especially the future.

epistle (i pis´ əl) *n.* A letter; a message.

equation (i kwā´ zhən) *n.* A mathematical statement that shows how two things are equal.

erratic (i rat´ ik) *adj.* Changeable; not reliable.

escort (es´ kort) *n.* A man who goes to a social event with a woman.

esperanto (es´ pə rän´ tō) *n. usually capitalized.* A language that was invented in hopes that all the people in the world could speak the same language.

estuary (es´ chōō er´ ē) *n.* A river mouth; where a river meets the sea.

etch (ech) *v.* To produce a design by making furrows on a hard surface.

ewer (yōō´ ər) *n.* A pitcher or jug.

ewer

excavate (eks´ kə vāt´) *v.* To dig out.

Word History

The word **excavate** comes from two Latin terms: *ex-*, which means "out of" or "from" and *cavate*, which means "to make hollow."

exhibition (ek´ sə bi´ shən) *n.* A public showing.

exigency (ek´ si jən sē) *n.* Urgency; the need to act immediately.

exquisite (ik skwiz´ it) *adj.* Having special or rare beauty.

extensively (ik sten´ siv lē) *adv.* Widely; to a great extent.

extent (ik stent´) *n.* The size; the amount.

extinct (ik stingkt´) *adj.* Not now existing.

F

falconer (fôl´ kə nər) *n.* A person who hunts by using falcons or hawks, both powerful birds of prey.

fanatic (fə nat´ ik) *n.* A person who is carried beyond reason by feelings or beliefs.

fare (fâr) *n.* Food.

fathomless (fath´ əm lis) *adj.* Extremely deep; bottomless.

feminist (fem´ ə nist) *adj.* Agreeing with equal rights for women.

fetter (fet´ ər) *n.* A chain binding the ankles.

flatiron (flat´ ī´ ərn) *n.* An iron that is not electric, used to press clothes.

flue (flōō) *n.* A chimney; a shaft for letting gases or fumes float out of a building.

fluted (flōō´ tid) *adj.* Having rounded grooves.

foe (fō) *n.* An enemy; an opponent.

folly (fol´ ē) *n.* Foolishness; lack of good sense.

foremost (for´ mōst´) *adj.* The most important.

fortunate (for chə nət) *adj.* Lucky.

frankincense (frang´ kin sens´) *n.* A substance with an aroma, burned as incense or used as perfume.

fraud (frôd) *n.* Someone who pretends to be something that he or she isn't; an imposter.

freeway (frē´ wā´) *n.* A highway.

frieze (frēz) *n.* An ornamental border around the walls of a room or the outside of a building.

frost heave (frôst´ hēv´) *n.* An area of soil that is raised due to the freezing of the moisture within the soil.

fungi (fun´ jī) *n.* A plural of **fungus** (fung´ gəs): A group of spongy plants that get their food from other dead or living plants; mushrooms, molds, and the like.

furl (fûrl) *v.* To roll up, as a flag or sail.

furrow (fûr´ ō) *n.* A depression made by a plow; a groove.

G

galley (gal´ ē) *n.* A ship's kitchen.

Pronunciation Key: at; l**ā**te; c**â**re; f**ä**ther; se**t**; m**ē**; **i**t; k**ī**te; **o**x; r**ō**se; **ô** in b**ou**ght; c**oi**n; b**ŏŏ**k; t**ōō**; f**o**rm; **ou**t; **u**p; **ū**se; t**û**rn; **ə** sound in **a**bout, chick**e**n, penc**i**l, cann**o**n, circ**u**s; **ch**air; **hw** in **wh**ich; ri**ng**; **sh**op; **th**in; **th**ere; **zh** in trea**s**ure.

garnet (gär´ nit) *n.* A deep red gem.

Word History

The word **garnet** comes from the French word *grenat*, which means "red like a pomegranate." This word can be traced back to the French words *pomme* and *grenate*, which mean "seedy apple." A pomegranate is a thick-skinned red fruit about the size of an orange.

gharial (gur´ ē əl) *n.* A gavial; a large reptile with an extra-long snout, in the crocodile family.

gibbon (gib´ ən) *n.* A small ape.

gingerly (jin´ jər lē) *adv.* Cautiously; warily.

glance (glans) *v.* To glide off an object instead of hitting it full.

glower (glou´ ər) *v.* To look or stare with sullen annoyance or anger.

glut (glut) *n.* An excess; too much of something.

Godspeed (god´ spēd´) *n.* Good luck; success.

guitarron (gi tä ron´) *n. Spanish.* A large guitar.

gunwale (gun´ l) *n.* The top edge of a boat's side.

gypsum (jip´ səm) *n.* A soft white mineral, or nonliving substance, that occurs in nature. The type of gypsum used in carvings and building is known as alabaster.

H

habitat (hab´ i tat´) *n.* The natural surroundings of a plant or animal; native environment.

Hail Mary (hāl´ mâr´ ē) *n.* A Roman Catholic prayer.

halflight (haf´ līt´) *n.* Dimmed light.

hamlet (ham´ lit) *n.* A small village.

harass (hə ras´) *v.* To pester; to annoy; to disturb.

Word Derivations

Below are some words derived from the word *harass*.

harassed   harassing   harassment

harpsichord (härp´ si kord´) *n.* A musical instrument like a small piano but with a more delicate sound.

harpsichord

henna (hen´ ə) *n.* A reddish-orange dye.

hermit (hûr´ mit) *n.* Someone who lives alone and stays away from others.

hew (hyōō) *v.* To cut with an axe.

hijo (ē´ hō´) *n. Spanish.* Son.

hobble (ho´ bəl) *v.* To make unable to walk by tying the legs together.

hoe (hō) *n.* A garden tool that has a thin flat blade with a straight edge used to break up ground.

hogan (hō´ gôn) *n.* The rounded, log and mud dwelling of the Navajo.

homage (hom´ ij) *n.* Duty; loyalty; devotion.

horde (hord) *n.* A large group of nomads.

hover (huv´ ər) *v.* To hang poised in the air.

husk (husk) *v.* To remove the outer leaves of an ear of corn.

I

ibis (ī´ bis) *n.* A large wading bird with a long bill that curves downward.

imam (i mom´) *n.* A prayer leader.

immortal (i mor´ tl) *adj.* Living forever.

imperial (im pir´ ē əl) *adj.* Relating to an empire or emperor.

implore (im plor´) *v.* To beg.

impoverished (im pov´ ər isht) *adj.* Very poor.

improvise (im´ prə vīz´) *v.* To write music without planning by just playing on an instrument.

inclined (in klīnd´) *adj.* Tending to be in favor of.

inconceivable (in´ kən sē´ və bəl) *adj.* Unbelievable; impossible to imagine.

inconsolable (in´ kən sō´ lə bəl) *adj.* Not able to be comforted.

incredulous (in krej´ ə ləs) *adj.* Not believing something; skeptical.

incubator (in´ kyə bā´ tər) *n.* An enclosure in which eggs are hatched by being kept at the right conditions.

indifference (in dif´ ər əns) *n.* A lack of interest.

indifferent (in dif´ ər ənt) *adj.* Not interested.

indignant (in dig´ nənt) *adj.* Angry; furious.

indispensable (in´ di spen´ sə bəl) *adj.* Necessary; essential.

inevitable (in ev´ i tə bəl) *adj.* Certain; sure.

inexistent (in´ ig zis´ tənt) *adj.* Not living; not being.

inferior (in fir´ ē ər) *adj.* Less than acceptable; not as good as others.

Word History

The word **inferior** comes from the Latin word *inferus*, which means "lower."

infertility (in´ fûr til´ i tē) *n.* The inability to bear young.

infinite (in´ fə nit) *adj.* Having no limits; endless; immense.

infuriated (in fyŏŏr´ ē ā´ təd) *adj.* Enraged; furious.

ingenuity (in jə nōō´ i tē) *n.* Cleverness.

ingratitude (in grat´ i tōōd´) *n.* A lack of thankfulness.

initial (in nish´ əl) *adj.* At the beginning; first.

insatiable (in sā´ shə bəl) *adj.* Unable to be satisfied; endless.

insensitive (in sen´ si tiv) *adj.* Not caring; not feeling sympathy.

intent (in tent´) *adj.* Fixed upon or bent upon; attentive to.

intoxicated (in tok´ si kā´ tid) *adj.* Highly excited.

intricate (in´ tri kit) *adj.* Made of many parts.

intrigue (in trēg´) *v.* To arouse curiosity.

inundation (in´ ən dā´ shən) *n.* A deluge; a flood.

irritable (ir´ i tə bəl) *adj.* Easily angered or annoyed.

J

jaeger (yā´ gər) *n.* A dark-colored seabird that is a hunter of other birds' prey, especially that of gulls.

jaeger

K

keen (kēn) *adj.* Fine; sharp.

ken (ken) *n.* Knowledge; understanding.

kittiwake (kit´ ē wāk´) *n.* A cliff-nesting gull of the northern seas.

km Kilometer.

knickers (nik´ ərz) *n.* Short, baggy trousers that end at the knees.

knight (nīt) *n.* A soldier in armor and on horseback, working on behalf of a feudal lord or a king or queen.

kohl (kōl) *n.* A dark powder, used as eyeliner or eye shadow.

L

lackey (lak´ ē) *n.* A footman; a manservant.

lamentation (lam´ ən tā´ shən) *n.* A vocal expression of grief or mourning.

lapis lazuli (lap´ is laz´ oo lē) *n.* A deep blue, semiprecious gemstone.

laurel (lor´ əl) *n.* A small, European evergreen tree with dark, glossy green leaves.

lave (lāv) *v.* To wash; to bathe.

lectern (lek´ tərn) *n.* A podium; a tall, narrow piece of furniture with a slanted top, which a speaker stands behind.

Word History

The word **lectern** comes from a French word that can be traced to a Latin word that means "to read."

lector (lek´ tər) *n.* A person who acts as a reader of Bible selections during a church service.

legibility (lej´ ə bil´ ə tē) *n.* The quality of being readable.

lethargy (leth´ ər jē) *n.* Slowness; sleepiness; dullness.

liberate (lib´ ə rāt´) *v.* To set free.

license (lī´ səns) *v.* To permit by law.

lichen (lī´ kən) *n.* A simple plant that grows on rocks and tree trunks.

logically (loj´ i kə lē) *adv.* In a reasonable way.

loom (loom) *v.* To appear larger than its surroundings.

loris (lor´ is) *n.* A slender primate with no tail.

lotus (lō´ təs) *n.* A kind of water lily that grows in Egypt and Asia.

lute (loot) *n.* An old-time stringed instrument like a guitar.

lyre (līr) *n.* A small harp used in ancient times.

M

magma (mag´ mə) *n.* The molten material that pours out of a volcano and hardens to become rock.

mahogany (mə hog´ ə nē) *n.* A hard, reddish-brown wood from a tropical tree.

malaria (mə lâr´ ē ə) *n.* A disease marked by fevers, caused by the bite of certain mosquitoes.

Word History

The word **malaria** comes from the two Italian words *mal* and *aria*, which mean "bad air."

mangrove (mang´ grōv) *n.* A tropical low-growing tree or shrub that grows in marshes or on tidal shores.

maritime (mâr´ ə tīm´) *adj.* Relating to the sea.

Marseillaise (mär´ sə lāz´) *n.* The national anthem of France.

mason (mā´ sən) *n.* A builder in stone, bricks, and tile.

mass (mas) *n. often capitalized.* The chief service of the Roman Catholic Church.

melancholy (mel´ ən kol´ ē) *adj.* Sad; moody.

mesa (mā´ sə) *n.* High, flat land like a plateau, but smaller.

mildew (mil´ doo´) *v.* To grow a coating of fuzzy mold.

mingle (min´ gəl) *v.* To interact with others; to mix together socially.

minstrel (min´ strəl) *n.* A bard; one who sings or recites poems.

mirage (mi räzh´) *n.* Something that appears but is not really there.

mock (mok) *v.* To make fun of; ridicule.

Word Derivations

Below are some words derived from the word *mingle*.

mingled   mingling   intermingle

---

modest (mo´dəst) *adj.* Having a moderate opinion of oneself.

molt (mōlt) *v.* To cast off or shed skin, scales, feathers, hair, or horns that are later replaced. Certain animals molt regularly.

monopoly (mə no´pə lē) *n.* Owned and controlled by only one person, group, or company.

monsoon (mon soon´) *n.* A wind that blows across south Asia seasonally, bringing heavy rains.

moonstone (moon´ stōn´) *n.* A pearly blue stone.

moonstruck (moon´ struk´) *adj.* Crazed as a result of the moon's influence.

moral (mor´ əl) *n.* The lesson taught by an experience.

mosque (mosk) *n.* The building in which Muslims worship publicly.

motley (mot´ lē) *adj.* Many-colored.

mottled (mot´ ld) *adj.* Spotted or blotched with different colors or shades.

mottled

mouth harp (mouth´ hârp´) *n.* A harmonica.

myriad (mir´ ē əd) *n.* An immense number.

myrrh (mûr) *n.* A fragrant, bitter resin used in medicine, perfumes, and incense.

N

nanny (nan´ ē) *n.* A woman hired to take care of a child.

nary (nâr´ ē) *adj.* Not any.

nationalist (nash´ ə nl ist´) *adj.* Patriotic; supporting one's country.

nocturnal (nok tûr´ nl) *adj.* Awake or active at night.

nomad (nō´ mad´) *n.* Someone with no permanent home who moves from place to place within a given area during different seasons.

noncommittal (non´ kə mit´ l) *adj.* Having no point of view; giving no opinion.

nosh (nosh) *v. informal.* To snack; to eat snacks.

Word History

Nosh is a Yiddish word that dates back to a German word that means "to eat on the sly."

---

nymph (nimf) *n.* A goddess of the sea, woods, or waters.

O

obelisk (ob´ ə lisk) *n.* A tall stone monument that is narrower at the top.

obese (ō bēs´) *adj.* Fat; overweight.

oblivion (ə bliv´ ē ən) *n.* The state of being unknown or totally forgotten.

obscurity (əb skyoor´ i tē) *n.* The state of being unknown.

observatory (əb zûr´ və tor´ ē) *n.* A place that is designed for astronomers to study the stars.

obsess (əb ses´) *v.* To fill one's mind; to focus one's thoughts on one thing.

offhanded (ôf´ han´ did) *adj.* Easygoing; careless; casual.

outing (ou´ ting) *n.* A trip for pleasure.

ovation (ō vā´ shən) *n.* Applause.

ozone (ō´ zōn) *n.* A form of oxygen with three atoms in each molecule instead of the usual two, often present in the atmosphere after a thunderstorm.

Pronunciation Key: at; lāte; câre; fäther; set; mē; it; kīte; ox; rōse; ô in bought; coin; bŏŏk; tōō; form; out; up; ūse; tûrn; ə sound in about, chicken, pencil, cannon, circus; chair; hw in which; ring; shop; thin; thēre; zh in treasure.

P

palanquin (pal′ ən kēn′) *n.* An enclosed structure stretched across four poles in which a person rides while four people carry the poles.

pallor (pal′ ər) *n.* Paleness.

palsy (pôl′ sē) *n.* Paralysis; numbness.

papa (pä′ pä′) *n. Spanish.* A potato.

passion (pa′ shən) *n.* Emotion.

patron (pā′ trən) *n.* One who supports an artist by giving money.

patron saint (pā′ trən sānt′) *n.* A saint who is the special guardian of a person or group.

patronage (pā′ trə nij) *n.* The attitude that one is granting a favor.

pedestal (pe′ dəs təl) *n.* The base on which a statue rests.

perpetual (pər pech′ ōō əl) *adj.* Lasting forever or for a long time.

pesticide (pes′ tə sīd′) *n.* A chemical used to destroy insect pests.

petition (pə tish′ ən) *n.* A written request to the government.

phenomenal (fi no′ mə nəl) *adj.* Amazing; incredible.

piazza (pē az′ ə) *n.* A porch or veranda.

piñon (pin′ yən) *n.* A kind of pine tree with seeds that can be eaten.

pitiless (pit′ i lis) *adj.* Having no mercy.

plait (plāt) *v.* To twine or braid.

plateau (pla tō′) *n.* A tract of high, flat land; a tableland.

pneumonia (nŏŏ mō′ nyə) *n.* A disease of the lungs caused by infection or irritation.

polecat (pōl′ kat) *n.* A skunk.

polystyrene (pol′ ē stī′ rēn) *n.* A clear plastic or a stiff foam used to make objects or used as insulation.

poncho (pon′ chō) *n.* A cloak with an opening for the head.

porcelain (por′ sə lin) *n.* A white ceramic material that can almost be seen through.

porter (por′ tər) *n.* A person who carries supplies.

pound (pound) *n.* A unit of money in England.

predator (pred′ ə tər) *n.* An animal that hunts and kills other animals for its food.

predatory (pred′ ə tor′ ē) *adj.* Preying on other animals for food.

predicament (pri di′ kə mənt) *n.* A difficult situation.

prehistoric (prē′ hi stor′ ik) *adj.* Belonging to a time before history was written down; very early in the history of humans.

prejudice (pre′ jə dəs) *n.* An unsupported negative opinion or attitude toward a person or group, often based on stereotypes.

première (pri mēr′) *n.* The first public performance of a work.

presume (pri zōōm′) *v.* To take for granted; to suppose.

Word History

The Italian word **piazza** comes from the Latin term *platea*, which means "broad street."

Word Derivations

Below are some words derived from the word *presume*.

presumed   presuming   presumedly

pilgrim (pil′ grəm) *n.* Someone who travels to a foreign land.

prodigious (prə dij′ əs) *adj.* Enormous; monstrous.

prodigy (prod´ i jē) *n.* A child with extraordinary talent.

profound (prə found´) *adj.* Of deep meaning.

proposed (prə pōzd´) *v.* To put forward a plan for possible future action.

prose (prōz) *n.* Written language that is not verse.

prostrate (pros´ trāt) *adj.* Lying flat.

pueblo (pweb´ lō) *n.* A group of adobe dwellings set into cliffs and reached by ladders.

puffin (puf´ in) *n.* A diving seabird with a beak like a parrot.

pumice (pum´ is) *n.* Light, porous lava.

puny (pyo͞o´ nē) *adj.* Smaller than normal.

purloin (pər loin´) *v.* To steal.

Q

quarry (kwor´ ē) *v.* To dig stone out of an open pit.

quell (kwel) *v.* To overcome by force; to crush.

queue (kyo͞o) *n.* A line.

R

rally (ra´ lē) *v.* To inspire or motivate a group to support a given cause.

rank (rangk) *adj.* Absolute; complete.

ransack (ran´ sak) *v.* To search a place looking for things to steal; to plunder; to pillage.

ration (ra´ shən) *n.* Food supply.

ravel (ra´ vəl) *v.* To separate or undo.

ravishing (rav´ i shing) *adj.* Extremely beautiful.

receipt (ri sēt´) *n.* A written statement that something has been received.

receipts (ri sēts´) *n.* The amount received; income.

reclamation (rek´ lə mā´ shən) *n.* The act of putting land back into a pure or healthy state.

reformer (ri for´ mər) *n.* A person who brings about change for the better.

regulate (reg´ yə lāt´) *v.* To adjust something to make it accurate.

Word Derivations

Below are some words derived from the word *regulate*.

regulated	regulation
regulating	regulatory

relativity (rel´ ə tiv´ i tē) *n.* A theory that says the values of certain things are not absolute but change according to different points of view. Those things whose values can be changed are time, space, velocity, motion, and mass.

relay (rē´ lā´) *n.* A race in which each member of a team takes a turn running a certain length of the course.

relic (rel´ ik) *n.* A surviving trace of something past or dead.

remote (ri mōt´) *adj.* Far off; distant.

rendezvous (rän´ də vo͞o´) *n.* An arranged meeting.

resentful (ri zent´ fəl) *adj.* Feeling that someone has caused insult or injury.

resin (rez´ in) *n.* The gummy sap of certain pine trees.

resound (ri zound´) *v.* To echo; to make a continuing sound, like ringing.

Word History

Resound comes from a French word that can be traced back to two Latin terms: *re-*, which means "again," and *sonare*, which means "to sound."

resistance (ri zis´ təns) *n.* Opposition.

restrain (ri strān´) *v.* To hold back; to control.

resurrection (rez´ ə rek´ shən) *n. usually capitalized.* The act of Christ rising from the dead.

retaining wall (ri tān´ ing wôl´) *n.* A wall constructed to keep earth from pouring over it.

reunion (rē yōōn´ yən) *n.* A meeting of family or friends after a period of absence.

reveille (rev´ ə lē) *n.* A bugle or drum signal used to call soldiers together in the morning.

revelation (rev´ ə lā´ shən) *n.* Something that had not been known before.

revenge (ri venj´) *n.* Vengeance; retaliation; the act of hurting in return for being hurt.

ridicule (rid´ i kyōōl´) *v.* To make fun of; to mock.

rivet (riv´ it) *v.* To have one's complete attention.

rural (rōōr´ əl) *adj.* Having to do with the countryside.

S

sanctity (sangk´ ti tē) *n.* A sacred or holy nature.

scale (skāl) *v.* To throw something at an angle so that it skips.

scoff (skof) *v.* To make fun of; to treat with contempt.

screen (skrēn) *v.* To keep something from being in clear view.

scribe (skrīb) *n.* A clerk with official status.

seditious (si dish´ əs) *adj.* Disloyal; unpatriotic.

segment (seg´ mənt) *n.* A part that breaks off naturally; a distinct part of something.

semaphore (sem´ ə for´) *n.* A system of signaling using flags in which the positions of the flags have different meanings.

sentinel (sent´ nəl) *n.* Guard; soldier watching for the enemy.

sentry (sen´ trē) *n.* A soldier on guard duty.

serenade (sâr´ ə nād´) *n.* A musical composition with several movements written for instruments.

semaphore

serial (sēr´ ē əl) *n.* A story published, told, or shown in successive parts.

sever (sev´ ər) *v.* To cut; to separate.

shaman (shō´ mən) *n.* A priest or priestess who uses magic.

Sherpa (shûr´ pə) *n.* A member of the people originally from Tibet who live on the high southern slopes of the Himalayas in eastern Nepal.

shirtwaist (shûrt´ wāst´) *n.* A woman's blouse or dress with a tailored front like a shirt.

shortwave radio (short´ wāv rā´ dē ō) *n.* A radio that sends and receives shortwaves, which are used for long-distance transmitting.

shun (shun) *v.* To have nothing to do with; to ignore.

sibling (sib´ ling) *n.* A brother or sister.

simulated (sim´ yə lā´ tid) *adj.* Imitated, as with a model of the real thing.

sinfonia (sin fō ne´ ə) *n.* A symphony, or instrumental piece, played as an introduction to an opera or oratorio.

sirdar (sûr´ där) *n.* A person holding a responsible position; the leader of the Sherpas on a mountaineering expedition.

siskin (sis´ kin) *n.* A small bird in the finch family.

skein (skān) *n.* Yarn or thread wound in a coil.

skirmish (skûr´ mish) *n.* A fast and lively encounter, or coming together, involving some conflict.

skirt (skûrt) *v.* To go along the edge of; to go around to avoid danger.

skua (skyōō′ ə) *n.* A large brown bird that is like a gull.

smote (smōt) *v.* A past tense of **smite:** To strike with a hard, sudden blow.

sneer (snēr) *n.* A smile that shows scorn or hate.

solace (sol′ is) *n.* Comfort; consolation.

solar (sō′ lər) *adj.* Concerning the sun.

solder (sod′ ər) *n.* A hot, melted blend of metals used to join pieces of metal together. —*v.* To join pieces of metal together by applying a blend of melted metals at the joints.

soloist (sō′ lə wist) *n.* One who performs alone.

soulful (sōl′ fəl) *adj.* Having deep feeling.

spa (spä) *n.* A health resort that has a mineral spring.

Word History

The city of Spa, Belgium, became so famous for its mineral springs that the term **spa** has been used for all health resorts with mineral springs.

spawn (spôn) *v.* To give rise to.

spectacle (spek′ ti kəl) *n.* Something unusual or entertaining that is put on display as a curiosity; an impressive public display.

sphere (sfēr) *n.* The area or environment of a person's life.

spiritless (spir′ it lis) *adj.* Without enthusiasm.

sprocket (sprok′ it) *n.* A wheel with tooth edges that grab another moving part.

stabilize (stā′ bə līz′) *v.* To make steady.

staff (staf) *n.* A rod; a long cane.

stalemate (stāl′ māt′) *n.* A position in which no action can be taken; a deadlock.

steep (stēp) *v.* To soak; to saturate.

stench (stench) *n.* A disagreeable odor.

steppe (step) *n.* A large area of land that is flat and treeless.

stipend (stī′ pend) *n.* A fixed salary.

straddle (strad′ l) *v.* To be positioned with parts on each side of something.

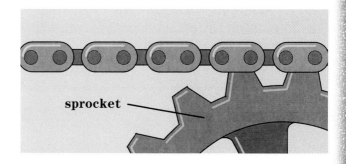

sprocket

strategic (strə tē′ jik) *adj.* Of great importance.

stucco (stuk′ ō) *n.* Plaster for covering outer walls.

Styx (stiks) *n.* In Greek mythology, the river that dead souls crossed.

subdivision (sub′ di vizh′ ən) *n.* A piece of land broken into separate lots for houses.

suffragist (suf′ rə jist) *n.* One who believes that women should have the right to vote.

sulphur or **sulfur** (sul′ fər) *n.* A yellow mineral substance with a sharp odor, used in medicine and chemistry.

summit (sum′ it) *n.* The highest point; the top.

summons (sum′ ənz) *n.* A signal that commands someone to approach.

suppress (sə pres′) *v.* To stop; to crush; to put down.

Word Derivations

Below are some words derived from the word *suppress.*

suppresses	suppressant
suppressing	suppression
suppressive	

sweat lodge (swet′ loj′) *n.* A building in which Native Americans cleanse themselves both spiritually and physically.

syncopated (sing′ kə pā′ tid) *adj.* Having a shortened, quick-sounding rhythm.

synthesize (sin′ thə sīz′) *v.* To make something by putting together parts or elements.

> **Pronunciation Key: a**t; l**ā**te; c**â**re; f**ä**ther;
> s**e**t; m**ē**; **i**t; k**ī**te; **o**x; r**ō**se; **ô** in b**ou**ght;
> c**oi**n; b**oo**k; t**oo**; f**or**m; **ou**t; **u**p; **ū**se; t**û**rn;
> **ə** sound in **a**bout, chick**e**n, penc**i**l, cann**o**n,
> circ**u**s; **ch**air; **hw** in **wh**ich; ri**ng**; **sh**op;
> **th**in; **th**ere; **zh** in trea**s**ure.

T

talon (tal´ ən) *n.* The claw of an animal or predatory bird.

tango (tang´ gō) *n.* The music for a Latin-American ballroom dance.

tenement (ten´ ə mənt) *n.* A run-down and crowded apartment building in a poor section of a city.

tern (tûrn) *n.* A web-footed water bird that resembles a gull.

terrain (tə rān´) *n.* The roughness or smoothness of a piece of land.

textile (tek´ stīl´) *n.* Cloth; fabric.

Word History

The word **textile** was first used in English in 1626 and comes from the Latin word *textilis*, which means "woven."

thatch (thach) *n.* Straw for a roof covering.

thicket (thi´ kət) *n.* A thick growth of bushes and small trees.

thrust (thrust) *n.* The force caused by the propellers or the jets of an airplane.

ticker-tape parade (ti´ kər tāp´ pə rād´) *n.* A type of parade during which narrow strips of long white paper are released.

tidal (tīd´ l) *adj.* Having to do with the rise and fall of the sea.

timidity (ti mid´ i tē) *n.* Shyness; fright.

tinder (tin´ dər) *n.* Any very dry material that can be set on fire by a spark.

tome (tōm) *n.* A large book; a scholarly book.

toxic (tok´ sik) *adj.* Poisonous.

transform (trans form´) *v.* To change completely.

transmission (trans mish´ ən) *n.* An enclosed box of gears that causes a transfer of forces from one part or machine to another.

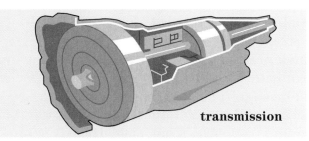

transmission

transmitter (trans mit´ ər) *n.* A device that sends out radio or television signals.

transparent (trans pâr´ ənt) *adj.* Easy to see through; clear.

traverse (trə vûrs) *n.* Crossing.

trawl (trôl) *v.* To catch with a large fishing net.

treacherous (tre´ chə rəs) *adj.* Having hidden dangers.

treat (trēt) *v.* To negotiate; to try to reach a settlement.

trek (trek) *n.* A trip, usually a difficult one.

trill (tril) *n.* A musical sound that goes quickly back and forth between two notes.

tripe (trīp) *n. slang.* Something that is worthless.

trowel (trou´ əl) *n.* A short-handled tool for spreading mortar or digging up plants.

Word History

The word **trowel** came into English usage about 600 years ago from the French word *truelle*, which goes back to a Latin word that means "ladle."

tundra (tun´ drə) *n.* A vast, treeless plain in the Arctic regions.

turquoise (tûr´ koiz) *n.* A semiprecious stone of bluish-green color.

U

unabashed (un´ ə basht´) *adj.* Bold; not embarrassed or ashamed.

uncharted (un chär′ tid) *adj.* Not mapped; not explored.

uncommitted (un′ kə mit′ id) *adj.* Not promised or bound to support a specific cause.

unfazed (ən′ fāzd′) *adj.* Not flustered or upset.

unguent (ung′ gwənt) *n.* An ointment or a salve, as a lotion.

unique (yo͞o nēk′) *adj.* Having no equal; one of a kind.

unison (yo͞o′ nə sən) *adj.* Together; as one.

universal (yo͞o′ nə vûr′ səl) *adj.* Known everywhere; belonging to everyone.

unlikeliest (un līk′ lē əst) *adj.* The least likely.

upright (up′ rīt′) *n.* A type of piano.

urn (ûrn) *n.* A large vase.

V

vague (vāg) *adj.* Not clearly seen.

vainglorious (vān glor′ ē əs) *adj.* Boastful; having too much pride.

vast (vast) *adj.* Extremely large; enormous.

venerate (ven′ ə rāt′) *v.* To respect or treat with reverence.

visage (vi′ zij) *n.* The face of a person.

vulnerable (vul′ nər ə bəl) *adj.* Weak; defenseless.

W

warehouseman (wâr′ hous′ mən) *n.* A person who works in a building where goods are stored.

warily (wâr′ ə lē) *adv.* In a watchful, slightly uncomfortable way.

warp (worp) *n.* A twist; a bend.

wash (wosh) *n.* An area of dry land that has been shaped partly by the action of water moving over it.

whickering (hwik′ ər ing) *n.* The sound of whinnying or neighing.

whilst (hwīlst) *conj. British.* While.

windfall (wind′ fôl′) *n.* An unexpected gain.

X

X-ray vision (eks′ rā vi′ zhən) *n.* A way of seeing through solid substances using a ray or beam that allows photographs to be taken of broken bones or other unseen objects.

Y

yucca (yuk′ ə) *n.* A plant with white flowers and large leaves shaped like swords in a cluster.

yucca

yurt (yûrt) *n.* A dome-shaped tent.

Z

zealot (zel′ ət) *n.* A person who shows too much enthusiasm for a cause.

zombie (zom′ bē) *n.* A person whose actions are mechanical and unemotional.

Acknowledgments *continued*

© 1994 by the Estate of Langston Hughes. Reprinted by permission of Alfred A. Knopf, Inc. "On Hearing a Flute at Night" from THE JADE MOUNTAIN by Witter Bynner. Copyright 1929 and renewed 1957 by Alfred A. Knopf, Inc. Reprinted by permission of the publisher. "The Weary Blues" from COLLECTED POEMS by Langston Hughes. Copyright ©1994 by the Estate of Langston Hughes. Reprinted by permission of Alfred A. Knopf, Inc.

Little, Brown and Company: From SAINT GEORGE AND THE DRAGON by Margaret Hodges. Copyright © 1984 by Margaret Hodges (Text); Illustrations © by Trina Schart Hyman. By permission of Little, Brown and Company.

Macmillan Library Reference USA, a Simon & Schuster Macmillan Company: "Sweeping Pittsburgh Clean" by Kathy Lynn Emerson. Reprinted with permission of Macmillan Library Reference USA, a Simon & Schuster Macmillan Company, from MAKING HEADLINES: A BIOGRAPHY OF NELLIE BLY by Kathy Lynn Emerson. Copyright © 1989 by Dillon Press.

Macmillan Publishing Company, a division of Simon & Schuster: "The Coin" by Sara Teasdale. Reprinted with the permission of Simon & Schuster from THE COLLECTED POEMS OF SARA TEASDALE. Copyright © 1920 by Macmillan Publishing Company, renewed 1948 by Mamie T. Wheless.

Margaret K. McElderry Books, an imprint of Simon & Schuster Children's Publishing Division: "The Search for Early Americans" by Sheila Cowing. Reprinted with the permission of Margaret K. McElderry Books, an imprint of Simon & Schuster Children's Publishing Division from SEARCHES IN THE AMERICAN DESERT by Sheila Cowing. Copyright © 1989 by Sheila Cowing.

Beverly McLoughland: "Crazy Boys" by Beverly McLoughland

in Lee Bennett Hopkin's HAND IN HAND: AN AMERICAN HISTORY THROUGH POETRY, copyright © 1994, Simon & Schuster, New York. Reprinted by permission of the author.

Melissa Milich: MR. EINSTEIN'S VIOLIN by Melissa Milich, from the January 1994 issue of *Cricket*, The Magazine for Children. Copyright © 1994 by Melissa Milich. Reprinted with permission of Melissa Milich.

Morrow Junior Books, a division of William Morrow & Company, Inc.: "Class Discussion" from SCHOOL SPIRIT by Johanna Hurwitz. Copyright © 1994 by Johanna Hurwitz. By permission of Morrow Junior Books, a division of William Morrow & Company, Inc. An excerpt from WINDOWS ON WILDLIFE by Ginny Johnston and Judy Cutchins. Copyright © 1990 by Ginny Johnston and Judy Cutchins. By permission of Morrow Junior Books, a division of William Morrow & Company, Inc.

Pantheon Books, a division of Random House, Inc.: "President Cleveland, Where Are You?" from EIGHT PLUS ONE by Robert Cormier. Copyright © 1965 and renewed 1993 by Robert Cormier. Reprinted by permission of Pantheon Books, a division of Random House, Inc.

Robert Priest: "Poem for the Ancient Trees" by Robert Priest. Copyright © by Robert Priest. Reprinted with permission of Robert Priest.

Laurence Pringle: "A Natural Force" from NATURAL FIRE: ITS ECOLOGY IN FORESTS by Laurence Pringle. Copyright © 1979 by Laurence Pringle. Reprinted with permission of Laurence Pringle.

Eric Protter: "A Gift for a Gift" from A CHILDREN'S TREASURY OF FOLK & FAIRY TALES, edited and adapted by Eric Protter. Translations copyright © 1961 by Channel Press, Inc. Reprinted with permission of Eric Protter.

Random House, Inc.: "The Sound of Flutes" from THE SOUND OF FLUTES AND OTHER INDIAN LEGENDS by Richard Erdoes. Copyright © 1976 by Richard Erdoes. Reprinted by permission of Random House, Inc.

Marian Reiner: "What is Jazz" and "Music" from WHAT IS THAT SOUND! by Mary O'Neill. Copyright © 1966 by Mary O'Neill. Copyright © renewed 1994 by Abigail Hagler and Erin Baroni. Reprinted by permission of Marian Reiner.

Scholastic: "The People on the Beach" from THE SECRETS OF VESUVIUS by Sara Bisel. Copyright © 1990 by Sara C. Bisel and Family and The Madison Press Ltd. Reprinted by permission of Scholastic Inc.

Simon & Schuster Books for Young Readers, an imprint of Simon & Schuster Children's Publishing Division: "The Fire Builder" by Gary Paulsen. Reprinted with the permission of Simon & Schuster Books for Young Readers, an imprint of Simon & Schuster Children's Publishing Division from HATCHET by Gary Paulsen. Copyright © 1987 Gary Paulsen.

Steepletop: "The Courage That My Mother Had" by Edna St. Vincent Millay. From COLLECTED POEMS, HarperCollins. Copyright © 1954, 1982 by Norma Millay Allis. All rights reserved. Used by permission of Elizabeth Barnett, literary executor. "To the Not Impossible Him" by Edna St. Vincent Millay. From COLLECTED POEMS, HarperCollins. Copyright © 1922, 1950 by Edna St. Vincent Millay. All rights reserved. Reprinted by permission of Elizabeth Barnett, literary executor.

Viking Children's Books, a division of Penguin Putnam Inc.: From A LONG WAY TO GO by Zibby Oneal, illustrations by Michael Dooling. Copyright © 1990 by Zibby Oneal, text. Copyright © 1990 by Michael Dooling, illustrations. Used by

permission of Viking Children's Books, a division of Penguin Putnam Inc.

Viking Penguin, a division of Penguin Putnam Inc.: From THE HUNDRED PENNY BOX by Sharon Bell Mathis, illustrated by Leo and Diane Dillon. Copyright © 1975 by Sharon Bell Mathis, text. Copyright © 1975 by Leo and Diane Dillon, illustrations. Used by permission of Viking Penguin, a division of Penguin Putnam Inc.

Franklin Watts, Inc.: "Digging Up the Past" from DIGGING UP THE PAST: THE STORY OF AN ARCHAEOLOGICAL ADVENTURE by Carollyn James. Copyright © 1989 by Carollyn James. Reprinted with permission of Frankilin Watts, Inc., New York.

Wayland Publishers Limited: An excerpt from GANDHI by Nigel Hunter. Copyright © 1986 by Wayland Publishers Limited, 61 Western Road, Hove, East Sussex BN3 1Jd, England. Reprinted with permission of Wayland Publishers Limited. An excerpt from PROTECTING WILDLIFE by Malcolm Penny. Copyright © 1983 by Wayland Publishers Limited, 61 Western Road, Hove, East Sussex BN3 1Jd, England. Reprinted with permission of Wayland Publishers Limited.

Writers House Inc.: THE DAY THEY PARACHUTED CATS OUT ON BORNEO: A DRAMA OF ECOLOGY by Charlotte Pomerantz. Text copyright © 1971 by Charlotte Pomerantz. Reprinted with permission of Writers House Inc. An excerpt from "I Have a Dream" by Martin Luther King, Jr., from A TESTAMENT OF HOPE: THE ESSENTIAL WRITINGS OF MARTIN LUTHER KING, JR., edited by James Melvin Washington. Reprinted by arrangement with The Heirs to the Estate of Martin Luther King, Jr., c/o Writers House, Inc. as agent for the proprietor. Copyright 1963 by Martin Luther King, Jr., copyright renewed 1991 by Coretta Scott King.

Photo Credits

7(br), ©The Library of Congress/PHOTRI; **8(1),** ©Spencer Swanger/Tom Stack & Associates; **11(tr),** ©The Hulton Getty/Liaison Agency, **11(br),** ©Corbis-Bettmann; **13(rc),** ©Charles Abbott; **15(tr),** ©Bob McKeever/Tom Stack & Associates; **48(t),** ©Ellen Young; **92,** ©The Library of Congress/PHOTRI; **93,** ©Wright State University; **95(t),** ©The Library of Congress/PHOTRI; **95(b),** ©Wright State University; **96,** ©The Library of Congress/PHOTRI; **99,** ©Wright State University; **101,** ©PHOTRI/Library of Congress; **104,** ©Wright State University; **107, 108,** ©Corbis-Bettmann; **109,** ©The Library of Congress/PHOTRI; **110-111,** ©Kim Westerkov/Tony Stone Images; **139,** ©CORBIS/David Muench; **141, 142,** ©John Gerlach/Tom Stack & Associates; **145,** ©National Park Service; **146,** Courtesy Department of Library Services American Museum of Natural History; **149,** ©Spencer Swanger/Tom Stack & Associates;

Photo Credits, continued

150, Courtesy Department of Library Services American Museum of Natural History; **152,** ©Spencer Swanger/Tom Stack & Associates; **155,** ©CORBIS/Ric Ergenbright; **156,** ©Ray Jones; **160,** ©Ancient Art & Architecture Collection Ltd.; **164,** Scala/Art Resource, NY; **166(b),** ©Ancient Art & Architecture Collection Ltd.; **171,** ©Jonathan Blair/Corbis; **173,** ©Giraudon/Art Resource, NY; **175,** ©Library of Congress/Corbis; **178,** ©Werner Forman/Art resource, NY; **181,** ©O. Louis Mazzatenta/National Geographic Image Collection; **182,** ©Jonathan Blair/Corbis; **183,** ©O. Louis Mazzatenta/National Geographic Image Collection; **184,** ©Jonathan Blair/Corbis; **185,** ©O. Louis Mazzatenta/National Geographic Image Collection; **187, 189, 190,** ©Jonathan Blair/Corbis; **191,** ©O. Louis Mazzatenta/National Geographic Image Collection; **238(b),** ©Cherie Fieser; **242-243,** ©Charlie Cole/SIPA Press; **285,** ©The Hulton Getty/Liaison Agency; **286,** ©Archive/American Stock; **288(t),** ©Flip Schulke/Corbis; **288(b),** ©The Hulton Getty/Liaison Agency; **289(tl),(cr),(bl),** ©Flip Schulke/Corbis; **289(tr),** ©UPI/Corbis-Bettmann; **312(t),** ©Stephen Blos; **314,** ©Popperfoto; **324,** ©AP/Wide World Photos; **326,** ©Popperfoto; **327,** ©Hulton-Deutsch Collection/Corbis; **331,** ©Corbis-Bettmann; **332, 335,** ©The Carnegie Library of Pittsburgh; **336-338, 341,** ©Historical Society of Western Pennsylvania; **358,** ©Archive Photos; **376(t),** ©Mike Liong; **408,** ©Frederic Reglain/Gamma Liaison; **409,** ©Arnaldo Magnani/Gamma Liaison; **411,** ©Debra Trebitz/The Gamma Liaison Network; **412(t),** ©Frederic Reglain/Gamma Liaison; **412(b),** ©Eric Pearle; **416,** ©1989 Charles Abbott; **417,** ©Walter H. Scott; **418,** ©SuperStock, Inc.; **419,** ©Jenna Soleo/The Juilliard School; **420,** ©Walter H. Scott; **421,** ©SuperStock; **423,** ©Walter H. Scott; **424(t),** ©SuperStock, Inc.; **424(b),** ©1988 Charles Abbott; **425,** ©1988 Charles Abbott; **438,** ©Dani/Jeske/Animals Animals; **439,** ©Doug Allan/Oxford Scientific Films; **440,** ©Doug Wechsler/Earth Scenes; **441(r),** ©Pavel Rahman/AP Wide World; **441(l),** ©James H. Robinson/Animals Animals; **442,** ©Jeff Lepore/Photo Researchers, Inc.; **443,** ©Louis Gagnon/Animals Animals; **444,** ©Michael Dick/Animals Animals; **445,** ©Garry McMichael/Photo Researchers; **446,** ©Carson Baldwin, Jr./Animals Animals; **447,** ©A. Osf Shay/Animals Animals; **448,** ©Stefan Meyers/Animals Animals; **449,** ©Joe McDonald/Animals Animals; **450,** ©E. R. Degginger/Animals Animals; **452,** ©Nigel J.H. Smith/Earth Scenes; **455,** ©Michael Dick/Animals Animals; **469, 470,** ©Joe Sebo/Zoo Atlanta; **471, 472,** ©Judy Cutchins; **473,** ©Joe Sebo/Zoo Atlanta; **474,** ©Judy Cutchins; **475,** ©Sea World of Texas; **476,** ©Bob Couey/Sea World, Inc.; **478,** ©Dennis DeMello/Wildlife Conservation Society; **479,** ©Everett H. Scott; **480, 481,** ©Wildlife Conservation Society headquartered at the Bronx Zoo; **482-485,** ©Judy Cutchins; **491,** ©Bob McKeever/Tom Stack & Associates; **487,** ©Bob Couey/SeaWorld, Inc.; ©**492,** ©Scott Blackman/Tom Stack & Associates; **493,** ©Bob McKeever/Tom Stack & Associates; **494,** ©J.R. Williams/Earth Scenes; **495(l),** ©David C. Fritts/Earth Scenes; **495(r),** ©Jim Steinberg/Photo Researchers, Inc.; **496,** ©Mickey Gibson/Earth Scenes; **497,** ©Gregory K. Scott/Photo Researchers, Inc.; **498(l),** ©John Gerlach/Tom Stack & Associates; **498(c),** ©John Shaw/Tom Stack & Associates; **498(r),** ©Wendy Shattil/Bob Rozinski/Tom Stack & Associates; **499(l),** ©J.H. Robinson/Earth Scenes; **499(r),** ©James H. Robinson/Earth Scenes; **501,** ©Bob McKeever/Tom Stack & Associates; **503,** ©Galen Rowell/Corbis; **504-513,** ©Richard R. Hewett; **514(l),** ©Richard R. Hewett; **514(r),** Courtesy the Predatory Bird Research Group/University of California at Santa Cruz; **515,** Courtesy the Predatory Bird Research Group/University of California at Santa Cruz; **517, 518(t),** ©Richard R. Hewett; **518(b),**©Richard Fish; **519,** ©Richard R. Hewett; **534(t),** ©Daniel Pomerantz; **542,** ©Velasquez/Archive Photos; **588(t),** ©Katy Peake; **598(b),** ©Ron Rinauldi; **616(t),** ©Jill Krementz; **616(c),** ©Bob Kuester; **628(t),** ©Carolyn Soto; **630-631,** ©Brendan Beirne/Tony Stone Images; **656(t),** ©Marcia C. Bell.

Unit Opener Acknowledgments

Unit 1 illustrated by Gail Piazza; **Unit 2** illustrated by Jan Adkins; **Unit 3** photograph by Charlie Cole/SIPA Press; **Unit 4** illustrated by David Wenzel; **Unit 5** illustrated by Diane Blasius; **Unit 6** illustrated by Laura Bryant.